SUBPRIM

Studies in Urban and Social Change

*Out of print

SUBPRIME CITIES

The Political Economy of Mortgage Markets

Edited by Manuel B. Aalbers

WILEY-BLACKWELL

A John Wiley & Sons, Ltd., Publication

Library of Congress Cataloging-in-Publication Data

Aalbers, Manuel.
    Subprime cities : the political economy of mortgage markets / Manuel B. Aalbers. – 1st ed.
       p.   cm.
    Includes index.
    ISBN 978-1-4443-3776-1 (hardback) – ISBN 978-1-4443-3777-8 (paper)
1. Subprime mortgage loans.   2. Mortgage loans.   3. Global Financial Crisis, 2008–2009.
I. Title.
    HG2040.15.A33 2012
    332.7′2–dc23

                                                          2011036441

A catalogue record for this book is available from the British Library.

Set in 10.5/12pt Baskerville by SPi Publisher Services, Pondicherry, India
Printed in Malaysia by Ho Printing (M) Sdn Bhd

1   2012

Contents

Figures

Tables

Notes on Contributors

Manuel B. Aalbers – a human geographer, sociologist, and urban planner – is Assistant Professor in the Department of Geography, Planning and International Development Studies at the University of Amsterdam. Manuel has been a guest researcher at Columbia University (New York), New York University, City University of New York, the University of Milan-Bicocca, and the University of Urbino (Italy). He is the author of *Place, Exclusion, and Mortgage Markets* (Wiley-Blackwell, 2011) and two Dutch books; the associate editor of the *Encyclopedia of Urban Studies* (Sage, 2010) and the journal *TESG*; and book review editor of Dutch urban planning journal *Rooilijn*. His main research interest lies in the intersection of housing and finance. Manuel has published extensively on redlining, social exclusion, financialization, gentrification, safety and security, and the Anglophone hegemony in academic writing. His website is http://home.medewerker.uva.nl/m.b.aalbers/.

Gary Dymski is Professor of Economics at the University of California, Riverside. He received his B.A. in Urban Studies from the University of Pennsylvania in 1975, and an MPA from Syracuse University in 1977. Gary received his Ph.D. in Economics from the University of Massachusetts, Amherst in 1987. From 2003 to 2009, Gary was the founding Executive Director of the University of California Center, Sacramento. Gary has been a visiting scholar in universities and research centers in Brazil, Bangladesh, Japan, Korea, Great Britain, Greece, and India. His most recent books are *Capture and Exclude: Developing Nations and the Poor in Global Finance* (Tulika Books, New Delhi, 2007), co-edited with Amiya Bagchi, and *Reimagining Growth: Toward a Renewal of the Idea of Development,* co-edited with Silvana DePaula (Zed, London, 2005).

Kevin Fox Gotham is a Professor of Sociology and Associate Dean of Academic Affairs in the School of Liberal Arts (SLA) at Tulane University. He has research interests in real estate and housing markets, urban redevelopment policy, gentrification, race and ethnicity, and the political economy of tourism. He is currently writing a book with Miriam Greenberg (University of California-Santa Cruz) on the federal response to the 9/11 and the Hurricane Katrina disasters (under contract with Oxford University Press). He is author of *Race, Real Estate and Uneven Development* (SUNY Press, 2002), *Authentic New Orleans* (NYU Press, 2007), *Critical Perspectives on Urban Redevelopment* (Elsevier Press, 2001), and dozens of peer-reviewed articles and book chapters on housing policy, racial segregation, urban redevelopment, and tourism.

Dan Hammel is Associate Professor and Director of the M.A. Program in the Department of Geography and Planning at the University of Toledo. His work focuses on structural and policy changes in the American city, particularly the operation of the housing market in driving nearly four decades of gentrification and other polarizing dimensions of neighborhood change. His research has been published in *Urban Studies, Urban Geography, Housing Policy Debate, Geografiska Annaler B*, the *Journal of Urban Affairs*, and *Environment and Planning A*.

David Harvey is a Distinguished Professor at the City University of New York (CUNY), Director of the Center for Place, Culture and Politics. He is the author of numerous books, most recently *The Enigma of Capital and the Crisis of Capitalism* (Oxford University Press, 2010), *A Companion to Marx's Capital* (Verso, 2010), and *Cosmopolitanism and the Geographies of Freedom* (Columbia University Press, 2009). He has been teaching Karl Marx's *Capital* for nearly 40 years. His research interests include: geography and social theory; geographical knowledges; urban political economy and urbanization in the advanced capitalist countries; architecture and urban planning; Marxism and social theory; cultural geography and cultural change; environmental philosophies; environment and social change; ecological movements; social justice; geographies of difference; utopianism.

Jesus Hernandez is currently completing his Ph.D. in Sociology at the University of California at Davis. His research focuses on how institutional structures and market interventions articulate the nexus between race and economy. For this volume, his work connects the current subprime loan crisis to historical processes of mortgage redlining and residential segregation, and demonstrates how racialized lending practices reproduce longstanding spatial and social patterns of inequality.

Markus Moos is Assistant Professor in the School of Planning at the University of Waterloo. His research and teaching focus on urban housing markets, commuting, labor market restructuring, and the relations between sustainability planning and social justice in cities. His publications have appeared in the *Journal of Urban Affairs*, the *International Journal of Urban and Regional Research*, *Urban Studies*, *Environment and Planning A*, and *Urban Geography*. He is a Co-Investigator on an international, major collaborative research initiative led by Roger Keil, focusing on global suburban dynamics of governance, land, and infrastructure.

Kathe Newman is Associate Professor in the Urban Planning and Policy Development Program at the Edward J. Bloustein School of Planning and Public Policy and Director of the Ralph W. Voorhees Center for Civic Engagement. Dr. Newman holds a Ph.D. in Political Science from the Graduate School and University Center at the City University of New York. Her research explores urban change, what it is, why it happens, and what it means. Her research has explored gentrification, foreclosure, urban redevelopment, and community participation. Dr. Newman has published articles in *Urban Studies*, *International Journal of Urban and Regional Research*, *Urban Affairs Review*, *Shelterforce*, *Progress in Human Geography*, *Housing Studies*, *GeoJournal*, and *Environment and Planning A*.

Saskia Sassen is the Robert S. Lynd Professor of Sociology and Co-Chair Committee on Global Thought at Columbia University. She is also a Centennial Visiting Professor at the London School of Economics. Her research and writing focuses on globalization (including social, economic and political dimensions), immigration, global cities (including cities and terrorism), the new networked technologies, and changes within the liberal state that result from current transnational conditions. In her research she has focused on the unexpected and the counterintuitive as a way to cut through established "truths." She's the author of many books, including *The Mobility of Labor and Capital* (Cambridge University Press, 1988), *The Global City* (Princeton University Press, 1991; 2nd edition, 2002), and *Territory, Authority, Rights: From Medieval to Global Assemblages* (Princeton University Press, 2006).

Herman Schwartz is Professor in the Politics Department at the University of Virginia, USA. His research focuses on economic development, change in the welfare state, and global capital flows. Before coming to the University of Virginia he taught on the Graduate Faculty of the New School for Social Research. He has also been a Fulbright scholar at Aarhus University (Denmark) and the University of Calgary (Canada). Dr. Schwartz's publications include *Subprime Nation: American Power, Global Capital Flows and the Housing Bubble* (Cornell), *States versus Markets* (Palgrave), and *In the Dominions of Debt* (Cornell), three edited volumes, *The Politics of Housing Booms and Busts* (Palgrave) with Leonard Seabrooke, *Crisis, Miracles and Beyond* (Aarhus) with Erik Albæk, Leslie Eliason and Asbjørn Sonne Nørgaard, and *Employment Miracles* (Amsterdam) with Uwe Becker, and over 40 articles and chapters. His website is http://www.people.virginia.edu/~hms2f.

Thomas Wainwright is a Postdoctoral Researcher in the Small Business Research Centre (SBRC) at Kingston University. He completed his first degree at the University of Leicester, and holds an MSc from the University of Nottingham. Tom completed his ESRC funded PhD in 2009 (University of Nottingham) where he investigated the UK mortgage market, wholesale banking, asset management and the unfolding of the credit crunch within the financial services sector. Tom then worked at the University of Nottingham as a Research Assistant on projects that examined wholesale-retail bank linkages and wealth management. His current research examines the effects of the credit crunch on small businesses and how individuals are becoming "olderpreneurs" to support themselves during retirement.

Elvin Wyly is Associate Professor of Geography and Chair of the Urban Studies Program at the University of British Columbia. He studies the inter-action of market processes and public policy in the production of social and spatial inequalities in North American cities. With Patricia A. McCoy, he guest edited a special issue of *Housing Policy Debate* (2004), "Market Failures and Predatory Lending." He has also published in *City & Community, City*, the *Journal of Urban Affairs, Urban Studies, Environment and Planning A*, the *Review of Black Political Economy*, and the *Journal of Ethnic and Migration Studies*.

Foreword
The Urban Roots of the Financial Crisis

David Harvey

Shortly after arriving in Baltimore in 1969, I became involved in a study
of inner city housing provision that focused mainly on the role of different
actors – landlords, tenants and homeowners, the brokers and lenders, the
FHA, the city authorities (Housing Code Enforcement in particular) – in
the production of the terrifying rat-infested living conditions in the areas
wracked by riots in the wake of the assassination of Martin Luther King
the year before. The vestiges of redlining of areas of low income African
American population were clearly visible but now justified as a legitimate
response to high credit risk (a view that the financial institutions and the
FHA clearly articulated). In several areas of the city, active blockbusting
practices were to be found. And there was a considerable scandal and
court suit over a practice called the "Land Installment Contract" that
purportedly was designed to give African American populations access to
the American dream of home ownership. Some takers made it (usually in
neighborhoods that were declining in value) but in unscrupulous hands
(and there were many) this turned out to be a particularly predatory form
of accumulation by dispossession on the backs of African Americans that
were otherwise excluded from mortgage finance. In the midst of this there
were still desultory attempts at urban renewal and neighborhood upgrad-
ing, funded with a good deal of help from the Federal Government that
accepted that it had a distinctively "urban crisis" on its hands and had
multiple programs on tap for urban up-grading. It was only in his State of
the Union address of 1973 that President Nixon declared the urban crisis
was over. I looked around the city and it then seemed no different to me.
What he meant, of course, was that he was cutting the money because
he needed it to close out the Vietnam War and keep US imperial
power intact.

When I go back to Baltimore now I find it looks even worse than
I remember, in part because the inequalities that are always written into any
urban landscape are now so much grosser and so much more blatant and

callous – as if nobody cared to try and conceal them anymore. Certainly it looks that way in *The Wire* too.

I had not read Marx or Engels when I arrived in Baltimore, but when I did I was struck by how useful it all was. Speaking to landlords about the distinction between use value and exchange value made a lot of sense to them (they were grateful that I was not an economist they said because I talked sense). The formulation that policies are least successful where they are most needed and most successful where they are least needed sounded exact to many housing inspectors. The bureaucrats and financiers found Engels' formulation in *The Housing Question* (1872) – that the bourgeoisie has no solution to the housing question, it only moves the problem around – devastatingly accurate. I did not say it exactly that way of course, and when I did confess to one New York banker, who found the formulation particularly appropriate, that I got it from Engels he surmised that Engels must be working at the Brookings Institution.

I mention all this for two reasons. Firstly, the impression probably emerges from my writings (now described by Dymski as canonical) that I applied Marx and Engels to the urban situation when the reality was that I actually learned what Marx and Engels meant and gained confidence in their formulations from the urban experience to which I was exposed during those years. I was and continue to be just a geographer trying to make sense of the world and change it. The second thing I had to learn was that the long history of racial discrimination could not be avoided as foundational. On the surface, this did not fit too easily with the emphasis on class relations in Marx and Engels. I had to learn to see the way, as Manning Marable (1983) puts it, that race becomes the prism through which issues of class are both experienced and seen in the United States, given the long history of white supremacy and racism. It is not only a question of race, of course. Gender issues are equally paramount and in many instances, particularly in US cities, ethnic identifications (as in East Baltimore) are crucial. However, it is very important to look through the prism, but in doing so to keep the class content very much in view.

I have not followed developments in the housing situation in Baltimore very closely since the late 1970s. But I do know that the land-installment contract scandal that drew a civil rights suit against certain landlords and financiers is now echoed by a civil rights suit against Wells Fargo on the grounds of predatory lending practices that particularly targeted African Americans and in many instances single-headed households, usually women. In between there are multiple scandals over "flipping" in the early 1990s. But at its foundation, and here I may sound dogmatic, we are dealing with a class relation in which those with money add to their pile by effectively robbing those with slender resources or who can easily be victimized. In this instance class, race, and gender overlap and intertwine. I cannot show exactly the connections, but when the Wall Street bonuses add up to roughly the amount that the African American population lost through predatory lending practices, then we have to rotate the prism and take another look: and there it is, just as Marx and Engels said, increasing concentration of wealth at one pole and increasing accumulation of misery, toil, and degradation at the other pole.

The crisis in subprime lending that triggered the financial crisis of 2008–2010 was widespread across the United States but particularly deeply rooted in the housing markets of California, Nevada, Arizona, and Florida. Overinvestment and speculative activity in the housing and property markets in Spain, Ireland, Britain, and elsewhere, complemented the bursting of the US housing bubble to engulf the world in first a financial and then a generalized crisis in the functioning of global capitalism. The crisis quickly spread to export producers who suddenly found themselves with drastic fall-offs in consumer demand that prompted lay-offs. But it has now gone on to trigger a fiscal crisis in state expenditures (everywhere from California to Greece) to deal with unemployment and to bail out the banks. The remedy for state fiscal shortfalls, in many parts of the advanced capitalist world, is draconian austerity with particularly dire consequences for the most vulnerable classes and for public sector unions (as dramatically witnessed in Wisconsin). The fact that much of the problem derived from financial shenanigans, and that the banks live in a world where their moral hazard is covered while everyone else pays up, is now cheerfully forgotten in a welter of complaints that it is the greedy public sector unions who are at the root of the fiscal crisis of the state. Prop up and give succor to the banks and sock it to the people has been the neoliberal tactic all along (it was done to New York City in 1975, then Mexico in 1982, and on and on).

Read backwards this says: current fiscal difficulties of the states (and proposed austerities) were derived from a global crisis of capitalism that arose out of the near collapse of a financial system that was caught in a tangled web of property market speculation that reflected malfunctioning processes of urbanization driven by the need to find outlets for overaccumulating capital. There has, prior to the publication of *Subprime Cities*, been very little concern for examining and interpreting this sequence of events and explaining the role of urbanization and financialization (along with rent-seeking) in this whole dynamic. What this book does is to begin the complex task of exploring and explaining the urban roots of crisis formation in general and of the dynamics of the most recent crisis in particular.

That capitalism exhibits a general tendency towards periodic crises of overaccumulation is indisputable. The stock market crash of 2001–2002, associated with the bursting of the "dot-com" speculative bubble (that saw major corporations like Enron and WorldCom bite the dust), left the world with a mass of surplus liquidity, of money capital desperately searching for some profitable place to go. That the surplus liquidity might flood into real estate, with potentially disastrous consequences, though not predetermined, was always on the cards. After all, it had done so many times before. Recent studies have revealed, for example, how real estate investments, both housing and commercial property, boomed speculatively during the 1920s in the United States before crashing just before the general stock market debacle of 1929. The dark economic days of the 1970s were ushered in by a collapse of property markets particularly in the United States and Britain in early 1973 (a full six months before the oil embargo put added pressure on Western economies). The effect was not only to bankrupt real estate investment trusts and other property investment vehicles, but also to stress out municipal finances (such that New York City, with one of the biggest public budgets in the world, went virtually bankrupt in 1975 in much the same way that Californian finances are close to total collapse now) and to put several banks worldwide on the brink of if not actually in failure. The turbulent years of neoliberalism since the late 1970s have witnessed multiple financial crises associated with property markets and urban development. The end of the Japanese boom of the 1980s was marked by a collapse of land prices, which is still ongoing. The Swedish banking system had to be nationalized in 1992 because of excesses in property markets. One of the triggers for the collapse in East and Southeast Asia in 1997–8 was excessive urban development in Thailand and Indonesia. The commercial property-led Savings and Loan Crisis of 1984–90 in the United States saw several hundred financial institutions go belly-up at the cost of some $200 billion to the US taxpayers (much of which was, however, eventually recouped as the 1990s boom set in).

This turbulent history runs totally counter to Robert Shiller's (the expert economist on housing) recent assertion in the *New York Times* (2011) that housing market crises are relatively rare and we really have nothing much to fear for the future (even as the housing market, like Japanese land prices, keeps on its downward spiral throughout much of the US). Several people saw the dangers early on. I certainly did. In *The New Imperialism* (2003a: 113) I wrote

> the most important prop to the US and British economies after the onset of general recession in all other sectors from mid 2001 onwards was the continued speculative vigor in the property and housing markets and construction … What happens if and when this property bubble bursts is a matter for serious concern.

It should be clear from this that the connectivity existing between urban processes and property development and macro-economic disruptions and shifts is deep and enduring. In the most recent case, what is termed the subprime foreclosure crisis was rooted in urban processes. Subprime lending, some of it highly predatory, was going on in many cities from the mid-1990s onwards. In some instances it could be clothed in benevolence towards the underprivileged and all those hitherto excluded from access to the American Dream. That it was really about accumulation by dispossession (although a lucky few made money in this situation) could all too easily be disguised. But it only led to financial collapse when it spread into more affluent places.

Urbanization has, however, just as often proven to be a solution to crises as it has been the locus of their unfolding. I have often cited the case of Second Empire Paris (e.g., Harvey 2003b), where a profound crisis of over-accumulation in 1848, in which surplus capital and surplus labor lay side by side with seemingly no way to put either back to profitable work, resulted in fierce revolutionary movements. In this case, Louis Bonaparte, wearing the mantle of his uncle, seized the moment, and took arbitrary powers in a *coup d'état* before declaring himself Emperor. But he knew all too well that he would not stay in power unless he put all that surplus capital and excess labor back to work. Part of the answer lay in the redesign and rebuilding of Paris, a process expertly managed by Haussmann with results that have lasted until today. Similarly, the state promoted and subsidized suburbanization wave that engulfed the United States after 1945 was a crucial element in ensuring that the United States (and the rest of the capitalist world which at that time depended upon the US as the locomotive of capital accumulation) did not fall back into the recession conditions that had bedeviled the 1930s. The construction industry had frozen up almost completely in the 1930s with very high rates of unemployment attached. It was precisely to counter that, that the mortgage finance reform was enacted in 1934, but it really did not gain traction until after 1945.

And in so far as there has been any exit from the crisis this time, it is notable that the housing and property boom in China along with a huge wave of debt-financed infrastructural investments there have taken a leading role not only in stimulating their internal market (and mopping up unemployment in the export industries) but also in stimulating the economies that are tightly integrated into the China trade, such as Australia with its raw materials and Germany with its high speed rail exports. In the United States, on the other hand, construction has been slow to revive with the unemployment rate in that industry more than twice that of the national average.

The virtue of housing and property markets from the standpoint of capital is that they have the capacity to absorb the vast amounts of surplus capital and surplus labor that capital perpetually produces. While investments in the land cannot move, property titles to them certainly can (as Marx noted when looking at the booms and busts in railroad investment in the nineteenth century). Surpluses of money capital in one place can easily be absorbed, therefore, by the building of a new geographical landscape for production, consumption, and daily life elsewhere. This does require, of course, adequate techniques of mediation in financial markets and the advent of securitization and various other financial instruments after 1980 or so certainly created new speculative possibilities (all of this being meticulously laid out in some of the chapters that follow). The big problem, however, is ascertaining when overinvestment is nigh. Urban investments typically take a long time to produce and an even longer time to mature so as to offer a return on capital. It is always difficult to determine, therefore, when an overaccumulation of capital has been or is about to be transformed into an overaccumulation of investments and asset values in the built environment. The likelihood of overshooting, as regularly happened with the railways in the nineteenth century and as the long history of building cycles and crashes shows, is very high. There is evidence mounting that China's investment spree in creating the built environment is getting closer and closer to a state of overaccumulation. The problem is that it is hard to see and control until it is too late. Asset markets invariably have a Ponzi character: one person invests in property and prices go up so another invests and so on. If and when over-investment is either feared or becomes apparent then the whole thing crashes. It is now difficult to see where all the surplus liquidity can go and where it will find a profitable outlet for investment. In the United States (as opposed to China), banks and businesses are stashing it away as cash reserves.

But what to do about all this? We can, of course, turn it all into a series of policy questions and seek a programmatic solution to the malfunctioning, the inequalities, the discriminations, and the like. I am a bit too old in the tooth, or maybe cynical, to go for that any more. All that will happen is that the problem will be moved around while those that have will learn to benefit at the expense of those that do not. I have lived through so many generations of anti-poverty initiatives (locally and globally) to realize that you cannot deal with the question of poverty without confronting the accumulation of wealth. If everyone drawn to an anti-poverty initiative converted to an anti-wealth campaign, an anti-capitalist politics, then we might get somewhere. But the city is a terrain where anti-capitalist struggle can flourish. The history of such struggles, from the Paris Commune through the Seattle General Strike to the movements of 1968 (and now we see them in Cairo) is stunning but also troubled. The "right to the city" may be an empty signifier but that does not mean it is irrelevant. It all depends who gets to fill it with meaning and then, as Marx puts it, between equal rights force decides.

An anti-capitalist struggle is about the abolition of the class relation between capital and labor and even when that struggle has to be seen through the kaleidoscopic prism of race, ethnicity, sexuality, and gender it still has to reach into the very guts of what a capitalist system is about and wrench out the cancerous tumor of class relations. This is, I recognize, another kind of project to that which is undertaken here in this volume. The diagnoses here are fine. We have here an astonishing and revelatory understanding of the urban roots of the fiscal crisis. But we need either another volume on what might be done in response or a set of evolving practices that change our urban world in radical anti-capitalist ways.

References

Engels, F. (1872) *The Housing Question*. Leipzig: Volksstaat.

Harvey, D. (2003a) *The New Imperialism*. Oxford: Oxford University Press.

Harvey, D. (2003b) *Paris, Capital of Modernity*. New York: Routledge.

Marable, M. (1983) *How Capitalism Underdeveloped Black America*. Boston: South End Press.

Shiller, R.J. (2011) Housing Bubbles Are Few and Far Between. *New York Times* February 5: BU5, http://www.nytimes.com/2011/02/06/business/06view.html (last accessed: February 23, 2011).

Series Editors' Preface

The Wiley-Blackwell *Studies in Urban and Social Change* series is published in association with the *International Journal of Urban and Regional Research*. It aims to advance theoretical debates and empirical analyses stimulated by changes in the fortunes of cities and regions across the world. Among topics taken up in past volumes and welcomed for future submissions are:

- Connections between economic restructuring and urban change
- Urban divisions, difference, and diversity
- Convergence and divergence among regions of east and west, north, and south
- Urban and environmental movements
- International migration and capital flows
- Trends in urban political economy
- Patterns of urban-based consumption

The series is explicitly interdisciplinary; the editors judge books by their contribution to intellectual solutions rather than according to disciplinary origin. Proposals may be submitted to members of the series' Editorial Committee, and further information about the series can be found at www.suscbookseries.com.

Jenny Robinson
Neil Brenner
Matthew Gandy
Patrick Le Galès
Chris Pickvance
Ananya Roy

Acknowledgments

Early in 2007 I sent around a call for papers for a conference session on "The Sociology and Geography of Mortgage Markets." At the end of that summer, very early drafts of some of the chapters of this book were presented at the annual RC21 conference that took place in Vancouver, Canada. In the months in between, the US mortgage market, and in particular the subprime market, had been falling apart, exactly what some of the authors of this book had suggested previously. Elvin Wyly, one of the contributing authors, was one of the local organizers of the conference. I would like to thank him and the other organizers for allowing us a forum to discuss the issues of this book, including but not limited to: subprime lending, the mortgage market crisis, securitization, and urban political economy. Subsequently, I organized a special issue for the *International Journal of Urban and Regional Research* (issue 33.2, June 2009) on "The Sociology and Geography of Mortgage Markets: Reflections on the Financial Crisis." I would like to thank the journal's editors, Roger Keil, Jeremy Seekings, and Terry McBride, not only for supporting the special issue but also for allowing us to include updated and expanded versions of the IJURR papers in this book. After the special issue was accepted, the idea of a book quickly came about. On the one hand, we were eager to update our papers and increase the dialogue between the different contributions. On the other hand, we were frustrated with most of the books that were being published on the financial crisis, as many of them still ignore or misrepresent what had been, and to some extent still is, taking place in the mortgage market. Along with the media, many of those books continued to spread subprime myths that we wanted to address. Personally, I was also eager to include more authors in this book than we had been able to include in the special issue. This allowed us to shift the focus to include more political economy perspectives, as represented by the chapters by Herman Schwartz and Gary Dymski. The idea of this book was fully supported by two fantastic book series editors, Jennifer Robinson and Neil Brenner, as well as by the people at Wiley-Blackwell, including Jacqueline Scott. Philip Ashton and Chris Pickvance assessed the draft manuscript and proposed a number of changes – most of which were excellent suggestions and have clearly improved the quality of the book and the connections between the different chapters. Finally, I would like to thank all the contributing authors, and in particular Gary Dymski who wrote the concluding chapter, for their work. Every time I asked them to adapt, expand, shorten, or update their chapters, they did. It was a pleasure to work with you, you have been great supporters of continuing this project, and I truly believe that thanks to all your work, the sum of the chapters of this book is greater than its parts.

Manuel B. Aalbers
Brooklyn, December 2010

Part I
Introduction

Subprime Cities and the Twin Crises

Manuel B. Aalbers

Introduction: Urban Political Economy

From the early 1970s to the late 1980s debates on homeownership and mortgage markets were at the center of urban sociology and human geography. Although the interest in mortgage markets in social science has waned since, the importance of mortgage markets to cities and societies has not. To the contrary: homeownership rates have steadily increased in most countries and mortgage markets have grown dramatically and now represent almost €12/$16 trillion worldwide. This expansion has happened at a time when most social scientists, including those in urban studies, have paid little attention to mortgage markets and have left the analysis to economists. The rise of subprime lending and securitization has resulted in a new interest among social scientists in mortgage markets; and this interest has only increased since the mortgage market crisis, and indeed the global financial crisis, of 2007–09. The authors represented in this book all started working on mortgage markets before the recent crisis, but their work, in many different ways, helps us to understand the origins and scope of this crisis.

Traditionally, the mortgage market has been the domain of economists. Other social scientists, most notably geographers, sociologists, and political scientists, have studied the mortgage market, but generally they were considered to work outside the mainstream and their work has largely been ignored by economists. There have been times when geographers and sociologists have contributed greatly to the understanding of mortgage markets. Usually this was at times of turmoil and change as well as when exclusion in mortgage markets was an important issue. One explanation for this may be that mainstream economics, with its obsession with equilibrium, has trouble understanding change. As the political economist Thorstein Veblen already observed 75 years ago, "The question is not how things stabilize themselves

Subprime Cities: The Political Economy of Mortgage Markets, First Edition. Edited by Manuel B. Aalbers.
© 2012 Blackwell Publishing Ltd. Published 2012 by Blackwell Publishing Ltd.

in a 'static state', but how they endlessly grow and change" (Veblen 1934: 8). It is here that some forms of heterodox economics (including some forms of political economy) shake hands with sociology and geography. It is, to some degree, also the difference between "clean models" and "dirty hands" (Hirsh *et al.* 1987): while mainstream economics prefers "clean, abstract, and parsimonious modeling," sociology and geography

> produce empirically rich accounts of concrete and socially situated economic processes; they each emphasize the essential diversity of economic phenomena, favoring context-rich explanations in which history is taken seriously; they each attach greater significance to plausibility and explanatory power than to elegance and predictive power; and they each strive to explain, and often improve, the characteristically messy economic worlds that they encounter. (Peck 2005: 132)

This is not, as some have interpreted it, a clash between quantitative and qualitative methods. Although clean models are generally very quantitative (and often have to do more with mathematics than with statistics), not all quantitative work fits the idea of clean models. Indeed, many sociologists and geographers have been getting their hands dirty by presenting both quantitative and qualitative research on issues like redlining and predatory lending (see Glossary). Many of them, in particular in the US, also got involved with local communities and the wider, national community reinvestment movement (e.g., Squires 1992).

Among the various non-economists who have worked on mortgage markets, the work of David Harvey from the late 1970s and early 1980s is probably most well known (e.g., Harvey 1977; 1985). It is part of a broader interest of mostly Northern American sociologists, geographers, political scientists, urban planners, and political economists in redlining and related forms of discrimination in mortgage markets from the 1970s onwards (e.g., Bradford and Rubinowitz 1975; Marcuse 1979; Shlay 1989; Dymski and Veitch 1996; Wyly and Holloway 1999; Gotham 2002; Stuart 2003; Aalbers 2007; 2011). Here, the discipline of political economy should not be taken too narrow. There are many schools of thought that call themselves political economy. Political economy is sometimes referred to as a specific group of heterodox economists, but also as a group of political scientists interested in the economy, often in what is called "international political economy" or "comparative political economy." In addition, there is also political economy within sociology and geography, which in its origins is heavily influenced by Marxist thinking as we can clearly see in the work of David Harvey. It is also related to the so-called "new urban sociology," which seeks to situate urban sociology within an equally emergent political economy, which requires urban sociology to be a more interdisciplinary enterprise (with economics and, to some degree, political science) than it has been. … By tying together urbanization, the quest for profit and domination, and the state's attempts to moderate domestic conflict between social classes, the new urban sociology achieves a coherence the field had lacked since Weber typified "the city." (Zukin 1980: 579)

What these different political economy traditions have in common is that they analyze "the economy within its social and political context rather than seeing it as a separate entity driven by its own set of rules based on individual self-interest" (Mackinnon and Cumbers 2007: 14). Therefore, political economists may come from different disciplinary backgrounds and they may be in dialogue with their "disciplinary home" more than with other political economy traditions, but each of these traditions is, almost by definition, interdisciplinary. This book includes a lot of work by academics who would often by referred to as urban sociologists and urban geographers, but they are all, to some degree, influenced by the political economic currents in their respective disciplines. In addition to these "urban political economists" this book also includes work by comparative political economist Herman Schwartz who has recently been seeking to establish a dialogue between comparative political economy and housing studies (Schwartz 2009; Schwartz and Seabrooke 2009) and by (political) economist Gary Dymski, who has been trying to build a relationship between economics and geography for a long time (e.g., Dymski 1996; 2009).

Presently we are living through another episode of turmoil and change in mortgage markets, and again the work of political economists of different traditions sheds new light on what is actually happening in the mortgage market. This book will not so much focus on how this crisis has spread to other sectors of the economy, but will look at the mortgage market and how problems have spread throughout mortgage markets. In all chapters, changes in the mortgage market have a central place. Some chapters present evidence of the changes that have resulted in what is often called the subprime mortgage crisis; others are more focused on some of the structural changes in the mortgage market than on the crisis itself.

The term "subprime mortgage crisis" is misleading, not only because the problem has spread throughout and beyond the mortgage market, but also because the problems did not start with subprime mortgages. Subprime loans (see Glossary) have been one important ingredient in the recent crisis, but other ingredients go beyond subprime lending. What the mortgage boom, at least in the US, has created, however, are "subprime cities:" cities modeled by the flow of capital in and out of neighborhoods. This dynamic of making profits on the production, and indeed reproduction (or revitalization, or gentrification), of the built environment has resulted in suboptimal or subprime cities. In the next section I will elaborate on the idea of the twin crises (subprime and financial) as an inherently *urban* crisis. In the later sections of this chapter I will look at the twin crises as a combination of a number of interrelated causes, including: (1) deregulation and re-regulation, (2) financialization and globalization, and (3) bubbles and poor credit ratings. Different media and most economists have focused mostly on the latter, but one cannot explain what went wrong without attention to the first two as they, together, explain in which context bubbles could develop. I do not present a full theory of the twin crises here, but I do present a framework in which the authors of this book move and in which we have to look not only for the causes of the crisis, but also for the solutions.

The Centrality of Cities in the Crisis

In a publication released in early 2008, Gregory Squires asks the question "Do subprime loans create subprime cities?" His answer is yes, in the US, they do. Unequal access to conventional financial services is linked to rising inequality of income and wealth, and intensified segregation by class and race. The resulting uneven development is not just costly to disadvantaged areas, but "to all parts of many metropolitan areas and to the U.S. economy as a whole" because it undermines "the political stability, social development, and economic growth of the entire region" (Squires 2008: 2–3). Indeed, cities, and in particular US cities, are central to this crisis for at least four reasons.

First, the urban is the site of racial and ethnic inequalities in housing that can be exploited by brokers and other local actors who have knowledge of these geographies of inequality. Decades of financial deregulation have not resulted in wider access to mainstream financial services, but in a two-tier banking system with mainstream finance in most places next to a landscape of financial exclusion and predatory lending where banking services and the number of bank accounts have declined while fringe banking (pawn shops, payday lenders, etc.) and predatory lending flourish (Caskey 1994; Dymski 1999; Immergluck 2009; Leyshon and Thrift 1997; Squires 2004). Both quantitative and qualitative research show that "subprime loans are making credit available in communities where credit likely historically has not been – and likely still is not – as readily available" (Goldstein 2004: 40). The old geography of place-based financial exclusion (redlining) has not disappeared, but has been replaced – and to a large extent *reproduced* – by a new geography of predatory lending and overinclusion (see the chapters by Wyly *et al.*, Newman, and Hernandez). Moreover, subprime lenders exploit uneven development that resulted from these earlier rounds of urban exclusion.

Second, cities take a special place in the subprime and foreclosure crisis because this crisis is not merely a financial crisis but also an urbanization crisis: at the root of this crisis is the real estate/financial complex (akin to the military/industrial complex) that fuelled both (sub-) urbanization and financialization. As David Harvey has argued, capital surplus has been absorbed into urbanization. Urban restructuring, expansion, and speculation are all ways to deal with this surplus. Indeed, cities have become huge building sites for capitalist surplus absorption – not only in the US but also elsewhere. In line with Harvey (1985), we can see how, through subprime lending, the urban has become the place of capital extraction (Wyly *et al.* 2006; Newman Chapter 8, this volume). Capital switching from the primary (production) to the secondary (built environment) circuit of capital may, at first sight, seem to benefit people who want to buy a house, but since it has resulted in dramatic increases in house prices, homeownership has simultaneously become more accessible *and* more expensive. The expansion of the mortgage market has not so much facilitated homeownership as it has facilitated capital switching to the secondary circuit of capital. By simultaneously expanding the mortgage market, by means of granting bigger loans, and by giving access to more households (so-called "underserved populations"), the growth machine (Logan and Molotch 1987) kept on working smoothly for a while. Yet, every growth machine or accumulation regime needs to keep on growing to function smoothly and it seems that the recent crisis has announced the beginning of the end of ever expanding mortgage markets (Aalbers 2008).

Third, the urban is the scale that matters for people who make decisions about housing and borrowing, and these decisions result in vast differences in mortgage supply. For example, in American Rustbelt cities subprime lending expanded first and foremost in neighborhoods of color; by contrast, the fastest-growing American Sunbelt cities became targets for the "exotic" loans targeted to middle-income and speculative house-flippers (see Glossary) as home prices crested. House prices can go down because of a structurally faltering economy, like in the Rustbelt, but also because they have been going up extremely fast, like in many cities in the Sunbelt. House prices in the Sunbelt were simply more inflated than elsewhere in the US: the housing bubble was bigger and more likely to bust. In addition, some local and regional economies in the Sunbelt also show signs of a declining economy, perhaps not structurally, as in the Rustbelt, but conjuncturally. Finally, high economic growth also meant a lot of new construction and more homeowners who had recently bought a house, thereby increasing the pool of possible victims of falling housing prices (Aalbers 2009).

Fourth, the securitization of mortgage loans (see below and Glossary) increasingly takes place in global cities: highly concentrated command points that function as a global marketplace for finance (Sassen 2001; see also Langley 2006; Pryke and Lee 1995), such as New York and London. It is here that securities, bonds, and swaps are designed and sent into the world. At the height of the crisis – fall 2008 – publications such as the *New York Times* and *New York Magazine* had headlines like "Wall Street, R.I.P." (Creswell and White 2008) and, with a reference to the novelist Tom Wolfe, "Good-bye, Masters of the Universe" (Cramer 2008). In a city where 20 percent of personal income tax and 45 percent of business income tax come from Wall Street, and many others are dependent on Wall Street employees' spending, the crisis has its own geographies. About a quarter of the 188,000 Wall Street jobs are said to be lost and, since every Wall Street job supports two others in the city, the loss of jobs turns out to be quite dramatic. Not only are the financial services sector and the housing market impacted by the crisis, the services industry – from luxury retailers to restaurants, and from nannies to hotels – is also highly impacted: one high-end massage therapist, for example, lost 50 percent of her Wall Street clientele (Dominus 2008). Cornell medical College received $250 million from Citigroup in 2007 and the New York Public Library $100 million from private equity group Blackstone – both gifts were cancelled in 2008 (Gapper 2008). These are just a few of many, many examples.

Deregulation and Re-Regulation

Land underlies all real estate.[1] Historically, the use of land, the desire to acquire it, and the need to regulate its transfer were among the fundamental reasons for the development of states. But land is also at the base of both power and wealth. Because land transaction administration and land surveys established the security and value of land, land not only became a secure investment, but it also became possible to borrow money based on the value of one's land. This is the basis for the formation of a mortgage market. A mortgage is "a conveyance of an interest in real property given as security for the payment of a debt" (Dennis and Pinkowish 2004: 386); it "gives a lender contingent property rights over an asset of the debtor, and in the event of default the lender may activate those rights" (Carruthers 2005: 365). Although the mortgage system has changed tremendously throughout the centuries, and continues to change, the idea of the mortgage loan is still the same as it was thousands of years ago: the state secures property rights, including land ownership and homeownership, and owners can get relatively cheap loans (i.e., low interest rates) because in case of default the lender can take possession of the property. To cut a long story short: no state regulation, no property rights, no mortgage market. In other words, regulation is a necessary component of (semi-)capitalist societies (Polanyi 1944).

The mortgage market is the outcome of an institutionalization process and a large part of this process is finding ways to stabilize and routinize competition, which is an inherently political process (DiMaggio and Powell 1991; Polanyi 1992; Fligstein 2001). Thus, mortgage markets are not only shaped and reshaped by mortgage lenders, but also by state institutions. Immergluck (2004) aptly speaks of "the visible hand of government" as many of the mortgage market institutions of today were designed by government and its institutions. Mortgage loan securitization, to which I will turn shortly, is essentially an invention designed by government and government-created institutions like Fannie Mae and Freddie Mac. The chapters by Gotham and, to a lesser extent, those by Schwartz, Dymski, Wyly *et al.*, and Newman show how the US mortgage market is politically constructed and reconstructed. They show how the state has been instrumental in designing and successfully implementing secondary mortgage markets and the use of securitization, but also how they have enabled the development of subprime and predatory lending. As the chapters by Wainwright and Aalbers show, American conceptions of risk and securitization not only needed to be adapted to fit European markets, but European mortgage markets also needed to be re-regulated – and not just deregulated – to enable securitization (see also Aalbers *et al.* 2011).

In the US, the banking crisis of the late 1980s was a decisive moment that opened up the mortgage market to widespread securitization, due to the new regulatory framework laid out by state institutions; for example, in the *Financial Institutions Reform, Recovery, and Enforcement Act* of 1989 that indirectly forced many lenders to convert from portfolio lending to off-balance lending. Deregulation also removed the walls between the different rooms of finance, thereby enabling existing financial firms to become active in more types of financial markets and providing opportunities for new mortgage lenders. Many of these new "non-bank lenders" had different regulators from traditional lenders and were also part of other, that is weaker, regulatory frameworks. In addition, it is not always clear which regulator watches what, and even when this is clear, this is no guarantee that regulators actually exercise their regulatory powers as they may be plagued by a lack of interest or a lack of manpower. Some similar re-regulation took place in the UK, as described by Hamnett (1994) and Wainwright (Chapter 4, this volume). In addition, global regulation by the Basel Committee on Banking Supervision in the so-called Basel Accord I (1988) established capital requirements for banks that encouraged them to place mortgages off-balance sheet, thereby stimulating securitization. The Basel Accord II (initially published in 2004 and to be fully implemented by 2015) has repaired this flaw, but with its Anglo-American bias it now stimulates risk management techniques, which could lead to an increasing use of credit scoring and risk-based pricing; methods that may promote safety, but can also be problematic in nature (see Aalbers 2011: chapter 3).

Globalization and Financialization

Globalization and financialization are not the same thing, but are often co-dependent: financialization needs globalization, and globalization, in turn, in part takes place through financialization. Financialization is a pattern of accumulation in which profit-making occurs increasingly through financial channels rather than through trade and commodity production (Arrighi 1994; Krippner 2005). In a finance-led regime of accumulation (Boyer 2000) risks that were once limited to a specific actor in the production–consumption chain become risks for all of the actors involved in that industry. In such a regime, the rules and logics of Wall Street are increasingly becoming the rules and logics outside Wall Street: on Main Street and anywhere else. It also involves the increasing integration and simultaneous expansion of different financial sub-markets; for example, the mortgage market and the securitization market. The financialization of mortgage markets demands that not just homes but also homeowners become viewed as financially exploitable. It is exemplified by the securitization of mortgage loans, but also by the use of credit scoring and risk-based pricing (Aalbers 2008).

The standardized mortgage loan was introduced in the US by two private, yet government-created and "government-sponsored," institutions and one public institution: the Federal National Mortgage Association, known as Fannie Mae; the Federal Home Loan Mortgage Corporation, known as Freddie Mac; and, the Government National Mortgage Association, known as Ginnie Mae (see Glossary). These organizations played a pivotal role in integrating mortgage markets throughout the US into one mortgage market, and were instrumental in implementing and institutionalizing three other important changes in mortgage markets: secondary mortgage markets, credit scoring, and risk-based pricing (see Glossary). In a primary mortgage market mortgages are closed between the borrower and the lender; in a secondary mortgage market investors can buy mortgage portfolios from lenders. Fannie Mae, Freddie Mac, and Ginnie Mae were created to buy or guarantee such mortgage portfolios. Mortgage portfolios sold in the secondary mortgage market are usually classified (and subsequently rated) by risk profiles, because risk determines their price. Therefore, mortgage lenders classify loan applicants according to the risks that they pose to both lenders and investors. The calculation of housing costs and other financial obligations in proportion to income determines the likelihood that an applicant will be *able* to pay a mortgage, but moneylenders also attempt to assess whether they are *willing* to pay it back (Stuart 2003; Aalbers 2011). Credit scoring uses available information to make predictions about future payment behavior; it is a form of customer profiling (Leyshon and Thrift 1999; Thomas 2000).

Credit scoring is not only indispensable if lenders want to sell their mortgage portfolios in the secondary market, it also facilitates risk-based pricing by charging higher interest rates for borrowers with low scores ("bad risk") and lower interest rates for borrowers with high scores ("good risk"): "As lenders become more confident about their ability to predict default, they also become more willing to issue credit, at a relatively high price, to higher-risk borrowers" (Ross and Yinger 2002: 23), as well as at a relatively low price, to lower-risk borrowers. The global implementation of credit scoring systems, originally developed in the US, illustrates how some of the institutions of mortgage markets have become more similar (Aalbers 2011: chapter 3). The chapters by Wyly *et al.* and, to a lesser extent, Hernandez and Aalbers go into credit scoring and risk-based pricing in more detail, while all chapters, but in particular those by Gotham, Sassen, Dymski, and Wainwright, will discuss the issue of secondary mortgage markets.

The globalization of mortgage markets is not only a result of the financialization of borrowers and markets, but also of the globalization of mortgage lenders, although the latter, according to Chapter 5 by Aalbers in this book, is empirically less important than the first two. It is the powerful combination of financialization and globalization that has been instrumental in the way the mortgage crisis in the US has turned into a financial crisis and then a general crisis, not only in the US but across the globe. It is the state that has re-regulated the mortgage market to enable economic growth: the US government was actively involved in making the trade in residential mortgage-backed securities (RMBS, see Glossary) possible, in de-linking investment from place, and in facilitating liquidity/tradability, thereby creating opportunities for both risk-averse and high-risk investors (Gotham 2006; Wyly *et al.* 2006). Because securitization increasingly connects the mortgage market to other financial markets, securitization embodies the financialization of the mortgage market. It increases the volatility of the mortgage market (and, as the recent crisis demonstrates, it also increases volatility in the wider credit market) because derivatives markets by their very nature are volatile markets. The restructuring of both welfare states and financial markets has resulted in a "great risk shift" (Hacker 2006) in which households are increasingly dependent on financial markets for their long-term security: due to the financialization of home, housing risks are increasingly financial market risks these days – and vice versa (Aalbers 2008).

Financialization demands that tradables become more liquid. Mortgages therefore need to be standardized so they can be priced in packages in secondary mortgage markets. Until the summer of 2007, the fastest growing part of the secondary mortgage market was the trade in subprime RMBS. The problem is that now the mortgage bubble has burst, RMBS (and not just subprime RMBS) – which in theory are supposed to be very transparent, liquid products – became illiquid because traders developed doubts about their value. Subprime lending and predatory lending (see Glossary for both terms) – a subset of subprime lending consisting of unsuitable loans designed to exploit vulnerable and unsophisticated borrowers – are at the center of many chapters in this book, most notably those of Newman, Hernandez, Dymski, and Wyly *et al.*

Most predatory loans are sold to borrowers who could have applied for cheaper loans (Immergluck 2009; Wyly *et al.* 2008). Residents are either offered loans that are more expensive than the risk profile of the borrower would suggest, or they are offered overpriced mortgage insurance that they often do not even need. As Wyly *et al.* argue in their chapter:

> the theory of risk-based pricing has become doctrine and ideology, used for well over a decade to blame consumers for the consequences of an abusive industry, to justify a de-regulatory stance that encourages usury as "innovation," and to sustain the mirage of an "American Dream" backed by high-risk, predatory credit.

This stance frequently leads to mortgage foreclosures at the individual level and housing abandonment at the neighborhood level, as Newman's chapter demonstrates. But it is not just borrowers being pushed unsuitable loans; it is also lenders allowing more risk in their organizations, as both default risk and liquidity risk have increased as a result of the restructuring of the mortgage market (Dymski Chapter 6, this volume; Lordon 2007). Most subprime lending is legal, although legislators have been trying to catch up by adapting the rules of the game for a number of years (McCoy and Wyly 2004; Squires 2004; Crump *et al.* 2008; Immergluck 2009).

To sum up the first two interrelated causes, the separate mortgage market of US Fordism (Florida and Feldman 1988) with its specialized, often regional, portfolio lenders working with an "originate and hold" model (pre-securitization) has been transformed into a neoliberal, financialized mortgage market characterized by a wider diversity of nationally operating mortgage lenders, including different types of banks and non-banks, that – since they are working with an "originate and distribute" model (securitization) – increasingly rely on the secondary market for equity and that, in their search for yield, have expanded both lending and securitization beyond the borders of what was sensible. The expansion of the mortgage market is not so much meant to increase homeownership, but to further the neoliberal agenda of private property, firms, and growing profits.

Few mainstream economists had expected a crisis in the mortgage market. One notable economist, behavioral economist Robert Shiller, had argued there was a housing bubble that would explode one day, but few realized the mortgage market was sick. In fact, most economists saw a blossoming market, thanks to financial liberalization. Several sociologists and geographers, but also a number of heterodox economists and academics with a background in law, had been warning about what was wrong with the mortgage market.

For more than a decade some had been working on subprime and predatory lending, and had suggested problems were on the rise. Defaults and foreclosures were rising year after year and, so they argued, would continue to rise due to the way the mortgage market was organized. The crisis of 2007–09 came as no surprise to them, although it is fair to say that probably none of them had expected this crisis would threaten to bring down the entire financial system. A crisis was also no surprise for another reason: financial deregulation, whether *de jure* or *de facto*, precedes the majority of crises, as an analysis of financial crisis since 1945 demonstrates (Kaminsky and Reinhart 1999).

Bubbles and Credit Ratings

The media have presented the subprime crisis as one in which homeowners took out risky loans that were pushed by greedy loan brokers and lenders who did not care about the riskiness of these loans as they would be packaged and sold as RMBS anyway. It continues to present a network of agents that have not paid enough attention to risk: not just borrowers and lenders, but also regulators, investors, and rating agencies. This image of the roots of the subprime crisis is not wrong, but it is limited and limiting because rather than looking at the roots of the crisis, it merely looks at what went wrong when the crisis was already in the making. Only with an idea of how deregulation, re-regulation, financialization, and globalization have shaped the mortgage market, can we begin to understand how the crisis could have happened. This is why this introductory chapter has started to briefly discuss these processes before discussing more common understandings of the twin crises. Only then can one understand how different agents could have made "mistakes" and fail to see the risky ventures in which they were involved.

The root of the mortgage crisis, according to some observers, is in the housing market: the rapid increase of house prices forced people to take out bigger loans (Shiller 2008). The housing bubble, like all bubbles, depended on a constant inflow of liquidity to sustain the rising market as well as the illusion that all participants in the market are winners (Lordon 2007). Once the housing bubble burst, homeowners got into trouble, not just because their homes were worth less, but also because so many of them had taken out big loans with small down-payments and high interest rates. Negative equity (see Glossary), default and foreclosure were some of the results. Indeed, there was a strong housing bubble, but this did not so much fuel the mortgage market: the mortgage market, in the first place, had fuelled the housing bubble. House prices increased first and foremost because mortgages allowed borrowers to buy more expensive homes, but since almost everyone could now afford a mortgage loan – and generally speaking a much bigger loan than ten or twenty years before – the expansion of the mortgage market resulted in higher house prices forcing people to take out ever-bigger loans. In that sense, the mortgage market created its own expansion. Thus, mortgage and housing markets fuelled one another, but it is crucial to understand that the driving force here is the mortgage market. As argued in the previous sections and in some of the subsequent chapters, this was enabled through deregulation and re-regulation.

Where did all these billions of dollars come from? We now know that an expanding mortgage market enabled homeowners to buy increasingly expensive houses, but where did the lenders get all this money? The answer is, by and large, from the securitization of mortgage loans. By selling RMBS, lenders cleaned up their balance sheets and were able to use the freed-up capital to grant even bigger loans to even more homeowners. Securitization also enabled new lenders to enter the market, many of which were less closely watched by regulatory agencies. Old and new lenders alike had an interest in making loans that could be sold off, and in loans that generated higher yields. This resulted in riskier loans with higher interest rates (sub-prime lending). Mortgage brokers were rewarded with higher fees if they sold loans with higher interest rates (often subprime loans). Many of these were not loans to buy a house, but refinanced loans and second mortgages, or, in other words, loans that did *not* contribute to the spread of homeown-ership. The higher risk of default on these loans was taken for granted, not just because they would be sold off, but also because default presented a risk to the borrower who would lose her or his home; the lender could repossess the home and sell it quite easily as house prices continued to rise.

There were enough investors who had an appetite for RMBS, first in so-called conforming loans (see Glossary) because of their low-risk, which was comparable to state obligations. But a few years later they also showed an interest in subprime loans issued as RMBS: in an ever-more competitive search for yield "each stage of market development replayed a dynamic of overspeculation based on competitive pressures to adopt riskier borrowers and loan products" (Ashton 2009: 1425). Investors, in turn, "had concen-trated risks by leveraging their holdings of mortgages in securitized assets, so [when the bubble burst] their losses were multiplied" (Mizen 2008: 532). Subprime loans were considered riskier, but this was compensated by higher returns and since the rating agencies still supplied high ratings, such RMBS were seen as low-risk/high-return. Rating agencies saw the increased likeli-ness of default on such loans, but, like the lenders, they did not see this as a major problem but more of an inconvenience.

What caused the rating agencies to be so late in realizing the risk of these securities? First, as I suggested above, they simply did not realize the risk as they believed in rising house prices, just like homeowners, lenders, and the media – like everyone essentially. Second, credit rating agencies get paid by the firms whose securities they have to rate. They had become so heavily involved with securities that their own growth now depended on rating more and more of them. Third, throughout the years the most basic RMBS were complemented by ever more complicated products that few had an understanding of, not even the rating agencies that investors trusted. It is sometimes argued that the rating agencies cannot be blamed for this as others in the mortgage network also did not understand the complexity and riskiness of these products, but, since it is their job to understand and then rate financial products, it could be argued (in an almost tautologically fashion) that the rating agencies are responsible for rating high-risk financial products as low-risk.

While in the past a mortgage bubble or a housing bubble would affect the economy through homeowners, the recent bursting of these bubbles affects the economy not just through homeowners, but also through financial markets. Because lenders are now national and international in scope this no longer affects only some housing markets, but all housing markets throughout the US. Housing markets may still be local or regional, mortgage markets are not. Since primary mortgage markets are national, the bubble in the national mortgage market affects all local and regional housing markets, although it clearly affects housing markets with a greater bubble more than those with a smaller bubble. In addition, secondary mortgage markets are global markets, which means that a crisis of mortgage securitization implies that investors around the globe, and therefore economies around the globe, are affected. Financialization in the form of securitization, does have borders (as Wainwright demonstrates in Chapter 4), but thanks to re-regulation it can transcend these borders. In the end, the mortgage market crisis affects the US economy on both sides of the mortgage lending chain – through homeowners and through financial markets – while it affects other economies in the world mostly through financial markets, not just because investors around the globe have invested in RMBS, but also because the mortgage market has triggered a whole chain of events that have decreased liquidity and this affects even agents in financial markets that have never been involved in RMBS. In this book we pay little attention to how the mortgage market crisis has widened into a major, global crisis, but many of the chapters look at the different sources and consequences of the structural changes in the mortgage market.

Post-Subprime Cities?

With the twin crises, subprime lending and subprime mortgage securitization have collapsed. Yet, it would be too easy to assume that subprime cities can return to being or finally become – depending on your perspective – prime cities. Subprime lending is not necessarily replaced by prime lending, but there is some evidence to suggest that redlining, that is place-based exclusion from mortgage loans, is back, not only in the US but also in Europe (Kane 2008; Markey 2010; Aalbers 2011). The havoc caused by subprime lending will plague neighborhoods and cities for years or even decades to come – we have learned as much from earlier urban crises. However, there are at least three other reasons to be skeptical about the post-subprime world.

Firstly, the city and state governments that have to deal with the post-crisis rubble and rumble are less able to do so than before the crisis. Government budgets have been heavily undermined by the twin crises. Many municipalities and states are already faced with lower incoming taxes (in particular real estate taxes) and cuts in funding of schools, social services, garbage collection, infrastructure, and so on. One complication in the US, and possibly elsewhere, is that municipalities as well as many states are not allowed to run a deficit. While the national government tries to stimulate the economy by spending more, municipalities and many states that are faced with decreasing revenues also have to cut back. This is by no means a marginal development. State revenues in New York, a state that in no way presents a worst-case scenario, have come down 36 percent in one year.[2]

Secondly, and following Harvey (2005), a crisis is often used to consolidate class power and this is exactly what the bailouts of the financial firms of Wall Street, as well as those of Detroit car companies, were doing. However the other "Detroits," the subprime cities and the many foreclosed homes, are not being bailed out. Under the Obama Administration there is a significant program to help people in foreclosure or to prevent foreclosure, but it cannot even keep up with the continuing high numbers of people losing their homes. So far, the program is a far cry from being a big success. In addition, the state is doing very little to allow bankruptcy judges to modify a mortgage on a primary residence to make it affordable. Oddly, "bankruptcy judges can cram down a mortgage on a second home or a yacht – both most likely owned by a rich person – but not on a primary residence" (Lobel 2008: 32). This suggests government is "aimed at aiding one class of Americans – the extremely wealthy" (ibid.).

Finally, new financial regulation is not only too late but also too little to deal with the excesses of the financial industry. Even the Dodd–Frank Wall Street Reform and Consumer Protection Act, which is often considered one of the most important steps, if not the crucial step, to creating a more responsible financial sector, is not without flaws. Although the Dodd–Frank Act, which was signed into law by US President Barack Obama on July 21, 2010 and consists of 2300 pages that direct regulators to create 533 new rules, is clearly an important step in the right direction, it could also be argued that it is a minimal improvement considering what is needed to patch up the previous system that enabled the financial crisis. Cassidy

(2010) argues that the measures actually taken were the least that could have been done. The Act has also been criticized for trying to forestall the last crisis rather than the next one – but this is intrinsic to post-crisis regulation. More problematic is that with the Dodd–Frank Act in place, the crisis of 2007–2009 would probably not have been forestalled. The Act was heavily lobbied by the financial sector. Partly as a result, some securities and derivatives are still exempt from new regulation, big banks face no effective limits to their debt pile and will still be "too big to fail" (and the biggest of them are now actually bigger than ever before), the credit rating agencies remain under-regulated, the situation of Fannie Mae and Freddie Mac and their implicit government backing remain unresolved, and finally the new Consumer Financial Protection Bureau will be part of the Federal Reserve Board and can be overruled by the Financial Stability Oversight Council, a council known for prioritizing bank profitability. *Tout ensemble*, the Dodd–Frank Act is a necessary but insufficient step in the direction of a more responsible financial sector.[3]

Overview

This book consists of four parts. The first part consists of the present chapter. The second and largest part focuses on the political economy of the mortgage market and its relation to the twin crises. The third part includes studies that explicitly focus on the urban elements of the crisis. The fourth part consists of one chapter: the conclusion to this book.

The second part of the book opens with the chapters of Kevin Fox Gotham and Herman Schwartz who both pay a great deal of attention to the role of the state in setting up the housing bubble, and thereby also the housing bust. First, Gotham situates the recent crisis in a series of ad hoc legal and regulatory actions taken in the US in the 1980s and 1990s that favored securitization. It is a key chapter for understanding many of the subsequent chapters. Second, Schwartz looks at the involvement of the state beyond securitization. In a way, his chapter contextualizes the American exceptionalism in mortgage lending. Next, Saskia Sassen argues that securitization has turned housing into an electronic instrument for high-risk finance. Her chapter clearly highlights the global–local nexus of the twin crises. We then move to Europe: Thomas Wainwright, partly based on interviews with key market actors, shows how US style securitization had to be reinvented and re-regulated to fit the UK's financial market, while Manuel Aalbers argues that despite all the rhetoric of globalization, primary mortgage markets and most mortgage lenders remain national in scope and only the market for RMBS has become globalized. The last chapter of the second part of this book, which also could have been the first chapter of the third part, is written by Gary Dymski who first describes how the subprime crisis was rooted in a long history of racial exploitation and exclusion in credit markets, and then goes on to dissect the microeconomic logic, the market dynamics, of the subprime lending crisis.

The third part of this book opens with a chapter by Jesus Hernandez who situates contemporary patterns of subprime and predatory lending in one century of exclusionary mortgage lending in Sacramento, California. Thanks to a combination of different research methods he is able to provide such a rich historical perspective. It is followed by Kathe Newman's chapter on subprime lending and foreclosures in Essex County (which includes the city of Newark), New Jersey; and the chapter by Elvin Wyly, Markus Moos, and Daniel Hammel that, based on an analysis of subprime and predatory lending across the US, debunks (1) the doctrine of risk-based pricing, (2) the homeownership myth, and (3) the idea of a discrimination-free mortgage market. Newman uses the relatively new method of mining property records to investigate neighborhood dynamics, while Wyly *et al.* use innovative statistical modeling to map the shifting cartographies of racial exploitation.

Together these chapters engage and extend some central and longstanding themes within urban political economy, but they also construct conceptual bridges between urban sociology and human geography on the one hand, and heterodox economics on the other.[4] Although many of the alternative approaches on economic issues – that is, alternatives to mainstream economics – share a great deal, they hardly ever enter into a dialogue with one another. More than any other chapter in this book, Gary Dymski's conclusion, which comprises the fourth part of the book, contrasts and compares the more socio-spatial approaches and the more economic approaches to mortgage markets and the twin crises. Finally, a Glossary that defines some of the commonly used concepts throughout this book is included.

Decades of social science have taught us that race and place are significant factors that impact on whether one gets a mortgage and, if so, on which terms. Capital extraction takes advantage of past and present forms of racial discrimination and reproduces past actions of race-based financial inequality. Mortgage securitization meant that things that were once local and distinctive (e.g., local housing markets, borrower–lender relationships) were now commensurable, so they could be traded as pure commodities. One of the things pulled out of context involves racial and ethnic relations. These vary widely across national and regional contexts. The mortgage market evolved in such a way that local actors could understand and exploit these racial, ethnic, and class variations, and then pass on the subsequent mortgage obligations to national and transnational institutions who did not really care about all those local variations. Racism was stripped out of local context, but the effects were intensified. This is clearest in the US as Dymski, Wyly *et al.*, Hernandez, and Newman all show: racial minorities and the neighborhoods inhabited by them are more likely to be targeted by subprime and predatory lenders. This has little to do with the discourse of expanding homeownership among groups traditionally excluded from homeownership and more with continuing patterns of racial discrimination and uneven development.

Notes

1 This paragraph is adapted from Aalbers (2011).
2 See the articles on "The crisis unfolds" in issues 34(3) and 34(4) of the *International Journal of Urban and Regional Research* (2010) for more examples of how cities are hit by the financial crisis and how they try to cope with it.
3 The situation is not necessarily better in the European Union (see, e.g., Posner and Véron 2010) or elsewhere.
4 I am heavily indebted to Philip Ashton's assessment of the book here.

References

Aalbers, M.B. (2007) Place-based and race-based exclusion from mortgage loans: Evidence from three cities in the Netherlands. *Journal of Urban Affairs* 29(1): 1–29.

Aalbers, M.B. (2008) The financialization of home and the mortgage market crisis. *Competition & Change* 12(2): 148–66.

Aalbers, M.B. (2009) Geographies of the financial crisis. *Area* 41(1): 34–42.

Aalbers, M.B. (2011) *Place, Exclusion and Mortgage Markets*. Oxford: Wiley-Blackwell.

Aalbers, M.B., E. Engelen, and A. Glasmacher (2011) "'Cognitive closure'" in the Netherlands: Mortgage Securitization in a hybrid European political economy. *Environment and Planning A* 43(8): 1779–95.

Arrighi, G. (1994) *The Long Twentieth Century: Money, Power, and the Origins of our Times*. London: Verso.

Ashton, P. (2009) An appetite for yield: The anatomy of the subprime mortgage crisis. *Environment & Planning A* 41(6): 1420–41.

Boyer, R. (2000) Is a finance-led growth regime a viable alternative to Fordism? A preliminary analysis. *Economy and Society* 29(1): 111–45.

Bradford, C.P. and L.S. Rubinowitz (1975) The urban-suburban investment-disinvestment process: Consequences for older Neighborhoods. *Annals of the American Academy of Political and Social Sciences* 422: 77–86.

Carruthers, B.G. (2005) The sociology of money and credit. In N.J. Smelser and R. Swedberg (eds.) *The Handbook of Economic Sociology. Second edition*. Princeton: Princeton University Press.

Caskey, J. (1994) *Fringe banking: Check-cashing Outlets, Pawnshops, and the Poor*. New York: Russell Sage.

Cassidy, J. (2010) The economy: Why they failed. *The New York Review of Books* 57(19) http://www.nybooks.com/articles/archives/2010/dec/09/economy-why-they-failed/ (accessed 24 November, 2010).

Cramer, J.J. (2008) Good-bye, Masters of the Universe. Hello, Ron Hermance of Paramus, New Jersey. *New York Magazine*, 29 September.

Creswell, J. and B. White (2008) Wall Street, R.I.P.: the end of an era, even at Goldman. *New York Times*, 28 September, BU1.

Crossney, K.B. and D.W. Bartelt (2005) The legacy of the Home Owners' Loan Corporation. *Housing Policy Debate* 16(3/4): 547–74.

Crump, J., K. Newman, E.S. Belsky, P. Ashton, D.H. Kaplan, D.J. Hammel, and E. Wyly (2008) Cities destroyed (again) for cash: Forum on the U.S. foreclosure crisis. *Urban Geography* 29(8): 745–84.

Dennis, M.W. and T.J. Pinkowish (2004) *Residential Mortgage Lending. Principles and Practices. Fifth edition.* Mason, OH: Thomson South-Western.

DiMaggio, P.J. and W.W. Powell (1991) Introduction. In W.W. Powell and P.J. DiMaggio (eds.) *The New Institutionalism in Organizational Analysis.* Chicago: University of Chicago Press.

Dominus, S. (2008) At massage office, business is a chart of Wall Street nerves. *New York Times*, 6 October, A22.

Dymski, G.A. (1996) On Krugman's model of economic geography. *Geoforum* 27(4): 439–52.

Dymski, G.A. (1999) *The bank merger wave: the economic causes and social consequences of financial consolidation.* Armonk, NY: Sharpe.

Dymski, G.A. (2009) Afterword: Mortgage markets and the urban problematic in the global transition. *International Journal of Urban and regional Research* 33(2): 427–42.

Fligstein, N. (2001) *The architecture of markets.* Princeton: Princeton University Press.

Florida, R.L. and M.M.A. Feldman (1988) Housing in US Fordism: The class accord and postwar spatial organization. *International Journal of Urban and Regional Research* 12(2): 187–210.

Gapper, J. (2008) The effects on the city of a drastically smaller Wall Street. *New York Magazine*, 29 September.

Goldstein, I. (2004) The economic consequences of predatory lending: a Philadelphia case study. In G.D. Squires (ed.) *Why The Poor Pay More. How to Stop Predatory Lending*, pp. 39–79, Westport: Praeger.

Gotham, K.F. (2002) *Race, real estate, and uneven development. The Kansas city experience, 1900–2000. Albany:* State University of New York Press.

Gotham, K.F. (2006) The secondary circuit of capital reconsidered: Globalization and the U.S. real estate sector. *American Journal of Sociology* 112(1): 231–75.

Hacker, J.S. (2006) *The great risk shift: The assault on American jobs, families, health care and retirement – and how you can fight back.* New York: Oxford University Press.

Hamnett, C. (1994) Restructuring housing finance and the housing market. In S. Corbridge, N. Thrift, and R. Martin (eds.) *Money, Power and Space.* Oxford: Blackwell.

Harvey, D. (1977) Government policies, financial institutions and neighbourhood change in United States cities. In M. Harloe (ed.) *Captive cities. Studies in the political economy of cities and regions.* London: John Wiley & Sons.

Harvey, D. (1985) *The Urbanization of Capital. Studies in The History and Theory of Capitalist Urbanization.* Oxford: Blackwell.

Harvey, D. (2005) *A Brief History of Neoliberalism.* Oxford: Oxford University Press.

Hillier, A. (2003) Redlining and the Home Owners' Loan Corporation. *Journal of Urban History* 29(4): 394–420.

Hirsch, P., S. Michaels, and R. Friedman (1987) "Dirty hands" versus "clean models": Is sociology in danger of being seduced by economics? *Theory and Society* 16: 317–36.

Immergluck, D. (2004) *Credit to the community. Community reinvestment and fair lending policy in the United States.* Armonk, NY: Sharpe.

Immergluck, D. (2009) *Foreclosed: High-risk Lending, Deregulation, and the Undermining of America's Mortgage Market.* Ithaca, NY: Cornell University Press.

Jackson, K.T. (1985) *Crabgrass frontier. The Suburbanization of the United States.* Oxford: Oxford University Press.

Kaminsky, G.L. and C.M. Reinhart (1999) The twin crises: the causes of banking and balance-of-payment problems. *American Economic Review* 89(3): 473–500.

Kane, M. (2008) Redlining redux: New mortgage industry policy could charge borrowers higher fees by zip code. *The Washington Independent*, May 15: http://washingtonindependent.com/view/reconsidering (accessed 24 November, 2010).

Krippner, G. (2005) The financialization of the American economy. *Socio-Economic Review* 3: 173–208.

Langley, P. (2006) Securitising suburbia: the transformation of Anglo-American mortgage finance. *Competition and Change* 10(3): 283–99.

Leyshon, A. and N. Thrift (1997) *Money/Space: Geographies of Monetary Transformation.* London: Routledge.

Leyshon, A. and N. Thrift (1999) Lists come alive: electronic systems of knowledge and the rise of credit-scoring in retail banking. *Economy and Society* 28(3): 434–66.

Lobel, M. (2008) A free and fair market. *Miller-McCune* September 16, http://www.miller-mccune.com/business_economics/a-free-and-fair-market-690 (accessed 24 November, 2010).

Logan, J. and H. Molotch (1987) *Urban Fortunes: The Political Economy of Place.* Berkeley, CA: University of California Press.

Lordon, F. (2007) Spéculation immobilière, ralentissement économique. Quand la finance prend le monde en otage. *Le Monde diplomatique*, Septembre.

Mackinnon, D. and A. Cumbers (2007) *An Introduction to Economic Geography. Globalization, Uneven Development and Place.* Harlow: Pearson.

Marcuse, P. (1979) The Deceptive Consensus on Redlining: Definitions Do Matter. *Journal of the American Planning Association* 45(4): 549–56.

Markey, E. (2010) Banks redline minority communities again. *City Limits*, May 14: http://www.citylimits.org/news/articles/3996/banks-redline-minority-communities-again (accessed 24 November, 2010).

McCoy, P.A. and E.K. Wyly (2004) Guest editors' introduction. *Housing Policy Debate* 15: 453–66.

Mizen, P. (2008) The credit crunch of 2007–2008: A discussion of the background, market reactions, and policy responses. *Federal Reserve Bank of St. Louis Review* 90(5): 531–67.

Peck, J. (2005) Economic sociologies in space. *Economic Geography* 81(2): 129–75.

Polanyi, K. (1944) *The Great Transformation: The Political and Economic Origins of Our Time.* Boston: Beacon.

Polanyi, K. (1992) The economy as instituted process. In M. Granovetter and R. Swedberg (eds.) *The Sociology of Economic* Life. Boulder, CO: Westview.

Posner, E. and N. Véron (2010) The EU and financial regulation. Power without purpose. *Journal of European Public Policy* 17(3): 400–15.

Pryke, M. and R. Lee (1995) Place your bets: towards an understanding of globalisation, socio-financial engineering and competition within a financial centre. *Urban Studies* 32(2): 329–44.

Ross, S.L. and J. Yinger (2002) *The Color of Credit: Mortgage Discrimination, Research Methodology, and Fair-Lending Enforcement.* Cambridge, MA: MIT Press.

Sassen, S. (2001) *The Global City: New York, London, Tokyo. Second edition.* Princeton: Princeton University Press.

Schwartz, H.M. (2009) *Subprime nation: American power, global finance and the housing bubble.* Ithaca, NY: Cornell University Press.

Schwartz, H.M. and L. Seabrooke (eds.) (2009) *The Politics of Housing Booms and Busts.* Basingstoke: Palgrave Macmillan.

Shiller, R.J. (2008) *The subprime solution.* Princeton: Princeton University Press.

Shlay, A. (1989) Financing community: Methods for assessing residential credit disparities, market barriers, and institutional reinvestment performance in the metropolis. *Journal of Urban Affairs* 11(3): 201–23.

Squires, G.D. (ed.) (1992) *From redlining to reinvestment: Community response to urban disinvestment.* Temple University Press, Philadelphia.

Squires, G.D. (ed.) (2004) *Why the poor pay more. How to Stop Predatory Lending.* Westport: Praeger.

Squires, G.D. (2008) Do subprime loans create subprime cities? Surging inequality and the rise in predatory lending. *EPI Briefing Paper*, February 28. Washington, DC: Economic Policy Institure.

Stuart, G. (2003) *Discriminating risk: The U.S. mortgage lending industry in the twentieth century.* Ithaca, NY: Cornell University Press.

Thomas, L.C. (2000) A survey of credit and behavioural scoring: forecasting financial risk of lending to consumers. *International Journal of Forecasting* 16(2): 149–72.

Veblen, T. (1934) *Essays in our changing order.* A.M. Kelley, New York.

Wyly, E.K. and S.R. Holloway (1999) "The color of money" revisited. Racial lending patterns in Atlanta's neighborhoods. *Housing Policy Debate* 10: 555–600.

Wyly, E.K., M. Atia, H. Foxcroft, D. Hammel, and K. Philips-Watts (2006) American home: predatory mortgage capital and neighbourhood spaces of race and class exploitation in the United States. *Geografiska Annaler B* 88: 105–32.

Wyly, E.K., M. Moos, H. Foxcroft, and E. Kabahizi (2008) Subprime mortgage segmentation in the American urban system. *Tijdschrift voor Economische en Sociale Geografie* 99(1): 3–23.

Zukin, S. (1980) A decade of the new urban sociology. *Theory and Society* 9(4): 575–601.

Part II

The Political Economy of the Mortgage Market

1

Creating Liquidity Out of Spatial Fixity
The Secondary Circuit of Capital and the Restructuring of the US Housing Finance System

Kevin Fox Gotham

Introduction

This chapter examines the current crisis within the US housing finance sector as an illustration of the contradictions of capital circulation as expressed in the tendency of capital to annihilate space through time. In his classic works, Karl Marx argued that one of the distinctive logics of capital accumulation is the tendency by capital to eliminate the spatial and temporal barriers to the realization of exchange values, to reduce to a minimum the time that it costs to produce and sell commodities. One of the major obstacles or barriers to realization of profit, as Marx noted, is the time involved in producing commodities, transporting them to market, and exchanging them for profit. In the case of land and housing, real estate's time in circulation can distend for months or years as capital is tied up for varying periods of time in the process of production and exchange, and hence cannot immediately be returned back to the capitalist in its enhanced form, M'. The longer the turnover time of real estate capital, the smaller the amount of surplus value. Speeding up and increasing the velocity of the circulation of capital and reducing the turnover time derives from the logic of the accumulation process. According to Marx,

> While capital must on one side strive to tear down every spatial barrier to intercourse, i.e. to exchange, and conquer the whole world for its market, it strives on the other side to annihilate this space with time, i.e. to reduce to a minimum the time spent in motion from one place to another. The more developed the capital ... the more does it strive for an even greater extension of the market and for greater annihilation of space by time. (1973: 539)

Subprime Cities: The Political Economy of Mortgage Markets, First Edition. Edited by Manuel B. Aalbers.
© 2012 Blackwell Publishing Ltd. Published 2012 by Blackwell Publishing Ltd.

Over the century Marx's ideas and theories have influenced countless scholars interested in understanding the growth-oriented, technologically dynamic, and crisis-prone nature of capitalism and its effects on urban space. During the 1960s and 1970s, Henri Lefebvre and David Harvey drew attention to the physical landscape and built environment as a source of and barrier to capital accumulation. For Harvey ([1975] 2001: 247) capitalism is a contradictory totality whose "crowning glory" is the creation of a built environment to further accumulation. At the same time, this built environment is a "prison" that can stifle profit-making as inherited networks and infrastructures can impede market formation, and erect barriers and impediments to capital circulation. As a contingent process of socio-spatial restructuring, capitalist development thereby has to negotiate a "knife-edge path" between preserving the fixed social structures that underpinned and supported past capital investments and destroying these structures in order to create new opportunities for investment. As a consequence, according to Harvey, we "witness a perpetual struggle in which capitalism builds a physical landscape appropriate to its own condition at a particular moment in time, only to have to destroy it, usually in the course of a crisis, at a subsequent point in time" ([1975] 2001: 247). Thus, the built environment that capitalism creates is a locus of fragmentation, polarization, and perpetual upheaval.

My basic argument is that the housing finance sector is permeated by significant contradictions and irrationalities that reflect the disruptive and unstable financial process of transforming illiquid commodities into liquid resources. In the sections below, I argue that over the past several decades the process of "securitization" – for example, converting opaque and illiquid assets into liquid and transparent securities – has become a major crisis-management strategy to remedy the contradictions of capital investment and circulation via the housing finance sector.

Securitization is designed to reduce the uncertainty of buying and selling atypical assets (leases, homes, loans, etc.) by transforming them into marketing investments that have common features and characteristics. As a mechanism for easing the spreading and trading of risk, securitization has been a major financial innovation that has allowed private and public actors to finance local property development and housing in the national and international capital markets. As a process of financial globalization, securitization consists in large part of homogenizing diverse commodities and weakening the institutional buffers between local, national, and global markets. Before the 1980s, consumer loans like home mortgage loans, automobile loans, student loans, and credit card receivables had been held in commercial and savings bank portfolio. In the 1980s and later, securitization enabled lenders and banking institutions to repackage these relatively illiquid assets into standardized, transparent, and interest-bearing securities for resale in global securities markets.

New legislation, regulatory strategies, and public policies have promoted the development and integration of securities markets, the formation of large pools of private investment capital, and the development of new real estate financing tools – for example, adjustable rate mortgages (ARMs), mortgage-backed securities (MBS), real estate investment trusts (REITs), among others. The potential advantages of securitization include enhanced flows of funds across borders; greater distribution of risk to lenders most willing to bear it, which reduces price of risk; and increased availability of credit. As noted in Wainwright's chapter, securitization is not a static thing but a historical process that has undergone relentless innovations as it has spread, albeit unevenly, across the globe.

As I point out, the securitization of real estate is a process of creating liquidity out of spatial fixity that is characterized by complex struggles and contradictory interests that reflect and reinforce the crisis-prone nature of capital accumulation and circulation in the built environment. I conceptualize spatial fixity as a condition of non-exchangeability, non-transferability, immobility, illiquidity, and long turnover times between buying and selling. Spatial fixity also refers to a commodity that has diverse, idiosyncratic, and inconsistent properties such that it is difficult for buyers and sellers to know the value and property of what they are exchanging. A liquid asset or resource, in contrast, has homogeneous, predictable, and standardized features that enable financial actors to convert it into cash quickly and easily. Exchangeability and marketability define liquid commodities. Liquidity is neither a psychological phenomenon nor an immutable or durable feature of an asset. As a social construction, liquidity is variable, contingent, and dependent on state actions and legal and regulatory frameworks to support the standardization, homogenization, and exchangeability of commodities. State policies, regulations, and legal actions can impede or facilitate the development of market liquidity. More important, creating markets for liquid capital reflect the politics of liquidity, including political struggles and conflicts over the formulation and implementation of housing finance policies and other socio-legal regulations pertaining to mortgage markets and financing instruments.

As far as possible, securitization attempts to standardize and rationalize non-transparent and localized commodities (like mortgages) so that different buyers and sellers in different places around the globe can understand their features and qualities and exchange them easily.

The securitization of mortgages is driven by a deep tension between local social relations and networks of real estate activity that generate knowledge about a home and its distinctive characteristics, and the reach of markets to extract that knowledge, reduce its unpredictability, and routinize and commodify it. Yet the spread of securitization to mortgages and other commodities is not a one-way process, nor is it necessarily functional, rational, or inevitable. Rather, securitization has developed as a result of substantial and ongoing legal and regulatory reforms that have been implemented on an ad hoc basis to remedy past economic crises. Such an account eschews a "capital logic" argument and examines the ways in which state policies and legal/regulatory actions to create and enhance the exchangeability of otherwise illiquid commodities are historically contingent, conflictual, and contradictory.

Past legal/regulatory actions have fed back into the US housing system by creating new financial flows, exacerbating uneven development, and destabilizing markets as recently revealed through the subprime mortgage crisis. Understanding the changing institutional linkages between housing finance, securitization, and state policy not only provides useful insights into the causes of the current financial crisis but also presents an opportunity for theoretical development into the sociology of mortgage markets. The conflicts over the securitization of illiquid assets – that is, the creation of liquidity out of spatial fixity – represent intense struggles over efforts to annihilate space through time within mortgage markets and the real estate rector more broadly.

I begin by describing the theoretical orientation that informs the analysis of the historical development and recent restructuring of the US housing finance system. I examine the rise of the New Deal system of housing finance and the growth of the savings and loan industry. I then describe the economic vulnerabilities of the savings and loan industry and the various policy reforms enacted during the 1960s through the 1980s to transform mortgages into liquid resources via the process of securitization. Next, I focus on two major regulatory drivers of the housing finance crisis: first, the expansion of private-label securitization and, second, the crucial role played by the US Treasury Department's Office of the Comptroller of the Currency (OCC) in nurturing the growth of a market for securitizing subprime loans. My historical analysis suggests that state strategies to guide investment in real estate and transform illiquid commodities into liquid resources have developed over time in conjunction with past political circumstances and sociopolitical struggles.

As I point out, the state plays a key role in the dialectics of spatial fixity and liquidity through a variety of policies, legal-regulatory actions, and infrastructural investment that can enhance the exchangeability of mortgages, and contribute to and exacerbate crisis tendencies within the finance and real estate sectors. I draw on recent theorizations of the secondary circuit of capital to illustrate the ways in which securitization has been both a response to and cause of financial crises. Whereas securitization was a major regulatory response to the savings and loan crisis of the 1980s and 1990s, today we recognize securitization as an important cause of the subprime mortgage crisis that has spread globally to affect mortgage and financial markets around the world. In conclusion, I suggest that we view recent state policies to mitigate the financial crisis as crisis management strategies designed to resolve the contradictions created by previous state-led interventions in the housing finance sector.

Real Estate, Housing, and the Secondary Circuit of Capital

My empirical interest in the housing finance system stems from a larger theoretical interest in understanding the links between recent regulatory reforms and structural changes within the "secondary" circuit of capital investment. Initial work by Henri Lefebvre (2003) and David Harvey (1978; 1985) drew attention to the use value and exchange value of real estate and the crucial distinction between the primary and secondary circuits of capital investment. The primary circuit involves capital moving in and out of manufacturing and industrial production, while the secondary circuit refers to capitalist investment in land, real estate, housing, and the built environment. Influenced by Karl Marx, Lefebvre and Harvey maintained that a central component of the overall dynamic of capitalist development lay in the production of the built environment and the process of city building. Both stressed the important influence of private and public financial structures in channeling capital into metropolitan development and the tendency towards crisis within the primary and secondary circuits. The secondary sector, according to Lefebvre, absorbs economic shocks that periodically affect capitalist societies. Harvey's oft-cited thesis attributed the growth of postwar US suburbs to the switching of capital out of the primary circuit, where crises of over accumulation were emerging at mid-century, into the secondary circuit of real estate investment (Harvey 1975). In particular, Lefebvre and Harvey drew attention to several theoretical components that laid the groundwork for understanding the importance of land and real estate in the production of space: the relation of the built environment to the sphere of production, the role of capital accumulation in the built environment, the mediation of financial institutions, and the cyclical nature of capital investment in the primary and secondary circuits (for an overview, see Gottdiener 1994).

Over the decades, the theoretical richness of Lefebvre's and Harvey's arguments have inspired scholars to investigate capital flows into and out of the real estate sector, identify the crisis tendencies and contradictions of the secondary circuit, and fashion new theoretical and analytical tools to examine real estate processes and their linkages with uneven metropolitan development. Early work by Feagin (1982; 1987) attempted to confront Harvey's thesis directly by examining the irrationality of accumulation and investment processes within the real estate sector. In her discussion of the "relative autonomy" of the primary and secondary circuits, Haila (1998; 1991) pointed to the mobilization of particular organized interests – for example, developers, local governments, financial institutions, and real estate brokers, among others – who are concerned not only with investing in property for speculative objectives but also in generating new investment opportunities distinct from those in the primary circuit. Beauregard's (1994) study of the 1980s building boom in the United States found little support for the capital switching thesis and, more important, pointed to the delinking of real estate investment from non-speculative investment criteria and use value considerations.

Recent research on the secondary circuit eschews a conception of real estate as a by-product or outgrowth of "industrial" capitalism and theorizes the real estate sector as having an intrinsic quality or *sui generis* character that forms an independent sector of the economy. Charney's (2001) case study of the Canadian real estate sector draws attention to how real estate companies attempt to capitalize on segmented real estate markets by using "three dimensions of capital switching" within the secondary circuit. Real estate companies can switch between modes of operation, between property types, and between geographical areas (i.e., spatial switching). More recently, Aalbers' (2007) examination of the Milan, Italy mortgage market suggests that capital switching does not necessarily reflect a post hoc response to economic crises per se. Capital switching can represent a proactive and consciously planned strategy taken by capital to exploit the lucrative opportunities that the built environment provides. Overall, the work of Charney, Aalbers, and others views the real estate sector as a conceptually separate and analytically distinct circuit of capital investment that is organized by diverse networks of actors, organizations, and laws and public policies (Gotham 2006; 2002). The secondary circuit is not the exclusive domain of separate real estate agents, but consists of a structure of banks, other financial conduits, and diverse modes of agency, such as monopolistic and small real estate and financial firms, appraisers, public and private investors, and homeowners (Feagin 1982; Gottdiener 1994: 185–94).

Conceptualizing and analyzing the dynamics of the secondary circuit suggests a theory of circulating capital that emphasizes the irrationalities of the circulation process and the systemic crises that periodically affect real estate markets. In Volume 3 of *Capital*, Marx (1991: 78) argued that capital creates institutional and financial structures and networks that can become sources of ruinous competition and obstacles to future investment: "The *true barrier* to capitalist production is *capital itself*," Marx theorized. From this perspective, real estate's time in circulation – that is, the period of time from the production of value to the realization of value in commodity exchange – can be both an opportunity and constraint to profitability.

Real estate can aid capital accumulation, if it is a profitable avenue for commercial investment and a source of mass consumption in the case of homeownership. Investment in real estate, housing, and land can be an important means of accumulating wealth and a crucial activity that pushes the growth of metropolitan areas in specific ways. Further, once built, residential real estate and housing provides access to other commodities; spatially embeds classes, races, and ethnic groups; and channels the spatial growth and movement of industrial capital.

Real estate can be a barrier to capital accumulation, however, when its enduring qualities render it outdated and anachronistic, or when financing needed to construct, sell, and rehabilitate it are unavailable. According to Gottdiener (1994: 191), investment in real estate generates bust-and-boom cycles of investment and "propels the never ending process of property turnover and spatial restructuring whether an area needs it or not." This process of "creative-destruction," of destruction and demolition, expropriation and rebuilding, and rapid and incessant changes in use as a result of real estate speculation and obsolescence are the most recognizable signs of uneven metropolitan development in the United States.

In short, the analysis of the secondary circuit of capital reveals a basic contradiction. On the one hand, real estate is by definition illiquid, spatially fixed and immobile, and defined by local particularities and idiosyncrasies. Geir Inge Orderud's (2006) analysis of the Norway housing sector suggests that home building is "a local business due to: a capacity restraint regarding local market knowledge; the interaction with local planning authorities; face-to-face meetings; and social relations." On the other hand, capital is abstract, nomadic, and placeless. Insofar as possible, capital seeks to eradicate local peculiarities and place distinctions that characterize the buying and selling of commodities and thereby eliminate the spatial barriers to the circulation of capital.

It is this duality, or inherent contradiction, between immobile properties and mobile capital that defines modern capitalist urbanization and uneven development. In Lefebvre's (2003: 159, 212) account of capitalist growth during the twentieth century, investment in the secondary circuit has assumed a life of its own as

> speculation henceforth becomes the principal source, the almost-exclusive arena of formation and realization of surplus value. Whereas the proportion of global surplus value amassed and realized in industry declines, the amount of surplus value created and realized in speculation and property construction increases. The secondary circuit thus supplants the primary circuit and perforce becomes essential.

Harvey (1985: 11) echoes this tendency in his assertion that urban growth has changed "from an expression of the needs of industrial producers to an expression of the power of finance capital over the totality of the production process."

Below, in my analysis of the historical development of the US housing finance sector, I show that creating liquidity out of spatial fixity is an uneven, multidirectional, and open-ended restructuring process that is frequently associated with crisis-generating breakdown and instability. Liquidity is both a social relation between buyers and sellers of risk, and a process of exercising financial power in and through certain political and institutional arrangements. While the logic of capital creates opportunities and obstructions for change, various actors and organized interests interpret and construct the rules of the game through politics, policies, laws, organizational procedures, and other regulatory strategies.

As I show with the savings and loan crisis of the 1980s and 1990s and the recent subprime mortgage crisis, the interpretations of and responses to accumulation crises create new openings and prospects for transformation as well as legitimating calls for new policies to extend and enhance existing institutional structures of liquidity. State policies and interventions ultimately create a "catch 22 loop" whereby "old" policies produce crises of liquidity that inevitably bring forth calls for "new" policies that, once implemented, create further contradictions and unforeseen crises, a situation that then generates a new round of calls for "reform," as we currently see with the subprime mortgage crisis and its spread to global capital markets. In this sense, the politics of liquidity take place on an aggressively contested institutional landscape in which past socio-spatial inequalities and regulatory arrangements interact with current political conflicts and struggles to control investment and accumulation. The establishment of new governance structures, state policies, and socio-legal arrangements to promote liquidity then provide a political arena in and through which class fractions and other organized interests battle to dominate and exploit markets, and control the accumulation process.

The New Deal Housing Finance System and Rise of the Savings and Loan Industry

The financial reforms of the New Deal represented the beginnings of federal involvement in establishing and subsidizing a national real estate sector and mortgage system that would last through the 1980s (for overviews, see Florida 1986b; Florida and Feldman 1988). Before the 1930s, federal involvement in housing markets was limited to the creation of a Federal Land Bank system in 1916 and the construction of military housing during the First World War. The establishment of the Federal Home Loan Bank Act (FHLB) in 1932, the Home Owners' Loan Act in 1933, and the Housing Act of 1934 represented the beginning of a multifaceted federal effort to rebuild the nation's housing and lending industries that had collapsed during the Great Depression. The Hoover Administration's FHLB included the creation of long-term amortized mortgages with low interest rates, and federal subsidies to aid private home building efforts and reduce housing construction costs (Radford 1996: 46–53; Davies 1958: 174–5; President's Committee on Home Building and Home Ownership 1932: 24; US Senate 1933). In addition, the FHLB created a system of federal home loan banks that could supply housing credit, and provide guidance, standards, and regulation over the private lending industry to expedite the flow of mortgage funds. The 1933 Act established the Home Owners Loan Corporation (HOLC), which systematized appraisal methods throughout the nation by devising a neighborhood rating system to assess the creditworthiness of the housing it financed (Harriss 1951). From 1933 to 1935, the HOLC refinanced approximately 20 percent of all outstanding mortgages on single family homes in the nation. This percentage amounted to one million loans worth approximately $3.1 billion. By 1935, the HOLC held 12 percent of the nation's outstanding residential mortgage debt, more than life insurance or commercial banks (Colton 2002: 4).

The Housing Act of 1934 provided for the establishment of a modern mortgage insurance system under which the newly created Federal Housing Administration (FHA) would provide insurance to private lenders to protect them against loss on home rehabilitation loans and mortgages for new homes (US House 1934a: 1). In addition to insuring home mortgages, the FHA created national mortgage associations to buy and sell FHA-insured mortgages in an effort to make mortgage insurance available on a nationwide scale and maintain a continuous and geographically even circulation of funds in times of short credit. Continuing a trend begun by the HOLC, the FHA required that all government-insured loans be long term, fixed rate, have high loan-to-value ratios, and be fully amortized with low down payments (10 percent or less of the total housing cost). The FHA also required all government-insured mortgages to conform to specific regulations pertaining to minimum property standards and inspections, design of the structure, quality of building materials and construction, appraisal procedures, condition and location of site, and subdivision planning. The effect of this new mortgage system was to standardize and systematize mortgage lending practices throughout the nation and transfer the risk of mortgage investment from the private sector to the federal government (US House 1934b). In addition, the 1934 Act established the Federal Savings and Loan Insurance Corporation (FSLIC) to insure the accounts of federal savings and loan (S&L) associations (Federal Housing Administration 1959). The significance of the 1934 Housing Act was that it represented the first concerted and large-scale federal intervention into the housing market to stimulate consumer demand and prime the private sector to increase housing supply.

Title III of the Housing Act of 1934 provided for the incorporation of private national mortgage associations to create a secondary mortgage market to provide greater mortgage market liquidity and enhance the financing of housing and real estate. In the "primary" mortgage market, borrowers obtain loans from mortgage originators. In the "secondary" mortgage market, mortgage originators and investors buy and sell mortgages as bonds or securities collateralized by the value of mortgage loans. Enhancing the liquidity of residential real estate proved difficult in the first few years as the lack of a central institution and socio-legal infrastructure mitigated against the transformation of mortgages into liquid resources. In 1938, the FHA chartered the National Mortgage Association of Washington, renamed the Federal National Mortgage Associate (FNMA), nicknamed Fannie Mae, to buy and sell mortgages as an expedient to pumping capital into the residential construction industry. A related purpose of Fannie Mae was to stimulate cash flow to enable mortgage banks, savings and loan associations, and commercial banks to make new loans. During the first decade of its existence, Fannie Mae purchased 66,947 FHA-insured mortgages and sold 49,048. In 1949, Fannie Mae expanded its activities to include buying and selling mortgages guaranteed by the Veterans Administration (VA). During these years, the volume of VA mortgages purchased by Fannie Mae skyrocketed, going from 6734 mortgages in 1948 to 133,032 mortgages two years later in 1950 (FNMA 1975).

Other New Deal reforms including the Glass-Steagall Act of 1933, the Securities and Exchange Act, and the Banking Act of 1935 erected rigid regulatory barriers between the various segments of the commercial banking and housing finance industries. Under the Glass-Steagall Act, Congress completely separated commercial banking and insurance, and prohibited banks from interstate operations and from offering insurance or securities. The Banking Act of 1935 created the Federal Deposition Insurance Corporation (FDIC) to protect depositors at FDIC-insured institutions and provide a means for insuring small depositors against losses arising from bank failure. The legislation also allowed the FDIC to review operations of those banks under its jurisdiction; issue regulations to promote safe and sound banking practices; and cancel insurance for banks engaged in unsafe and unlawful banking practices.

Through this New Deal housing system, housing finance became insulated from the national financial system. Highly localized and small savings and loans became the source of capital for housing finance while Congress designed the FHA to provide housing credit on a long-term basis. The savings and loan (S&L) or "thrift" industry, as it emerged after the 1930s, became the chief source of mortgages as the federal government protected the emerging industry from more volatile flows of funds in national capital markets by shielding savings deposits.[1] With financing from deposits, S&Ls

made conventional fixed, long-term loans to home buyers. Federal and state regulations limited the spatial investment reach of these lenders, restricting interstate banking activities and mandating thrifts to make mortgages in small local areas – within 50 miles of the home office until 1964, and within 100 miles after. From 1950 to 1977, the percentage of residential mortgage debt outstanding held by savings and loan associations increased from 36 percent to 65 percent (Colton 2002: 9). In subsequent decades, life insurance companies and commercial banks saw their share of the market for residential mortgage debt decline while the thrift industry grew at an astonishing rate, doubling their assets every five years and increasing their market share from less than one-fifth to almost one-half of all savings deposits (Hendershott and Villani 1977). By the mid-1950s, a system of specialized mortgage finance institutions had become a "second banking system" (Florida 1986a: 52), controlling a huge pool of resources and functioning under the jurisdiction of the federal government.

New Deal housing policies transformed the home building and loan lending industries by promoting economies of scale through suburban housing construction, a development related to federal efforts to promote the concentration of capital (home builders). The FHA's home building subsides, underwriting standards, and land-planning policies encouraged large builders to expand the scope of operations and market share by enhancing the financial feasibility of single-family homes. Community developers and large builders whose housing plans conformed to FHA standards were able to get a government-insured mortgage for all homes they built (Weiss 1987). Once the FHA subsidy was obtained, builders rapidly increased the size of their operations, producing a high volume of quality, moderately priced dwellings in suburban areas. In 1938, large builders accounted for five percent of all new housing starts. This figure increased to 24 percent in 1949 and 64 percent by 1959. Builders who could promise a large quantity of mortgages and new homes were the principal beneficiaries of federal housing subsidies while smaller builders were driven from the market due to their small-scale operations. For large builders, the FHA offered billions of dollars of credit and insured loans up to 95 percent of the value of the house. In Long Island, NY, the William Levitt and Son Company was able to get FHA subsidies to finance 4000 houses before clearing the land to build Levittown (Checkoway 1984:158–9). Overall, the level of housing production rose significantly after the Second World War, from 209,000 units in 1945, to more than a million units by the end of the decade, to as high as 2,379,000 units by the early 1970s. On an annual basis, production levels during the 1950s, 1960s, and the early 1970s were equally impressive, remaining above seven dwelling units per 1000 population during these years, reaching a peak of 11.4 in 1972 (Rowe 1995: 184). Overall, New Deal housing policies and tax provisions allowing homeowners to deduct mortgage interest and property tax payments from taxable income fueled rises in homeownership, from 48 percent to 63 percent of all households between 1930 and 1970.

Economic Crisis and the Decline of the Savings and Loan Industry

Sharp swings in interest rates, changes in the availability of funds, and unstable production cycles characterized the New Deal housing system during the 1950s and 1960s, leading to calls for major reforms in governing regulations pertaining to housing (Guttentag 1961). Between 1962 and 1969, rising interest rates and plummeting housing starts prompted the Federal Home Loan Bank Board (FHLBB) to authorize a study into the vulnerability of the S&Ls to economic downturns and to recommend changes in the system of housing finance (President's Committee on Federal Credit Programs 1963). This FHLBB study, directed by Irwin Friend, recommended that the federal government promote economies of scale within the S&L industry, encourage industry consolidation through mergers and acquisitions, and develop new mortgage instruments such as gradual payment mortgages and variable-rate mortgages (Friend 1969). New savings inflows to S&Ls plummeted from $8.4 million in 1965 to just $3.6 million in 1966. Through the middle to late 1960s, residential construction declined dramatically experiencing a 23 percent decline between the first quarter of 1966 and the first quarter of 1967. This liquidity crisis prompted Fannie Mae to escalate its mortgage financing activities, purchasing $2 billion in mortgages in an effort to stabilize the housing market (Green and Wachter 2005). By this time, political and economic elites recognized that a fundamental problem facing housing finance was the "maturity mismatch" between long-term mortgage credit and the short-term deposits that banks used to finance mortgages.

Relying on short-term deposits to fund long-term mortgages exposed the Achilles heel of the New Deal housing system and, in the context of the residential construction crisis of the 1960s, aggravated liquidity problems. In response, the federal government passed the Housing Act of 1968, which, among other policy innovations, removed Fannie Mae from the federal budget and privatized the agency as a shareholder-owned company. The legislation also created the Government National Mortgage Association (Ginnie Mae) to assume the management functions of Fannie Mae and guarantee FHA and VA mortgages. Two years later, the federal government created the Federal Loan Mortgage Company, or Freddie Mac, to compete with Fannie Mae in attracting investors to finance housing through an expanded secondary mortgage market. Legislation passed in 1968 and 1970 authorized Fannie Mae, Freddie Mac, and Ginnie Mae to issue securitized bonds to sell to private companies and institutional investors, and represented a bold experiment to attract investment funds to the field of mortgage investment.

To ease the spread and trading of risk via mortgages, federal officials offered a "double guarantee" to create a liquid security, the mortgage pass-through security, that diverse buyers and sellers could understand and exchange. First, pools of securities would contain mortgages insured by the FHA or the VA to protect the investor if the homeowner defaulted. Second, these pools would protect investors if a bank that issued the securitized bonds defaulted. By decoupling risks from profits, the federal government during the 1970s was involved in developing a new housing finance tool, the mortgage-backed security, to promote investment in housing and enhance the marketability or liquidity of mortgages.

The turbulent recessions of 1969–70 and 1974–75, the oil crisis of 1973–74, and the collapse of the Bretton Woods system of fixed exchange rate destabilized the New Deal housing finance system and spurred legislators to enact sweeping reforms to remedy the spreading liquidity crisis. In 1979, the Federal Reserve implemented new regulations to restrict the growth of money supply, a development that caused interest rates to skyrocket. Between June 1979 and March 1980, short-term interest rates rose by more than six percentage points, from 9.06 percent to 15.2 percent. Borrowing at high interest rates to carry mortgages at lower rates caused Fannie Mae to lose millions of dollars and had contagion effects within the broader credit and financial markets.

To remedy the housing finance crisis, in the early 1980s, the US Congress passed the Depository Institutions Deregulation and Monetary Control Act (DIDMCA) of 1980 and the Garn-St. Germain Depository Institutions Act of 1982 that eliminated deposit rate ceilings, enabled S&Ls to invest in commercial banking, and allowed S&Ls to offer competitive money market type accounts. Also in 1982, Congress passed the Alternative Mortgage Transactions Parity Act (AMTPA), which preempted state laws to allow banks throughout the nation to use variable rate terms and balloon payments. These statutes also allowed S&Ls to offer adjustable interest rate mortgages (ARMs) to unload some of the credit risk onto consumers and help mortgage lending institutions match investment returns with interest expenses (see Chapter 8).

Rather than remedy the problems of the S&Ls, however, the regulatory initiatives passed in the 1980s destabilized markets and contributed to the demise of the thrift industry. New legislation and regulations raised interest rates on deposits, reduced rates on old mortgages, and allowed S&Ls to invest heavily in real estate speculation and the junk bond market. The relaxing of regulations and the rise of speculative financing caused catastrophic bank failures and eroded the multi-decade market dominance of S&Ls as suppliers of mortgage credit. In 1981 and 1982 combined, the S&L

industry reported almost $9 billion in losses. On average during 1982–84, one S&L and one commercial bank failed every week. In 1983, the FDIC's list of problem banks grew by 25 institutions per month. Within a year, the rate of bank failures was increasing by three banks a week with the size of receivership assets owned by the FDIC at $10 billion (Kane 1985: 2–3). Overall, bank failures increased from only 22 in 1980, 99 in 1983, 180 in 1985, 262 in 1987, 470 in 1988, and 534 in 1989.[2] From the 1930s through the 1970s, S&Ls provided nearly three-quarters of all new mortgage origina- tions. By the early 1980s, this had declined to just one-fifth of new residential credit (Florida 1986a; 1986b). In short, the elimination of rate ceilings, the development of the adjustable rate mortgage and other loan instruments, and a lessening of legal restrictions that expanded the geographical areas in which individual banks could operate all worked together to inject a new form of competition into the housing sector that undermined the economic power of S&Ls and destabilized the New Deal housing system.

Securitization as Crisis Management Strategy

The savings and loan crisis of the 1980s and early 1990s caused major disruptions in the flow of mortgage capital and mobilized political and economic elites to pass legislation to increase the liquidity of mortgages through securitization and encourage the growth of the secondary mortgage market. Federal officials viewed the S&L crisis as a housing finance problem caused by the dominance of deposit-taking portfolio lenders in the mortgage market. Relying on savings deposits for mortgage loans limited the volume of loans S&Ls could originate. As noted by Baily, Litan, and Johnson (2008: 22), "securitization was seen as a solution to the problems with the S&L model, as it freed mortgage lenders from the liquidity constraint of their balance sheets."

Federal statutes passed during the 1980s to expand the secondary mort- gage market aimed to allow S&Ls and other lenders to sell mortgages to a third-party, take them off their books, and use the money from the sale to generate more loans for homeowners (for overviews, see MacDonald 1995; 1996). In 1984, Congress passed the Secondary Mortgage Market Enhancement Act (SMMEA) that removed statutory restrictions on invest- ments in private MBSs by federal chartered depository institutions. Congress designed this legislation to expand the secondary mortgage market to increase the supply of funds available to mortgage borrowers, transform mortgages into liquid financial instruments, and facilitate the trading of mortgages. The Tax Reform Act of 1986 authorized Real Estate Mortgage Investment Conduits (REMICs), a financial tool that separated groups of mortgages (i.e., mortgage pools) into different risk classes as well as different maturity classes, thereby insulating the financial performance of securities issued from the financial position of the issuer. A year later, Fannie Mae began using REMICs to attract investors not traditionally interested in mortgage-related investments.

The Financial Institutions Reform, Recovery and Enforcement Act of 1989 (FIRREA) established the Resolution Trust Corporation (RTC) to liquidate the assets of hundreds of failed banks and moved S&L regulatory authority from the Federal Home Loan Bank Board to the Office of Thrift Supervision (OTS) (US House of Representatives 1989a; 1989b). One of the primary goals of the FIRREA, and later amendments, was to bolster the supply of mortgage credit by requiring S&Ls to sell mortgages held in portfolio to the secondary mortgage market. The FIRREA also created a board of directors to supervise Freddie Mac and appointed HUD as the major oversight body of the GSE. The supervisory and regulatory structure of the FIRREA was further rationalized through the Federal Housing Enterprises Financial Safety and Soundness Act (FHEFSSA) of 1992. This legislation created the Office of Federal Housing Enterprise Oversight (OFHEO) as a new regulatory office within HUD with the responsibility to "ensure that Fannie Mae and Freddie Mac are adequately capitalized and operating safely."[3] The FHEFSSA established risk-based and minimum capital standards for Fannie Mae and Freddie Mac, and established HUD-imposed housing goals for the financing of affordable housing. Overall, the passage of legislation and the establishment of federal policies and regulations helped define a legal infrastructure for regulating market transactions and enforcing contractual relations to expand the secondary mortgage market.

By the beginning of the millennium, institutional conditions were in place to enhance the liquidity of mortgages thereby providing incentives to domestic and foreign investors to invest capital in residential real estate (Gotham 2006). By this time, securitization had become the primary vehicle for financing the buying and selling of mortgages in the United States. Over the last two decades, the creation and institutionalization of new financial instruments such as the MBS, structured investment vehicles (SIV), the collateral mortgage obligation (CMO), the collateral debt obligation (CDO), and others have uprooted or disembedded the financing of real estate from local networks of accumulation and enmeshed real estate financing within global capital markets. Unlike the MBS that permits the bundling homogeneous risks in the securitization process, SIVs combine many forms of debt and risk to sell to different investors. CMOs are a more complex and sophisticated variation of the MBS that differs in the temporal structure of the expected payments. With a CMO or a CDO (collateralized debt obligation), payments are divided into tranches, with the first one receiving the first set of payments and the later ones taking their turn. CDOs and CMOs are assets and bonds that represent pools of MBSs and other securities that banks and lenders have collected and resecuritized.

As resecuritized securities, CDOs are intended to further diversify investor risk. Mortgage companies and financial institutions can structure CDOs in a variety of ways and can include complex "multi-tranche" structures that complicate refinancing and expose different investors to different degrees of risk. CDOs can be securitizations or re-securitizations of commercial loans, corporate bonds, other types of residential MBSs, commercial MBSs, and debt. The development of structured securities such as the MBS, CMO, and CDO is a process of enhancing the liquidity and exchangeability of mortgages by dividing and subdividing the cash flows into separate "strips" or "tranches" with different yields, maturities, and credit quality and risks (for overviews, see Chapters 4 and 8; Green and Wachter 2005).

We can view the "tranching process" of dividing and subdividing securities, securitizing and re-securitizing securities ad infinitum, and creating multi-tranche securities as a complex and unpredictable process of commodity rationalization, differentiation, and fragmentation. SIVs, CMOs, CDOs, and so on, transform risk in unique ways by generating exposures to different "slices" or tranches of the securitized mortgage, a process that is designed to distribute risk to different parties and thereby improve the trading of different assets. The assumption underlying securitization and tranching is that the partitioning of a commodity into separate securities can enhance the liquidity, or exchange-value of the overall mortgage. Yet mortgages have maturities that are non-standardized, unpredictable, and uncertain. As illiquid commodities, mortgages require messy maintenance and labor-intensive upkeep to assess risk and maintain their value. Collecting monthly payments, making sure real estate taxes are paid, keeping track of slow-pay and no-pay borrowers, and sending out annual statements of interest and taxes paid all require a costly infrastructure of institutions and networks of organizations. Thus, the development of securitization and other financial tools to transform illiquid assets into liquid securities – for eaxample, MBSs, CDOs, CMOs, and so on – represent attempts by economic actors and financial institutions to minimize and eliminate the obscurity and opaqueness of the mortgage commodity and enhance their exchangeability.

In short, the expansion of securitization has been a major crisis management strategy to address the crisis of accumulation within the S&L industry. As a mechanism for responding to the problem of under consumption within the housing finance sector, securitization expresses the relentless formation and reformation of financial instruments to extend purchasing power and mitigate the omnipresent threat of devalorization. As the subprime mortgage crisis illustrates, however, the process of securitization has introduced new problems and contradictions that are destabilizing markets, reinforcing inequalities, and perpetuating patterns of uneven development.

The Subprime Mortgage Crisis and the Role of the US Federal Government

One popular view shared by many journalists and researchers is that the subprime mortgage crisis can be explained with reference to "deregulation" or lax regulation by federal and state agencies.[4] Immergluck's (2009) account of the rise of subprime mortgage lending argues that financial innovations, deregulation, and failure of regulators to maintain control over new mortgage products facilitated excessive risk taking that harmed different populations and communities. The deregulatory fervor that marked the passage of legislation during the 1980s later lessened the constraints to buying and selling mortgages in the secondary mortgage market and facilitated a vast expansion of credit (see Chapter 3). Securitization is an outgrowth of various deregulation measures that have broken down the institutional and legal barriers to international exchange and encouraged the buying and selling of risk. Deregulation does not mean withdrawal of the state from regulating society. Nor does this term suggest or signify a reduction or diminution of state power and authority. Rather, deregulation is a conscious policy decision that reflects an application of state power to transform property rights and rules of exchange to enable actors in markets to engage in profitable exchange.

In addition to focusing on the significance of deregulation and failure to regulate, it is also important to direct attention to the ways in which different state institutions and agencies formulate and implement various policies, statutes, and legal-regulatory frameworks to encourage and facilitate subprime lending. As Aalbers notes in his introduction, "no state regulation, no property rights, no mortgage market." As we have seen, state activity has always been involved in the deregulation and reregulation of mortgage markets and state policies have been critical to the financialization of the economy. The state promoted the growth of the New Deal housing system that enabled suburban development, deregulated the S&L industry causing catastrophic results, and reregulated the mortgage market through the development of the MBS and other structured finance tools that created new incentives for risk-averse and high-risk investors. By increasing the demand for, and supply of, mortgage capital, according to Newman, "national housing, macroeconomic and tax policies have expanded the importance of banking and finance within the global and national economy" (2009: 314; see also McCoy and Renault 2008). In short, deregulation and reregulation have combined and worked in tandem to encourage the subprime mortgage crisis. The erosion of lending standards and the dismantling of socio-legal regulations to protect consumers have interacted with the new legislation to fuel the rise of exploitation and speculative lending practices.

Before the mid 1990s, the vast majority of mortgages bundled into securities were traditional prime loans that lenders sold to consumers who could prove they were affluent enough to buy homes. Beginning in the late 1990s, however, lenders began bundling "subprime mortgages" into private-label MBS that did not have the federal government's backing. To create a market for their products, many lenders engaged in a variety of deceptive and "predatory" lending practices to sell mortgages to borrowers with poor credit. Some were misrepresenting the terms of loans, giving huge loans to people who could not repay, creating loans with deceptive "teaser" rates that later ballooned, packing loans with undisclosed charges and fees, or even paying illegal kickbacks (see Chapter 8). In one publicized case, EMC Mortgage, a subsidiary of Bear Stearns, serviced hundreds of thousands of subprime mortgages and hit customers with unauthorized fees, misrepresented how much money homeowners owed, harassed consumers with property inspections, neglected to keep track of loan balances, escrows, and payment histories, and failed to tell national credit report bureaus that borrowers were disputing false reports.[5] To combat the surge in predatory lending, several state legislatures passed anti-predatory legislation. In 1999, the state of New York sued Delta Funding Corporation for predatory lending. In 2002, attorneys general from all 50 states entered into a settlement with Household Finance that resulted in restitution of $484 million to victims of predatory lending. In 2006, attorneys general and banking regulators in 49 states settled a $325 million lawsuit with Ameriquest Mortgage Company for engaging in predatory lending practices. During these years, state legislatures in North Carolina (1999), Georgia (2002), and New York (2003) passed anti-predatory lending laws to curb exploitative banking practices.[6]

National banks and their lending subsidiaries bitterly fought these new state regulations and embarked on an aggressive campaign to prevent state governments from passing and enforcing laws to halt predatory lending practices. In 2001, the U. Treasury Department's Office of the Comptroller of the Currency (OCC) ruled that banks' "operating subsidiaries" should not be subject to state control. Two years later, the OCC issued a series of formal opinions and new rules that negated all state predatory lending laws, thereby rendering them unenforceable. With state laws nullified, national banks and their state subsidiaries could engage in a variety of exploitative lending practices that states had hoped to stamp out. In response, all 50 state attorneys general, and all 50 state banking superintendents, actively fought the new rules and launched suits against the OCC. The national banks and their allies maintained that an unduly burdensome patchwork of state rules and regulations was stifling profits and denying access to credit for consumers. The states argued that their role was lawful and necessary to protect consumers from predatory lending practices and other potential violations. In the end, in 2007, the US Supreme Court ruled in a five to three decision that states could not regulate the mortgage-lending subsidiaries of national banks.[7] By this time, however, the OCC had successful created the legal conditions to encourage predatory lending and permit the aggressive mass marketing of unaffordable and exploitative mortgage products to vulnerable consumers.

From the late 1990s through 2005, rising housing prices contributed to a liquid mortgage market characterized by low loan default rates, increasing homeownership, and escalating subprime lending. A major vulnerability of subprime lending was the optimistic assumption that home values and prices would increase indefinitely (Immergluck 2008). Nationally, average housing prices peaked in the second quarter of 2006 and entered into a period of decline. Once housing prices stopped rising, subprime borrowers could not refinance their homes to pay off their loans before they adjusted to higher and unaffordable interest rates; a condition that produced a vast supply of foreclosed, vacant, and unsold homes. By 2008, the United States was facing huge increases in loan delinquencies and housing foreclosures, a perilous situation that has contributed to widespread bank losses, and declining tax revenues and major budget deficits for local and state governments.[8] The crisis in home lending reached a major milestone in March 2008 with a report from the Mortgage Bankers Association (MBA) finding that 2.04 percent of outstanding mortgages were in foreclosure in the fourth quarter of 2007; an all time high. The announcement came shortly after a Federal Reserve study showing that the ratio of owner equity to debt in US homes fell below 50 percent in 2007, a first since 1945.[9] Today, we witness a crisis of overaccumulation and devaluation in the financial and real estate markets, in which the consumers cannot afford homes to own or rent and banks and mortgage companies have reduced their lending in times of uncertainty.

Discussion

The above points resonate with Harvey's famous thesis in the *Limits to Capital* (1999: 83) that capital "as value in motion" is always under the threat of devaluation through decelerated turnover time. Production and realization of profits through real estate takes time: entrepreneurs and firms have to invest capital prior to the production of the built environment, and they can only realize profits after the completion of production and the selling of the spatially fixed commodity. Thus, there is always a time lag between investment and payoffs in real estate. On the one hand, the long turnover time of real estate can provide an attractive linchpin for capital at times when the average rate of profit is low, due to its long amortization, diverse use values, and heterogeneous markets. On the other hand, the long turnover time of real estate increases its risk due to the unpredictability and uncertainty of the economic and political environment. As capital immobilized in space, real estate always faces intersecting and multiple crises of realization, repayment, and falling rates of profit. To solve this contradiction, the state must liberate capital from its spatial fixity, reduce the uncertainty and unpredictability of exchange, raise the rate of profit to make room for new investments, and promote flows between territories. As a mechanism for extracting and stripping wealth from the homeowner, subprime mortgages – especially so-called exotic mortgages with interest-only payments, negative amortization, and adjustable rates – are tools of exploitation that reflect a long history of attempts by banking and financial institutions to increase profits, mitigate omnipresent crises of accumulation, and exploit markets.

Transforming mortgages and other long-term debt into liquid securities is an attempt to bring greater rationalization, standardization, and exchange-ability to the difficult and conflictual process of buying and selling complex commodities that have a variety of use values and exchange values. The major contradiction is that these financial tools reflect and reinforce the cyclical dynamics of overaccumulation and devalorization that are *sine qua non* of capitalism. In the New Deal housing system, S&Ls originated mortgage loans and financed housing through savings deposits of customers, a process that concentrated risk within the lending agencies and limited the volume loans they could finance. At the same time, this localized system of mortgage finance reduced information asymmetries between the originator of the loan and the lenders who held the underlying risk, a system that encouraged sound risk analysis. As noted by Immergluck (2008), by holding the loans for up to 30 years, the S&L originators had a financial incentive to monitor their quality, investigate whether borrowers could repay the mortgage, avoid high risk lending, and invest in gathering information about borrowers and communities. In contrast, the securitization of mortgages creates and exacerbates information asymmetries between originators of the mortgage and investors, as the former have little financial or reputational incentive to engage in rigorous and thorough risk analysis since the loans will eventually be sold to a third party within the secondary mortgage market.

With the development and expansion of securitization, the various steps in the origination, servicing, and investing in mortgages were unbundled and broken up into differentiated and autonomous steps controlled and managed by different institutional actors. In the securitized system, brokers process mortgage applications, lenders originate the loans, large mortgage banking organizations purchase the loans and aggregate them into pools, investment banking firms issue securities based on these pools, and investors from around the world purchase the securities. Unlike the primary mortgage market where the source of profit is the payment of the mortgage to the bank that originated the home loan, the source of profit in the secondary market for securitized mortgages is the sale of mortgage pools that contain hundreds or thousands of individual mortgages. It is interesting, as Sassen notes in Chapter 3, that it is not the creditworthiness of the homebuyer that is important in this securitized system, but the opportunity and capacity to maximize profits through the global circulation of the pooled mortgages.

As we have seen with predatory lending and the subprime mortgage crisis, securitization has created new windows of opportunity for financial actors to engage in speculative and exploitative financial activities, displace risks onto vulnerable groups, and evade accountability. Not surprisingly, a variety of studies, including the chapters by Hernandez, Sassen, Newman, Wyly, *et al.*, and Dymski in this volume, show that racial and ethnic minorities are more likely than Whites to get subprime mortgages and, therefore, bear the brunt of negative consequences of subprime-induced mortgage market downturns and financial crises (see also Squires 2004; Bond and Williams 2007; Williams, Nesiba, and McConnell 2005; Squires, Hyra, and Remer 2009). In their study of the racial distribution of subprime mortgages, Calem, Gillen, and Wachter (2004) found that, even after controlling for a variety of socio-economic factors and other characteristics, all-Black census tracts had a share of subprime mortgages that was 24 percentage points higher than an otherwise equivalent White census tract. In July 2007, the National Association for the Advancement of Colored People (NAACP) filed a discrimination suit against 11 of the largest lenders in the United States, arguing that racial minorities are steered toward subprime loans more than Whites, even after controlling for all risk factors.[10]

The above points suggest that securitization is an inequality-reinforcing process that reflects and reinforces the historically contradictory dynamics of capitalist investment in the built environment. As we have seen, securitization is associated with a series of regulatory dilemmas. On the one hand, securitization can serve as a basis for the accumulation process as mortgages and other illiquid commodities are transformed into liquid assets. On the other hand, securitization can operate as a barrier to accumulation as different state policies and regulatory strategies undermine previously stable patterns and networks of exchange and social reproduction. For this reason, and as we have seen with the historical development of the US housing finance system, securitization has not only helped create new opportunities for capital investment and growth but has also introduced new instabilities that are destabilizing mortgage markets and national economies around the world. Today, as the subprime mortgage crisis morphs into a global financial crisis, political and economic elites have become embroiled in a controversial politics of liquidity in which pressures to discard and rework extant institutional frameworks and regulatory strategies has become particularly intense. We now find ourselves in a period of institutional searching and regulatory experimentation in which diverse actors, organizations, and political alliances are promoting a variety of competing financial models and policies. Thus, the current politics of liquidity reflects the politically contested interaction between past institutional forms and policy frameworks that underpinned the securitization process and emergent strategies of state policy and regulation that seek to remedy the problems and crisis tendencies of securitization.

Conclusions

The subprime mortgage crisis has exposed the inability of securitization to address the long running problems of uneven development and endemic financial crisis that affect capitalist economies. Over the last few years, the subprime crisis has mushroomed into a worldwide financial crisis. Vast quantities of capital are being devalued as financial firms cannibalize and liquidate each other in a battle to undermine competition and dominate mortgage markets. We cannot deduce the specific regulatory arrangements and policy outcomes in advance because they are the product of inter- and intra-class conflicts over the formulation and implementation of state policy. Today, the combination of increasing concern with exploitative loan practices, housing foreclosures, bank failures, and persistent housing afford-ability problems are igniting a new round of regulatory battles over housing finance. In 2008, the Federal Reserve proposed new rules to curtail abuses in mortgage lending, including barring lenders from penalizing subprime borrowers who pay their loans off early, forcing lenders to make sure that subprime borrowers set aside money to pay taxes and insurance, restricting loans that do not require proof of a borrower's income.[11] Mortgage industry officials, on the other hand, have bitterly fought these rules and proposed alternative plans and policies. Thus, current battles pit housing activists and advocates for victims of subprime and predatory lending against powerful corporate banking interests bent on shaping new regulations to promote free markets and entrepreneurialism. Speculative investments, untraceable financial schemes, and complex international financial networks make up this entrepreneurialism and, when combined with an increasingly global investment environment and deregulated system, exacerbate the potential for an even deeper crisis in housing finance than that which we have seen in recent years.

Overall, the development of the MBS, CDO, CMO, and other struc-tured finance instruments underscores capital's relentless drive to annihilate space by time, to increase the liquidity of illiquid assets like mortgages. As active participants in promoting new financial innovations, banks and financial institutions have created new liquidity enhancement tools to reduce the turnover time of capital by increasing the fluidity and velocity of market transactions. In buying the original mortgages and then buying the tranches for the CDOs, powerful banks and lending institutions could lev-erage diverse kinds of investments and profit enormously. Financial giants such as Bear Stearns, Lehman Brothers, J.P. Morgan, Merrill Lynch, and other lending institutions originated, packaged, and sold subprime mortgages to diverse buyers including British hedge funds, German savings banks, oil-rich Norwegian villages, and Florida pension funds, among others. While securitization and the tranching process multiplied investors' options and flexibility, they offered only a short-term temporal fix to the crisis-prone nature of capitalism. The negative consequences of securitization include greater instability in the mortgage market, greater speculative investment, and increased levels of indebtedness. In the United States, the rise and fall of the subprime mortgage market has followed a conventional boom–bust lending trajectory, in which intense growth and profit-making leads to market paralysis, financial sector imbalances, and accelerating inequalities. Fears over MBSs, CDOs, and CMOs, are raising doubts about the resilience and robustness of mortgage markets and fueling a contagion effect, with investors now shy of a wide range of securitized products. Thus, the subprime mortgage crisis is instructive in the impact of state laws and financial regulations in exacerbating the economic problems that they were supposed to remedy.

The empirical analysis and theoretical arguments I have laid out in this chapter provide a challenge to accounts that maintain that mortgage finance policy and securitization strategies have been successful in promoting efficient markets and optimal economic development. Mainstream economics assumes the existence of market equilibrium, harmony, and optimization; promotes the idea that market forces of supply and demand promote efficiency and overall social betterment; and views land use and metropolitan development as resulting from the operations of a self-regulating "free market" that is unfettered by the actions of power groups or elites.[12] Yet, the subprime mortgage crisis suggests that disequilibrium, instability, and cycles of boom and bust (overaccumulation and devalorization) are more valid for explaining the dramatic and chaotic transformations that are affecting cities and metropolitan areas. In contrast to mainstream work in economics, which has sought to discover the stable and progressive aspects of capitalism, the account I have offered here exposes the limits and contradictions of the securitization process. Thus, the subprime mortgage crisis reveals the intense destructive power that lurks behind the facade of societal progress and economic affluence. Just as capital continually renders obsolete and irrelevant the built environment and socio-spatial structures it creates, capital continually mobilizes new territories and spaces as sources of investment and profit. In this sense, the creation and destruction of mortgage markets and financing tools are premised upon the "production of space" (Lefebvre [1974] 1991).

Finally, my conceptualization of securitization as a process of creating liquidity out of spatial fixity dovetails with theoretization that emphasizes the conflictual, contested, and deeply contradictory nature of uneven geographical development. Many scholars have noted that uneven development is endemic to capitalism and represents a key expression of capital's insatiable drive to mobilize spaces, places, and territories as forces of production (Harvey 1985; Brenner and Theodore 2002; Smith 1984). Uneven development is both a medium of intercapitalist competition and class struggle, and an evolving socio-spatial organization through which the process of securitization has unfolded. At the same time, securitization is permeated by tensions, antagonisms, and conflicts that are destabilizing the process of capital accumulation and circulation within the real estate sector. Just as capitalist regulation and profit-making occur as systems of rules, habits, and norms that constrain action, securitization is a set of socio-legal relations that define mortgages and tranches as standardized and exchangeable commodities (securities). As a result, securitization has developed through the production of historically specific patterns of socio-spatial organization, uneven development, and legal-regulatory policy. Today, the profitability and efficacy of securization is being questioned as the specter of devalorization rattles financial markets, and financial firms and banks raise doubts about the long-term resilience and robustness of market liquidity. Thus, securitization has become contested terrain, a political arena in and through which struggles over the regulation of housing finance and real estate, and their associated contradictions, are being articulated and fought out both domestically and internationally.

Notes

1   I use "thrifts" and "savings and loans" interchangeably to refer to federally insured savings institutions that have traditionally provided home mortgage loans.
2   See Federal Deposition Insurance Corporation (FDIC). Historical Statistics on Banking; Bank and Thrift Failure Reports. http://www2.fdic.gov/hsob/SelectRpt.asp?EntryTyp=30 (accessed January 15, 2008).
3   About Fannie Mae. Our Charter. http://www.fanniemae.com/aboutfm/charter.jhtml (accessed September 30, 2008).
4   CBS News. October 5, 2008. "A Look at Wall Street's Shadow Market." http://www.cbsnews.com/stories/2008/10/05/60minutes/printable4502454.shtml; Weissman, Robert. January 22, 2008. "Deregulation and the Financial Crisis." Huffington Post. http://www.huffingtonpost.com/robert-weissman/deregulation-and-the-fina_b_82639.html (accessed October 15, 2008); Toplin, Robert Brent. August 20, 2007. "The Housing Crisis: Caused by Lax Regulation." History News Network. http://hnn.us/articles/41986.html; Knox, Noelle. February 16, 2007. "Some Subprime Woes Linked to Hodgepodge of Regulators." *USA Today.* http://www.usatoday.com/money/economy/housing/2007-03-16-subprime-usat_N.htm (accessed October 15, 2008).

5 Harney, K.R. September 20, 2008. "Settlement Sheds Light on Boom's Bad Practices." *Washington Post*. P. F1.
6 Bagley, N. January 24, 2008. "Crashing the Subprime Party." *Washington Post*. Spitzer, E. February 14, 2008. "Predatory Lenders' Partners in Crime." *Washington Post*. P. A25; Day, K. "Villians in the Mortgage Mess? Start at Wall Street. Keep Going." *Washington Post*. P.B1.
7 Barnes, R. and El Boghdady, D. April 18, 2007. "High Court Sides With Banks on Mortgage Rules States Can't Regulate Loan Subsidiaries." *Washington Post*, p. D01.
8 For information, data sources, and analysis of housing foreclosures and subprime lending, see Center for Responsible Lending. http://www.responsible-lending.org/index.html (accessed October 15, 2008); see also Wyly, Atia, Foxcroft, Hammel, and Phillips-Watts (2006).
9 Merle, R. and Tse, T.M. March 7, 2008. "Mortgage Foreclosures Reach an All-Time High." *Washington Post*.
10 Ford, D. November 26, 2007. "Minorities Hit Hardest By Housing Crisis." Reuters News Release. http://www.reuters.com/article/inDepthNews/idUSN0 936310120071126?feedType=RSS&feedName=inDepthNews (accessed January 15, 2008).
11 Aversa, J. July 13, 2008. "Fed Poised to Curb Shady Home-Lending Practices." *USA Today*. http://www.usatoday.com/news/washington/2008-07-13-2483477143_x.htm (accessed October 25, 2008).
12 See Dymski's chapter for an overview of neoclassical explanations of the subprime and financial crises.

References

Aalbers, M.B. (2007) Geographies of housing finance: the mortgage market in Milan, Italy. *Growth and Change*, 38(2): 174–99.

Baily, M.N., Litan, R.E., and Johnson, M.S. (2008) *The Origins of the Financial Crisis*. Washington, DC: Brookings Institution.

Beauregard, R.A. (1994) Capital switching and the built environment: United States, 1970–89. *Environment and Planning A*. 26: 715–32.

Bond, C. and Williams, R. (2007) Residential segregation and the transformation of home mortgage lending. *Social Forces* 86(2): 671–98.

Brenner, N., and Theodore, N. (eds.) (2002) *Spaces of Neoliberalism: Urban Restructuring in North America and Western Europe*. New York and London: Blackwell Publishing.

Calem, P., Gillen, K., and Wachter, S. (2004) The neighborhood distribution of subprime mortgage lending. *Journal of Real Estate Finance and Economics* 29: 393–410.

Charney, I. (2001) Three dimensions of capital switching within the real estate sector: A Canadian case study. *International Journal of Urban and Regional Research* 25(4): 740–58.

Checkoway, B. (1984) Large builders, federal housing programs and postwar suburbanization. In: W.K. Tabb and L. Sawyers (eds.) *Marxism and the Metropolis: New*

Perspectives in Urban Political Economy. Second Edition. New York: Oxford University Press, pp. 152–73.

Colton, K.W. (2002) Housing finance in the United States: The transformation of the US housing finance system. Joint Center for Housing Studies, Harvard University W02–5.

Davies, P.J. (1958) *Real Estate in American History*. Washington, DC: Public Affairs Press.

Feagin, J.R. (1982) Urban real estate speculation in the United States: implications for social science and urban planning. *International Journal of Urban and Regional Research* 6: 35–60.

Feagin, J.R. (1987) The Secondary Circuit of Capital: Office Construction in Houston, Texas. *International Journal of Urban and Regional Research* 11: 172–92.

Federal National Mortgage Association (FNMA). (1975) *Background and History*. Washington, D.C.: FNMA.

Florida, R.L. (1986a) The origins of financial deregulation: The CMC, Heller Committee, and the Friend Study. In: R.L. Florida (ed.) *Housing and the New Financial Markets*. New Brunswick: Center for Urban Policy Research, State University of New Jersey, pp. 49–65.

Florida, R.L. (1986b) The political economy of financial deregulation and the reorganization of housing finance in the United States. *International Journal of Urban and Regional Research* 10(2): 207–31.

Florida, R.L. and Feldman, M.M.A. (1988) Housing in US Fordism. *International Journal of Urban and Regional Research* 12(2): 187–210.

Friend, I. (1969) *A Study of the Savings and Loan Industry: Summary and Recommendations*. Washington, DC: Federal Home Loan Bank Board.

Gotham, K.F. (2002) *Race, Real Estate, and Uneven Development: The Kansas City Experience, 1900–2000*. Albany, NY: State University of New York Press (SUNY).

Gotham, K.F. (2006) The secondary circuit of capital reconsidered: Globalization and the U.S. real estate sector. *American Journal of Sociology* 112(1): 231–75.

Gottdiener, M. (1994) *The Social Production of Urban Space*. Second Edition. Austin, TX: University of Texas Press.

Green, R.K. and Wachter, S.M. (2005) The American mortgage in historical and international context. *Journal of Economic Perspectives* 19:(4): 93–114. http://ssrn.com/abstract=908976 (Accessed November 29, 2007).

Guttentag, J. (1961) The short cycle in residential construction, 1946–59. *American Economic Review* 51(June): 275–98.

Haila, A. (1991) Four types of investment in land and property. *International Journal of Urban and Regional Research* 15: 343–65.

Haila, A. (1998) The neglected builder of global cities. In: O. Kalltopr, I. Elander, O. Ericsson, and M. Frazen (eds.) *Cities in Transformation – Transformation in Cities*. Aldershot: Ashgate Publishing.

Harriss, C.L. (1951) *History and Policies of the Home Owners Loan Corporation*. New York: Bureau of Economic Research.

Harvey, D. (1975 [2001]) *Spaces of Capital: Towards a Critical Geography*. New York: Routlege.

Harvey, D. (1978) The urban process under capitalism: A framework for analysis. *International Journal of Urban and Regional Research* 2: 101–31.

Harvey, D. (1985) *The Urbanization of Capital: Studies in the History and Theory of Capitalist Urbanization*. Baltimore, MD: Johns Hopkins University Press.

Harvey, D. (1999) *The Limits to Capital*. New Edition. Oxford: Blackwell.

Harvey, D. (2001) Globalization and the "spatial fix." *Geographische Revue* 2: 23–30.

Hendershott, P. and Villani, K. (1977) *Regulation and Reform of the Housing Finance System*. Washington, DC: American Enterprise Institute.

Immergluck, D. (2008) From the subprime to the exotic: Excessive mortgage market risk and foreclosures. *Journal of the American Planning Association* 74(1): 59–76.

Immergluck, D. (2009) *Foreclosed: High-Risk Lending, Deregulation, and the Undermining of America's Mortgage Market*. Ithaca, NY: Cornell University Press.

Kane, E.J. (1985) *The Gathering Crisis in Federal Deposit Insurance*. Boston, MA: MIT Press.

Lefebvre, H. ([1970] 2003) *The Urban Revolution*. Minneapolis, MN: University of Minnesota Press.

Lefebvre, H. ([1974] 1991) *The Production of Space*. Oxford: Blackwell.

MacDonald, H. (1995) Secondary mortgage markets and federal housing policy. *Journal of Urban Affairs* 17(1): 53–79.

MacDonald, H. (1996) The rise of mortgage-backed securities: Struggles to reshape access to credit in the USA. *Environment and Planning A* 28(7): 1179–98.

Marx, K. (1973) [1857]) *The Grundrisse: Foundations for the Critique of Political Economy*. Translated by Martin Nicholas. New York: Vintage Books.

McCoy, P. and Renault, E. (2008) *The Legal Infrastructure of Subprime and Nontraditional Home Mortgages*. UCC08–5. Cambridge: Joint Center for Housing Studies.

Newman, K. (2009) Post-industrial widgets: Capital flows and the production of the urban. *International Journal of Urban and Regional Research* 33(2): 314–31.

Orederud, G.I. (2006) The Norwegian home-building industry — locally embedded or in the space of flows? *International Journal of Urban and Regional Research* 30(2): 384–402.

President's Committee on Federal Credit Programs. (1963) *Report of the President's Committee on Federal Credit Programs*. Washington, DC: US Government Printing Office.

President's Committee on Home Building and Home Ownership. (1932) *Final Report of the Committee on Large-Scale Operations*. Washington, DC: US Government Printing Office.

Radford, G. (1996) *Modern Housing for America: Policy Struggles in the New Deal*. Chicago: University of Chicago Press.

Rowe, P.G. (1995) *Modernity and Housing*. Cambridge: MIT Press.

Smith, N. (1984) *Uneven Development: Nature, Capital and the Production of Space*. New York: Blackwell.

Squires, G.D. (ed.) (2004) *Why the Poor Pay More: How to Stop Predatory Lending*. Westport, CT: Greenwood Publishing Group.

Squires, G.D., Hyra, D.S., and Remer, R.N. (2009) Segregation and the subprime lending crisis. Paper presented at the 2009 Federal Reserve System Community Affairs Research Conference. Washington, DC, April 16, 2009. Version 6.11.09. Available at: http://www.kansascityfed.org/carc2009/pdf/carc2009%20Hyra%20 paper.pdf (accessed October 6, 2009).

US House of Representatives. (1989a) *Administrative Plan to Resolve the Savings and Loan Crisis*. Committee on Banking, Finance and Urban Affairs. 101st Congress. 1st Session. Washington, DC: US Government Printing Office.

US House of Representatives. (1989b) *Financial Institutions Reform, Recovery, and Enforcement Act of 1989, pts. 1 and 2.* Committee on Banking, Finance and Urban Affairs, Subcommittee on Financial Institutions Supervision, Regulation and Insurance. 101st Congress. 1st Session. Washington, DC: US Government Printing Office.

US House. (1934a) The National Housing Act. 73rd Congress, 2nd Session. Committee on Banking and Currency (CBC). Hearings on H.R. 9620. May 18– June 4, 1934. Washington, DC: US Government Printing Office.

US House. (1934b) Hearings on H.R. 8403 (S. 2999). A Bill to Guarantee the Bonds of the Home Owners Loan Corporation, etc. Committee on Banking and Currency. 73rd Congress. 2nd Session. March 7, 1934. Washington, DC: US Government Printing Office.

US Senate. (1933) Hearings on S. 1317. The Home Owners Loan Act. Committee on Banking and Currency. 73rd Congress, 1st Session. Washington, DC: US Government Printing Office and University of Chicago Press.

Weiss, M.A. (1987) *Rise of the Community Builders: The American Real Estate Industry and Urban Land Planning.* New York: Columbia University Press.

Williams, R., Nesiba, R., and McConnell, E.D. (2005) The changing face of inequality in home mortgage lending. *Social Problems* 52(2): 181–208.

Wyly, E.K., Atia, M., Foxcroft, H., Hammel, D.J., and Phillips-Watts, K. (2006) American home: Predatory mortgage capital and neighborhood spaces of race and class exploitation in the United States. *Geografiska Annaler* 88 B(1): 105–32.

2

Finance and the State in the Housing Bubble

Herman Schwartz

Introduction

To what extent was the housing bubble a geo-political phenomenon? Most of the chapters in this volume analyze highly localized or specific phenomena. But the subprime mortgage fiasco and the housing bubble were more than the consequence of massive over-leveraging by investment and commercial banks or financial predation on American minorities. Every level of the global economy was marked by the same combination of excessive leverage and extensive maturity mismatches that marked the subprime sector. And at every level, the US state played a substantial role in arranging and supporting both leverage and maturity mismatch, often in ways that go beyond the creation of the global market for mortgage backed securities described by Gotham in Chapter 1. A set of nested political concerns paralleled these leveraged positions. At the highest geopolitical level, leverage enabled a resurgence of US economic power. At the local level, American political parties sought permanent majorities by delivering housing-based wealth to new, largely minority, constituencies. In the middle, connecting the other two levels, US financial firms sought to expand their control over global profit flows by marketing claims on this new housing wealth (Seabrooke 2006).

I make four linked points in this chapter. First, I argue that the US economy was losing global "market share" during the 1970s and 1980s. US state elites changed policy to reverse this relative decline. These policy shifts inadvertently created the conditions for a housing led economic boom during the long 1990s (1991–2005). The Clinton administration's pursuit of fiscal balance accelerated disinflation, which in turn created fictitious capital by boosting housing prices. Second, the US state supported a global leveraging up of the US economy in which the US borrowed short term at low

Subprime Cities: The Political Economy of Mortgage Markets, First Edition. Edited by Manuel B. Aalbers.
© 2012 Blackwell Publishing Ltd. Published 2012 by Blackwell Publishing Ltd.

interest rates from the rest of the world, while investing back into the world on a long-term, high return basis. Housing based securities and Treasury bonds were the major vehicles for this leveraging. The implicit guarantee for various forms of Government Sponsored enterprise (GSE, that is, Fannie Mae and Freddie Mac) debt enabled the US to borrow in global markets at low interest rates. In turn, this generated above OECD-average GDP and employment growth in the US, reversing US relative decline. Third, financial deregulation enabled banks to create novel derivative products that re-packaged mortgages, as well as novel vehicles to hold those derivatives. The Bush Administration's deliberate regulatory forbearance permitted banks to leverage their holdings of those new mortgage based products at levels well above prior practice. Fourth, narrower partisan considerations permitted a regulatory environment that encouraged excessive production of private, subprime mortgages and residential mortgage backed securities (RMBS) as the raw material for these new derivatives. The Clinton administration expanded the Community Reinvestment Act and encouraged Fannie and Freddie to expand lending to poor urban areas in order to link those communities to the regulated banking industry in a politically visible way. At the same time, the Republican Party wanted to use increased rates of homeownership among Blacks and Latinos to lure a slice of these culturally conservative but economically excluded groups away from the Democratic Party and towards themselves. The conclusion notes that the housing boom and bust, thus, grew out of a set of intersecting geopolitical and partisan political imperatives. This makes a rerun of the housing bubble unlikely. Nevertheless, housing and housing finance will remain at the center of efforts to restart the US economy, even though, or especially because, housing finance has now been resocialized.

Relative Growth and Global Power

From the 1950s to the end of the 1980s, the United States suffered a decline in its relative geo-economic power, defined as its share of global output, its ability to escape the normal constraints economies face, and the control exerted by US based firms over global commodity chains. In some respects part of this decline was inevitable as other countries recovered from the Second World War. Nevertheless, this decline posed a substantial geo-economic policy problem for the US state. State actors sought to reverse this decline through a number of deliberate policy initiatives. These initiatives inadvertently created a temporarily virtuous cycle of housing-led growth for the United States and other countries with similar housing finance systems. This section defines geo-economic power and describes the decline and recovery of US power. Put simply, disinflation after 1989 filtered through the US housing finance system to generate differential growth – relatively faster economic growth – for the United States. Differential growth both generated large volumes of profit that could be used to take control of critical nodes in production chains, and encouraged and validated investment in new production processes related to those critical nodes. Control assured continued profitability. Differential growth attracted foreign capital inflows, removing the normal constraints on the US economy. Yet these processes were not fully independent, as foreign capital inflows – a substantial part of which came as purchases of RMBS – also helped activate US differential growth.

From 1950 through 1982 the US share of gross world product fell from 27.7 percent to 20.9 percent, and its share of rich country GDP (gross domestic product) declined from 46.6 percent to 37.8 percent (Groningen database).[1] Both shares then stabilized at roughly those levels through 1990. US multinational companies (MNCs) continuously expanded their control over global production into the 1980s, sparking a range of alarmed books about the American Challenge and widening dependency in the third world. Yet the emergence of MNCs from other rich countries, and the sharp increase in their direct investment in the US economy in the 1980s relatively diminished US firms' control. While US-based MNCs accounted for nearly all global foreign direct investment (FDI) in the 1950s, by the early 1980s they accounted for only 28.1 percent and by the late 1980s they accounted for only 14.3 percent, well below the US share of the global economy (UNCTC 1991: 10). Finally, the ability of the United States to escape the normal economic constraints also diminished through the 1960s. Normally an economy experiences a trade-off across consumption, domestic investment, and foreign investment. The only way to escape this constraint is to borrow. Foreign willingness to hold a net position in dollar denominated assets – the essence of an escape from constraint and a pre-condition for use of the dollar as an international reserve dollar currency – wavered in the 1970s and 1980s. By the end of the 1980s, the US share of global official reserves had fallen below 50 percent and the dollar's position as a reserve currency was in question.

US policymakers responded to American relative decline in a variety of ways. The Nixon administration famously terminated the Bretton Woods gold-dollar standard in 1971, and less obviously began reshaping the global trade regime. But it also responded to the erosion of US superiority in the manufacture of "dumb" machinery through a whole range of largely covert policies designed to promote a shift towards an information technology and biotechnology based economy (Hurt 2009). The Carter Administration began a long process of service sector deregulation, continued by the Reagan Administration. Both also promoted a ferocious attack on inflation from 1979 onwards and consolidated the shift towards an information technology economy. These facilitated the later supply chain revolution. The George H. W. Bush and Clinton Administrations matched this with a process of fiscal consolidation later undone by George W. Bush. All these initiatives produced an upturn in the rate of productivity and, thus, output growth by the 1990s. While most of these gains – disinflation, the supply chain revolution, mobile telephony, etc. – were shared by America's peer rivals, the US economy outperformed the OECD average in the long 1990s, from 1991 to 2005. This outperformance stabilized US economic power globally, and expanded it relative to its rich country peer rivals.

From 1991 onwards, the United States escaped the usual economic constraints, and was able to expand consumption (including government consumption), domestic investment, and investment overseas faster than the underlying expansion of the US economy. From 1991 to 2005 consumption expanded from 65 percent to 70 percent of US GDP. Simultaneously the share of domestic gross fixed capital formation in GDP also grew by 5 percentage points, from 14 percent to 19 percent. Theoretically this simultaneous expansion might be possible if the United States redirected capital flows that had gone overseas into domestic consumption and investment. But, in fact, a cumulative and non-trivial $7 trillion dollars flowed out of the United States into overseas investments during this period. How did the US escape the usual constraints on consumption, domestic investment, and foreign investment?

The United States escaped the usual constraints in the usual way – borrowing abroad. US net foreign debt expanded absolutely to roughly $3 trillion and relatively to about 25 percent of GDP during the long 1990s. How can this rising debt be squared with the claim that US economic power rose during those years? Curiously, despite its rising net foreign debt, the United States – aggregated into one accounting identity – made money on its international investments. Rising US foreign debt enhanced US growth and power rather than diminishing it. Foreign borrowing financed both rapid US economic growth and expanded control over global commodity chains by firms headquartered in the United States.

During the long 1990s, the $7 trillion investment outflow from the United States increased US entities' control over foreign firms and global commodity chains. From 1994 to 2006, the US owned share of the Morgan-Stanley MSCI All Country World ex-US market index rose from 10 percent to 24 percent of total global market capitalization (Heckman 2008). By contrast, foreign holdings of US equities rose more slowly from 5.1 percent to 9.7 percent of US market capitalization. US firms also grew faster overseas than foreign firms grew in the US market, 1995–2004. Despite a 10 percent increase in the dollar's exchange rate through 2004 (which diminishes measures of overseas activity), overseas value added by US based MNCs increased by 40 percent, while turnover nearly doubled to 7.8 percent

Table 2.1 Population adjusted rates of growth, 1991–2005 or 2006

	United States	OECD average	Germany	Japan
GDP per capita (2005)	33.5	28.1	17.3	13.3
Gross fixed capital formation (2005)	79.9	48.2	2.7	−13.5
Real output per hour in manufacturing (2006)	106	71	68	64
Total manufacturing output (2006)	74	52	16	15

Source: Based on Schwartz, H. (2009a) *Subprime Nation: American Power, Global Capital and the Housing Bubble*. Ithaca, NY: Cornell University Press.

of gross world product (UNCTC 2006: 332–333; BEA 2007: 45; OECD 2008: 378, 382). Moreover, despite slower growth in other rich countries, the ratio of US MNCs' overseas sales to sales in the US by firms doing FDI into the US also rose from 1.3 to 1.5, during 1995–2004, while the ratio of value added increased from 1.4 to 1.6. Finally, the share of global outward FDI controlled by US based firms recovered to 21.4 percent (UNCTC 2008: 257).

Foreign capital inflows also accelerated US economic growth, enabling the United States to out-grow its rich country peers. Indeed, those rich country peers accounted for half of global lending to the United States, slowing growth in their own economies. Table 2.1 presents growth rates adjusted for differences in population growth. (Keep in mind that the United States had far stronger population growth than the other countries, which implies even larger absolute increases in all of these indicators.) Massive foreign lending to the United States provided 10–20 percent of total lending in US credit markets annually after 1994; by 2005 it accounted for 25 percent (D'Arista and Griffith-Jones 2006: 64). Foreigners lent against collateral, or so they thought, buying huge volumes of US RMBS and Treasuries. With the nominal market value of US houses rising by about $14 trillion, and mortgage debt rising by nearly $7 trillion from 1991 to 2006, there was plenty of collateral to go around. This inflow of foreign capital helped the US economy maintain its share of global GDP at 20 percent, despite rapid contemporaneous economic growth in China, India and other developing countries. Equally important, the US share of OECD GDP increased by 4.2 percentage points to 42.7 percent, reversing the post 1950 fall.[2] The big relative losers in terms of shares of global output were Germany and Japan, even though they generated large export surpluses. These surpluses reflected domestic growth deficits and a growing reliance on external demand for growth.

Why did the United States outgrow its peer competitors? US policymakers responded to US decline with a variety of policy responses. These helped reverse US decline, but their effects were widespread and arguably should have helped other countries as well. Some Carter and Reagan era technology projects accelerated improvements in chip design and fabrication, lowering IT costs for the broad economy; other projects generated the digital signal processing chips at the heart of the mobile telephony revolution. Yet the roll-out of new technologies in the 1990s did not automatically guarantee relatively *faster* US growth per capita as compared to its rich country peers. Everyone had access to new thinking about supply chain management, to mobile telephony, and to the internet. Arguably, European economies adapted to and utilized mobile telephony more quickly than did the US economy. Similarly, the Clinton Administration's successful reduction of the US fiscal deficit led the US Federal Reserve Bank to lower interest rates. This too had positive externalities for all economies. Nominal long-term interest rates fell from 8.7 percent to 4.0 percent, during 1990–2003, in the United States (*OECD Factbook 2005*). But they fell farther and lower in Europe, with Euroland nominal long-term interest rates dropping from 11.2 percent in 1990 to 3.5 percent by 2005. While real interest rates did not fall, studies show that house prices are much more sensitive to nominal rates than real rates (Green and Wachter 2007: 9).

Arguably, falling nominal interest rates should have propelled all economies forward. Yet the United States, Scandinavia, Netherlands, Britain, and Australia did better than other OECD economies. The difference between the two groups was in part a function of their housing finance systems, which interacted with the same environmental decline in nominal interest rates to produce different growth outcomes. Four features characterized the faster growing systems: high rates of private homeownership; high levels of mortgage debt relative to GDP; low transaction costs for obtaining mortgages, cashing out home equity, and transferring property; and high rates of securitization of new mortgages. The more these four institutional features were present, the greater the degree to which falling nominal interest rates could be translated into new aggregate demand and, thus, growth (MacLennan, Muellbauer, and Stephens 1998).

The level of homeownership determines how many households can potentially gain from rising housing prices. The scale of mortgage debt in relation to GDP determines how much purchasing power can be activated if debt payments are reduced. Low transaction costs for refinance and the possibility of securitization determine whether it is actually possible to reduce those payments. Thus, these features can be thought of as the sources for the breadth, depth, and likelihood of increased aggregate demand. When all four features were present, sometimes with an additional fillip from tax subsidies for mortgage interest, they enabled a relatively straightforward process of Keynesian demand stimulus to operate. When they were not present, the disinflation of the 1990s did not trigger increased aggregate demand. In the United States, the average new homeowner buying between 1999 and 2005 saw an increase in median net wealth from $11,100 to $88,000, mostly in home equity, while incumbent households' median net wealth nearly doubled from about $152,400 to $289,000. And Americans spent this fictitious wealth, withdrawing an average of $300 billion per year via home equity loans and the like. While prices also rose in many continental European countries, housing finance systems in those countries did not allow incumbent homeowners to tap into their nominally higher equity. As Schwartz (2009a) shows, these differences in housing finance structures thus explain much of the difference in growth rates – but not the absolute growth rate – among OECD economies in the 1990s.

Rising housing prices allowed all levels of American society to indulge in leveraged investment at foreign expense. American households and firms used rising housing prices to leverage themselves up. Interest rates on US mortgages are usually pegged to the ten year Treasury Bond, whose rates fell steadily through the 1990s. Americans used home equity withdrawal to pay down much higher interest rate credit card debt, to avoid somewhat higher automobile purchase debt, and to pour money into domestic and international mutual funds. US firms borrowed cheaply in foreign markets and reinvested abroad; US based FDI increased by $2.76 trillion during 1990–2008, versus only $1.88 trillion of inward flows or reinvestment. US financial firms borrowed cheaply by issuing asset backed commercial paper to the money markets in order to fund purchases of longer term, higher yielding sub-prime mortgages. Finally, as noted above, the United States at a macro-economic level also leveraged up, creating new and low yielding housing based mortgage assets that could be exchanged with foreigners for higher yielding equity claims on those foreign economies. Housing related debt made all of this possible. This highest level aggregates all the other flows, so the next section explores how deregulation enabled the US to create massive amounts of marketable housing related debt, and in turn enabled the United States to exploit global capital flows.

Deregulation and Securitization

As the Gotham and Aalbers chapters note (Chapters 1 and 5, respectively), prior to widespread securitization, banks held mortgages to maturity and made money from the interest rate spread between deposits and loans. Without a change in regulation and behavior, these illiquid loans could not be sold to anyone. Deregulation of US financial markets enabled these dead loans to become live securities. By 2007, GSE RMBS and borrowing accounted for nearly half of outstanding US residential mortgage debt of $11.1 trillion. A further quarter of outstanding mortgage debt was privately securitized, leaving only 25 percent in the traditional, illiquid bank-held format (Credit Suisse 2007; FNMA 2006); FHLMC 2006; Federal Reserve Bank 2008). As the third section shows, overseas sales of these RMBS helped energize the US economy, enabling the United States to maintain high rates of growth and positive net international investment income even as US net foreign debt was rising. Fannie and Freddie's securitization of mortgages, thus, played a crucial supply side role in the process of foreign debt-financed, housing-driven US growth. By 2007 roughly 60 percent of all US credit was being securitized (Anderson 2009). While securitization was not specifically aimed at enabling foreign capital inflows, securitization did enable overseas sales of mortgage assets to a wide range of customers, including central banks.

In the absence of securitization, foreign funds could only enter the US market if foreign banks established a presence in the market, or if US banks accepted exchange rate risks and borrowed offshore. In 2001, foreign holdings of GSE RMBS amounted to $133 billion. By 2007 foreign holdings exceeded $1 trillion, with foreign official institutions – that is, Asian central banks – holding the majority (Department of the Treasury 2007: 11). Without a standardized product and liquid markets, foreigners would have been less willing to buy mortgage assets from the US, making it harder for the US to fund its trade deficit. (Private RMBS, the vast majority of which packaged subprime and Alt-A mortgages, did not become important until 2004–07, and apparently were largely held by off-shore subsidiaries of US financial firms.) Treasury bonds alone could not supply enough assets on the scale observed in the 1990s, because the underlying fiscal deficit corresponding to that outflow of Treasury bonds would have spooked international investors, just as US fiscal deficits scared foreign (and domestic) investors in the late 1980s and early 1990s.

In other words, massive sales of Treasury debt would have driven investors away from the dollar much sooner than the more opaque sales of GSE RMBS. Massive sales of corporate equities to foreigners would also have provoked a political backlash, just as in the late 1980s when Japanese investment into the United States surged. Instead housing-related debt filled the gap. Sales of GSE RMBS and then privately generated RMBS filled the gap. At mid-2007 total GSE debt amounted to nearly twice marketable Treasury debt, because GSE debt typically constitutes a third of all marketable US-debt securities, public and private. Fannie and Freddie also played a crucial demand side role, absorbing new mortgages generated by the relentless upward trend in housing prices and the equally relentless extraction of home equity. Foreign holdings of GSE mortgage backed securities amounted to about $260 billion (or 7 percent of the outstanding amount) by 2000, and about $1.5 trillion (or 21 percent) by 2008. The foreign share of corporate bonds in 2008 was similar at $2.8 trillion and 22.6 percent, though much corporate bond debt to "foreigners" is actually holdings by US firms operating through subsidiaries chartered in off-shore tax havens (US Treasury 2009: 5).

The two waves of deregulation documented by Gotham in Chapter 1 made securitization possible and profitable. Deregulation gave the emerging national banks an incentive to sell their assets (loans) to the securities market in order to shift from generating profits through an increasingly narrower interest rate spread toward generating profits from increasingly larger fee and transaction income. Thus, deregulation created a larger supply of securitizable mortgages. Fannie Mae and Freddie Mac provided the demand for these mortgages, securitizing $95 billion of mortgages in 1988 and $430 billion by 1993. In this phase, securitization performed a socially useful function by reducing maturity mismatches for banks. Banks otherwise would have had to fund long-dated assets (mortgages) with short-dated liabilities (consumer deposits). Instead, securitization allowed organizations like pension, insurance, and mutual funds to match long-term assets against long-term liabilities to their clients. But when private securitizers entered the market after 1999, they inverted this system. Deregulation gave securities firms direct access to the raw material for RMBS; banks now had their own outlets for RMBS and could bypass Fannie Mae and Freddie Mac. By 2004, private securitizers (i.e., not Fannie Mae, Freddie Mac, or Ginnie Mae) were creating more than half of the $1.8 trillion in RMBS issued that year. This allowed them to use securitization for socially useless purposes, by deliberately creating maturity mismatches. Investment banks borrowed in short-term money markets to fund purchases of collateralized debt obligations (CDOs) composed of long-dated mortgages.

The George W. Bush Administration gave financial firms even more running room. A series of well publicized events in 2001 showcased the head of the Office of Thrift Supervision (OTS), which is one of several federal government regulators of savings banks, and the Federal Deposit Insurance Company (FDIC) using a chainsaw to cut through a stack of regulatory manuals with the help of representatives of bank lobbying associations. In 2004 the Bush Administration ordered the Office of the Comptroller of the Currency to pre-empt all nationally chartered banks from stricter state-level anti-predatory lending laws and other restrictions on their ability to issue mortgages (Ding, Quercia, and White 2009). These banks promptly took advantage of regulatory laxity to issue high interest rate loans even though borrowers most likely could not service these loans. The share of high cost loans in pre-empted states tripled from 16 percent to 46 percent, during 2004–07, creating the problems documented in other chapters in this volume. Deregulation and pre-emption freed banks to generate a cumulative

$1.7 trillion in subprime and Alt-A loans from 2004 to 2007. Seabrooke (2006) has argued that the economic power of US financial institutions rests in part on their ability to transform incomes at the bottom of the income distribution into liquid assets. These assets enabled US financial firms to regain their prominence *vis-à-vis* the Japanese and German banks that went global in the 1980s. While Seabrooke is undoubtedly correct about the period before 2004, the subsequent three years saw an unstable exaggeration of this process. Nevertheless, the steady stream of securitized assets over the entire 1990s enabled the United States to engage in a global system of arbitrage, which is the subject of the next section.

US Leverage in Global Markets: A House of Cards or Playing the Housing Card?

How could the United States be both a large net foreign debtor and the recipient of net positive international investment income since the early 1990s? In 2007, removing six zeros, this was rather like a private investor, who owed $20,082 while holding investments worth only $17,640, somehow managing to pay out only $726 on the investor's debts while earning $818 from his or her own investments, and thus receiving net income of $92. It is perfectly plausible that a savvy individual investor might be able to borrow money, invest only part, and still net a positive return. But it is implausible that on average every US investor is smarter than every foreign investor. It is even less plausible that every US investor suddenly became even smarter after the US became a net debtor, as data from Gourinchas and Rey (2005) suggest. They calculate that from 1960 to 2001, US overseas assets earned an annualized rate of return two percentage points higher than US liabilities to foreigners, at 5.6 percent versus 3.6 percent. Furthermore, the gap expanded after 1973, as US assets yielded 6.8 percent while liabilities cost only 3.5 percent. This is one reason why, despite five years of cumulating trade deficits, US net foreign debt was the same 20 percent of GDP in 2007 as it had been in 2002.

The United States generated net international income by operating a global system of financial arbitrage and leverage. Arbitrage occurs when an intermediary exploits price differences between similar commodities on two different markets, buying and selling that commodity at the same time. Differences in political, regulatory, and housing market finance structures produced these price differences. The differences allowed the United States to leverage itself up and create a global maturity mismatch. At the macro-economic level, the United States systematically borrowed short term at low interest rates from the rest of the world, and then turned

Table 2.2 Stock of international investment positions, 2007

	1	2	3	4	5
$ Billion	FDI[a]	Portfolio equities	Portfolio debt[b]	Loans	**Total**
United States into world	5,148	5,171	1,478	5,002	16,799
Rest of world into US	3,524	2,833	6,965	4,982	18,304
of which, central banks			2,931	406	3,337
% shares					
United States into world	30.6	30.8	8.8	29.8	100
Rest of world into US	19.3	15.5	38.1	27.2	100
of which, central banks			16.0	2.2	18.2

Source: Data from BEA, International Investment Position. http://www.bea.gov/international/
index.htm#iip, date accessed August 1, 2008.
[a]Market valuation; [b]omits trivial US holding of currency and foreign holdings of US currency
totaling $279 billion.

around and invested back in the rest of the world in longer term, higher
risk, higher return, active investment vehicles. At the micro-economic level
US financial institutions transformed cheap short-term foreign borrowing
into a huge variety of higher yield, longer term RMBS and collateralized debt obligations (CDOs). Physically, US arbitrage transformed cheap
overseas credit into outsized domestic investment and in particular into
(literally) outsized housing. This mismatch between the US and foreign
investment positions can be seen in Table 2.2. About three-fifths of US
outward investment is composed of high yielding equities and direct investment (columns 1 and 2), while over three-fifths of foreign investment in the
United States is composed of bonds and loans (columns 3 and 4), which
yield less income.

Mortgage backed securities and GSE debt in general played two starring
roles in this process. Foreigners overwhelmingly invested in US Treasury
debt and GSE debt and RMBS. The first by definition has low yields –
Treasury debt provides the global reference rate – while the second is
largely indexed against the first. By June 2006, foreign investors held 52
percent of marketable US Treasury securities and 16.8 percent of outstanding GSE debt (US Treasury 2007: 3, 5). Asian central bank recycling of
trade surpluses during the late 1990s and early 2000s depressed yields on ten
year US Treasury debt by about 90 basis points, or almost one percentage

point, and as much as 150 basis points in 2005 (Warnock and Warnock 2006). European and oil exporter acquisitions of dollar denominated portfolio assets should have had much the same effect in the early to mid 1990s, when those groups primarily funded the US trade deficit.

Consequently, foreign purchases of US RMBS energized a giant circle: foreign purchases of Treasuries depressed the reference rate for mortgage interest rates, causing the issue of new mortgages through refinancing or purchase; the new mortgages were then bundled into RMBS and sold to foreigners; their eager purchases further depressed mortgage rates, helping banks to fund the roughly $7 trillion increase in US mortgage debt from 1991 to 2006. This debt corresponded to both an upward valuation of existing housing and a wave of new construction. The United States built 17.7 million units of housing during 1990–2000, and an additional 10 million units through mid-2006, which helped the US create half of the OECD's new jobs for 1991–2005. As Ronald MacKinnon notes, Asia provided much of the cash driving this cycle. Japan and China accounted for 46 percent of foreign holdings of GSE RMBS – plus a much smaller slice of riskier private RMBS – and 51 percent of foreign Treasury holdings at mid-2007 (MacKinnon 2009). Why couldn't this virtuous cycle continue indefinitely? Ultimately all this debt had to be validated through payments on mortgages, yet new entrants to the housing market – the subjects of Chapter 7 by Hernandez and Chapter 9 by Wyly *et al.* – were increasingly income-constrained. The next section discusses how partisan political strategies intersected with financialization of the housing market to create the housing boom and bust.

The Intersection of the Micro-Politics of Race with the Macro-Economics of Housing

Why housing?

Logics of state – restoring US global economic power – intersected with narrower party-political strategies precisely over housing finance. Partisan struggles over housing provision in the United States thus helped to both accelerate the US housing boom and then tip it into a bust. Put simply, both Democrats and Republicans respectively sought increased homeownership to cement or attract the votes of parts of the Black and Latino populations. While US politicians did not promote homeownership with quite the same vigor as British politicians (Watson 2009), they did embark on partisan policies promoting home ownership, particularly for poor Black, Latino, and White voters. Democrats used the Community Reinvestment Act to try to cement Black voters' loyalty and secure Latino voters' loyalty though increased access to bank-originated mortgages. Republicans similarly tried to detach some – not all – Black and Latino voters from the Democratic coalition by tolerating a huge expansion of subprime lending by non-depository institutions. (Unlike a bank, a "non-depository" financial firm is not covered by federal deposit insurance, and consequently is not required to hold the same level of reserves.) Neither strategy was solely responsible for the explosion of subprime lending after 2004, given that most Alt-A, and some subprime, loans were taken out by non-minority groups. But both strategies allowed subprime loans to magnify the scale of the housing bubble.

These competing housing policies reflected the state of play in US presidential elections. By the 1990s, the Republicans had succeeded in taking nearly all southern White Protestants and many northern urban Catholics out of the Democratic Party's coalition, leaving the parties evenly balanced. Generally speaking, US elections have been won by the party that captures most of the votes of the one-third of White US families that have incomes over $100,000, as the Democrats did twice in the 1990s and the Republicans did twice in the 2000s. Yet both parties sought to turn tenuous majorities into permanent majorities. The Democrats – whose hold on the well-to-do slice of America has always been more tenuous than their hold on poorer, darker slices of America – sought a permanent majority by removing the race issue. Democrats sought to defuse White voters' fears that redistribution inevitably favored Blacks by reforming social assistance programs and moving more Blacks into middle class properties and occupations through housing and other policy.

For their part, Republicans had a firmer grasp on the White electorate, winning 54 and 58 percent of white votes in 2000 and 2004 respectively. But Republican strategist Karl Rove sought to create a permanent Republican majority by taking away part of the Democratic party's non-White base (Balz and Allen 2004). Republicans had captured 44 percent of Latino votes in the 2004 election, and swelling immigrant populations in all states, and especially the southwest, made this bloc even more attractive. If the Republicans could capture an additional 10–20 percentage points of this vote, the Democrats faced electoral doom in the southwest. Equally so, shaving ten percentage points off the Democrats' share of the Black vote would endanger the Democrats' majority in crucial states like Florida, Ohio, and Michigan. In Rove's analysis, Latinos and Blacks were cultural conservatives and, thus, halfway to the Republican Party. Economic issues, though, drove them towards the Democrats. Like Margaret Thatcher in the UK, Rove reasoned that turning some Latinos and Blacks into homeowners would help transform them into economic conservatives as well. Indeed, the drop in the Democrat's Latino vote share from 62 in 2000 to 53 percent in 2004 indicated that this group was biddable.

Homeownership was a plausible hook to catch these two groups because real wages had stagnated for the bottom 60–70 percent of the US workforce from the 1980s onwards. Homeownership thus became an increasingly important part of people's current consumption and retirement security; homeowners typically had five to ten times the net worth of non-homeowners (Gramlich 2007: 80–2). Housing wealth also provided Americans with a cushion against unforeseen medical or accident expenses not covered by insurance, by allowing them to borrow against their home equity. Even in the bottom quartile of US households by income, the median family had $80,000 of home equity in 2007, almost as much as the next two quartiles (Harvard JCHS 2009: 14). Yet homeownership was unevenly distributed. Among elderly households (65–74 years old), in 1980 only 59 percent of Black households owned their home, versus 76 percent of White households. By 1990 both groups had moved up to 64 and 82 percent respectively, but the gap persisted (Masnick 2001: 29). Moreover, among younger households the rate of ownership was falling and the gap was expanding. Whereas, respectively, 57 and 30 percent of White and Black households aged 25–34 owned (mortgaged) homes in 1980, by 1990 only 52 and 24 percent did (Masnick 2001: 29). Housing policy thus became an important lever to capture biddable voters. Moving non-homeowners into homeownership, and moving owners at the bottom of the housing ladder upward, seemingly bestowed huge financial rewards on those groups. The party that could take credit for these rewards would win votes.

Democratic Party initiatives

The Clinton administration tried to expand minority homeownership and close the ownership gap. While lower relative income among Blacks and Latinos was a continuing cause for lower ownership rates, so too was outright discrimination. Housing finance in the post-war period had produced and reproduced homogeneous, predominantly White, suburban households and housing products, as the chapters by Newman, Hernandez, Dymski, and Wyly *et al.* note (Chapters 8, 7, 6, and 9 respectively). Government agencies like the Federal Housing Administration and Fannie Mae, as well as private banks, had "redlined" Black neighborhoods, meaning that they simply refused to make loans to potential Black owners regardless of their income or creditworthiness. They also explicitly sought to preserve the character of existing neighborhoods by refusing loans to Blacks seeking to move into White neighborhoods. The 1968 Fair Housing Act made these practices illegal, requiring banks to lend on the basis of objective measures like credit scores and documented income. *De facto*, though, both practices continued up into the 1970s. The Carter Administration thus passed the 1977 Community Reinvestment Act (CRA) to force banks to behave, first by applying the same lending criteria to all borrowers and second by recycling depositors' money back into depositor neighborhoods. The CRA bound only depository institutions – that is, those whose deposits were covered by federal deposit insurance. The CRA produced a modest improvement in minority homeownership, which reached 42.3 percent of all Black households and 41 percent of Latino households by 1994 (Harvard JCHS 2009: 37).

In 1994, the Clinton Administration publicly committed to raising homeownership rates to 67.5 percent of households by 2000, and amended the CRA in 1995 to force banks to stop limiting lending in "redlined" communities. These amendments did not force banks to make high risk loans, and the amended CRA did not have specific lending targets. However, statistically speaking, residents of poorer neighborhoods were more likely to have insecure incomes, shaky credit histories, and smaller down payments. Banks consequently scrutinized these borrowers carefully, knowing that the resulting loans would have to stay on their books, and thus constitute a credit risk for the bank. Given that the CRA contained no penalties for non-compliance (aside from the normal anti-discrimination issues), why did banks comply with CRA? Regulators could use non-compliance to block the bank mergers that proliferated in the wake of financial deregulation in the 1990s. The CRA thus motivated banks to extend credit to low income households. In addition, the Clinton administration pressed Fannie Mae and Freddie Mac to securitize a wider range of loans – though not subprime loans. By 2000, homeownership rates among Blacks and Latinos reached 47.6 and 46.3 percent respectively, versus an average US rate of 67.4 percent (Harvard JCHS 2009: 37). The Clinton policy created a tight nexus between banks, the community groups that monitored their CRA compliance, and Democratic Party politicians in Congress. It, thus, tied minority elites more firmly to the Democratic Party, by showing that the party could deliver jobs and wealth to minority communities. To an extent this was a cyclical phenomenon: in the 1990s gently falling interest rates, gently rising incomes at the bottom, and a robust employment market created a virtuous cycle in which successful homeownership and income stability reinforced each other.

To what extent did this expansion of credit and homeownership create the conditions for the later crisis? While the 1995 CRA revisions permitted securitization of subprime loans, non-depository institutions – those not covered by depositors insurance – were already securitizing these loans in 1995, and CRA securitizations did not start until 1997. The CRA unquestionably facilitated growth in this market, but largely at the margin. CRA lending accounted for only 6 percent of the total volume of outstanding subprime lending in 2007, and CRA loans did not default at rates above the entire pool of subprime loans, indicating that they were not excessively risky

(Duke 2009). Instead, the problems with subprime clearly emerged from the Republican Party's deregulation of depository institutions and *non-regulation* of non-depository financial firms and national banks after 2000.

Republican Party initiatives

Like the Democrats, the Republicans used housing policy for partisan purposes. George W. Bush publicly set a goal of 5.5 million more minority homeowners, subsidizing first time purchases by low income buyers through the American Dream Downpayment Act of 2003. Despite this, and unlike the Democrats, the Republicans sought a market based policy that would reward their campaign contributors with lavish profits. As noted above, the Bush Administration eased regulation of financial firms in 2001 and pre-empted stricter state-level laws in 2004. Lenders used this permissive environment to originate and securitize a vastly expanded volume of subprime loans, as well as a vastly expanded and increasingly risky range of mortgage products. Thus, for example, OTS supervised banks originated about $255 billion in so-called Option ARM (adjustable rate mortgage) loans in 2006, which amounted to one-sixth of the entire stock of subprime loans at the time the crisis hit (Appelbaum and Nakashima 2008). In an Option ARM, the borrower is free to reduce his or her payment in any given month and have the shortfall added to the principal of the mortgage debt. These borrowers were thus vulnerable to both the risks that interest rates might rise (because the rate was adjustable)and that their payment would rise to amortize the new, larger principal. Banks could market Option-ARMs, and ARMs in general, as having very low "teaser" interest rates to customers whose income was too low to qualify them for a prime or conforming Fannie Mae mortgage. On the other side, the Bush Administration pressured Fannie Mae and Freddie Mac to securitize more subprime mortgages as a way of rescuing increasingly troubled private mortgage originators.

Similarly, the Bush Administration made a decision in 2005 *not* to regulate the rapidly proliferating non-depository financial institutions that were originating the bulk of the subprime and Alt-A (intermediate between prime and subprime) loans, even though voices in the Office of the Comptroller of the Currency (OCC – which regulates nationally chartered banks) and the Federal Reserve were warning that rising defaults on these loans posed a considerable threat to the financial system (Gramlich 2007). The pattern of subprime lending explains part of this non-decision. Subprime lending was concentrated in areas rich in presidential electoral votes as well as rich in poor minority voters. Latinos account for at least 30 percent of the electorate in Arizona, California, Texas, and New Mexico, 25 percent in Nevada, and 20 percent in Florida. By 2006, roughly one half of all mortgages made to Blacks and Latinos were in the subprime categories. Nevertheless,

Fannie Mae estimated that roughly half of those subprime loans could have qualified for lower interest rate prime or near prime loans (Squires and O'Connor 2001).

The flood of easily available, but expensive, mortgage money these policies made possible easily exceeded that of the Clinton Administration, but with more modest results. Under Clinton, subprime originations rose from $65 billion in 1995 to $138 billion in 2000, and produced an increase in homeownership rates of 3.4 percentage points (Chomsisengphet and Pennington-Cross 2006: 37). Under Bush, subprime originations rose to $332 billion in 2003 and then peaked at $625 billion in 2006, while increasing their share from 8.6 percent to 20 percent of originations.[3] But this produced only an additional 1.6 percentage point gain in homeownership before round-tripping back down to the Clinton era level. Among Blacks, the 5.1 percentage point increase under Clinton was succeeded by a temporary 2.1 percentage point gain under Bush. Only among Latinos did a similar 5.1 percentage point gain give way to a more durable 2.8 percentage point gain (Harvard JCHS 2009: 37). These gains came at an extremely high macroeconomic cost. Unlike the more sustainable Clinton boom, where rising incomes caused median house prices to fall relative to median incomes, the flood of mortgage money in the 2000s caused house prices to rise more rapidly than income (Schwartz 2009b). From 2000 to 2007 the ratio of the median price for owner-occupied housing to median family income rose from 2.4 to 3.2 – a 32 percent jump – across the entire United States. But these increases were even greater in the politically salient states: 108 percent to 8.3 for California, 84 percent to 5.1 for Nevada, 64 percent to 4.2 for Arizona, and 83 percent to 4.2 for Florida (Lucy and Herlitz 2009). Unsurprisingly, these states led the pack in terms of the percentage of homes in foreclosure in 2008, with California, Florida, Nevada, and Arizona accounting for 62 percent of all foreclosures that year.

Conclusions

We can now close the loop between what we observed at the macro-level (US differential growth), the meso-level (securitization), and the micro-level (subprime). The US housing finance system more readily translated the disinflation of the long 1990s into increased aggregate demand. This increased demand created a temporarily self-sustaining upward cycle. Falling nominal interest rates lured new homebuyers into the market, putting gentle upward pressure on housing prices. Incumbents cashed out their gains with home equity loans and spent this money, increasing aggregate demand further. A buoyant economy drew more people into the labor market, creating more new homebuyers. As the US economy began to outpace the other large OECD economies, capital flowed from those economies into the US to capture higher returns than their own domestic markets offered, even though those returns were lower than the returns US investors captured through their own outward investment. A substantial portion of the foreign capital inflow purchased the ever growing pool of securitized mortgages.

What broke this virtuous cycle? Like all such economic cycles it eventually would have exhausted its basic inputs – disinflation, a steady stream of new homebuyers at the bottom, and foreign willingness to fund an ever increasing US trade deficit. This would have produced the normal recession. Yet the 2007–09 global financial crisis presents more than the normal cyclical recession. US policy decisions under the G.W. Bush Administration clearly exaggerated the normal cycle, by combining fiscal incontinence with excessive regulatory forbearance at a time when interest rates were low. This supercharged the housing market, producing the flood of subprime and Alt-A mortgages that investment banks packaged into RMBS and then repackaged into collateralized debt obligations (CDOs). As the inevitable recession moved many of the underlying mortgages into default, these CDOs unraveled, bringing down the financial system, rather than simply tipping the economy into a normal recession.

What now? Deliberate deregulation of finance and other sectors helped propel the United States in front of its peer rich country rivals, while preventing erosion relative to the rapidly growing developing country giants. Deregulation enabled the US housing finance system to provide the US economy with extra growth. But going forward it is unlikely that housing finance will play the same role it played in the long 1990s. That role was contingent on environmental, social, and political factors – disinflation, household receptivity to increased debt, and deregulation – that are unlikely to recur together. Instead, regulators are tightening lending standards and households are deleveraging. Though many prognosticators fear inflation from the massive bailouts and liquidity injections of 2007–10, deflation remains a significant problem in a global economy plagued by overcapacity and a US economy with far too many empty housing units.

Instead, housing finance is likely to remain the province of the state for some time. Both Fannie Mae and Freddie Mac have returned to state ownership. Along with the Federal Home Loan Banks, they were the primary providers of new money to the US mortgage market from 2007 to 2010. In 2007, the two GSEs accounted for 75 percent of new mortgage money; adding in the FHLBs increased that share to 90 percent. From 2006 to 2009, FHLB advances to their member banks nearly doubled to $1 trillion (*Economist* 2009). For their part, the two GSEs relied heavily on the Federal Reserve to absorb their RMBS and allow them to finance those new mortgages. In 2009, the Fed was the primary buyer of RMBS, adding nearly $700 billion in RMBS to its balance sheet. Consequently, the subprime market has returned to its formerly marginal place in the larger mortgage market, constraining the number of new buyers stepping onto the housing ladder. Instead, vanilla mortgages conforming to the GSE underwriting standards dominate the market.

This pattern implies that the layered pattern of excessive leverage and maturity mismatches characterizing the housing market and global economy at all levels will disappear. Regulators and firms alike will fear overextension. While maturity mismatches necessarily occur – this is the province of banking after all – securitization seems likely to return to its original function of reducing rather than amplifying mismatches. To the extent that deleveraging US households decrease their consumption and, thus, also decrease the trade deficit, the inflow of foreign capital to the United States will fall. This limits the potential for the US arbitrage described in the third section. Smaller capital inflows flow mechanically from lower consumption because imports have been and will be shrinking in volume. (This is an accounting identity: net capital inflows must equal the net deficit on goods, services, and factor income flows.)

All this tells us what has gone, rather than what will be. Nevertheless, it has clear implications for the housing market and housing finance. Housing debt comprises the single largest chunk of private debt in the United States, and the overwhelming majority of household debt. Conversely, housing wealth typically exceeds corporate equity holdings for the average household. Both sorts of households can no longer rely on rising housing prices to build retirement or other savings. Instead, they will have to build savings out of income. If incomes grow, these savings will keep real mortgage rates low for years. If deflationary pressures persist, these savings might keep nominal rates low as well. If incomes don't grow, deflationary pressures will exert considerable downward pressure on housing prices, bank balance sheets, and US economic growth. A geo-economic perspective thus suggests that the US state should be looking for ways to restart income growth and shift some income back down to the bottom of society. "Should," however, generally bows to power in politics – and the nature of state responses to the 2007–10 crisis suggest that it is the financial sector that has the power. Will they give up short-term income to restart long-term growth?

Notes

1 Rich countries are defined here as the high income constituents of the Organization for Economic Cooperation and Development (OECD) net of the eastern European countries, Greece, Korea, Mexico, and Turkey.

2 Calculated from the EU-KLEMS database at http://www.euklems.net/, using purchasing power parity GDP in constant 1990 Geary-Khamis dollars, which controls for fluctuations in exchange rates and inflation.

3 By contrast, the total volume of securitized mortgages in Europe for 2005 was roughly €326 billion, and the cumulative volume during 2000–05 was roughly

€1072 billion, versus a cumulative $1690 billion in securitized subprime and Alt-A mortgages and $6691 billion in securitized prime mortgages in the United States (Aalbers, this book; Schwartz 2009a: 103).

References

Anderson, J. (2009) Debt-market paralysis deepens credit drought. *New York Times* October 7, 2009. http://www.nytimes.com/2009/10/07/business/economy/07shadow.html.

Appelbaum, B. and E. Nakashima (2008) Banking regulator played advocate over enforcer; agency let lenders grow out of control, then fail. *Washington Post* November 23, 2008, p. A01. http://www.washingtonpost.com/wp-dyn/content/article/2008/11/22/AR2008112202213_pf.html.

Balz, D. and M. Allen (2004) Four more years attributed to Rove's strategy despite moments of doubt, adviser's planning paid off *Washington Post* November 7, 2004. http://www.washingtonpost.com/ac2/wp-dyn/A31003-2004Nov6.

BEA (Bureau of Economic Analysis). (2007) An ownership based framework of the US current account, 1995-2005. *Survey of Current Business.*

Chomsisengphet, S. and A. Pennington-Cross (2006) Evolution of the subprime market. *Federal Reserve Bank of St. Louis Review* 88(1): 37-8.

Credit Suisse. (2007) *Mortgage Liquidity du Jour: Underestimated no More,* June.

D'Arista, J. and S. Griffith-Jones (2006) The Dilemmas and Dangers of the Build-up of US Debt. In: J. J. Teunissen and A. Akerman (eds.) *Global Imbalances and the US Debt Problem.* The Hague: Fondad, pp. 53-86.

Ding, L., R. Quercia, and A. White (2009) Federal preemption of state anti-predatory lending laws. University of North Carolina at Chapel Hill, at http://www.ccc.unc.edu/documents/Phase_I_report_Final_Oct5,2009_Clean.pdf.

Duke, E.A. (2009) Stabilizing the housing market: Focus on communities. February 16, 2009 at http://www.federalreserve.gov/newsevents/speech/duke20090216a.htm.

Economist. (2009) America's mortgage agencies: Government sponsored anxiety. January 29, 2009, at http://www.economist.com/businessfinance/displaystory.cfm?story_id=13036784.

Federal Reserve. (2008) *Flow of Funds of the United States: Second Quarter 2008.* Washington DC, September.

FHLMC. (2006) *Annual Report.* Washington DC: FHLMC.

FNMA. (2006) *Annual Report.* Washington DC: FNMA.

Gourinchas, P.-O. and H. Rey (2005) From world banker to world venture capitalist: US external adjustment and the exorbitant privilege. NBER Working Paper 11563, Chicago: NBER.

Gramlich, E. (2007), *Subprime Mortgages: America's Latest Boom and Bust.* Washington D.C.: Urban Institute.

Green, R. and S. Wachter (2007) The housing finance revolution. Federal Reserve Bank 31st Economic Policy Symposium, Jackson Hole, WY.

Groningen database at http://www.euklems.net/.

Harvard University Joint Center for Housing Studies. (2008) *The State of the Nation's Housing.* Cambridge, MA: Harvard University JCHS.

Harvard University Joint Center for Housing Studies. (2009) *The State of the Nation's Housing.* Cambridge, MA: Harvard University JCHS.

Heckman, L. (2008) Insight: Refuge may be found via new frontiers. *Financial Times.* 13 February 2008, http://www.ft.com/cms/s/0/234aaafe-da4e-11dc-9bb9-0000779fd2ac.html.

Hurt, S. (2009) *Institutionalizing Food Power: United States Foreign Policy, Intellectual Property Rights, and the Agricultural Biotechnology Industry (1972–1994).* New York, NY: New School for Social Research, unpublished PhD dissertation.

Lucy, W. and J. Herlitz (2009) Foreclosures in states and metropolitan areas: Patterns, forecasts and policy challenges. unpublished paper, Department of Urban and Environmental Planning, University of Virginia.

MacKinnon, R. (2009) The world dollar standard and globalization: New rules for the game?' In: E. Helleiner and J. Kirshner (eds.) *The Future of the US Dollar.* Ithaca, NY: Cornell University Press.

MacLennan, D., J. Muellbauer, and M. Stephens (1998) Asymmetries in housing and financial market institutions and EMU. *Oxford Review of Economic Policy* 14(3): 54–80.

Masnick, G. (2001) Home ownership trends and racial inequality in the United States in the 20th Century. Harvard University Joint Center for Housing Studies working paper W01–4.

OECD. (2005) *OECD Factbook, 2005.* http://www.sourceOECD.org.

OECD. (2008) *Measuring Globalization: Activities of Multinationals, II, 2008.* Paris: OECD.

Schwartz, H. (2009a) *Subprime Nation: American Power, Global Capital and the Housing Bubble.* Ithaca, NY: Cornell University Press.

Schwartz, H. (2009b) Origins and consequences of the US subprime crisis. In: H. Schwartz and L. Seabrook (eds.) *The Politics of Housing Booms and Busts.* Basingstoke: Palgrave Macmillan.

Seabrooke, L. (2006) *Social Sources of Financial Power: Domestic Legitimacy and International Financial Orders*, Ithaca, NY: Cornell University Press.

Squires, G. and S. O'Connor (2001) *Color of Money.* Albany: State University of New York Press.

UNCTC (United Nations Conference on Trade and Development). (1991) *World Investment Report, 1991.* New York: United Nations.

UNCTC (United Nations Conference on Trade and Development). (2006) *World Investment Report, 2006.* New York: United Nations.

UNCTC (United Nations Conference on Trade and Development). (2008) *World Investment Report, 2008.* New York: United Nations.

US Treasury. (2007) *Report on Foreign Portfolio Holdings of US Securities, June 2006.* Washington DC.

US Treasury. (2009) *Report on Foreign Portfolio Holdings of U.S. Securities, June 2008.* Washington D.C.

Warnock, F.E. and V.C. Warnock (2006) International capital flows and U.S. interest rates. FRB International Finance Discussion Paper No. 840, September.

Watson, M. (2009) Boom and Crash: The politics of individual subject creation in the most recent British house price bubble. In: H. Schwartz and L. Seabrook (eds.) *The Politics of Housing Booms and Busts.* Basingstoke: Palgrave.

3

Expanding the Terrain for Global Capital
When Local Housing Becomes an Electronic Instrument

Saskia Sassen

Beyond its social and political role, housing has long been a critical economic sector in all developed societies. There have historically been three ways in which it played this economic role: as part of the construction sector, as part of the real estate market and as part of the banking sector in the form of mortgages (see Aalbers 2008; Wyly *et al.* 2004; Gotham 2006, among others). In all three sectors it has at times been a vector for innovation. For instance, in the early stages of development solar energy was largely applied to housing rather than offices or factories. Mass construction has used housing as a key channel to develop new organizational formats, and so has the industrial production of prefabricated buildings, which has mostly been about housing. Finally, mortgages have been one of the key sources of income and innovation for traditional-style banking. The 30-year mortgage, now a worldwide standard, was actually a major innovation for credit markets. Japan earlier and China today have instituted, respectively, 90- and 70-year mortgages to deal with a rapidly growing demand for housing finance in a situation where it takes three generations to cover the cost of housing in a boom period – the 1980s in Japan and the 2000s in China.

Today, housing has become the instrument for yet another innovation: a financial instrument that has lengthened the distance between itself and the underlying asset (housing) to an extreme that is usually associated with high-risk innovative finance. This is not the first time the financial sector has used housing for such an instrument: the first residential-mortgage-backed securities were produced in the late 1970s. The original intention was quite reasonable: to generate an additional source for funding the mortgages of

Subprime Cities: The Political Economy of Mortgage Markets, First Edition. Edited by Manuel B. Aalbers.
© 2012 Blackwell Publishing Ltd. Published 2012 by Blackwell Publishing Ltd.

modest-income households, besides the traditional one of bank deposits. The particular distortion of the original concept of the subprime mortgage at issue today is in substantial part a result of the selling logic and practices in the US during a short but intense period, mostly from 2003 to 2007.

Conceptually I situate the current disastrous outcome – millions of households losing their homes largely through the dubious, including illegal, practices of mortgage sellers – in a larger framing of *logics of expulsion* (Sassen 2010). In the larger project I develop the thesis that our post-1980s global age has now taken on a clear systemic shape. Notwithstanding its multiple exclusions, the Keynesian period of the mid-twentieth century brought with it an active expansion of the population systemically valued as "workers and consumers." Today's phase of advanced capitalism does not. In the last two decades there has been a sharp growth in the numbers of people that have been "expelled," numbers far larger than the newly "incorporated" middle classes of countries such as India and China. I use the term "expulsions" to describe a diversity of conditions: the growing numbers of the abjectly poor, of the displaced who are warehoused in formal and informal refugee camps in the Global South, of the minoritized and persecuted warehoused in prisons in the Global North, of workers who have been reduced to laboring bodies, often rendered useless at far too young an age. My argument is that these multi-sited logics of expulsion, with strong elements of what Harvey (2003) has called accumulation by dispossession, are actually signaling a deeper systemic transformation that has been documented in bits and pieces but remains insufficiently theorized.

Elsewhere (Sassen 2008a: chapters 1, 8, and 9) I develop a theory of change that has as one core dynamic the fact that condition x or capability y can shift organizing logics and, thereby, actually change valence even if it may look the same: thus, for instance, I posit that this massive expulsion of people is not simply more of the same. I argue that the organizing logic of this post-Keynesian period is now making legible its shape: at the center of this logic is not the "valuing" of people as workers and consumers, but the expulsion of people and the destruction of traditional capitalisms to feed the needs of the new capitalism, one dominated by the interests of high finance and the needs for natural resources. The particular case of the so-called subprime mortgage crisis can be conceptualized as one instance of systemic expulsion through an extension of an advanced mode of capitalist relations of production – the financializing of non-financial domains. Extending this particular mode to modest-income households worldwide emerges as a possibility given low levels of home-ownership in many countries (e.g., Sassen 2008b, 2011: chapters 2, 5, and 8).

Here I examine the character of this innovation and its global potential for subjecting modest-income households to this mode of extraction. One major effort is to situate the particularity of the subprime mortgage crisis that exploded in August 2007 in a larger context of crisis that culminates with the September 2008 credit-default swaps crisis, another major innovation of this period. It is this particular type of swap, which had reached $62 trillion by 2007, compared to $800 billion of the subprime mortgage market that threatened to bring the financial system down. The subprime mortgage crisis was a crisis for mortgage holders, and, in my analysis, a mere crisis of *confidence* for the world of high finance. The second major effort is to compare the incidence of household debt, especially residential mortgage debt, in a range of countries in order to underline the enormous differences across countries. For instance, in Sao Paulo, a high share of residents own their houses, but few have used mortgages – housing is bought with cash. These differences signal the variable potentials for growth in the selling of this particular type of distortion of the original concept of the subprime mortgage. It is important to see this as a mere signal of a potential and a danger. The enormous diversity of economic, financial, and social cultures through which housing is accessed across the world points to diverse levels of potential use.

Situating the Subprime Mortgage Crisis in a Larger Landscape

The geographic expansion and systemic deepening of capitalist relations of production over the last 20 years have led to one of the most brutal divisions of the winners and losers. The so-called subprime mortgage crisis can be conceptualized as an extension of an advanced mode of capitalist relations of production – the financializing of non-financial domains. One way of putting it is that capitalism is undergoing a deepening of advanced capitalism predicated on the destruction of more traditional forms of capitalism. The financializing of non-financial domains is one such form of deepening. Extending this to modest-income households is equivalent to peasant economies being subjected to early capitalist modes of capitalism.

Marx saw a specific type of shift whereby pre-capitalist modes of production were incorporated into capitalist relations, a process marked by violence, destruction, and appropriation. Here I posit another specific type of shift: the destruction of traditional capitalisms in order to extract what can be extracted for the further deepening of advanced capitalism (Sassen 2008a: chapters 4 and 5). I use this term to capture a phase dominated by a financial logic, a condition that recurs and historically signals a decaying phase (Arrighi 1994). Built into this proposition is the fact of diverse phases of capitalist development and, hence, the possibility that in today's global phase the extension of capitalist relations has its own distinct mechanisms and that these need to be distinguished from older imperial phases.

The marxist category "primitive accumulation" points not only to a logic of extraction that can expropriate and impoverish, but also, and more importantly, to a mode of incorporating non-capitalist economies into capitalist relations of production. In this regard PA is part of the historic expansion of capitalist relations. This would suggest *prima facie* that the category is not applicable today since most of the world has basically been incorporated into capitalist relations of production (Amin 2000, 2010).[1]

For Marx, PA hinged on earlier modes of production becoming factors in the making of capitalist relations of production. Marx's definition of PA in terms of the theory of capitalism has at its center the notion of a historical process that separates people from the means that allow them to live and produce.[2] Amin (2000) mentions the idea that primitive accumulation is not something confined to the early stage or prehistory of capitalism. Harvey (2003: 137–82) writes that Marx's use of "primitive" or "original" accumulation is misleading since the history of capitalism contains repeated instances of this kind of accumulation. He recasts the term as accumulation by dispossession, and develops its multiple instances. One of these is as a safety valve against over-accumulation crises, since it allows lowering the prices of consumer commodities (thereby raising the propensity for general consumption); this, in turn, is made possible by the considerable reduction in the price of production inputs. Harvey (2003) makes a crucial contribution to the understanding of the current era by emphasizing the ongoing appropriation of non-capitalist economies and their incorporation into capitalist relations of production. Harvey opens up the concept to a wide range of processes.

> These include the commodification and privatization of land and the forceful expulsion of peasant populations; the conversion of various forms of property rights (common, collective, state, etc.) into exclusive private property rights; suppression of rights to the commons; commodification of labour power and the suppression of alternative (indigenous) forms of production and consumption; colonial, neocolonial, and imperial processes of appropriation of assets (including natural resources); monetization of exchange and taxation, particularly of land; the slave trade [which continues particularly in the sex industry]; and usury, the national debt and ultimately the credit system as radical means of primitive accumulation. The state, with its monopoly of violence and definitions of legality, plays a crucial role in both backing and promoting these processes. (2003: 145)

This is a point I develop in the context of the making of regulations and laws in the post-1980s decades (2008a: chapters 4 and 5). Central to my analysis is that inside capitalism itself we can characterize the relation of advanced to traditional capitalism as one marked by PA. At its most extreme this can mean the immiseration and exclusion of growing numbers of people who cease being of value as workers and consumers. But it also means that traditional petty and national bourgeoisies cease being of value.[3] This is part of the current systemic deepening of capitalist relations, as is the financializing of mortgages for modest-income households aimed at building a new circuit for high finance for the benefit of investors and a total disregard for the homeowners involved. The "subprime mortgage crisis" is but one of a wide range of instances that all involve logics of expulsion from older forms of capitalism. For example, elsewhere (2010) I use this framing to examine how territory is systemically repositioned in growing parts of the Global South, away from representing nation states and towards representing "needed" resources. Here I extend this argument to a range of territorial sites in the Global North, particularly the US (e.g., neighborhoods devastated by home foreclosures). It can be extended to more instances than the one focused on in this chapter (for instance, central Detroit devastated by the disassembling of manufacturing production).[4]

I emphasize the *making* of these capitalist relations of production: whether those of early or of advanced capitalism.[5] I think it is critical to go beyond questions of power and powerlessness and to recover the work and innovations that it takes to produce these outcomes. It is not simply a function of power – to make these destructive instruments it took state work, the innovations of lawyers and accountants, and so on. It is a process I describe as the making of complexities to produce elementary brutalities (2010). In what follows I discuss some of the work that it took to destroy a more traditional type of home mortgage in order to expand the operational space of advanced capitalism. These are system-changing practices and projects within capitalism.[6]

Expanding the Operational Space of Advanced Capitalism

The 1980s saw the financial industry produce multiple innovations that allowed the securitizing of all sorts of debt (for a discussion of the issues and the pertinent bibliography see Sassen 1991: chapter 4). These innovations also addressed small debts, notably individual consumer debt, through the bundling of millions of such small debts, from auto loans to credit card debt. When it came to mortgages, these were mostly owned by highly regulated institutions. Deregulation became the critical step to enable securitization: mortgages had to be pulled out of their protective encasements (Aalbers 2008; Newman Chapter 8 in this volume; Miles 2007).[7]

Two features of the current innovation make the particular type of subprime mortgage at issue here different from traditional mortgages. One is the extent to which these mortgages function purely as a financial instrument, in that they can be bought and promptly sold (Aalbers 2008;

Gotham 2006). In a fast moving market of buying and selling, ownership of the instrument may last for just two hours. Thus, when an investor has sold the instrument, what happens to the house itself becomes irrelevant to that investor; indeed, the subprime lenders who went bankrupt in the 2007 subprime mortgage crisis where those who did not sell these mortgages and hung on to them. Those who did sell them to investors made significant profits in the years before the crisis erupted. Further, these mortgages were mostly divided into hundreds of slices, which were then mixed up with high-grade debt and distributed across diverse investment packages; they could then be sold as asset-backed securities, no matter how thin and how dubious that slice of a mortgage representing an actual material asset. There is no single component in such a package that actually represents the whole house. In contrast, the owner loses the house if unable to meet the mortgage payments for a few months no matter who owns the instrument, because there is always some investor or "servicer" who owns it and hence can make claims.

The second difference from traditional mortgages is the fact that the source of profit for the investor is not the payment of the mortgage itself plus interests. It is, rather, the desirability of having an actual asset (a bit of a house) backing the security in a period of extreme speculation when asset-backed securities had become rare in the high-finance circuit. The aim of the innovation is to delink investor profits from the creditworthiness of the subprime mortgage borrower – the investor could benefit even if the mortgaged household went bankrupt. The critical condition to make it work for the high-finance investment circuit is securing a large number of subprime mortgage contracts to reach the volumes needed. These two features suggest that the 2 billion modest-income households worldwide are a potential global market for what has become a dangerous instrument not aimed at helping such households but rather at filling a demand in the high-finance circuit (Sassen 2008b, 2010). They can become a major target when the source of profit is not the payment of the mortgage itself but the sale of a highly liquid financial package with a bit of material asset. What counts, is not the creditworthiness of the borrower but crossing a threshold in terms of numbers of mortgage contracts sold to, and often pushed onto, households.

Much has been made, especially in the US media, of the subprime mortgage crisis as a source of the larger crisis. These mostly modest-income families unable to pay their mortgage were often represented as irresponsible for having taken on these mortgages. But the facts show another pattern. The overall value of the subprime mortgage losses was too small to bring this powerful financial system down. The crisis was triggered by another complex financial innovation: the so-called credit default swaps.

In an accelerated history that took off in the early 2000s, we can identify three distinct crises. A first one is a crisis of home foreclosures that in 2006 sent over a million households into poverty, downgraded housing, and often homelessness. As 2007 saw another 2.2 million foreclosures, an increase of 75% over 2006, this crisis of foreclosures became a crisis of confidence for investors in August 2007. By then the sharp growth and vast spread of slices of subprime mortgages had made it impossible to identify foreclosed mortgages, the so-called toxic asset. In other words, the complexity needed to delink borrowers' creditworthiness from investors' profit had become the source of the crisis of confidence in the financial system. This in turn fed the third crisis, when those who had bought complex types of derivatives named credit-default swaps and sold as insurance against financial crises called in to collect that "insurance." By 2007, the outstanding value of credit-default swaps stood at $62 trillion, more than the $54 trillion value of global GDP (ISDA 2009; Varchaver and Benner 2008). But the cash was not there to cover the claims. It should be noted that all along this process, many financial actors made vast amounts of profits.

Credit-default swaps are part of what has come to be referred to as the shadow banking system (http://www.huffingtonpost.com/saskia-sassen/obama-and-volcker-economi_b_161249.html). According to some analysts this shadow banking system accounted for 70 percent of financial transactions at the time the crisis exploded. The shadow banking system is not informal, illegal, or clandestine. Not at all: it is in the open, but it has thrived on the opaqueness of the investment instruments. The complexity of many financial instruments is such that nobody can actually trace what is bundled up in some of them. Eventually this meant that nobody knew exactly or could understand the composition of their investments, not even those who sold and bought the instruments. This shadow banking system has thrived on the recoding of instruments, which, at the limit, allowed illegal practices to thrive. For instance, it is now clear that credit-default swaps were sold as a type of insurance. But they were actually derivatives. In order to be an actual form of insurance the law requires they be backed by capital reserves and be subject to considerable regulation. Making them into derivatives was a *de facto* deregulation and eliminated the capital reserves requirement.

Credit-default swaps could not have grown so fast and reached such extreme values if they were actually insurances. None of the financial firms had the capital reserves they would have needed to back $60 trillion in insurance. Because they were re-coded as derivatives, they could have an almost vertical growth curve beginning as recently as 2001. Finally, their growth also indicates the extent to which interpretation is a strategic function in financial markets. Those who sold these swaps did not see the crisis coming and bet on many more years of speculative growth. Those who bought the swaps, as insurance, were getting worried about the prospects of ongoing financial growth.[8] It is important to emphasize that the viral infection of subprime mortgages originated in the United States but spread to other countries via the globalization of financial markets (Aalbers Chapter 5 in this volume; IMF 2008). This spread was helped by the fact that non-national investors are, as a group, the single largest buyers of some of the weakest types of mortgage instruments (for more detail see Sassen 2008b; IMF 2008). Together with banks, non-national mortgage buyers make up over a third of all subprime mortgage holders. Foreign ownership strengthens the potential for spillover effects well beyond the United States.

A critical contextual feature bringing it all together was the growing demand among investors for asset-backed securities at a time of sharp growth in the financializing of economies. Actual assets had become increasingly attractive by the early 2000s given a financial market dominated by derivatives with an outstanding value of $630 trillion, equivalent to fourteen times the value of global GDP. The total value of *financial* assets in the US stood at almost five times (450 percent) the value of its GDP in 2006, before the crisis was evident; the UK, Japan, and the Netherlands all had a similar ratio (see McKinsey 2008: 11).[9] In one year alone, 2005–06, the total value of the world's financial assets grew by 17 percent (in nominal terms, 13 percent at constant exchange rates) reaching $167 trillion. This is not only an all-time high value, it also reflects a higher growth rate in 2006 than the annual average of 9.1 percent since 1980 – in other words, a sharp growth in financial deepening (Sassen 2011: chapters 5 and 8). The total value of financial assets stood at $12 trillion in 1980, $94 trillion in 2000, $142 trillion in 2005, and $167 trillion in 2006.[10]

This is the context within which even subprime mortgage debt on modest housing became of interest to financiers (see also Wyly *et al.* 2004; Hernandez Chapter 7 in this volume, on the limits of this option, e.g., redlining).[11] It took complex mixes of innovations and vast numbers of these mortgages to make it all work for high-finance investors. Sellers of these mortgages needed at least 500 such subprime mortgages to make it work. As the demand for asset-backed securities grew, so did the push by subprime mortgage sellers to have buyers sign on, regardless of capacity to pay the mortgage. This combination of demand and a supply of increasingly low-quality assets meant mixing slices of low-quality mortgage debt with high-quality debt. The result was an enormously complex instrument that was also enormously opaque. These new types of mortgage-backed financial instruments allow lenders to overlook creditworthiness and aim at a quick sale, since what matters is the number of mortgages that can be bundled and sold on the secondary financial circuit. This is the logic that made low-quality subprime residential mortgages into an efficient mechanism for the high-finance investment circuit (Sassen 2008b), an accomplishment on its own terms.

Given the ensuing crisis of confidence once high rates of foreclosure became visible, the current period makes legible a third asymmetry. At a time of massive concentration of financial resources in a limited number of super-firms, the one that owns a good share of the subprime mortgages when the mortgage default crisis hits, gets stuck with massive losses. In an earlier period, ownership of mortgages was widely distributed among a large number of banks, savings and loans associations, and credit unions, resulting in a wider distribution of losses. The fact that large, powerful firms have also felt that they could get by with high-risk instruments has further raised their losses. Ruthless practices, the capacity to control these markets and the growing interconnectedness of markets have made these super-firms vulnerable to their own power in a sort of network effect (Sassen 2008a: 348–65).

The Selectivity of Subprime Mortgage Lending

Modest neighborhoods became a strategic space in this process, pushing the role of urban space as a source of profit well beyond the gentrification dynamic. This asymmetry between the worlds of investors (only some will be affected) and homeowners (once they default, they can lose the house and whatever they have already paid on it regardless of what investor happens to own the instrument at the time) creates a massive distortion in the housing market and the housing finance market. Most investors can escape the negative consequences of home mortgage default because they buy these mortgages in order to sell them; there were many winners among investors for several years and only a few losers before the crisis broke in August 2007. But homeowners unable to meet their mortgage obligations cannot escape default. The fact that investors could have a positive view of subprime mortgages (poor-quality instruments) was bad for potential homeowners. We see here yet another sharp asymmetry in the position of the diverse players "enacting" an innovation.[12]

Extending mortgages to modest-income households, in itself a worthy objective, became a dangerous innovation. Since creditworthiness is not the issue with these mortgages, but numbers sold is, the likelihood that a borrower would eventually be unable to pay the mortgage was high. As with home equity loans, lenders often pushed these mortgages onto households, without full disclosure of the risks and changes in interest rates involved, and without taking account of the capacity of a household to meet the monthly mortgage payments.

Under these conditions, subprime and similar kinds of mortgages for modest-income households became a mechanism for extracting something from those households, a sort of primitive accumulation (Sassen 2010). At

Table 3.1 New York City, rate of subprime lending by borough, 2002–06 (in percent)

	2002	2003	2004	2005	2006
Bronx	14.2	19.7	28.2	34.4	27.4
Brooklyn	9.2	13.9	18.4	26.1	23.6
Manhattan	1.3	1.8	0.6	1.1	0.8
Queens	7.7	12.6	17.8	28.2	24.4
Staten Island	7.2	11.1	13.9	19.9	17.1
NYC total	7.0	10.8	14.9	22.9	19.8

Source: Furman Center for Real Estate & Urban Policy, 2007, State of New York City's housing and neighborhoods (http://furmancenter.org/research/sonychan/2007-report/, accessed November 28, 2008).

Note: A further breakdown by neighborhoods (community districts) in New York City shows that the worst-hit ten neighborhoods were poor – and between 34 and 47 percent of all mortgages bought by residents were subprime mortgages (see Table 3.2).

its most brutal, the object of this extraction was a contract (the mortgage agreement) that represented an asset. And all that was needed, given financial engineering, was for the household to sign that contract – nothing more and nothing less. The available evidence does suggest that race and locality are one of the variables at work in this process. Newman (Chapter 8, this volume) provides an important datum in this regard: a significant share of those who got subprime mortgages could have qualified for regular mortgages.

Tables 3.1, 3.2, and 3.3 show clearly that race and income level matter: African Americans and low-income neighborhoods show a disproportionately high incidence of subprime mortgages as a share of all the mortgages bought by each of these groups from 2000 to 2007 (see also Chapters 7, 8, and 9). Table 3.1 shows the extreme difference between Manhattan (one of the richest counties in the whole country despite having significant pockets of poverty) and other New York City counties: in 2006 less than 1 percent of mortgages sold to Manhattan home-buyers were subprime compared to 27.4 percent in the Bronx. This table also shows the sharp rate of growth over the years of subprime mortgages in all boroughs except Manhattan.

Finally, we see a similar pattern if we control for race (see Table 3.3; Newman Chapter 9 in this volume). Whites, who have a far higher average income than all the other groups in New York City, were far less likely to have subprime mortgages than all other groups. Thus, of all mortgages bought by Whites in 2006, 9.1 percent were subprime, compared with 13.6 percent for Asians, 28.6 percent for Hispanics, and 40.7 percent for Blacks.

Table 3.2 Ten New York City community districts with the highest rates of subprime lending, 2006

Sub-borough area	Percent of home purchase loans issued by subprime lender
University Heights/Fordham (Bronx)	47.2
Jamaica (Queens)	46.0
East Flatbush (Brooklyn)	44.0
Brownsville (Brooklyn)	43.8
Williamsbridge/Baychester (Bronx)	41.6
East New York/Starrett City (Brooklyn)	39.5
Bushwick (Brooklyn)	38.6
Morrisania/Belmont (Bronx)	37.2
Queens Village (Queens)	34.6
Bedford Stuyvesant (Brooklyn)	34.2

Source: Furman Center for Real Estate & Urban Policy, 2007, State of New York City's housing and neighborhoods (http://furmancenter.org/research/sonychan/2007-report/, accessed November 28, 2008).

Table 3.3 Rate of conventional subprime lending by race in New York City, 2002–06 (in percent)

	2002	2003	2004	2005	2006
White	4.6	6.2	7.2	11.2	9.1
Black	13.4	20.5	35.2	47.1	40.7
Hispanic	11.9	18.1	27.6	39.3	28.6
Asian	4.2	6.2	9.4	18.3	13.6

Source: Furman Center for Real Estate & Urban Policy, 2007, State of New York City's housing and neighborhoods (http://furmancenter.org/research/sonychan/2007-report/, accessed November 28, 2008).

Table 3.3 also shows the much lower growth rate in subprime lending from 2002 to 2006 among Whites compared with the other groups. In the most acute period, 2003–06, it doubled from 4.6 percent to 9.1 percent for Whites, but basically tripled for Asians and Hispanics, and quadrupled for Blacks.

The costs extend to whole metropolitan areas. The loss of property tax income for municipal governments varies across different types of cities and metro areas. One study of the ten metro areas with the largest losses of real GMP (Gross Municipal Product) for 2008 due to the mortgage crisis estimates their total economic loss at over $45 billion (Global Insight 2007).[13] New York City losses were estimated at $10 billion in 2008, Los Angeles at $8.3 billion, and Dallas, Washington, and Chicago each at about $4 billion (see generally SAIS 2009).

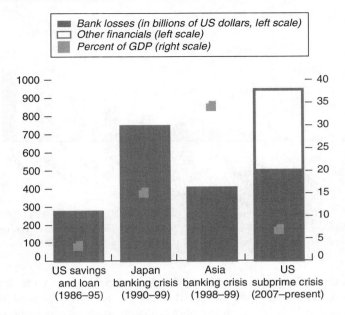

Figure 3.1 Comparison of financial crises

Sources: World Bank and IMF staff estimates. IMF Financial Stability Report 2008, Chapter 1: "Assessing Risks to Global Financial Stability." Available at http://www.imf.org/external/pubs/ft/gfsr/2008/01/PDF/chap1.pdf, last accessed July 2011. Reproduced by permission of the International Monetary Fund.

Note: US subprime costs represent staff estimates of losses on banks and other financial institutions from Table 3.1. All costs are in real 2007 dollars. Asia includes Indonesia, Korea, the Philippines, and Thailand.

Subprime Mortgages: A New Global Frontier for Finance

When we compare the current crisis to earlier crises in the global phase that began in the 1980s, we can see some interesting differences. Figure 3.1 shows that financial leveraging added another 20 percent to the underlying banking crisis, thereby bringing the current financial crisis up to an equivalent of 40 percent of global GDP, compared to earlier crises, which rarely went beyond 20 percent.

Innovations in housing finance in advanced economies over the last half century have changed the role of the housing sector in the economy at the local, national, and, more recently, global levels. This results partly from the growing value of mortgage capital, expressed as a ratio to a range of variables: GDP, household credit, household disposable income, total private credit in an economy, and so on. And it results from the expansion

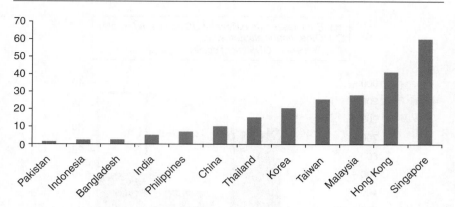

Figure 3.2 Ratio of residential mortgage debt to GDP: Emerging Asia, 2007
Source: Warnock, V.C. and Warnock, F.E., Markets and Housing Finance (February 2008).
Available at SSRN: http://ssrn.com/abstract=981641, retrieved August 24, 2008.

of secondary mortgage markets (where financial instruments based on mortgages, rather than the houses themselves, get sold). Both of these, in turn, contribute to considerable spillover effects to other economic sectors.[14]

The extremely high value of mortgages measured as a ratio to national GDP in the United States, Switzerland, Denmark, Australia, Sweden, and the Netherlands is generally seen as an indication that these countries have the most flexible and "complete" mortgage markets. One key explanation for this is clearly the level of housing market deregulation with the associated possibility of securitizing mortgages, and how long they have been deregulated (Gotham 2006; and the chapters by Aalbers, Gotham, and Wainwright in this volume).

A comparison of the pre-crisis value of all residential mortgage debt (from high- to low-quality mortgages) as a ratio to national GDP across developed countries shows sharp variation. The average for the period 2001–06 stood at around a ratio of 20 percent to GDP for Italy and Austria; closer to 30 percent for France and Belgium; 40 percent for Finland, Sweden, and Germany; 60 percent for Spain, Portugal, and Ireland; 80 percent for the UK and the Netherlands, and so on (see Figure 3.2) (IMF 2007: chapter 3; Miles 2007; Wainwright Chapter 4 in this volume).[15] To some extent the variation in this value is a function of the timing of processes. In the US, the UK, and Australia the housing market has long been private and many households have paid off their mortgages. More mature markets in Asia show a higher ratio of residential mortgage debt to GDP: 59 percent in Singapore, 39 percent in Hong Kong, and 26 percent in Taiwan (see Figure 3.2).

An important distinction is that between the ratio of residential mortgages to GDP (see, for example, Figure 3.1), on the one hand, and the growth rate of residential mortgage finance, on the other. Thus, the former is very low in countries with young housing markets, such as India and China, where it stands at 10 percent. In contrast, in more mature markets in Asia that value can be much higher, but the growth rate much lower. The average annual growth of housing loans between 1999 and 2006 in India and China was extremely high and above the growth of other types of loans; both countries have rapidly growing housing markets and they are at the merest beginning of a whole new phase in their economies. While most other Asian countries have not had the extremely high growth rates of India and China in the mortgage market, they nonetheless had a doubling in such loans from 1999 to 2006.

Understanding the weight of the residential mortgage market in the rapidly growing and diversifying world of lending, including household credit, gives us an indication of the growth potential of mortgage finance. Tables 3.4 and 3.5 provide some comparative data on the incidence of residential mortgage loans to total loans in several highly developed and in so-called emerging market countries well before the current mortgage crisis. Developed countries with multiple different financial circuits, such as the US and the UK, clearly show that, compared to other types of loans, mort-gages are a relatively small share of all loans even if most households have mortgages. It is important to distinguish that the same low level of mortgage loans to total loans in economies marked by a small elite of superrich, has a very different meaning from that in the US and UK: hence, Russia's extremely low incidence of residential to total loans in the economy is an indication of a narrow mortgage market (mostly for the rich and very rich) and the fact that there are vast financial circuits centered on other resources.

Critical measures for gauging the potential growth of residential mortgage capital are: (1) the ratio of overall household credit to household disposable income; (2) the share of household credit in total private sector credit in the national economy; and (3) the ratio of household credit to GDP. All three measures have grown over the last decade, indicating a financial deepening in the household sector and in the use of the household sector for financial deepening. While still low, these measures also show growth in emerging market economies. By the end of 2005, a good year before the subprime crisis became visible to investors, the average ratio of residential mortgages to all loans stood at 32 percent in developed markets (Table 3.4) and at 14 percent in emerging markets (Table 3.5).

The ratio of household credit to personal disposable income (see Table 3.6) shows sharp increases in some countries, especially in Eastern Europe: for instance, in the Czech Republic it grew from 8.5 percent in 2000 to 27.1 percent in 2005, in Hungary from 11.2 percent to 39.3%, while in South Korea it rose from 33 percent to 68.9 percent. This growth is also evident, for instance, in India, where the initial level was a low 4.7 percent

Table 3.4   Ratio of residential real estate loans to total loans, developed markets (December 31, 2005)*

Country	Residential real estate loans to total loans (%)
Australia	56.46
Austria	13.11
Belgium	—
Canada	58.94
Denmark	—
Finland	33.79
France	42.00
Germany	17.82
Greece	—
Hong Kong SAR	—
Ireland	13.87
Italy	17.37
Japan	—
Netherlands	28.62
New Zealand	—
Norway	61.53
Portugal	28.25
Singapore	22.01
Spain	25.85
Sweden	34.48
Switzerland	—
United Kingdom	20.05
United States	39.46*
Average	32.10

Source: International Monetary Fund, Coordinated Compilation Exercise (CCE) for Financial Soundness Indicators (FSIs): data – individual economy tables selected by topic (Table A) http://www.imf.org/external/np/sta/fsi/topic.asp?table=A. Reproduced by permission of International Monetary Fund.

*Compiled on a domestic consolidation basis unless otherwise noted; one of the International Monetary Fund's Financial Soundness Indicators.

in 2000, but had doubled to 9.7 percent in 2004. In mature market economies, this ratio is much higher but it grew at a far lower rate than in emerging markets. For instance, in Japan it grew from 73.6 percent to 77.8 percent between 2000 and 2005, and in the US from 104 percent to 132.7 percent. Spain had one of the highest increases, from 65 percent in 2000 to 112.7 percent in 2005, as did Australia, growing from 83.3 percent to 124 percent.

An important question raised by these patterns is to what extent other developed and developing countries will follow the troublesome

Table 3.5 Ratio of residential real estate loans to total loans, emerging markets (December 31, 2005)*

Country	Residential real estate loans to total loans (%)
South Africa	19.92
Russian Federation	9.15
Poland	12.91
Luxembourg	7.17
Latvia	18.81
Croatia	17.47
South Africa	19.92
Russian Federation	9.15
Poland	12.91
Average	14.16

Source: International Monetary Fund, Coordinated Compilation Exercise (CCE) for Financial Soundness Indicators (FSIs): data – individual economy tables selected by topic (Table A) http://www.imf.org/external/np/sta/fsi/topic.asp?table=A. Reproduced by permission of International Monetary Fund.

*Compiled on a domestic consolidation basis unless otherwise noted; one of the International Monetary Fund's Financial Soundness Indicators.

"development" path of the US. That path ultimately has become yet another way of extracting value from individuals, in this case through home mortgages that even very modest households are invited to buy. As indicated earlier, this is partly because once the sellers get enough mortgage contracts they just bundle them up with high-grade debt and sell the package to an investor. This passes on the risk and it no longer matters whether the homeowner goes bankrupt or manages to hang on to the house.

In my analysis of the subprime crisis, two dynamics of financial markets have come together and they signal a potentially global expansion in the use of these problematic tactics (Sassen 2008b). Both arise out of the interlinking of markets. One is usually described as a spillover effect; in this case, it is a spillover from US markets to the rest of the world. The second, less noted, is the network effect that arises from the fact that more and more firms use financial instruments that are meant to export risk: in electronically linked markets this becomes a network effect that hits all firms back (Sassen 2008a: 358–65).

The financializing of mortgages has broadened the spillovers from the housing sector to the rest of the economy and, given poor quality mortgage contracts, it has raised the use of derivatives and expanded their use onto wider and wider domains, as I have discussed regarding credit-default swaps.[16]

Table 3.6 Ratio of household credit to personal disposable income, 2000–05 (in percent)

	2000	2001	2002	2003	2004	2005
Emerging markets						
Czech Republic	8.5	10.1	12.9	16.4	21.3	27.1
Hungary	11.2	14.4	20.9	29.5	33.9	39.3
Poland	10.1	10.3	10.9	12.6	14.5	18.2
India	4.7	5.4	6.4	7.4	9.7	...
Korea	33.0	43.9	57.3	62.6	64.5	68.9
Philippines	1.7	4.6	5.5	5.5	5.6	...
Taiwan	75.1	72.7	76.0	83.0	95.5	...
Thailand	26.0	25.6	28.6	34.3	36.4	...
Mature markets						
Australia	83.3	86.7	95.6	109.0	119.0	124.6
France	57.8	57.5	58.2	59.8	64.2	69.2
Germany	70.4	70.1	69.1	70.3	70.5	70.0
Italy	25.0	25.8	27.0	28.7	31.8	34.8
Japan	73.6	75.7	77.6	77.3	77.9	77.8
Spain	65.2	70.4	76.9	86.4	98.8	112.7
United States	104.0	105.1	110.8	118.2	126.0	132.7

Source: IMF staff estimates based on data from country authorities, CEIC, OECD, and Bloomberg. International Monetary Fund, "Global Financial Stability Report, Market Developments and Issues," *IMF: World Economic and Financial Surveys*, September 2006, Table 2.4, p. 56. Reproduced by permission of International Monetary Fund.

Conclusion

In this chapter I have sought to show that the critical feature in the subprime mortgage crisis is the combination of: (1) the delinking of profit-making for lenders and investors from the capacity of the borrower to pay for the mortgage; (2) the development of instruments that allow for the splicing of individual mortgages and the bundling of these low-grade mortgage bits with high-grade debt; and (3) the interest of investors in asset-backed securities at a time when extremely complex instruments such as derivatives on interest rates were becoming dominant. The fatal flaw for mortgage borrowers is, in my reading, the delinking described in the first point, even though this is the condition that makes it attractive for investors. Clearly, this asymmetrical relation can only be activated if the second and third are also present. Securitizing mortgages in itself is not necessarily bad, especially if it allows lenders to provide mortgages to modest-income households. Delinking profitability from the borrower's creditworthiness is bad – initially for borrowers and eventually, as it turns out, for investors.

A second issue developed here is what we might think of as a new global space for the deployment of subprime mortgages: the billions of households in much of the world where residential mortgage capital has extensive room to grow. Although in many countries households tend to use cash to buy their homes, modest-income households with little disposable cash emerge as prime candidates for faulty mortgages. One indication of this growth potential is the low ratio of residential mortgage capital to GDP in Eastern Europe and Asia.

The third issue addressed in this chapter has to do with the interlinking of financial markets and the rapid internationalization of financial capital. This includes the growing incidence of foreign-currency borrowing by households worldwide. The intermediaries that provide this credit might be credit card companies of a variety of banks and financial institutions. Foreign firms are one key agent in the financial deepening of much of the world, including the growth of household credit in relation to household disposable income. This interlinking also includes a great potential for spillover and network effects – that is to say, a potential for both enhanced growth and enhanced losses. While the subprime mortgage crisis originates in the US, its negative effects easily spread to Europe via the investment circuit. Investors bought instruments typically rated as high-grade given the mix of slices of subprime mortgages with high-grade debt. As lenders in the US delinked the granting of these mortgages from borrowers creditworthiness, the resultant escalating foreclosures alerted investors to the presence of "toxic" components.

The so-called "subprime mortgage crisis" is, strictly speaking, the result of the worries of investors about the composition of these mixed instruments and the impossibility of tracing that composition – the lack of transparency of these instruments. It exploded in August 2007, when banks as diverse as the Bank of China and Paribas discovered they had invested in troubled instruments. It was investors' crisis of confidence; whether the investors were banks or individuals. This crisis needs to be distinguished from the foreclosure crisis, which is a crisis of households and has repercussions on neighborhoods, whole cities and regions, and municipal governments.

Finally, notwithstanding the costs to particular types of investors, the subprime mortgage is not going to disappear. From the perspective of banks and financial firms, a market comprising potentially billions of modest-income households worldwide is too good a thing to relinquish. Today's subprime mortgage, like the "junk bond" of the 1980s, will be fixed and redeployed. Lawmakers, regulators, and citizens groups need to be on the alert. From other perspectives, refining this instrument and subject-ing it to regulations that protect the weakest parties – the modest-income households – is not necessarily a bad idea. But that would require some serious work on the part of legislators and regulators worldwide.

Notes

1　This is particularly so if we take a simple and direct definition such as "a primitive accumulation preceding capitalistic accumulation; an accumulation not the result of the capitalistic mode of production, but its starting point" (Marx 1992: 873).

2　"The capitalist system pre-supposes the complete separation of the labourers from all property in the means by which they can realize their labour. As soon as capitalist production is once on its own legs, it not only maintains this separation, but reproduces it on a continually extending scale. The process, therefore, that clears the way for the capitalist system, can be none other than the process which takes away from the labourer the possession of his means of production; a process that transforms, on the one hand, the social means of subsistence and of production into capital, on the other, the immediate producers into wage-labourers. The so-called primitive accumulation, therefore, is nothing else than the historical process of divorcing the producer from the means of production. It appears as primitive, because it forms the pre-historic stage of capital and of the mode of production corresponding with it" (Marx 1992: 874–5).

3　I have long been interested in expanding the analytic terrain within which we understand some classical categories, from citizenship to primitive accumulation, as a way to a) make these older categories work to elucidate novel conditions, and b) to identify, potentially, the limits of these older categories to explain current conditions, hence making visible the need for new categories (Sassen 2008a).

4　In my earlier research (e.g., Sassen 1982, 1988, 1991) I conceptualized these types of operations in the Global North – a mix of organizational complexity and destitution/disempowerment – as "peripheralization at the core." In many ways this concept captures the particularity of the short and brutal history of this particular type of subprime mortgage.

5　For instance, the growing informalization of work in major global cities of the North beginning in the 1980s is often described as a mechanism to lower costs of production. It is that, but it is also a more complex dynamic that contributes to the deepening of advanced capitalism. In my research I find that some (not all) of the components of this informalizing of work are the systemic equivalent of the deregulation of major advanced economic sectors, notably finance and telecommunications. It adds particular forms of "flexibility," i.e., needed components of production and work for the advanced sectors that could not function/survive formally. (Sassen 2008a: chapters 5 and 6).

6　Elsewhere (2008b, 2008c) I examine a range of cases through a specific lens: the assemblages of specific processes, institutions, and logics that get mobilized in this systemic transformation/expansion/consolidation. Comparing the current assemblage of elements that enables the operations of "PA" as systemic deepening with those of the original in Marx also is a way of establishing the differences – the specific historical and systemic differences. Focusing on assemblages of elements involved in these shifts, rather than positing more deterministic dynamics, also enables factoring in contingency.

7 I examined the implications of this for urban economies in the first edition of *The Global City* (Sassen 1991: chapter 4). In the US this began with the (in) famous and much debated phasing out of interest rate controls under Regulation Q in the 1980s, which also led to the destruction of the Savings and Loans institutions and a massive bailout by taxpayers. These destructions generated a series of innovations – new types of mortgage instruments, of which the current generation of so-called structured-investment instruments is but the latest. The overall effect was a vast expansion of credit in the mortgage sector in the 1980s, long before the current phase. It is extraordinary how regulators and legislators failed to learn a lesson from this.

8 Elsewhere I have examined the strategic role of interpretation in finance, notably the diverse technical cultures of interpretation (2008a: chapter 4 generally and chapter 7, especially pp. 352–65).

9 The financial deepening of economies has become one of the major dynamics characterizing advanced economies. The number of countries where financial assets exceed the value of their gross national product more than doubled from 33 in 1990 to 72 in 2006 (McKinsey 2008). Securitizing a broad range of types of debt is a key vehicle for this financial deepening. The extension of securitization into consumer debt, including mortgages, took off in the 1980s in the US. The sharp growth of mortgages to enable the massive housing construction boom in developed countries in the decades following the Second World War produced a vast money pool, which became a prime object for securitization in the 1980s.

10 The trends in financial globalization point to geopolitical shifts. Before the loss of value of the financial crisis of September 2008, the US, still the largest financial power, had $56.1 trillion assets, almost a third of the world's financial assets. Europe's Eurozone financial markets were almost $40 trillion; including the UK's $10 trillion and Eastern Europe's $14 trillion puts Europe close to the US. The Euro had by then become a strong alternative global currency to the dollar, with the value of euro currency in circulation surpassing the latter in mid-2007; it was and is also the top currency for issuing of international bonds. Japan, China, India, and several other Asian countries are a fast growing third financial block. The composition of financial assets in these major national and regional financial markets varies sharply. Before the devaluing of the crisis, the largest components in the US were equity securities and private debt securities, which together accounted for seventy percent of the financial market. In contrast, in China, bank deposits account for 55 percent of financial assets.

11 The high incidence of homeownership in the US partly explains why the banking and financial industries generated innovations so as to expand their markets. Ultimately, this logic led to the invention of mortgages aimed at modest- and low-income households – the remaining potential market. But before this current innovation there were the so-called home equity loans based on homeownership, which also expanded the financial market centered on homeownership. Mortgage lenders succeeded in developing a whole

industry around secondary mortgages, often persuading reluctant homeowners to sign on.

12   According to the Federal Reserve's flow of funds data, as of 2008: Q1, "U.S. households and nonprofits held about $22 trillion in real estate assets (mostly residential properties), and businesses (corporations and non-corporate entities) held $16 trillion; these sums do not include foreign or government holdings. Supporting these real estate assets is nearly $15 trillion in mortgage debt. For purposes of comparison, households owe about $2.5 trillion in consumer debt, and U.S. businesses (nonfarm and nonfinancial) owe about $11 trillion" (FRBSF 2009).

13   For an explanation of how these estimates were reached please see Global Insight 2007. This report contains a full list of GMP estimated losses for all 361 metros (Appendix, Table A2, pp. 8–16). The estimate is that that 128 metros will see slow real GMP growth of less than 2 percent in 2008, and that growth will fall by more than a third in 65 metros, and by more than a quarter in 143 metros.

14   According to the Federal Reserve's flow of funds data, as of 2008: Q1, "U.S. households and nonprofits held about $22 trillion in real estate assets (mostly residential properties), and businesses (corporations and noncorporate entities) held $16 trillion; these sums do not include foreign or government holdings. Supporting these real estate assets is nearly $15 trillion in mortgage debt. For purposes of comparison, households owe about $2.5 trillion in consumer debt, and U.S. businesses (nonfarm and nonfinancial) owe about $11 trillion" (FRBSF 2009).

15   These measures are based on several sources: IMF national accounts data, European Mortgage Federation, Hypostat Statistical Tables, the US Federal Reserve, the OECD Analytical Database, Statistics Canada, and IMF staff calculations.

16   There are two features of derivatives that matter for my argument here. The first, frequently overlooked both in general commentaries and in more academic treatments, is that their distinctive characteristic is not so much that they reduce risk, as is commonly believed, but that they transfer it to less risk-sensitive sectors in the economy. This aspect is easily lost in academic fields centered on firms. Insofar as firms remain central to a model, it makes sense to confine observation to the fact that firms use derivatives to hedge and thereby reduce their risks. This is correct, but only partially. What has been left out of this picture, I argue, is that in the context of electronically linked markets and an absolute predominance of derivatives as the instrument of choice for most firms in today's financial markets, the transfer of risk by individual firms becomes a collective transfer of risk to the market. In so doing, trading in derivatives produces a network effect that is a new type of risk: market risk (Sassen 2008a: 358–65). The crucial contextual variable contributing to this network effect is that derivatives are used by firms in all financial markets and account for the vast majority of financial transactions.

References

Aalbers, M.B. (2008) The financialization of home and the mortgage market crisis. *Competition & Change* 12: 148–66.

Amin, S. (2000) Economic globalism and political universalism: conflicting issues? *Journal of World-Systems Research* 6(3): 582–622.

Amin, S. (2010) Exiting the crisis of capitalism or capitalism in crisis? *Globalizations* 7(1–2): 261–73.

Arrighi, G. (1994) *The long twentieth century: money, power, and the origins of our times, Part I*. London: Verso.

FRBSF (Federal Reserve Bank of San Francisco). (2009) FRBSF Economic Letter: Housing Prices and Bank Loan Performance, 2009–06; 6 February 2009 [WWW document]. URL http://www.frbsf.org/publications/economics/ letter/2009/el2009–06.html (accessed May 1, 2009).

Furman Center for Real Estate and Urban Policy. (2007) *State of New York City's housing and neighborhoods* [WWWdocument]. URL http://furmancenter.org/research/sonychan/2007-report/ (accessed November 28, 2008).

Global Insight, Inc. (2007) The mortgage crisis: economic and fiscal implications for metro areas. Research paper, United States Conference of Mayors and the Council for the New American City.

Gotham, K.F. (2006) The secondary circuit ofcapital reconsidered: globalization and the US real estate sector. *American Journal of Sociology* 112: 231–75.

Harvey, D. (2003) *The New Imperialism*. Oxford: Oxford University Press.

IMF (International Monetary Fund). (2006) Household credit growth in emerging market countries. In: *Global Financial Stability Report, Market Developments and Issues* (2007). Washington DC: IMF.

IMF Coordinated Compilation Exercise (CCE) for Financial Soundness Indicators (FSIs): data — individual economy tables selected by topic (Table A) [WWW document]. URL http://www.imf.org/external/np/sta/fsi/topic.asp?table=A (accessed August 28, 2008).

IMF (International Monetary Fund). (2008) *Containing systemic risks and restoring financial soundness*. IMF World Economic and Financial Surveys: Global Financial Stability Report, Market Developments, IMF, Washington, DC, [WWW document]. URL http://www.imf.org/external/pubs/ft/gfsr/2008/01/index.htm (accessed August 28, 2008).

ISDA (International Swaps and Derivatives Association). (2009) Data on Credit-Default.Swaps.

Marx, K. (1992) *Capital*, vol. 1, Part VIII. London: Penguin Classics, chapters 26–31: 873–931.

McKinsey & Company. (2008) Mapping global capital markets fourth annual report. McKinsey Global Institute [WWW document]. URL http://www.mckinsey. com/mgi/reports/pdfs/Mapping_Global/ MGI_Mapping_Global_full_Report.pdf (accessed November 28, 2008).

Miles, D. (2007) European economics: financial innovation and European housing and mortgage markets. *Morgan Stanley Research Europe* 18 July. Morgan Stanley [WWW document]. URL http://www.germany-re.com/files/00034800/ MS%20Housing%20Report%202007.pdf (accessed August 28, 2008).

SAIS Review. (2009) Special Issue on "Cities," *SAIS Review* 29(1): 1–173.

Sassen, S. (1982) Recomposition and peripheralization at the core. In: *The New Nomads: Immigration and Change in the International Division of Labor*, M. Dixon and S. Jonas (eds.) San Francisco, CA: Synthesis, pp. 88–100.

Sassen, S. (1988) *The Mobility of Labor and Capital*. Cambridge: Cambridge University Press.

Sassen, S. (1991) *The global city: New York, London, Tokyo*. Princeton, NJ: Princeton University Press (second edition 2001).

Sassen, S. (2008a [2006]) *Territory, authority, rights: from medieval to global assemblages*. Princeton, NJ: Princeton University Press (updated edition).

Sassen, S. (2008b) Mortgage capital and its particularities: a new frontier for global finance. *Journal of International Affairs* 62(1): 187–212.

Sassen S. (2008c) Two stops in today's new global geographies: Shaping novel labor supplies and employment regimes. *American Behavioral Scientist* 52(3): 457–96.

Sassen, S. (2010) A savage sorting of winners and losers: Contemporary versions of primitive accumulation. *Globalizations* 7(1–2): 23–50.

Sassen, S. (2011) *Cities in a World Economy*. Thousand Oaks, CA: Sage/Pine Forge 4th Updated Ed.

Varchaver, N. and Benner, K. (2008) The $55 trillion question: special report issue 1: America's money crisis, *CNNMoney.com* http://money.cnn.com/2008/09/30/magazines/fortunre/varchaver_derivatives_short.fortune/index. htm.

Warnock, V.C. and Warnock, F.E. (2008) Markets and housing finance, February [WWW document]. URL http://ssrn.com/abstract=981641 (accessed August 24, 2008).

Wyly, E.K., Atia, M., and Hammel, D. (2004) Has mortgage capital found an inner-city spatial fix? *Housing Policy Debate* 15: 623–86.

4

Building New Markets

Transferring Securitization, Bond-Rating, and a Crisis from the US to the UK

Thomas Wainwright

Introduction

Northern Rock's a good example, because it's, a very prudent Securitizer …
if you're a shareholder in Northern Rock then it's brilliant, there's no risk for
you, you're just getting paid, it's almost risk free (Interview: Director, large
UK retail bank, February 2007) … customers queued up to withdraw their
savings from the UK mortgage lender after it was rescued by the Bank of
England … shares in Northern Rock plunged more than 30 per cent. (*Financial
Times* September 15, 2007:1)

In July 2007, newly appointed British Prime Minister Gordon Brown called
for banks to increase their use of structured finance and the capital markets,
in order to fund new 25 year fixed-rate mortgages. The aim was to fund
new mortgage products that would assist first time buyers in the purchase of
their new home (BBC 2007a). Between 1997 and 2007, the average house
price in the UK had increased by 193 percent, from £76,103 in 1997 to
£223,405 in 2007 (Department for Communities and Local Government
2009). Like their US counterparts, many British homeowners became real
estate speculators as housing often became the most valuable asset possessed
by families, whilst those entering retirement frequently planned to use the
equity within their homes to fund their retirement (Rowlingson 2006). The
rapid increase in house prices, fuelled in part by the ability of mortgage lenders to access cheap money from the capital markets, came to an abrupt halt
when it became clear that the UK was not insulated from the effects of the
US subprime mortgage crisis. On 10 September 2007, the small mortgage
lender Victoria Mortgages, which borrowed money from financiers to fund

Subprime Cities: The Political Economy of Mortgage Markets, First Edition. Edited by Manuel B. Aalbers.
© 2012 Blackwell Publishing Ltd. Published 2012 by Blackwell Publishing Ltd.

mortgage issuance as opposed to using consumer deposits, became the first fatality of the UK mortgage industry (Banham 2007). Four days later it was revealed that Northern Rock, one of the UK's largest mortgage lenders, had been forced to go to the Bank of England to seek emergency funding as its financiers had withdrawn their credit lines, which formed the majority of the bank's funding (Thal Larsen 2007).

As the credit crunch began to take hold of the UK's banking system, the financial press began to report how several funds around the world – that were backed by US subprime mortgages – were rapidly losing value. It became immediately apparent that the repercussions from the US subprime crisis had spread far beyond the US borders. Subsequently, many UK mortgage lenders found themselves cut off from the capital markets – or had their access to capital severely curtailed – as a flight-to-quality ensued. Mortgage lenders began to withdraw products that were aimed at riskier consumers and, by September 2007, lending approvals in the UK fell to the lowest level seen in two years (Strauss 2007). The effect of the crisis varied between UK mortgage lenders. Those worst affected had borrowed heavily from the wholesale markets to fund mortgage production and their business models had become reliant on their ability to sell their mortgage assets to investors through a process called securitization.

This chapter has four aims. First, it seeks to explain how securitization is implicated in the globalization of international finance and how it facilitated the movement of the credit crunch to the UK. Second, the chapter aims to uncover how securitization was adapted for use in the UK, where it was reengineered and became responsible for channeling international capital into the UK's urban landscape. This links to the third aim of the chapter, which is to build upon the work of David Harvey, by providing a nuanced and cultural understanding of capital switching, whilst highlighting the prominence of financiers in coordinating flows between circuits of capital. The final aim, draws upon Sidaway's (2008) call that financial crises narratives, such as the credit crunch, should be attentive to space. As such, this chapter seeks to provide a spatially sensitive examination of the UK's experience of the "global" crisis, whilst highlighting the transmission mechanism that transferred the US subprime crisis to the UK. The remainder of this chapter is as follows: part two gives an explanation of what securitization is, which actors are involved in its production, and how it functions. Part three discusses how Harvey's work on the circuits of capital can be expanded upon with regard to the construction of securitization and the role of financiers in producing urban space. In part four, the chapter explains how securitization, a key financial innovation, was transferred from the US to the UK, where it became an important tool for UK mortgage lenders. Part five outlines how the transfer of US bond-rating agencies into London aided the expansion and internationalization of the UK's RMBS market.

Part six suggests a narrative to explain how the US subprime crisis spread from the US and triggered the credit crunch, which produced instability for the debt capital markets, financial institutions, and the UK consumers. Part seven concludes the chapter.

At the time of writing, the implications of the credit crunch are still being unraveled and there is a limited quantity of academic literature on this topic, especially with regard to the UK's experience. Consequently, the chapter relies heavily on empirical evidence that was collected in 2007. Forty semi-structured interviews were conducted in the UK, the duration of which varied between 45 minutes and two hours. Respondents were sought from the UK's leading mortgage lenders based on the volumes of mortgages produced, according to information from the Council of Mortgage Lenders, whilst all major investment banks, laws firms, and trustees were contacted through snowballing based on retail bank contacts, or trade publications. The organizations approached included retail banks, centralized lenders, investment banks, bond rating agencies, credit referencing agencies, law firms, trustee firms, and investors. The interviews were conducted with directors and associates who work across the different stages of mortgage production and securitization.

Securitization: Opening the Black Box

Securitization is a complex financial process that was developed in the US in the 1980s and has undergone relentless innovations as it has spread, albeit unevenly, across the globe. Until the mass media recently pushed the neologism securitization into popular consciousness as a result of the credit crunch, it was a word used mainly by bankers involved in the capital markets. Langley (2006: 283) argues that securitization can be understood as a "practice of 'bundling' together a stream of future obligations arising from mortgage repayments to provide the basis for the issue of, and the payment of principal and interest on securities." According to Leyshon and Thrift (2008) securitization provides three key benefits. First, securitization as a cheap way of borrowing as a company, or lender, can realize its income streams early. Second, there is a demand for securities, backed by stable income streams, from large institutional investors – a demand that is partly satisfied by securitization. Third, banks can accelerate the circulation of their capital as the off-balance sheet nature of securitization means that they can circumnavigate capital adequacy requirements.

Dymski (Chapter 6) argues that lenders also benefit from the off-balance sheet nature of securitization, which has led some banks to originate profitable, high-risk mortgages as the credit risk is shifted from their balance sheets to investors.

Securitization involves the sale of a set of assets, such as residential mortgages, but can also include credit cards, consumer loans, car finance, and infrastructure, which are generically known as asset-backed securities (ABS). There are several organizations involved in the production of residential mortgage-backed securities (RMBS). The production begins with the mortgage lender, called the originator, who produces mortgage assets and collects the monthly repayments. The lender's treasury department then sells the assets to a special purpose vehicle (SPV) (Langley 2006). Legally, SPVs function like any normal company; they produce annual reports and pay tax but effectively outsource all of their operations as they do not have offices or employees and are managed by independent trustee managers (Ferran 1992; Langley 2006). A series of SPVs are used in the transactions where each SPV provides a different function, such as holding the mortgage assets, issuing the notes, and acting as a funding provider. SPVs are used because the originator needs to sell the assets to another party, for the sale of assets to be legal; however, they cannot be sold to the investors as they do not buy the assets but a series of financially engineered income streams, as will be explained later. Subsequently, the SPVs collectively act as a third party that holds the transaction's assets.

Investment banks are central to securitization as they promote the deals and provide "structured finance" services (Langley 2006). Existing social science research has failed to appreciate the importance of structured finance services that have contributed to securitization's development, which this chapter argues is imperative to understanding how the credit crunch emerged as the financial engineering provided by investment banks failed to contain the credit risk of subprime mortgages. The key technology behind securitization is produced through a network of socio-cultural technological practices (Pryke and Lee 1995) and is known as the "waterfall structure," which is produced by the investment bank. The waterfall structure is produced using mathematical modeling where the revenue streams from individual assets are (re)engineered. Instead of trying to spread the credit risk from the assets, the structure concentrates the risk of default into specific tranches, or fractions of capital. The interest and principal repayments from mortgage assets are not divided up evenly and distributed to investors. Instead, the repayments flow like a waterfall down through the top of this hypothetical structure, filling-up the different tranches from top to bottom.

The aim is that the least risky AAA notes are paid first whilst the remaining capital flows down to the BB tranche. The rationale behind tranching is that if there is a financial crisis – where many consumers default on their mortgages – the more junior notes at the bottom are not repaid, whereas the investors with the larger proportion of senior notes at the top are protected. This is known as subordination where the credit risks – and potential losses – are squeezed into the junior notes and a reserve fund.[1] The waterfall structure theoretically allows low yield, high quality notes to be engineered from riskier assets, whilst also providing a smaller proportion of riskier notes that pay a higher return to investors who want to take on more risk. However, in the US market, lenders began to originate mortgage products that carried increasingly more credit risk and so the defaults that emanated from the US subprime mortgage crisis occurred on a greater scale than had been predicted by investment bank and bond-rating analysts, a consequence of information asymmetries. Subsequently, the analysts miscalculated the necessary subordination required for many transactions, which failed to contain the higher than predicted credit risk within the junior notes, causing losses to spread into the senior, "low risk" notes.

Investors are the key actors who consume the securitized notes. As the securitized structures became more complex and diversified, they attracted a diverse range of investors, beacuse the deals provided different levels of risk and returns. This made securitization popular with investors including pension funds, insurance funds, hedge funds, structured investment vehicles (SIVs), and retail banks. Bond-rating agencies, to be discussed in more detail later, provide a key role by producing independent risk metrics for the securitized notes. Research by Sinclair (1994a, 1994b, 2005) discusses how bond-rating agencies exercise governance across the financial system by providing risk metrics for financial products, such as RMBS, which are used by investors when they make investment decisions. This chapter argues that bond-rating agencies also assist the development of new RMBS markets, by attempting to provide transparency to non-local investors.

Capital Switching or Capital Switchers?
Producing Urban Space

Academics studying economic geography and the built environment have frequently made reference to the seminal work of Harvey (1973, 1974, 1978, 1982, 1985) who has consistently argued that capitalism has made use of urban space in an attempt to overcome its internal contradictions. Harvey (1982) argues that capitalists succeed in delaying financial crises by channeling capital into the secondary circuit (the built environment), which averts overaccumulation in the primary circuit (manufacturing sector) accompanied by the overproduction of commodities, falling profits, and the emergence of surplus labor. Harvey (1985) maintains that capital switching funded the US's postwar suburbanization, a practice used to offset over-accumulation (Dymski and Veitch 1996), although capital switching can also be integrated with a spatial fix, across two scales (Harvey 1982). First, MacDonald (1996) discusses how capital can be switched from the regional to the national scale. Early US housing credit was organized through local and regional markets, which were later reorganized and mediated through a national market that was used to switch capital between regions of overaccumulation into regions suffering from capital shortages. Second, Hamnett (1994) and Pryke (1994) discuss capital switching from the national to the global scale, illustrated by US investment banks that implanted securitization programs within the UK's mortgage markets, which constituted an international spatial fix.

Harvey has provided a theoretical framework that has informed urban research, and contemporary accounts have built upon Harvey's focus on the primary and secondary circuits of capital. For example, Charney (2001: 741) has argued that the real estate sector can be seen not as an overspill for excess capital, "but rather as an investment channel in its own right" providing diversification for portfolios as well as attractive incomes. Both Beauregard (1994) and Charney (2001) have highlighted how the real estate industry is an independent and dynamic sector, which is organized and (re)produced by specific companies, not abstract market forces, and although Harvey has explored how financial markets articulate a central role in switching capital into the urban environment, there is a lacuna in knowledge as to how this is achieved in practice.

This chapter seeks to build on the work of Harvey and Charney to explore how the practice of securitization became increasingly more important for financial institutions as a technique for facilitating increased capital switching into the UK's urban environment. In doing so, the chapter aims to demonstrate how financial elites have sought to refine and (re)engineer securitization, in order to produce a financial tool that could enhance the profitability of the UK's mortgage market; providing attractive returns for mortgage lenders, investment banks and investors. This investigation will attempt to offer insight into the politics surrounding securitization's transfer to the UK, and how the integration of the UK's built environment into the international circuits of capital is motivated by fresh capital accumulation and regulatory arbitrage to increase lending and profitability. In order to achieve this, the chapter has scrutinized the development of UK securitization through a social lens, to emphasize the roles of individuals, practices, technologies, and knowledge in the articulation of financial products and markets (Knorr-Cetina and Bruegger 2002; Pryke and du Gay 2007), in order to uncover how London emerged as the European center of securitization.

A Historical Geography of Securitization

This chapter does not seek to provide an in-depth discussion on the development of securitization in the US, which is discussed in more detail by Gotham (2006 and Chapter 1 in this volume), where he explains how government sponsored entities (GSEs) developed secondary mortgage markets. Gotham's account of embryonic securitization differs from the UK's experience in that the British government had no direct intervention in the development of a secondary market for UK mortgages. This market was established solely by financial institutions. This chapter will argue that securitization emerged in the UK because it was compatible with the recently deregulated political economy and existed as an efficient and useful tool for mortgage lenders. In this regard, the foundations for the UK's securitization market were established in 1986 when the UK's financial markets were reregulated, which inadvertently made the UK's banking infrastructure compatible with a variant of US securitization.

Before 1986, the only financial institutions permitted to offer mortgages to consumers in the UK were building societies, but in 1986 the Financial Services Act was passed, opening up the markets to a myriad of new financial institutions such as banks and centralized lenders; while the Building Societies Act (1986) allowed building societies, to demutualize and become banks (Leyshon and Thrift 1997; Martin and Turner 2000). This deregulation had two implications for UK securitization. First, US investment banks were able to establish mortgage lending subsidiaries in the UK, whilst retail banks, which would later become the largest securitizers in the UK, began originating mortgages. Historically, London has existed as an important financial center, but it became more important with the emergence of the Euromarkets in the 1960s prior to the disintegration of the Bretton Woods System (Thrift 1994; Sassen 2001). Deregulation in the 1970s had ended regulation that had limited the operations of foreign banks (Plender 1986), whilst the 1980s witnessed the adoption of new technological innovations – for example, electronic trading – leading to the development of new markets. These transformations enabled US investment banks to expand their operations in London, which enabled them to introduce new financial products like securitization to the UK. Pryke and Allen (2000) argue that the social relations between experts in financial centers are vital in the construction of financial products in what they call socio-financial engineering. The arrival of US investment banks enabled epistemic communities to form who could align their knowledge, practices, texts, skills, vocabularies (Thrift 1994), and mathematical skills to construct the waterfall structures of the first UK securitizations.

The successful implementation of securitization in the UK hinged on the ability of localized, decentralized networks of bankers to embed the alien idea of securitization into the UK's political economy. We need to view securitization, in the case of RMBS, as being simultaneously an idea, a technology, and an investment vehicle. Securitization, as an idea, refers to the theory of securitization as a tool which homogenizes heterogeneous income streams into standardized products (Gotham 2006) that allows mortgage debt to be removed from a lender's balance sheet. This concept traveled relatively freely from the US to the UK in the 1980s, as American investment banks – experienced in performing securitization – began to promote securitization to UK lenders. Securitization as a technology refers to the practices involved in converting securitization from an idea into an organizational framework and product. These technologies are the synthesis of a complicated and contested relationship between the translations of a series of US designed financial practices into a process that would be compatible with the UK legal system, whilst being of use to UK lenders and investors. Despite claims that deregulation will lead to deterritorialization and homogenization (O' Brien 1992), mortgage markets are still subject to specific configurations of law and tax (Gotham 2006; Aalbers 2008) so securitization as a product had to be redesigned. Finally, securitization as an investment vehicle explains how UK RMBS products were structured so that they would develop an international demand from investors.

Early adopters that helped establish securitization in the UK included: Chemical Bank (US), Canadian Imperial Bank of Commerce, Salomon Brothers (US), and the Bank of Ireland (Hamnett 1994). Salomon Brothers introduced securitization to the UK in 1986 by setting up The Mortgage Corporation, which issued mortgages to be structured by Salomon and sold to investors in the UK (Lewis 1989; Pryke and Whitehead 1994). The introduction of securitization to the UK was just one of many financial innovations and tools that were developed in the US and later spread to the UK in a milieu of restructuring in the 1980s and 1990s (Leyshon and Pollard 2000).

Traditionally, mortgage origination requires substantial amounts of capital, both to fund the mortgages and to maintain the extensive bank branch infrastructure to acquire consumer deposits. The US investment banks unveiled a cheaper method of funding and issuing mortgages, called the centralized lender model that sold mortgages through established intermediaries like estate agents, and later the internet, eliminating the need for a branch network. The money to fund the mortgages was borrowed from a "warehouse line," which is effectively a short-term overdraft offered by investment banks who would frequently own the mortgage lender. The lenders sell the revenue streams of the mortgage repayments to investors through securitization, and the money from the sale of these assets is then used to repay and clear the warehouse line before the process of mortgage origination restarts. The lenders profit from the deals by taking a commission from the debt sale, but they also profit by acting as a "servicer" who manages the mortgage accounts on behalf of the investors – although professional servicers are also beginning to provide this role.

The development of securitization in the UK was by no means a simple process. Securitization existed as an idea, but its implementation required the involvement of a series of different banking and legal institutions, many of which had no prior experience of securitization. The following experiments in securitization and subsequent innovations meant that the development of securitization in the UK was a multidimensional and problematic process that would cause securitization's US structure to change in order to adapt to UK laws.

> We worked with a US law firm ... who had a lot of experience with securitization in the US, so the legal framework was different ... the solutions to the problems were quite different ... very detailed points on how payments are made ... arrears are dealt with ... making sure that the securitization vehicle is tax neutral. (Interview: Partner, Large City law firm, July 2007)

It was necessary for the bankers to liaise with lawyers who understood how to resolve the tensions that would develop between the US securitization structures and UK law. The legal issues included differences in tax liabilities, legal ownership, securities law, and contractual obligations. Many new transactions would rely on US expertise to understand the technology behind securitization as it had to be reconfigured using a series of expert skills and artifacts to readjust the technology around UK law.

> [My boss said] find someone who thinks it's a good idea ... and I went off around the American investment banks and eventually rolled into X, and there was a very nice guy there who said this is a seriously interesting idea ... we wrote a combined feasibility study ... [and] they brought over a whole team of boffs who had experience in the US and spent enormous amounts of time ringing people up in the States ... we were about to axe the project because it had got so completely out of control ... it was completely different from an American securitization, because of the tax, the law ... there was nothing about it that was straight forward. (Interview 21: Director, ex-commercial bank, July 2007)

Important innovations at the time included the use of wcomputers, to model the waterfall structure, and of cash flow probabilities, to manage the huge amounts of data needed to devise these theoretical structures. Innovations in accountancy were also needed to interpret how the assets should be represented in company accounts. The initial success of securitization and centralized lenders was soon challenged. During the1990s centralized lenders experienced heavy losses from the UK housing crash and many bankers doubted securitization's viability as a useful tool. By 1996 The Mortgage Corporation had been sold and securitization's reputation as a celebrated banking tool had been thrown into disrepute:

> the centralized lender-securitized funding model was just not profitable, and it experienced higher repossessions, losses, arrears than the industry average. It can be argued that the early 90s recession finally killed the idea ... if you

look back to the early 90s ... the scoring systems weren't very good. (Interview: Director, Large UK retail bank, October 2007)

Until the late 1990s, securitization had been used exclusively as a funding tool and as retail banks and building societies used customer deposits to fund their mortgage issuance, they had no interest in securitization. However, securitization underwent a second transformation in the UK and was soon used as a tool to overcome capital adequacy regulation. The introduction of capital adequacy ratios in 1988, called Basel, was a policy developed by the Bank of International Settlements, applied and enforced by national governments.[2] The ratios were used to dictate the size of a bank's capital reserves to curb the disastrous effects of illiquidity problems experienced by commercial banks after the developing world debt crisis (Leyshon and Thrift 1997). The capital ratio for a bank's mortgage assets was calculated by multiplying 8 percent of the mortgage portfolio's value by a risk weighting of 0.5. For example, if a bank had £1 billion in mortgage assets – and it is not uncommon for *single* RMBS issues to be measured in *billions* – it would have had to have retained £40 million in capital reserves under the Basel regulation. Retail banks realized that the capital regulations required substantial amounts of cash to be held in reserves – cash that could be earning a return elsewhere. Furthermore, loans under 365 days did not need capital backing under Basel 1 regulation, which acted as a further incentive to securitize mortgage assets and to transfer them "off balance sheet" to SPVs; freeing up millions of pounds for retail banks:[3]

> it was a fairly small industry compared to what it is today, but it was all done for capital adequacy risks, i.e. Basel. (Interview: Director, ex-commercial bank, July 2007)

There were two ways that retail banks gained the expertise and knowledge required to experiment with securitization. First, retail banks would approach investment banks to develop small, one-off securitizations to see if this tool was useful for them, or the retail banks would use staff from centralized lenders that they had acquired after the early 1990s housing market crash.

> [We bought an intermediary] and it had an in-built system that could cope with securitization and that had managers who knew securitization ... so I was able to latch onto the in-built skills in the business. (Interview: Director, large UK retail bank, October 2007)

Retail banks began to experiment with smaller securitization structures, which grew as bankers became more confident that securitization could circumvent capital adequacy regulation. They realized that by issuing notes backed by mortgage assets, they could retain profits on servicing the mortgage accounts with the option of buying back some of the notes. Securitization was still problematic for retail banks in the UK, as setting up the transactions took time and the process was expensive. The question that many bank treasuries began to ask themselves was – is it worth the effort?

> [Securitization has a] high cost of funding ... which could only be pulled back if you saw how much regulatory capital came of the balance sheet. (Interview: Director, large UK retail bank, October, 2007)

The structures of securitization evolved during the late 1990s as the UK adopted what is known as the Mastertrust structure, which had lower operating costs. Earlier RMBS structures, known as Amortizing structures, repaid investors their principal and interest from a fixed pool of assets until they matured. Once the securitization's asset pool became depleted, the lender had to perform a new securitization and establish new SPVs in which to house the new assets; an expensive strategy as some securitizations can cost around £2 million in fees to develop. On the other hand, Mastertrusts – originally used in US credit card securitizations – allow a securitization structure to continue to operate indefinitely. Mastertrusts are designed so that if any mortgages – backing the RMBS notes – are repaid or refinanced, the lender can transfer single, replacement mortgages into the asset pool. Subsequently, the securitization does not amortize as its mortgage pool is never depleted and, once the bonds held by investors are repaid, the lender can arrange for new notes to be issued from the securitized structure so that the mortgage issuer does not have to develop an expensive new securitization.

This had a second implication that was to add to securitization's appeal for investors. Securitization became more of an investment vehicle as the technologies and structures changed over time and new tranches were added that would appeal to a growing range of investors. Initially, selling RMBS notes to overseas investors was problematic, as US investors were used to buying RMBS notes in the US where securitization was more established and had a proven track record of repayments.

> What we didn't have in the UK was a repayment history ... and I couldn't go to the US [investors] and say rely on that. (Interview: Director, large UK retail bank, October 2007)

To entice US investors into purchasing RMBS notes that had a short record of repayments was more problematic. It was important to sell the notes to the international market to expand the number of UK RMBS investors, as increased investor demand lowers the yield paid on the notes – making securitization cheaper to fund and more profitable for the lender. Mastertrusts enabled an extra feature to be added to the securitization technology, which became known as a "bullet." A bullet payment means that an investor receives their entire principal investment back on a set date, instead of being paid back in small amounts over the life of the note, which investors were more comfortable with as it provided greater certainty as to when their investment would be repaid. This feature could be accommodated by the Mastertrust structure as there is sufficient liquidity to repay the principal beacuse the assets are repeatedly replaced.

The development of bullet payments enticed additional investors from a wider geographical arena, with the aid of bond-rating agency metrics, to buy UK RMBS notes. This innovation stimulated the expansion of UK mortgage lending and the profitability of securitization, which dramatically increased the reliance of the UK mortgage market on the liquidity of RMBS markets and an abundance of low-priced capital obtained through the global capital markets. Such innovations, despite contributing to the initial success and profitability of the UK mortgage market, enhanced the exposure of the UK economy to systemic risks from the global markets, which exacerbated the devastating effects experienced by the UK retail finance sector and its consumers once the consequences of the credit crunch began to unfold.

As the RMBS market expanded and securitization became firmly established amongst the financial community, two additional financial products were devised by investment banks, which used the idea of securitization and some of its technologies to produce new funds. SIVs, known as structured investment vehicles, are funds that purchase RMBS and other ABS products, as well as corporate bonds, but tend to purchase low risk prime RMBS notes such as AAA through to BBB. SIVs are unique as they are able to purchase larger and more diverse volumes of assets than a smaller investor could, beacuse they leverage these funds by borrowing cheap money through the interbank markets to purchase additional assets. In this sense, the SIV fund's assets – long-term RMBS notes – are funded through short-term interbank borrowing that provides SIV fund investors with high returns. SIV managers also pass the revenue streams from the assets they purchase through a waterfall structure, to provide additional protection to investors. Investors then purchase low-risk commercial paper, rated as AAA to BBB, from SIVs that mature over a couple of years.

CDOs, or collateralized debt obligations, are funds that invest in the high-risk tranches of RMBS subprime notes and other ABS deals, frequently investing in non-investment grade notes, rated by bond-rating agencies as BBB, or below. CDOs pass the revenue streams through a waterfall structure and are reliant on their ability to successfully (re)securitize the income streams from the high-risk paper to enhance the stability of the income streams. The advantage of CDOs is that they theoretically transform high-risk paper into tranches of low-risk AAA paper, which provide higher returns than AAA RMBS subprime bonds, because CDO notes are backed by high-risk bonds that pay higher yields. More exotic CDOs use this technology to develop new CDOs out of junior CDO debt producing what are commonly known as CDO squared and CDO cubed:

> in the last two or three years there has been a huge increase in CDOs and SIV type investors ... where the bank was hoovering up triple B assets, re-rating that using rating agency methodologies, to get a tranch of triple A and single A [notes] ... entirely legal ... using leverage to drive strong returns. (Interview: Director, UK centralized lender, September 2007)

The popularity of the bonds issued by SIVs and CDOS, backed by RMBS assets, amplified the demand for UK RMBS notes further, increasing the reliance of UK mortgage lenders on the liquidity of the capital markets, which exacerbated the adverse effects of the credit crunch for these lenders. The effects of the credit crunch within the UK's financial sector were also exacerbated by the development of CDOs and SIVs, backed by European investment banks. These funds purchased US subprime RMBS, as well as UK RMBS, which later exposed many UK financial institutions to the contagion of US subprime credit risk embodied within the US RMBS notes. In effect, these investment vehicles increased the exposure of the UK's economy to the systemic risks of the international finance system as the SIVs and CDOs acted as spatial conduits, conveying US credit risk into UK financial institutions.

Migrating Metrics and the Arrival of US Bond-Rating Agencies in the UK

We have seen how financial innovations such as the introduction of the bullet payment, enticed US investors into purchasing UK RMBS notes, but this chapter will now explore the role that bond-rating agencies played in the internationalization of the UK's securitization market. Bond-rating agencies fulfill a key function in the operation of debt capital markets by providing independent opinions in the form of risk metrics to investors. The aim is to provide an independent assessment of the risks embodied within financial products and tradable debt securities. As such, bond-rating agencies have performed a central role in the financialization of Anglo-American capitalist economies (Erturk *et al.* 2004), through their judgments on the quality of investment products. The agencies attempt to provide investors with the ability to overcome information asymmetries and avert losses (Sinclair 2005), an activity facilitated through the calculation of an estimate of the probability that borrowers, or debt issuers, will not fulfill their borrowing obligations (Ferri *et al.* 1999).

The circulation of these agencies' ratings, predominantly Standard and Poor's or Fitch and Moody's, has led to the emergence of a new private mode of financial surveillance, leading to a regime of governance, not government. Subsequently, these institutions have enabled states to minimize formal legislation in favor of "light touch" regulation, pleasing advocates of neoliberalism (Sinclair 1994a, 1994b; Augar 2000). The expansion of bond-rating agencies from their North American homeland into Latin America, Europe, and Asia, along with a regime of financial governance, has been accompanied by a more controversial history. Bodenman (1996), for example, has argued that the metrics provided by these companies have weakened the quality of living at the municipal level in some of the America's poorest cities, whilst Ferri *et al.* (1999) have criticized the agencies for their role in exacerbating the East Asia crisis in the 1990s. More recently, the bond-rating agencies have received criticism from representatives of national governments, in particular German Chancellor Angela Merkel who believes that low risk ratings were given to US subprime RMBS notes when they should in fact have been classified as higher risk investments (BBC 2007b). Merkel feels that these ratings misled investors, especially as there is a conflict of interest between bond-rating agencies and the issuers of bonds, as the latter pay the fees of the bond-rating agencies, which some commentators believe coerced the agencies into providing more favorable ratings for RMBS notes.

To what degree this conflict of interest affects the rating agencies in practice, if at all, is unclear. After all, the independent reputation of bond-rating agencies is a key asset and if it were damaged then they would cease to successfully fulfill their role in global governance. Despite these issues, bond-rating agencies have developed a powerful role in global finance by providing greater transparency and risk analytics to investors. In doing so, they have enabled the development of disintermediated financial markets and the growth of cheap credit raised directly from investors (French and Leyshon 2004). It is argued here that bond-rating agencies provided an additional role in nurturing the expansion of the UK RMBS market in its early days, by providing international investors with access to "local" knowledge, enabling them to minimize the information asymmetries involved in RMBS investments whilst increasing the nascent market's transparency. The early UK RMBS bonds, whilst created by US based investment banks, financial elites, and centralized lenders, were purchased predominantly by UK based investors in notes that were denominated in sterling, as the following interviewee said:

> [The buyers were] pretty much banks, pension funds and insurance compa-
> nies, it was an entirely a professional market, it was very localised, we did the
> deal in sterling, so anyone who wasn't a sterling based house wouldn't have
> bought those bonds. (Interview: Director, ex-commercial bank, July 2007)

The UK RMBS market was initially a small local one, unlike the global market that it had become prior to the credit crunch. The development of securitization in the UK was set against a backdrop of technological innovation and the supposed displacement of London's "gentlemanly capitalism" as a consequence of the "Big Bang" in the late 1980s (Leyshon and Thrift 1997). However, the importance of trust, reputation, and social bonds, continued. These virtues, synonymous with gentlemanly capitalism, continued to be important within the early UK securitization market. Early risk metrics from the rating-agencies were useful, in terms of deciding the strength and respectability of the issuer backing the transaction, but as the market was new and largely unknown, investors did not have a detailed understanding about the performance of securitization. As such, the reputation of bankers and trust in their respective institutions was significant in understanding whether the bonds were stable or not, as suggested below:

> people who were taking senior credit risk needed to understand what an asset-backed security was, and what the risk was, but buying triple A, if you say, look the risk profile of this is better than the British Government, or as good as the British government, and even if you don't understand what the devil it's about, as long as someone tells you that, and they are prepared to stand up and say that's the case, and you have [Bank X]a bloody great, triple A bank behind it, you think, it works, you can't get higher than [Bank X] ... in the early days, the beginning of the 90s ... there were probably, top side, 30 people in the whole of Europe that knew what the hell securitization meant, it was not exactly a huge industry. (Interview: Director, ex-commercial bank, July 2007)

The depth of investor research into the credit quality of RMBS bonds prior to their purchase varies. Some investors may visit the mortgage lender and explore how mortgages are issued and repossessed, which may be complemented by the modeling of economic scenarios, whilst others may simply purchase notes from a lender that they have bought from before, using the bond-rating as a proxy to identify how "risky" the bond is. Investors tend to conduct less research into the credit quality of AAA notes due to their perceived stability, but for investments in subprime transactions issuing BBB to B, or the equity piece, the investors may spend more time scrutinizing the transactions. Investors who are investing in AAA notes, or who are not based in the UK and are unfamiliar with the market, may place more reliance on bond-rating agency metrics. Whilst the bond-rating agencies have an established history in the US, their operations were limited in Europe during the British banking community's experiments with securitization and the first UK agency offices served mainly as conduits of information to the technical expertise of its analysts in the US.

SandP had two or three people, they were in Finsbury Square, but that was a bucket shop of an office, I mean basically, they did not have European operations, they were learning too, that was what made it so amazing, we were all sort of sitting there, thinking, how do you [do this?], I mean the analysis was done in the States, the details of the portfolio were sent through. (Interview: Director, ex-commercial bank, July 2007)

It was not until later that these offices developed the in-house analysts who would provide the ratings for UK RMBS issues, and later, those issued from continental Europe and Russia. As UK mortgage issuers found securitiza- tion to be a useful funding tool, the technologies evolved and the market became more complex as new features and additional note classes were built into these financially engineered structures. The expansion of bond-rating agencies and their calculative practices into the UK provided new investors with transparency into the increasingly complex UK RMBS bonds, while enabling existing investors to quickly compare the potential risks between different RMBS bonds through ratings and reports. It can be argued that bond-rating agencies were instrumental in developing the UK market as UK issuers began to produce innovative bonds that appealed to overseas investors, but required internationally recognized ratings. The ultimate effect of this was to expand the size of the UK RMBS market, which increased the ability of UK lenders to sell more RMBS notes, reducing the cost to them in raising funds, and making it possible for them to increase their lending and profits. This enhanced reliance on the international demand for RMBS notes and liquid capital markets exposed the UK to the shocks that would later emanate from the US subprime crisis.

Building a Crisis: The "Credit Crunch" of 2007–?

It is argued here that the US subprime crisis and the credit crunch are two different – but intimately connected – events. The emphasis on this distinc- tion is necessary as the UK's experience of the credit crunch is not related to direct investments made by UK banks into US subprime RMBS, but rather to the geographical contagion of risk through the international financial system. The deterioration of the US mortgage market was a consequence of the underestimation of the credit risk posed by subprime borrowers – either through ignorance – or through the deliberate miss-selling of unsuitable products to consumers by lenders and mortgage intermediaries (Gotham 2006; Hernandez Chapter 7 in this volume; Immergluck 2008). On the other hand, the deterioration of the UK mortgage market is due to the global evaporation of liquidity, on which the sector had become dependent – through securitization. The credit crunch in the UK was not linked directly to the credit quality of its borrowers, or dramatic increases in the Bank of England Base rate, but was due to an escalation in the cost of mortgages and the reduction of riskier mortgage products – a consequence of the capital markets becoming illiquid due to the US subprime crisis (Langley 2008).

This chapter will not discuss the unraveling of the subprime crisis in the US, as it is discussed elsewhere in this book, but perhaps the most appropriate way to understand the UK's experience of the credit crunch is to trace the effects on UK consumers back through the financial institutions and capital markets to the US, the source of the crunch. This framework can be used as the starting point to unravel how UK consumers have been adversely affected by the credit crunch, especially as their savings, investments, and debts have become deeply entwined in an increasingly more complex financial system (Langley 2008). UK consumers have been affected by the credit crunch in three key ways. First, the initial credit crunch has affected the value of UK pension funds. Historically, banks have delivered high returns to institutional investors and pension portfolios have developed large exposures to financial organizations. As financial institutions have suffered in the credit crunch their value has dropped dramatically, lowering the value of pension funds, which was exacerbated as the credit crunch began to affect the wider economy and the share prices of companies outside the financial sector. Second, as the London Interbank Offered Rate (LIBOR) increased the prices of mortgages increased. Historically, mortgage rates were based on the Bank of England base rate, but lenders who borrowed heavily from the capital markets were exposed to changes in high LIBOR rates – passed onto consumers – as the capital markets became illiquid. The third effect has been the withdrawal of credit for consumers, particularly subprime borrowers. Mortgage lenders who provided products for customers with a less than perfect credit history modeled what the effect of increasing interest rates would have on their consumers, and the results indicated that there would be an unacceptable increase in the rate of defaults – leading to the widespread withdrawal of many subprime products (BBC 2007c, 2007d), a strategy known as credit rationing. Unlike credit scoring (Pollard 1996; Leyshon and Thrift 1999; Burton *et al.* 2004) where money is allocated to consumers who meet specific criteria – and are not expected to default - credit rationing sees "good" risk customers hierarchically ranked in order of quality, as there is not enough capital to issue credit to all "good" risk consumers and only the lowest risk customers are able to obtain credit. Combined with the withdrawal of banking infrastructure, the current lack of financial provision has led to favoritism, or a "flight to quality" (Leyshon and Thrift 1995; Midgley 2005). Credit rationing has had its greatest effect upon first time buyers and the low paid. In 2009, two years after the "run" on Northern Rock began, the arrears and repossession rates of property had only just begun to stabilize (CML 2009a). Many of the mortgage deals on offer to new borrowers or those on low incomes, if available, required deposits of 20–40 percent, far beyond the value of the savings and assets of these groups. The CML revealed that since the credit crunch began to unravel in the UK in 2007 the average age of a first time buyer, not using financial assistance from family members, had increased from 33 to 37 years of age (CML 2009b).

The impact on mortgage lenders is uneven as retail banks, with the exception of Northern Rock, use retail deposits to fund the majority of their mortgages and do not need to borrow money to lend. On the other hand, centralized lenders who usually offer subprime products, do not take deposits from customers like banks beacuse extensive branch networks and infrastructure are expensive (Leyshon and Thrift 1999; Langley 2008). The credit crunch generated two key consequences for the centralized lenders. First, they had to increase the price of mortgages and, second, they had to withdraw riskier mortgage products. The UK RMBS secondary market is relatively illiquid, but uncertainty from the crisis eliminated the demand for all RMBS notes. The lenders who relied on warehouse lines were unable to refinance their debts with investment banks and were unable to issue new mortgages. As a result they have less capital to lend, and are lending it to the safer borrowers.

> I know there are companies that have gone from [a warehouse line of £]200 million in origination to [£]35 [million] and that's not because that's where they want to be … there has been [£]15 billion of monthly origination taken out of the market, that's one in five, so one in five people who were getting mortgages will not be getting them today. (Interview: Director, UK central-ized lender, September 2007)

This was detrimental to Northern Rock, who had become dependent on deep capital markets, and the bank found itself unable to raise more capital to continue issuing mortgages, forcing it to seek emergency funding from the Bank of England in September 2007. The second problem for centralized lenders was that investment banks began to close or decrease the size of the warehouse lines, reducing their capacity to issue mortgages, leading many to abandon the issuance of new mortgages.

The next question is why have the investment banks reduced the amount of money available, and why has it become more expensive through LIBOR? The answer is that investment banks had sponsored SIVs and CDOs in an attempt to enhance the profitability of RMBS notes, but it soon became clear that the technology of securitized technology of CDOs were flawed as the new notes issued to investors were fundamentally based on higher risk subprime notes, while the performance of SIVs were sensitive to LIBOR rates. Initially, CDOs and SIVs appeared to operate successfully, offering attractive yields, but many investors did not fully understand the risks embodied in these products and placed too much reliance on the ratings produced by bond rating agencies (Interview: Director, UK centralized lender, September 2007). Many investors assumed that CDOs with high bond ratings would be as safe as other prime ABS products, although this was not the case as the underlying assets carried far more credit risk. As the US subprime crisis began to escalate, the repayments passing through subprime waterfall structures began to diminish to such an extent that the senior CDO and SIV notes were not being repaid in full. By June 2006, it emerged that funds run by Bear Stearns had been heavily exposed to defaulting assets based on US subprime mortgages. Bear was the first investment bank to admit that it had problems before it collapsed, while other investment banks began to admit their unprecedented losses. Investment banks realized that they needed cash to cover their losses on their SIVs, CDOs, and subprime RMBS investments and they responded by hoarding money, which reduced the supply of money available in the interbank money markets.

As such, the interbank money markets began to close, as investment banks and retail banks became suspicious about which institutions were facing an imminent collapse, due to exposure to their toxic US investments. The credit risk of US mortgages had begun to travel through the international financial system as investment banks such as Lehman's – deemed too large to fail – collapsed and any available money became exceptionally expensive. This problem was compounded by the UK's domestic mortgage banks, such as Northern Rock, HBOS, Bradford and Bingley, and Alliance and Leicester that could no longer fund their mortgage production with cheap money through RMBS issuance, or the interbank money markets, and started to struggle as consumers began to withdraw their deposits. Subsequently, the origins of the credit crunch's illiquidity can be attributed to the inability of US subprime borrowers to repay their mortgage lenders, who in turn failed to pass on their mortgage receivables to RMBS investors, such as investment banks, CDOs, and SIVs, which witnessed the effective geographical transference of the US subprime crisis though to the UK's economy via these complex investment vehicles.

Conclusion

Securitization has been identified as a tool that is instrumental in liquefying fixed capital and funneling it between, and within, different circuits of accumulation (Aalbers Chapter 5 in this volume; Gotham Chapter 1 in this volume). This chapter has sought to problematize and build upon Harvey's theoretical work on circuits of capital by using a sociological lens to uncover how circuits of capital become integrated – not as an overspill to overaccumulation from the primary circuit of capital – but because funding mortgage production is profitable - illustrated through the establishment of securitization within the UK. Although securitization's history is rooted in the US, the idea was transferred to the UK in the 1980s, where it was adjusted and reconfigured to become compatible with the UK's political economy. This was not a simple process: it required a series of translations and relied on expertise from epistemic communities in law, finance, mathematics, and computing combined with a favorable macroeconomic environment. Initially, securitization was used to fund UK mortgage origination, although this model would became temporarily unsustainable due to the high level of defaults that centralized lenders experienced during the housing crisis of the 1990s.

Securitization did not remain a stable entity but carried on evolving as the milieu in which it existed continued to change. Securitization re-emerged, not as a tool for funding, but as a way of subverting capital adequacy ratios for retail banks. Other innovations in structured finance such as Mastertrusts increased the demand for UK RMBS, as the UK financial sector became progressively more reliant on securitization and the capital markets. During this time, the transfer of bond-rating agencies to the UK enabled the development of metrics for UK RMBS bonds, which sought to reduce the information asymmetries between issuers and investors. This development helped expand the geographic market of UK RMBS bonds, as international financial institutions became significant investors; also amplifying the reliance of UK mortgage lenders on the international capital markets. The increased integration of global financial institutions through warehouse lines, CDOs, SIVs, and US subprime income flows exposed the world's financial institutions, directly and indirectly, to the credit risk of US consumers through the sale of mortgage debt. The ill-perceived stability of US subprime assets, undermined by the inability of US consumers to repay unrealistic debts, led to the destabilization of the international financial system culminating in a credit crunch. The main brunt has been felt by consumers who are overindebted and embedded within the subprime markets of the US and UK, who will no doubt find credit progressively more expensive, or impossible to access, as financial institutions withdraw their subprime products.

Notes

1   More cash is funneled through the waterfall structure than is necessary to repay the investors, known as over-collateralization. This excess cash is stored in a reserve fund that can be used to cover any temporary shortfalls in future mortgage repayments. Additionally, short-term loans can be made available by other

financial institutions to repay investors, which cover temporary shortfalls that are larger than the value of the reserve fund.

2   The regulation became known as Basel, named after the place where the ratios were developed. These ratios are currently being replaced with new capital regulations, known as Basel II which are more sensitive to the particular risks of individual assets.

3   Off balance sheet refers to a process where financial institutions transfer their ownership of assets to another company or subsidiary, literally moving the assets off their balance sheet. This transfer of legal ownership means that a financial institution no-longer has any direct claim over the assets – or any of the liabilities associated with the assets – although it may still manage or administer the assets on behalf of the new owner.

References

Aalbers, M.B. (2008). The Financialisation of Home and the Mortgage Market Crisis. *Competition and Change* 12(2): 148–66.

Augar, P. (2000). *The Death of Gentlemanly Capitalism*. London: Penguin.

Banham, M. (2007). Time for someone to walk the Victoria and Northern Rock plank? *Financial Times*. 9 October: 3–3.

BBC. (2007a). More 25-year fixed-rate mortgages? Retrieved 14/04/2009, from http://news.bbc.co.uk/1/hi/business/6292266.stm.

BBC. (2007b). Merkel censures ratings agencies. Retrieved 10/10/09, from http://news.bbc.co.uk/1/hi/business/6970302.stm.

BBC. (2007c). Timeline: sub-prime problems. Retrieved 31/08/07, from http://news.bbc.co.uk/go/pr/fr/-/1/hi/business/6945672.stm.

BBC. (2007d). UK lender pulls sub-prime range. Retrieved 22/11/2007, from http://news.bbc.co.uk/go/pr/fr/-/1/hi/business/7107921.stm.

Beauregard, R. (1994). Capital switching and the built environment: United States 1970–89 *Environment and Planning A* 26: 715–32.

Bodenman, J. (1996). The relationship between municipal bond-ratings and the quality of life in American cities 1970–1990. *Middle States Geographer* 29: 17–24.

Burton, D., Knights, D., Leyshon, A., Alferoff, C., and Signoretta, P. (2004). Making a market: the UK retail financial services industry and the rise of the complex sub-prime credit market. *Competition and Change* 8(1): 3–25.

Charney, I. (2001). Three dimensions of capital switching within the real estate sector: A Canadian case study. *International Journal of Urban and Regional Research* 25(4): 741–58.

CML. (2009a). First-time buyers – are they really getting older? Retrieved 11/10/09, from http://www.cml.org.uk/cml/publications/newsandviews/45/152.

CML. (2009b). Possessions fall and arrears flatten in second quarter." Retrieved 03/10/09, from http://www.cml.org.uk/cml/media/press/2357.

Department for Communities and Local Government. (2009). Housing market: simple average house prices, United Kingdom." Retrieved 14/04/09, from http://www.communities.gov.uk/documents/housing/xls/141038.xls.

Dymski, G. and Veitch, J. (1996). Financial transformation and the metropolis: booms, busts, and banking in Los Angeles. *Environment and Planning A* 28(7): 1233–60.

Erturk, I., Froud, J., Johal, S., and Williams, K. (2004). Corporate governance and disappointment. *Review of International Political Economy* 11(4): 677–713.

Ferran, E. (1992). *Mortgage Securitisation: Legal Aspects.* London: Butterworths.

Ferri, G., Liu, L.-G., and Stiglitz, J. (1999). The procyclical role of rating agencies: evidence from the East Asian crisis. *Economic Notes* 28(3): 335–55.

French, S. and Leyshon, L. (2004). The new, new financial system? Towards a conceptualisation of financial reintermediation. *Review of International Political Economy* 11(2): 263–88.

Gotham, K. (2006). The secondary circuit of capital reconsidered: globalisation and the US real estate sector. *The American Journal of Sociology* 112(1): 231–75.

Hamnett, C. (1994). "Restructuring housing finance and the housing market," *in* S. Corbridge, R. Martin and N. Thrift. *Money, Power and Space* Oxford, Blackwell: 281–308.

Harvey, D. (1973). *Social Justice and the City.* London: Edward Arnold.

Harvey, D. (1974). Class monopoly rent, finance capitals and the urban revolution. *Regional Studies* 8: 239–55.

Harvey, D. (1978). The urban process under capitalism: a framework for analysis. *International Journal of Urban and Regional Research* 2: 101–31.

Harvey, D. (1982). *The Limits to Capital.* Oxford: Blackwell.

Harvey, D. (1985). *The Urbanization of Capital.* Oxford: Basil Blackwell.

Immergluck, D. (2008). From the subprime to the exotic: excessive mortgage market risk and foreclosures. *Journal of the American Planning Association* 74(1): 59–76.

Knorr-Cetina, K. and Bruegger, U. (2002). Trader's engagement with markets. *Theory, Society and Culture* 19(5): 161–85.

Langley, P. (2006). Securitising Suburbia: The transformation of Anglo-American mortgage finance. *Competition and Change* 10(3): 283–99.

Langley, P. (2008). *The Everyday Life of Global Finance: Saving and Borrowing in Anglo-America.* Oxford: Oxford University Press.

Lewis, M. (1989). *Liar's Poker.* London: Coronet.

Leyshon, A. and Pollard, J. (2000). Geographies of industrial convergence: the case of retail banking. *Transactions of the Institute of British Geographers* 25: 203–20.

Leyshon, A. and Thrift, N. (1995). Geographies of financial exclusion: financial abandonment in Britain and the United States. *Transactions of the Institute of British Geographers* 20(3): 312–41.

Leyshon, A. and Thrift, N. (1997). *Money Space: Geographies Of Monetary Transformations.* London: Routledge.

Leyshon, A. and Thrift, N. (1999). Lists come alive: electronic systems of knowledge and the rise of credit-scoring in retail banking. *Economy and Society* 28(3): 434–66.

Leyshon, A. and Thrift, N. (2008). The capitalism of almost everything: the future of finance and capitalism. *Theory, Society and Culture* 24: 97–115.

MacDonald, H. (1996). The rise of mortgage-backed securities: struggles to reshape access to credit in the USA. *Environment and Planning A* 28(7): 1179–98.

Martin, R. and Turner, D. (2000). Demutualisation and the remapping of financial landscapes. *Transactions of the Institute of British Geographers* 25: 221–41.

Midgley, J. (2005). Financial inclusion, universal banking and post offices in Britain. *Area* 37(3): 277–85.

O' Brien, R. (1992). *Global Financial Integration: The End of Geography*. London: Royal Institute of International Affairs.

Plender, J. (1986). London's big bang in international context. *International Affairs (Royal Institute of International Affairs 1944–)* 63(1): 39–48.

Pollard, J. (1996). Banking at the margins: a geography of financial exclusion in Los Angeles. *Environment and Planning A* 28(7): 1149–338.

Pryke, M. (1994). Urbanizing Capitals: towards an integration of time, space and economic calculation. In: S. Corbridge, R. Martin, and N. Thrift. *Money, Power and Space*. Oxford: Blackwell, pp. 218–52.

Pryke, M. and Allen, J. (2000). Monetized time-space: derivatives- money's "new imaginary." *Economy and Society* 2: (264–84).

Pryke, M. and du Gay, P. (2007). Take an issue: cultural economy and finance. *Economy and Society* 36(3): 339–54.

Pryke, M. and Lee, R. (1995). Place Your Bets: Towards an understanding of globalisation, socio-financial engineering and competition within a financial center. *Urban Studies* 32(2): 329–44.

Pryke, M. and Whitehead, C. (1994). An overview of mortgage-backed securitisation in the UK. *Housing Studies* 9(1): 75–102.

Rowlingson, K. (2006). "Living poor to die rich"? Or "Spending the kids" inheritance? Attitudes to assets and inheritance in later life. *Journal of Social Policy* 35(2): 175–92.

Sassen, S. (2001). *The Global City: New York, London, Tokyo*. Princeton: Princeton University Press.

Sidaway, J. (2008). Subprime crisis: American crisis or human crisis. *Environment and Planning D: Society and Space* 26: 196–98.

Sinclair, T. (1994a). Between hegemony and market: hegemony and institutions of collective action under conditions of international capital mobility. *Policy Sciences* 27: 447–66.

Sinclair, T. (1994b). Passing judgement: credit rating processes as regulatory mechanisms of governance in the emerging world order. *Review of International Political Economy* 1(1): 133–59.

Sinclair, T. (2005). *The New Masters of Capital*. New York: Cornell University Press.

Strauss, D. (2007). Mortgage approvals at two-year low. *Financial Times*: Retrieved 20/11/07, from URL http://www.ft.com/cms/s/0/6887225e-860d-11dc-b00e-0000779fd2ac.html

Thal Larsen, P. (2007). Scramble to quit UK bank. *Financial Times*: September 15: 1–1.

Thrift, N. (1994). On the social and cultural determinants of international finance centers: the case of the City of London. In: S. Corbridge, R. Martin, and N. Thrift. *Money, Power and Space*, Oxford: Blackwell, pp. 327–55.

5

European Mortgage Markets Before and After the Financial Crisis

Manuel B. Aalbers

Introduction

Economic globalization in combination with deregulation will lead to a deterritorialization of economic activities and the prevalence of the global over the local, regional, and national (Wachtel 1986; Ohmae 1990; Levine 1997); some have even proclaimed *The End of Geography* (O'Brien 1992). This position is dominant in mainstream, neoclassical, and orthodox economics, but has been challenged by many others, most notably human geographers and international political economists, who claim that deterritorialization and convergence claims are not only theoretically simplistic, but also empirically inaccurate (e.g., Porter 1990; Corbridge *et al.* 1994; Hirst and Thompson 1996; Cox 1997; Hollingsworth and Boyer 1997; Storper 1997; Scott 1998; Whitley 1998). For example, despite the extensive growth in foreign direct investment since the 1950s (Dicken 1998), direct international investment was relatively more important before 1914 than it was in the early 1990s (Koechlin 1995; see also Bayoumi 1997); most sectors of the economy today continue to be dominated by nationally based firms. Against mainstream economic theory, political economists and geographers have argued that globalization does not diminish the significance of economic organization. The increasing internationalization of economic activities has not replaced existing forms of capitalism and nationally constructed business systems; globalization processes are path dependent and reflect (national) historical legacies (Whitley 1998; see also Hudson 2003).

Subprime Cities: The Political Economy of Mortgage Markets, First Edition. Edited by Manuel B. Aalbers.
© 2012 Blackwell Publishing Ltd. Published 2012 by Blackwell Publishing Ltd.

Others, like Sassen, have argued that globalization does indeed take place, in particular in the financial services industry; however, that it does not lead to the end of geography, but to a new geography witnessed by a simultaneous movement of deterritorialization and reterritorialization as "the increased mobility of capital brings about new forms of locational concentration, which are as much a part of this mobility as is geographic dispersal" (Sassen 2001: 34). From the perspective of global cities like New York, London, Tokyo, Frankfurt, and Paris, the increasing concentration of global financial markets and firms in global cities is a process of reterritorialization, but from the perspective of other places it constitutes deterritorialization (Sassen 1998, 2001; see also Hudson 2003). The resulting concentration in markets and of firms is stronger than before economic globalization. Rather than becoming flattened, the economic landscape gets hillier and the international financial system has actually become more social, more reflexive, and more interpretative (Leyshon and Thrift 1997: 292). Sassen and others have shown empirically how, where, and why financial markets have become more concentrated, but most analyses overlook one dominant financial market: the mortgage market. Do globalization and Europeanization lead to the deterritorialization of European mortgage markets?

Mortgage markets are not just important due to their sheer volume – €4.7 trillion outstanding mortgage loans in the European Union at the end of 2004; €11.3 trillion worldwide (EMF 2005) – but also because most homeowners depend on them, because they fuel the economy both directly and indirectly (through equity withdrawal [see Glossary]) and because they serve an ideological purpose in the neoliberal age. Mortgage markets – and credit markets more generally – have been "liberalized" in order to widen access to mortgage markets and, thus, to fuel economic growth and increase homeownership rates. That is, the "liberalization" of mortgage markets is not just a goal in itself, but also a means to further the neoliberal agenda of private property, firms, and growing profits. It comes as no surprise then that this neoliberalization of mortgage markets took place earlier in the US than in the UK, and earlier in the UK than in most of continental Europe. In this process, households have become more dependent on financial markets. Old arrangements of social rights have been replaced and continue to be replaced by new arrangements in which social rights and guarantees are made dependent on financial markets. Indeed, the restructuring of welfare states has resulted in a "great risk shift" in which households are increasingly dependent on financial markets for their long-term security (Hacker 2006). Due to the commodification and financialization of housing, housing risks are increasingly financial market risks these days (Aalbers 2008). It is, therefore, no surprise that the recent economic crisis originated at the intersection of housing and finance and that this crisis feeds into the wider economy both through defaults and foreclosures (see Chapters 7, 8, and 9 by Hernandez, Newman, and Wyly *et al.*, respectively, in this volume) on the one hand, and a liquidity crisis and government bailouts on the other.

Financial markets are the most international, most globalized markets in the world – at least that is the dominant conceptualization, whether one follows O'Brien's strong convergence thesis (O'Brien 1992) or Sassen's "new geography" thesis (Sassen 2001). Highly mobile capital moves unimpeded to friendlier regulatory environments in search of higher profits, but not all capital is highly mobile and not all capital moves as if there are no borders. In this chapter I argue that despite financial globalization, mortgage markets remain national markets even in a "Europe without borders." Rather than explaining how differences between different systems have developed – which is the focus of the comparative housing literature (for an overview see Kemeny and Lowe 1998) – this chapter looks at the factors that facilitate and impede the globalization and Europeanization of mortgage markets. Contrary to the two extremes in comparative housing research, I do not focus on the particularities of "unique cases" nor assume that all countries are equally subject to the same overriding imperatives. My interest is also not in constructing typologies of housing systems. My main concern is to what extent globalization and Europeanization have affected the existing differences between countries. I describe the differences between European mortgage markets, the globalization and Europeanization of market players (actors), market regulation and markets themselves, and the reasons for continued territorialization as well as those for deterritorialization. Since many mortgage lenders are banks, a great deal of attention is paid to the internationalization of banks.

In this chapter I see globalization as the growing interdependence and unfolding of networks across national borders steered by economic and political actors impacting not just on the national and supranational scales, but on all scales. Globalization involves a "complex re-articulation of socio-economic space upon multiple geographical scales" (Brenner 2000: 366) and takes place deep inside the territories and institutional domains where global changes are often codified as national, resulting in a scaling or rescaling of the global (Agnew 1993; Massey 1993; Swyngedouw 1997; Sassen 2003). Europeanization, then, refers to similar processes taking place at the European level and enabled, and often stimulated, by the flattening of intra-European regulation. Globalization and Europeanization are not replacing national regulation, but are superimposed on existing regulation, adding layers to and restructuring national regulation. In other words, the increasing significance of the EU does not signify a reproduction of national territorial orders at a larger scale, and globalization and Europeanization are not necessarily eating away existing nation states, but rather transforming them (Mamadouh 2001). European Union policies to create a single European market are often seen in the light of economic globalization; in fact, processes of Europeanization and globalization intertwine, as the EU seeks to erode territorially specific forms of capitalism, but also seeks to make European firms and markets more competitive in the face of globalization, for instance by facilitating the emergence of EU-based multinational corporations (Hudson 2003; see also Ziltener 2004); therefore, the EU strategy can be characterized as one of parallel liberalization and consolidation (Leyshon and Thrift 1997: 115).

Here, I make a distinction between three different types of globalization and Europeanization: the globalization and Europeanization of *firms*, the globalization and Europeanization of *markets*, and the globalization and Europeanization of *regulation* (Drahos and Braithwaite 2001). The globalization or Europeanization of firms refers to firms that start working in one country and spread their operations to other countries. A global or European market is a market where buyers and sellers from one country can transact business with buyers and sellers from another country. The globalization or Europeanization of regulation "involves the spread of some set of regulatory norms" (ibid.: 103). By and large Drahos and Braithwaite refer to regulatory norms as legal and administrative arrangements, but I take a wider, more sociological view on regulation including social adjustments motivated by the economy (Dijkink 2000), the maintenance of "systemic equilibrium" (Hancher and Moran 1989), and dominant norms and conventions in the industry – that is, both formal and informal regulation. One could also speak of a "mode of social regulation," which is a systematic way of speaking of political and social relations, including state action, social institutions, behavioral norms and habits, and political preferences, to ensure capital accumulation. Regulation school theorists argue that stability in the (global) economic system is dependent on the mode of social regulation (Aglietta 1979; Scott 1988). Yet, since the mode of social regulation is dependent on institutions, different forms "can exist at virtually any territorial level – local, regional, national, global" (Storper and Walker 1989: 215).

The examples I provide to illustrate my argument often come from the Dutch and Italian mortgage markets. This is because these two markets, as I will argue in the next section, in many respects offer opposite trajectories: "Italy is the world's most affluent large country that has such a low level of mortgage activity" (Ball 2005: 95), while the Netherlands has the largest mortgage market in the world relative to its population size or GDP. Considering the use of mortgage credit the countries could not be much more different; yet, these two markets are becoming increasingly like one another due to processes partly located at the European and partly at the global level. That is, different mortgage market trajectories are not necessarily a barrier to the implementation of similar formal and informal credit regimes. Different national trajectories are still significant, but rather than preventing convergence, they slow down or mould convergence.

The following section highlights the key differences between European mortgage markets. The subsequent section examines the extent of globalization and Europeanization of firms, markets, and regulation. It notes how internationalization has been limited despite factors pushing for less national and more supranational regulation, and in particular factors pushing for a "single European mortgage market." Next, the slow pace of deterritorialization is explained. The concluding section argues that we should still speak of *European mortgage markets* rather than of *a European mortgage market*. Yet, it also argues that the recent mortgage crisis is in part a US crisis and in part a global crisis as the globalization of mortgage markets is, and will remain, partial.

Differences and Similarities in European Mortgage Markets

In this section I will pay attention to the differences and similarities in European mortgage markets. I do this by first presenting some statistical data on European mortgage markets and second by looking into the relationship between the expansion of the mortgage market and the rise in house prices. The first sub-section is very descriptive: the differences that are described here will make more sense after the analysis in subsequent sections.

Quantitative differences between European mortgage markets

The differences between European mortgage markets can be illustrated by statistics. The selection of countries presented here largely depends on the availability of reliable and comparable data, which implies that we can sometimes compare 8 or 12 countries and sometimes 25. Firstly, typical and maximum loan-to-value-ratios (LTV-ratios) differ greatly between countries; out of the eight European countries shown in Table 5.1, the Netherlands has the highest average and maximum LTV-ratios and Italy the lowest. There is a strong correlation between LTV-ratio and loan-to-income-ratio (LTI-ratio). The Netherlands and Denmark have the highest LTI-ratios and Italy and Belgium the lowest out of nine European countries (Table 5.2). As a result, average mortgage debt tends to be higher in countries with high LTV- and LTI-ratios; again the Netherlands is on top of the list and Italy at the bottom (Table 5.2). The LTV and LTI figures are strongly related to the average loan term: higher LTVs take longer to repay. The average loan term in Italy is half that of the Netherlands

Table 5.1 LTV-ratio, average loan term, and default rate in eight EU countries, ordered by LTV-ratio, respectively 2001 and 2003

Country	Typical LTV-ratio	Maximum LTV-ratio	Average loan term in years	Default rate
Netherlands	90	115	30	0.6
Portugal	83	90	27	1.8
Denmark	80	80	30	1.3
Spain	70	100	20	6.0
UK	69	110	25	1.0
France	67	100	17	2.8
Germany	67	80	23	missing
Italy	55	80	15	5.2

Sources: EMF 2001; Low *et al.* 2003; ECHP 2004.

Table 5.2 LTI-ratio and mortgage debt in nine European countries, ordered by LTI-ratio, 2003

Country	Typical LTI-ratio	Typical loan term in years	Average mortgage debt per recent buyer in €
Netherlands	3.4	30	103,204
Denmark	3.2	30	89,156
Spain	2.7	15–20	47,589
UK	2.2	20–30	71,950
Ireland	2.1	20–30	76,512
France	1.4	15–20	35,830
Austria	1.3	20–25	32,466
Belgium	0.9	15–20	40,532
Italy	0.9	10–15	11,019

Sources: Neuteboom 2003, 2004. Used by permission of Taylor & Francis.

and Denmark. One would expect default rates to be high in countries with high LTV- and LTI-ratios, but in a comparison of 12 European countries between 1994 and 2001, default rates were the lowest in the Netherlands, followed by Austria, UK, Luxembourg, and Denmark; and were the highest in Finland, followed by Spain, Ireland, Italy, and Belgium. The differences between the countries are remarkably large, as Table 5.1 shows for some of these countries.

From a comparison of 25 EU countries (all EU countries except the most recent member states Romania and Bulgaria) and the US, we can see that homeownership rates vary widely across Europe (Table 5.3). Most countries with low homeownership rates have either a large social housing stock

Table 5.3 Mortgage debt in the European Union and in the US, ordered by home-ownership rate, 2004

Country	Homeownership rate	Total value of mortgage debt, in million €	Mortgage-debt to-GDP ratio	Per capita mortgage debt in €
Germany	42	1,157,026	52.4	14,019
Sweden	47	147,163	52.7	16,396
Czech Republic	49	6,576	7.6	644
Poland	50	10,686	5.5	280
Netherlands	53	518,115	111.1	31,868
Denmark	53	174,300	89.7	32,292
France	56	432,300	26.2	7,217
Austria	57	48,064	20.3	5,905
Finland	60	56,522	37.8	10,829
Cyprus	64	2,182	17.6	2,988
Latvia	66	1,273	11.5	549
Portugal	66	70,834	52.5	6,762
Luxembourg	66	8,797	34.3	19,480
UK	70	1,243,261	72.5	20,835
Belgium	72	88,434	31.2	8,506
Malta	74	1,236	28.6	3,090
Ireland	77	77,029	52.7	19,125
Slovakia	80	2,032	6.1	380
Italy	80	196,504	14.5	3,395
Estonia	81	1,500	16.6	1,110
Slovenia	82	387	1.5	194
Greece	83	34,052	20.6	3,084
Lithuania	84	1,258	7.0	365
Spain	85	384,631	45.9	9,083
Hungary	93	7,767	9.6	768
EU15	65	4,566,198	46.4	11,931
EU25	68	4,670,736	45.3	10,223
US	69	7,568,200	64.5	25,772

Source: EMF 2005. Hypostat 2004. European Mortgage Federation, Brussels.

(Sweden and the Netherlands) or a large subsidized private-rented sector (Germany). The comparison also shows that in absolute terms the UK and Germany are by far the largest mortgage markets in the EU, followed by the Netherlands, France, and Spain. Small countries in Central and Eastern Europe (CEE) have the smallest markets. The US market was more than 1.5 times the size of the total EU market by the end of 2004, although this had dropped significantly by the end of 2008 due to a weaker US dollar and a stronger Euro. If we relate the size of the mortgage market to GDP, the Netherlands turns out to have the largest mortgage market, followed by Denmark and the UK (all significantly larger than the US); again, small markets are found in CEE. Outside CEE, Austria, Greece, and, in particular, Italy have low mortgage-debt-to-GDP ratios (Table 5.3). Per capita mortgage debt is by far the highest in Denmark and the Netherlands (and again higher than in the US) and the lowest in CEE, followed by Greece and Italy. Another difference lies in the interest rate variability: Portugal, the UK, and Spain show a predominance of variable interest rates and short periods of fixed rates; Denmark shows a high share of long fixed periods; other countries show a mixture of short and long fixed periods (EMF 2003; Low *et al.* 2003).

The distribution of mortgages in the all eight countries examined by Low and colleagues is dominated by bank branches: in Italy almost 90 percent of mortgages are distributed through bank branches, in Germany (where mortgages are mostly offered by specialized mortgage banks) and France this is 80 percent, in Portugal and Denmark just over 60 percent, and in the Netherlands, the UK, and Spain around 50 percent. Mortgage intermediaries (brokers, independent agents) play a more significant part in the latter countries that are characterized by a greater variety in and complexity of mortgage products – product differentiation and the emergence of niche markets is facilitated by mortgage intermediaries, and the growth in the number of mortgage intermediaries is enabled by product differentiation. In Greece, Sweden, and Finland there are almost no intermediaries active in the mortgage market (Forum Group 2004). In all the eight above-mentioned countries, mortgage intermediaries are gaining market share. Changes in the Italian mortgage market, for example, have resulted in the increasing importance of intermediaries in recent years. In addition, Italian and French real estate agents play a significant role in steering homebuyers to certain lenders. Other differences exist in the level of transaction costs, the average time to register a mortgage, and average repossession times. The last two are indicators of process efficiency, which is highest in Denmark and the Netherlands, and lowest in Italy followed by Portugal.

Market concentration also differs: in general, in smaller countries the largest five mortgage lenders together tend to have a bigger market share than in bigger countries. Denmark shows the highest concentration because the five largest lenders control 80–95 percent of the market, depending on the source (EMF 2003; Low *et al.* 2003; ECB 2004). Italy is the only big country with a high degree of concentration: 65–75 percent, the same as for a small country like the Netherlands. Concentrations in other large countries, such as Germany, Spain, and the UK, are lower: 45–60 percent. The five largest mortgage lenders in the EU together have a market share of 24 percent, clearly lower than the 37 percent of the US (ibid.). Calculations based on the Herfindahl concentration index – a measure of the size of firms in relationship to the industry and an indicator of the amount of competition among them – come to similar results (Low *et al.* 2003). A high degree of concentration is not necessarily related to a small number of mortgage lenders: because of the wide variety of minor players in the Dutch market, there are about as many lenders active as in the British market.

Expansion of the mortgage market and the rise in house prices

Strikingly, the size of the mortgage market is relatively small in many countries with a large owner-occupied sector (Table 5.3). In many Southern European countries, homeownership is the norm and renting the exception. Castles and Ferrera (1996) argue that there is a distinctive Mediterranean culture that explains the significance of homeownership in Southern Europe. (In the Southern group, we could again include Belgium whose inhabit-ants, it is said, are "born with a brick in their stomach" indicating the Belgians' preference for building their own homes.) Here, most homeowners have either paid off their mortgage loan or even bought a house without a mortgage. This is enabled by intergenerational transfers of both property and equity (Allen *et al.* 2004; Aalbers 2007), as well as by self-promotion and self-provision of housing (Arbaci 2002; Allen *et al.* 2004). Throughout the EU15 (i.e., including Southern Europe), 24 percent of households held a mortgage in 1996, compared to 13 percent in the Southern EU mem-ber states (Allen *et al.* 2004: 25). Northern European countries, in general, have a younger homeownership tradition and intergenerational transfers are less significant. Therefore, the share of the owner-occupied market in most Northern European countries is significantly smaller, yet most homeowners have taken out a mortgage loan to buy a house. The UK largely follows the path of Northern Europe, but is different in one important aspect: it has a relatively high homeownership rate. This is, contrary to Southern European countries, not a historical characteristic, but the result of a conscious policy shift in favor of private property, the resulting "right to buy," and the related opening up of mortgage markets, including the development of subprime markets, to enable these political desires. The consequence of these political choices – a large and highly developed mortgage market – fits well in the Northern European trajectory with high outstanding mortgage debt, high LTV-ratios, high LTI-ratios, and long maturity periods.

One might argue that house prices are lower in Southern Europe than in Northern Europe and that as a result people do not need to take out a mortgage loan. This is, however, not the case: on an *international comparative level* there is no relationship between house prices and the aggregate value of outstanding mortgage loans if we control for income levels. Southern European countries, in general, have had high homeownership levels for much longer than Northern European countries, thus decreasing the need to extend credit possibilities and increasing the importance of the family in the south. In the north of Europe, on the other hand, the family plays a less important role and extended credit possibilities were needed to be able to increase the political and economic goal of higher homeownership rates. In addition, credit tended to be cheaper in Northern Europe, with its low inflation rates, than in Southern Europe, with its high inflation rates. This resulted in much many options in the mortgage markets of Northern Europe than in those of Southern Europe.

An important development is that the extension of the mortgage market is related to the extension of the owner-occupied sector. This seems logical: if prices rise, most households will need a larger mortgage loan to finance the purchase of a house. Yet, the argument can also be reversed: because mortgage lenders allowed people to take out higher loans, households were able to afford more expensive houses, but as this was the case for most households the increase in demand led to an increase in prices in a feedback loop. What we see is a co-evolution in which the growth of owner-occupied market (in volume or price levels) fuels the mortgage market, and the growth of the mortgage market (in volume and loan conditions) fuels the owner-occupied market. On a *national level*, house price increases are not just the result of average income growth, economic booms, and housing shortages, but also and mostly the mortgage market's expansion. In order to understand the expansion of mortgage markets we have to stop viewing this expansion as the result of rising house prices and start paying attention to the interconnections between the housing and mortgage markets: the mortgage market does not simply enable homeownership, but moulds the housing market by fuelling prices that in turn fuel the demand for mortgage loans. (Rising house prices do not lead to a declining homeownership rate because there are often few alternatives in the rental market and because selling a house as a rental property generally generates less capital than selling an empty house intended for owner-occupation.)

Although we can witness the co-evolution of mortgage markets and housing markets in most European countries, I do not argue that sub-national and supranational variations do not make a difference. On the sub-national level, variations in economic growth and in housing shortages and surpluses make a real difference and this enables sometimes large discrepancies in rising house prices and mortgage markets between different regions within one country. On the supranational level, there is no connection between the level of house prices in one country and the size of the mortgage market in that country *compared to other countries*. Only for each country by itself can we argue that when looking at *changes over time*, the expansion of the mortgage market leads to higher house prices. Two examples can illustrate this point.

First, in the Netherlands the rapid increase in house prices in the 1990s, and in particular in the late 1990s, was only partly a result of high economic growth and exploding stock markets, and was largely a result of more favorable mortgage loan conditions. The Dutch national bank has calculated that in five years time the maximum loan amount for the "average household" (with one income of €30,000 and one income of €12,000) increased by 86 percent (DNB 2000). This is not only because mortgage lenders allowed significantly higher LTI-ratios and slightly higher LTV-ratios, but also because they started granting mortgage loans based not on just one income but on the incomes of both partners. Low interest rates and the state's favorable tax treatment and the related promotion of homeownership played an additional role, but they have served more to *sustain* than to *extend* homeownership and mortgage markets, because they had been in action for a number of decades and have not changed significantly throughout the 1990s. This enabled house price increases far greater than income increases, but also a faster rise in outstanding mortgage credit than in house prices.

Second, in Italy, where the mortgage market is traditionally characterized by constraints to mortgage lending, the last 15 years have seen dramatic changes (Aalbers 2007) partly as a result of EU and European Monetary Union (EMU) induced regulation. Most importantly, the LTV-cap was abolished resulting in higher LTV-ratios; banks were allowed to grant mortgages (while this had been the exclusive terrain of specialized credit institutions until 1990); and both European and national regulation forced bank restructuring resulting in increased competition and the entry of foreign players in the Italian mortgage market. In addition, interest rates went down. Lending not only became much cheaper, but it also became possible to take out loans with higher LTV-ratios, higher LTI-ratios, and longer maturities. Even though the Italian economy in the last five years has witnessed a more serious crisis than most other European countries, the mortgage market has expanded rapidly and house price increases have been significant. This mirrors earlier developments in other European countries where the loosening of mortgage requirements made it possible for households to acquire more expensive properties, but also resulted in higher house prices. The banks pursued a "policy of cheap money:" to "keep the market going," mortgage requirements were loosened further (DNB 2000; Aalbers 2007). The price boom(s) associated with the expansion of credit possibilities created a situation in which homeowners with outstanding mortgage debts also began to carry more risk (Stephens 2003).

Europeanization and Globalization of Mortgage Markets

There is not one European mortgage market, there are many. Each national mortgage market is conditioned by national rules and regulations as well as by a set of shared ideas about the mortgage market demonstrated by rules of thumb shared by actors in those national markets as well as a shared analysis of market conditions. The rules and regulations structure the shared ideas, but are also structured by them; this is the *internal dynamic*, which is related to informal regulation. For example, a national rule that does not allow loans exceeding four times annual income, as until recently in place in Italy, structures the rules of thumb used by mortgage market actors, but a shared idea that a loan of four times annual income is not that high and that it is possible to supply mortgage loans up to five times annual income without necessarily exceeding acceptable risk levels, as in the Netherlands, may – over time – lead to a change in national regulation. There is also an *external dynamic* that is formed by both state and non-state regulation, as well as by international market developments. Examples of regulation include EU initiatives to open up markets and the global spread of risk management policies such as credit scoring (Aalbers 2011: chapter 3) made possible by ICT devices and applications. Examples of international market developments are cross-border joint ventures, and mergers and acquisitions. Foreign players may push national players to redefine their shared ideas. Of course, developments in other markets, both financial and non-financial, also play a part. For example, Dutch mortgage lenders are less willing to take up high-risk loans today than five to ten years ago because rising unemployment rates and the financial crisis cast a shadow on the mortgage market.

Regulation

It is important to realize the difference between harmonization and globalization: "Countries can adapt the same regulatory standards or principles and yet construct different rule-based systems of regulation" (Drahos and Braithwaite 2001: 104). This is indeed what is happening to many EU and EMU rules and regulations: they are implemented to harmonize the different European mortgage markets and, thus, enable "a market without borders," but in their implementation they often take a different turn because EU and EMU rules and regulations are "filled in" differently in the legal and economic framework of each country. In addition, big differences exist in contractual rules (Forum Group 2004) as well as in tax and subsidy schemes (Scanlon and Whitehead 2004). Important differences are related to the level of national regulation of mortgage lenders and markets, and to direct government intervention. Government intervention is substantial in Germany, France, and Portugal, but limited in Spain, the UK, and Italy. The Netherlands has introduced guarantees through a private non-profit institution backed by government that has the same effect as private mortgage insurance, namely the externalization of payment risk resulting in a greater willingness among lenders to grant loans on relatively cheap houses. In Denmark, finally, "there is a high degree of regulation of mortgage banks, but little direct government intervention" (Low *et al.* 2003: 21).

In addition to EU, EMU, and national regulation, global regulation also plays its part. The most important of these are the regulations and requirements established by the Basel Committee on Banking Supervision. The Basel II Accord specifies the "internal rating based" method as the new system for measuring solvency as of 2007. This means that providers who apply credit risk management will receive higher solvency scores from the National or European Central Bank than providers who do not, and they will, therefore, require less equity. This will create both internal and external incentives to apply credit risk management. The adoption of credit risk management techniques provides an example of the globalization of financial regulation, as more and more actors in the credit market are being encouraged to apply similar methods. The aim of this worldwide standardization is to increase the liquidity of the market, so that financial actors can know the risks and certainties of particular investments, and thus the prices of financial products, irrespective of their location (Carruthers and Stinchcombe 1999; Gotham 2006). The global spread of credit risk management due to formal regulation such as Basel II is tightly connected to the spread and institutionalization of credit risk management. The spread of credit risk management – and in particular one form of it, known as credit scoring, a quantified risk-selection technique used to minimize default and other types of risk – from the US throughout the world can be seen as the embodiment of the globalization and standardization of financial regulation (Aalbers 2011; see also Braithwaite and Drahos 2000: chapter 8; De Goede 2004).

Firms

At first sight the globalization and Europeanization of firms seems to be very limited: international corporate ownership is low (Wójcik 2002) and foreign markets' shares in different national mortgage markets tend to be low. In most Northern European countries the market shares of foreign credit institutions are rather small and together they are well below 20 percent – and in some cases even below 10 percent. If we look only at mortgage products, market shares of foreign mortgage lenders drop even further. In the Netherlands, for example, the market share of all foreign players together is around 5 percent, most of which is taken up by the Belgian bank Argenta, the Bank of Scotland (HBOS), and the American mortgage lender GMAC RFC. In the UK, foreign credit institutions play a significant role in the credit market with a market share of almost 50 percent, but in the mortgage market their share is below 10 percent. GMAC, with a market share of 2.2 percent (the tenth position) is the most important foreign mortgage lender active in the UK (CML 2005). The situation is not very different in other Northern European countries; in Germany the foreign market share is minimal, but recently growth has set in due to the entry of Dutch bank ING and Italian bank Unicredit's acquisition of German mortgage bank HVB.

In Southern Europe, the situation is quite similar in the sense that foreign mortgage lenders tend to have market shares of less than 10 percent altogether. In addition, in some countries, most notably Italy, acquisitions by foreign banks have been blocked for years. In 2005, Dutch bank ABN-AMRO was the first to gain access to the Italian market when it was allowed to buy the Italian Banca Antonveneta. But this only happened after a protracted battle for the bank in which the governor of the Bank of Italy had initially blocked ABN-AMRO's attempts, and had favored a small financially unsound Italian bank in its attempt to take over Antonveneta. Only after the involvement of Consob, the Italian market regulator, and of magistrates, were the attempts of Banca Popolare di Lodi (BPL) – ABN-AMRO's rival – blocked because of market manipulation, insider dealing, and illegal pacts. As a result of the battle, the governor of the Bank of Italy resigned and is now being prosecuted, while BPL's chief executive is charged with a number of violations and is imprisoned. Not much later French bank BNP Paribas was able to take over the Italian Banca Nazionale del Lavoro. The merger and acquisition wave in Italy may soon increase foreign market shares above the current 10 percent. Currently, the Spanish Banco Santander (operating under its subsidiary Abbey National), British lender Woolwich, Deutsche Bank, and Dutch bank ING are the most important foreign players in the Italian mortgage market. In the meantime, and after a failed merger with Barclays (UK), ABN-AMRO was bought by a consortium of three European banks. Bank of Scotland (UK) and Banco Santander (Spain) take over ABN-AMRO's foreign operations in 62 countries, including those in Italy (Santander), while the Belgian–Netherlands bank Fortis takes over most of its operations in the Netherlands. Santander then sold Interbanca, a part of Antonveneta, to General Electric Commercial Finance (US) and the rest to Monte di Paschi di Siena (Italy), which claims to be the oldest surviving bank in the world.

In small European countries as well as in CEE, credit markets are dominated by foreign players. In the Czech Republic, Estonia, Hungary, and Luxembourg foreign credit institutions have a market share of more than 90 percent. This is largely a result of the international expansion of some Western European (and to a limited degree also American) banks. Aside from CEE, the Netherlands, the UK, and Italy have seen the largest number of foreign entrants into their mortgage markets. In general, while banks and other financial institutions have become international and are present not only in the EU but also in the rest of the world, their mortgage companies remain national: "the internationalisation of finance has comparatively little impact on mortgage systems" (Stephens 2003: 1018). Wójcik's conclusion on the low level of credit market integration in Europe is also valid in one of its sub-markets, the mortgage market, but Wójcik's claim that what we see is Americanization rather than Europeanization (Wójcik 2002: 486) does not hold in European mortgage markets as US (-owned) mortgage lenders have only very small market shares. In addition, we see how a number of, mostly large, European banks, like their counterparts in the US, have globalized their operations to other, mostly less developed countries, not just in CEE, but also across Latin America and parts of Asia. In that sense, some of the European banks that grant mortgage loans are more globalized than an analysis of intra-European lending reveals.

Markets

Since most national mortgage markets in Northern and Southern Europe are dominated by national mortgage lenders, one could easily assume that mortgage markets are also not very globalized or Europeanized. This would be jumping to conclusions. Many mortgage lenders get part of their capital from countries other than their home countries (see also Chapter 3 by Sassen). If we take the example of Dutch pension funds: they are small players in the Dutch mortgage market but large players in global investment and have important stakes in some American financial institutions (Engelen 2003); ABP, the largest Dutch pension fund, and the world's second or third largest, has a global investment portfolio of over €215 billion, exemplifying a growing concentration of market power in large institutional investors like pension funds and insurance companies.

In addition, the importance of the secondary mortgage market has increased over the last ten years. In the secondary market so-called residential mortgage-backed securities (RMBS) are sold to investors. This process, called "securitization," provides liquidity to lenders because loans are placed "off-balance sheet;" it moderates the cyclical flow of mortgage capital; it assists the flow of capital from surplus areas to deficit areas; and it decreases the geographical spread in interest rates and allows for portfolio diversification because risks are spread geographically (Dennis and Pinkowish 2004: 208–09). Securitization requires not only a vastly expanding market, but also the deregulation and internationalization of domestic financial markets (Sassen 2001: 72) leading to a rapid growth in trade of securities, of which mortgage-backed securities are only one element. Because securitization increasingly connects the mortgage market to the stock market, securitization embodies the financialization of the mortgage market (Aalbers 2008). It increases the volatility of the mortgage market (and as the recent crisis demonstrates, it also increases volatility in the wider credit market) because stock markets by their very nature are volatile markets.

Table 5.4 Securitization issuance in Europe, 1996–2005

Year	Billion €
1996	29.5
1997	41.0
1998	27.9
1999	57.4
2000	58.4
2001	112.0
2002	124.0
2003	203.0
2004	248.7
2005	326.4

Sources: ESF 2006; IFS 2006.

Securitization of mortgage loans takes different dimensions in different countries. In the US, secondary mortgage markets have grown tremendously and now represent up to two-thirds of the mortgage market. Close to its peak in 2003, RMBS have been issued for a value of over 3 trillion (i.e., 3000 billion) US dollars. In 2004–07, issuance in the US was down to about $2 trillion a year; almost half of it handled by Fannie Mac, Freddie Mac, and Ginnie Mae (see Glossary). The decline in RMBS issuance had settled in three years before the crisis. In Europe, RMBS were introduced much later, but were also growing in number and volume in the years before the financial crisis hit; the volume tripled in less than four years to €326 billion (Table 5.4). In the early twenty-first century, mortgage market securitization has become more established in the UK, Spain, the Netherlands, and Italy, and to a lesser extent also in Germany, France, and Portugal (Table 5.5) (Forum Group 2004; IFS 2006). In the Netherlands, 15 percent of the mortgage market was securitized in 2005 and this share is increasing each year; RMBS issuance in that year valued €36 billion. In the UK, RMBS were issued for a value of €145 billion in 2005; in Spain issuance valued €42 billion; and in Italy €33 billion (ESF 2006). The development of securitization has been enabled and promoted by the state as Gotham explains in Chapter 1 for the case of the US, Wainwright in Chapter 4 for the UK, and Aalbers *et al.* (2011) for the Netherlands.

RMBS are sold to both national and foreign investors, and today there exists an international market for mortgage-backed securities that is highly transparent and accessible, "even though the integration of the various domestic markets involved is still quite limited" (Sassen 2001: 68). Securitization increasingly takes places in highly concentrated command points that function as a global marketplace for finance: Sassen's global

Table 5.5 Securitization in Europe per country, total issuance 2000–05

Country	Billion €	share %
UK	428.6	40.0
Italy	154.8	14.4
Spain	137.8	12.8
Netherlands	101.3	9.4
Germany	52.3	4.9
France	38.8	3.6
Pan-Europe	69.6	6.5
Other countries	89.2	8.3
Total	1072.4	100.0

Sources: ESF 2006; IFS 2006.

cities. Most European securitizations are handled by a London-based team of banks and financial service companies, including the London offices of some non-UK banks such as Deutsche Bank; Frankfurt only plays a secondary role. London also handles half of Australia's RMBS market (with a total value of &Euro;62 billion in 2005) as well as a small but (for London) significant share of US and Asian RMBS issuance – non-European issuance in London totals &Euro;309 million (IFS 2006).

This is possible because RMBS are, in theory, more transparent than mortgage products in the primary market. Local knowledge, which is so important in the primary market and a barrier for foreign mortgage lenders, is much less important in the secondary market because products have been standardized and made more transparent to make them more interesting for investors (cf. Clark and O'Connor 1997). Investors, in return, have the ability to compare the price, risk, and expected profitability of RMBS between countries, but also to compare them to other possible investments. As a result of securitization, mortgage markets indirectly become more globalized, not through mortgage lenders in the primary market, but through investors in the secondary market. While the primary mortgage markets remain firmly national; the secondary market becomes globalized, but also Europeanized or, perhaps more correct, "Londonized."

The recent mortgage market crisis demonstrates that many RMBS are actually not as transparent as they are in theory. As a result, the reduced liquidity of mortgages in the secondary market will make it harder for lenders to securitize loans. And considering that two-thirds of the US mortgage market is securitized, the impact can only be massive. This is why major bank lenders are hit hard and have lost billions of dollars in the crisis, but the ones going bankrupt (e.g., New Century Financial Corporation) or closing down (e.g., American Home Mortgage) are the non-bank lenders that fully rely on the secondary mortgage market to sell their portfolios. In addition, many investors in RMBS, both inside and outside the financial sector, are announcing losses of billions of dollars. Although securitization was designed to limit risk by spreading it over a wider area and to increase efficiency as a result of economies of scale, it now turns out that the spread expands the impact of the crisis, not only affecting sub-prime loans, but also prime loans; not only affecting mortgage markets, but also other credit markets; and not only affecting the US, but also other places around the globe (Aalbers 2009). It could be argued that without the globalization of secondary mortgage markets (through securitization) the mortgage crisis in the US could have developed into a national crisis, but that the global effects would have been limited. Yet, this is only true to some degree: even if non-American investors had not invested in US RMBS, the global credit crunch could have happened because, as a result of securitization in the US on the one hand and the existence of a global market for credit on the other hand, US mortgage markets affect US credit markets and, thereby, credit markets around the world.

Why Has Deterritorialization Been So Slow?

Deterritorialization of European primary mortgage markets has been slow for various reasons. First, as suggested above, harmonization of rules does not imply that markets also work in a similar manner. Large differences exist, for example, in tax and regression (repossession) laws. It is relatively easy for mortgage lenders in the Netherlands and the UK to take possession of the properties of households that default on their mortgage loan, but very hard or almost impossible in some Southern European countries such as Italy. In addition, double taxation may occur, discouraging cross-border mortgage transactions (Forum Group 2004: 42). Tax differences combined with cultural and structural differences may be the most important: together they result in different risk mentalities among households and mortgage lenders, as well as different mortgage products. Product differences between countries are largely a result of tax differences and to a lesser extent of innovative lenders, and of the potential for product cross-sales and cross-subsidies. For example, the potential to cross-sell insurance and mortgages results in a different "design" of mortgage products compared to a situation in which this potential is lacking.

Second, in most European countries, mortgages are primarily sold through the branches of banks. Foreign mortgage lenders lack a branch network and consequently have problems entering foreign markets. In Italy, Dutch bank ING offers loans through the internet and in a very small number of "boutique offices." As a brand, however, ING is not well known in Italy resulting in low consumer confidence and consequently a very low market share. ABN-AMRO realized that it needed to have a branch network in order to play a significant role in Italian financial markets (not only the mortgage market) and, therefore, bought shares in two Italian banks before it was able to acquire one of them. The added benefit of taking over a local bank is that the brand is already known. Many foreign lenders also make use of mortgage intermediaries, agents and brokers. In many countries, their number is small but increasing. For the time being this provides foreign mortgage lenders with a very limited alternative to distribution through bank branches.

In other countries, notably the Netherlands, but also the UK, intermediaries cover a much larger share of the distribution of mortgages. In the Netherlands, a few large franchise companies of mortgage intermediaries and a large number of independent mortgage intermediaries exist. The five largest franchise companies together have a market share of 35 percent in the distribution of mortgages through intermediaries. The existence of such franchise companies and independent intermediaries makes it relatively easy for foreign lenders to enter the Dutch market because they do not need to build up a branch network and can distribute their mortgages through mortgage intermediaries. In this way Argenta, Bank of Scotland, and GMAC have been able to gain market share. In relative terms, Argenta has been the fastest growing mortgage lender in the Netherlands, but their share of the market is still only a few percent. Some Dutch mortgage lenders also distribute most or even all of their mortgages through these intermediaries, while others, such as market leader Rabobank, prefer to distribute mortgages through their branch network. To tap into the intermediary chain Rabobank started a joint venture with ABP Pension Fund under the name of Obvion. In the last decade Obvion has had a market share of 4–7 percent. Some years ago ABN-AMRO decided to stop distributing mortgages through intermediaries, but a significant loss of market share, coupled with a growth in overall distribution through intermediaries, forced the bank to improve relations with the intermediaries in 2005. Some of the large franchise companies, however, indicated that they were not interested in working with ABN-AMRO anymore because they already had a full variety of mortgage products on offer.

Third, in some countries foreign lenders are blocked by the state. The initial problems of ABN-AMRO in Italy are a clear example of this. Italy has a history of government-engineered mergers and did not welcome foreign intervention. Until the recent announcement of the nationalization of the Bank of Italy, there was an explicit protection of commercial banks by the national Bank, not least so because the Italian commercial banks together own the national bank.

Fourth, foreign mortgage lenders have an information deficit. They lack knowledge of tax differences, cultural and structural factors, and the assessment of local real estate. It is possible to overcome these barriers, but it is a question of whether the costs outweigh the benefits. Moreover, in some countries foreign mortgage lenders do not have access to credit, collateral, and land registers because states prohibit them from acquiring such information.

Fifth, some of the European mortgage markets are considered saturated. This is the case in well-developed markets such as the British, Dutch, and Danish markets that already offer a full range of mortgage products for a wide range of customers. According to Low *et al.* (2003) the UK market is the most complete market as regards product range, borrower type and purpose, distribution, and information and advice; the Dutch and Danish market follow it closely. Saturated markets coupled with moderate profits make these markets relatively uninteresting for foreign mortgage lenders. Only a few years ago, the Danish and, especially, the Dutch markets were considered to have some room for growth in the subprime market. In the early 2000s, foreign lenders such as GMAC and ELQ (part of Lehman Brothers) started offering subprime loans in the Netherlands. These loans were based on risk-based pricing in which higher risks are priced higher and lower risks lower. As a result of the financial crisis both GMAC and ELQ stopped granting new mortgages in the Netherlands in March 2008. GMAC and ELQ were not the only foreign lenders that recently entered the Dutch mortgage market with "new" products: the Bank of Scotland entered the market offering loans with high LTV-loans while Argenta competes on prices by offering cheaper loans to low-risk households. Other national markets, such as the German and the French, show low levels of profit (as a share of outstanding mortgage credit) (Low *et al.* 2003) which may discourage foreign players unless they see ways to make more profit than the mortgage lenders already active in those markets.

But not all European markets are considered saturated: according to the European Mortgage Federation, the biggest potential growth markets are those in Southern Europe, CEE, and Germany (EMF 2004). In absolute terms Germany, Italy, Spain, France, Poland, and the Czech Republic offer the biggest opportunities for expansion. In relative terms all CEE countries, followed by Italy and Germany, present the largest untapped market growth potential. Absolute potential (in Euros) may be more important for foreign lenders than relative potential (as a share of GDP) because high fixed costs in entering a new market make it necessary to reach economies of scale. The CEE markets are considered growth markets because mortgage markets are very small there compared to the size of the owner-occupied market (partly because in many of these countries, many housing units were sold to the tenants at prices far below the market value in the early 1990s), while first-time buyers have a need for credit resulting in an expanding market. In Hungary, Poland, and Latvia, mortgage lending grew by more than 100 percent in 2002 and 2003 (EMF 2004). Overall, the EU15 have experienced an average yearly growth rate of 8 percent in mortgage debt between 1991 and 2003; while in the ten new EU member states the average growth was 50 percent per year (Forum Group 2004). Italy is considered a growth market because its mortgage market is not only small compared to its owner-occupied market and its GDP (for the various reasons mentioned above; and in Aalbers 2007), but also because there is a growing need among first-time buyers to get a mortgage loan since intergenerational transfers have been delayed and house prices have been rising. Germany already presents a large market, but German mortgage lenders ask for high down-payments and offer low LTI-ratios. Together with the rising homeownership rate and the fact that Germany is by far the largest European country in population size (82 million people compared to less than 60 million separately in France, the UK, Italy, and other European countries), this makes Germany a growth market as well.

The Future of European Mortgage Markets

Whitley (1998) has argued that for globalization and shifts in business systems to occur, (1) foreign firms need to control economic resources and activities, (2) national economies need to depend on foreign firms' large investments, (3) foreign firms need to come predominantly from one kind of business system, and (4) foreign firms need to be substantially independent of local institutions. The insignificant presence of foreign mortgage lenders in most countries does not constitute the globalization of firms, but it does result in a globalization of non-state regulation and also in the restructuring of national institutions, despite the fact that foreign mortgage lenders in most cases only have a small market share, do not control vital resources, do not necessarily come predominantly from one kind of business system, and are not substantially independent of local institutions. In Italy, for example, British and Dutch mortgage lenders only possess a small market share and are dependent on local intermediaries and nationally defined rules of the game; yet, they have triggered the restructuring of the Italian mortgage market in many ways: mergers and acquisitions, changes in state regulation, changes in the rules of the game and in rules of thumb, and changes in the mentality of lending and the related increased use of credit scoring techniques (Aalbers 2007). Whitley (1998) argues that weakly standardized and regulated, less cohesive, relatively poorly integrated, and peripherally linked characteristics of business systems are more prone to the effects of capital market internationalization, but in Italy these changes took place in a highly regulated, state controlled, cohesive, strongly integrated, and centrally linked banking sector. The presence of foreign mortgage firms may be insignificant in numbers, but the symbolic and competitive presence is highly significant. I agree with Whitley that this has not, and will not, result in one global business system; yet, it is a sign of globalization without deterritorialization, but with national reform and structural changes – "nationally codified globalization," to paraphrase Sassen (2003). The globalization of regulation and of mortgage markets takes place without large-scale deterritorialization and without large-scale globalization of firms.

European mortgage markets are quite different from one another in many respects. EU policies have not resulted in a single European mortgage market; in most countries national lenders continue to dominate the market even though regulation itself has been internationalized to some extent. More generally, despite liberalization, deregulation, and leveling the playing field, the EU does not constitute one market, but a patchwork of (mostly national) markets (e.g., Therborn 1999; Wójcik 2002; Ziltener 2004). Deterritorialization has been slow for various reasons: tax, law, cultural, and structural differences play a part, but the limited market share of mortgage intermediaries and the unequal treatment of foreign mortgage lenders in some countries also form a barrier. Globalization and Europeanization processes have been selectively absorbed and have led to both divergence and continued convergence. Path dependent trajectories are highly important, but can sometimes be bypassed by global processes such as the development of secondary mortgage markets, or downplayed by the entry of foreign firms, as the Italian example shows. Or, in other words: securitization and the entry of foreign firms may very well constitute critical junctures in which actors make contingent choices that set a specific trajectory of institutional development and consolidation that is difficult to reverse. Does this imply that globalization and Europeanization effects will stay limited and that European mortgage markets will not integrate into one European mortgage market?

First, it can be expected that after several bank merger and acquisition waves *within* countries, the second European supranational bank merger and acquisition wave is now in the making, resulting in the globalization or Europeanization of firms (see also Dymski 2002). This merger and acquisition wave is mixed, however: we see cross-border M&A activity, but also the break-up of internationally oriented banks along national lines. The first European supranational bank merger and acquisition wave (see also Gardener and Molyneux 1990; Leyshon and Thrift,1997: chapter 3), reflecting high socio-cultural thresholds in acquiring banks in significantly different yet highly established financial systems, is embodied by acquisitions of CEE banks by Western European banks as well as by cross-border mergers in small, relatively similar countries (in culture, language, and market regulation) that, for example, resulted in the Nordea Group and the Fortis Group.

Nordea is the result of the 1997 merger of the Finnish Merita Bank and the Swedish Nordbanken (see also Lindblom and Von Koch 2002), who then in 2000 merged with the Danish Unidanmark. Subsequently the Norwegian Christiana Bank Kreditkassen and the Swedish Postgirot Bank, as well a Russian and a Latvian bank, were acquired. It is now, by far, the largest financial institution in the Nordic countries. The Fortis Group is the result of the 1990 merger of the Belgian AG Group, Dutch bank VSB, and Dutch insurance company AMEV. Fortis Bank was created in 1999 as the result of a merger of the banks that are part of the Fortis Group: the Belgian banks ASLK, BPC, and Generale Bank and the Dutch banks Mees Pierson and VSB. In 2006, the insurance companies of the Fortis Group merged into Fortis ASR insurances. But then the backlash of the overpriced acquisition of the Dutch parts of ABN-AMRO in combination with the crisis forced the Dutch government to buy out the Dutch parts of Fortis (including the Dutch parts of acquired ABN-AMRO). Yet, most of the Belgian parts of Fortis were acquired by BNP-Paribas. Thus, while the Dutch parts of both ABN-AMRO and Fortis went back into Dutch hands – that is, the Dutch state – the Belgian parts of Fortis became part of a French bank; representing both the brake-up of banks along national lines and cross-border M&A activity.

The second European supranational bank merger and acquisition wave was set in motion by ABN-AMRO's acquisition of Antonveneta, but is now being followed in Italy by acquisition attempts of Spanish, French, and German banks. As Rijkman Groenink, ABN-AMRO's chairman at the time, explained: "the hunting season has opened, it is eat or to be eaten." In this sense, ABN-AMRO's acquisition was both offensive (growth strategy) and defensive in scope. But we all know how this story ended: despite having a healthy – perhaps more than healthy – appetite, ABN-AMRO got eaten itself. Part of the bank went back into Dutch hands, while the investment banking parts that Bank of Scotland had acquired only increased this bank's problems in the financial crisis. Banco Santander resold parts of Antonveneta to the Italian bank Monte di Paschi di Siena and will merge the Brazilian parts of ABN-AMRO with their own subsidiary in Brazil. Nonetheless, it is to be expected that more cash-stripped banks will be prey to acquisitions of big European, American, and perhaps also Asian banks. One result of the financial crisis has been a consolidation in the banking sector. Another result has been the stripping of several banks, some of them now in government hands, which sooner or later will be up for grabs. If such acquisitions take place by banks that offer mortgages, it is likely that they will enter the mortgage market in the country of acquisition. As mentioned above, mergers and acquisitions have the added benefit of acquiring local knowledge and branch networks.

Second, even without mergers and acquisitions, lenders will get widened access to foreign markets contributing to the globalization and

Europeanization of firms. The internet plays a bigger part today than it did ten years ago and it will play an even bigger part in ten years time. More importantly, the role of intermediaries will stay strong in countries like the Netherlands and the UK, but is on the rise in most other countries, and will increasingly start to offer a viable alternative to mortgage lenders without a branch network. In both cases, foreign lenders either try to offer products cheaper (price competition) or try to reach untapped market segments by offering mortgages to households formerly excluded, for example high-risk households. In Italy, foreign lenders entered the market offering higher LTV- and LTI-ratios as well as longer maturities. Until recently it was believed that subprime lending based on risk-based pricing offered the biggest market potential in other countries, because this segment is only fully developed in the UK. But after the subprime debacle in the US (and to some degree the UK), it is unlikely that the rise of subprime lending in Europe will be very fast, as both lenders and borrowers are now more aware of the risks. This will, however, not completely impede the rise of subprime in Europe, as some types of subprime loans will include households formerly excluded from mortgage loans, for example entrepreneurs and free-lancers, while lenders will again see possibilities for profits.

Third, we can expect further globalization and Europeanization of markets as a result of mortgage value chain unbundling, or vertical disintegration. A full-scale mortgage company is not just a lender, but also a funder, a servicer, and a distributor. The unbundling of the value chain means that different functions are offered by different companies. It is important to realize that only the distribution (sales) of mortgages has to be a local affair. The other functions can take place at other levels. This means that globalization and Europeanization become easier as a result of unbundling. The increasing numbers of mortgage intermediaries in some countries take over distribution functions from mortgages lenders, and although securitization may go out of fashion during the crisis years, it is already on the rise again in many countries implying that investors take over funding functions from mortgage lenders. Servicing concerns what we could call the "maintenance" of mortgage loans, often done by the back offices of mortgage lenders. European lenders typically service mortgages in-house; third party servicing is only popular in the Netherlands and UK, but it can be expected that more securitization and more foreign lending in time will make other markets ripe for third party servicing, which in return makes it easier for lenders to enter foreign markets. In the US, the unbundling of the mortgage value chain is much more progressed than in any European country. This also enables smaller companies (in employee size and equity size) to enter the mortgage market as long as they focus on a specific function in the market.

It is useful here to couple the unbundling of the mortgage value chain to Clark and O'Connor's typology of financial products (1997). Their typology builds on the simple idea that some knowledge, some information, is locally specific and that, as a result, not all financial products are traded at global markets, but that there is scope for local and national products and markets in finance. Or in their words:

> financial products often have a distinct spatial configuration of information embedded in their design. ... Even if markets were strongly efficient in the sense that they were comprehensively and completely spatially and economically (price) integrated, arbitragers with local market-specific information can still make profit. (Clark and O'Connor 1997: 95)

Their typology presents three types of products – transparent, translucent, and opaque – that have different probable market scopes – global, national, and local respectively. In Table 5.6, we can see these types of products, their characteristics and how they apply to the mortgage value chain. To Clark and O'Connor's "probable market scope," I have added "prospects for internationalization" because the nature of a product may fit a different market scope than the possibilities offered in the mortgage market. For example, foreign lenders can successfully penetrate a market by acquiring national and local knowledge by taking over a national bank with a local branch network, which enables them to fulfill lender and distributor functions.

Distribution through intermediaries remains largely national.[1] In-house servicing can become international in the same way as bank branch distribution, while third party servicing is not only a solution for foreign lenders, but can itself become international as well. The start-up costs for going down an international path are high, but can be compensated by high levels of standardization within a national market, provided that economies of scale are reached. Two of the largest servicers in Europe, the Dutch companies Stater and Quion, only operate in the Netherlands, but both have indicated that expansion to other countries is a likely possibility in the near future. This means that servicing can be done by global companies, but that markets for servicing remain national. Likewise, global *firms*, such as Banco Santander and HBSC, can do lending but the *market* for lending – the primary mortgage market – remains national. Lending also requires local knowledge of real estate valuation and the structural and cyclical workings of national and local housing markets. Funding in a global market can only be offered by highly specialized firms located in global cities.[2]

The US mortgage crisis, resulting in a global credit crunch, has shaken up mortgage markets in different places. It will decelerate the spread of subprime lending, not only in the US but around the world. As a result of the crisis, securitization has slowed down, with RMBS issuance down by 50 percent in EU countries in 2008. But in time we will see a renewed interest in securitization based on improved risk ratings. RMBS may become less complicated

Table 5.6 Mortgage value chain and prospects for globalization

Value chain	Lending	Distribution	Funding	Servicing
Type of product	Translucent	Opaque	Transparent	Opaque/ translucent
Key characteristics	Standardized nationally, but non-standardized internationally; differentiated over space and time; variation in observed risk and actual returns	Asymmetrically distributed information; transaction-specific information; relational investing; heterogeneous; requires detailed local knowledge	Functionally and spatially homogeneous; standardized; simply and cheaply observable; average returns	Specialist expertise; standardized nationally, but heterogeneous internationally; differentiated over space and time; requires detailed local knowledge
Probable market scope	National, because mortgage products in the primary market are national in design	Local, in the sense of being produced at a particular site relying upon transaction-specific clients	International, relying on both national and international investors	National, relying on nationally operating lenders
Prospects for internationalization	Possible through acquiring national knowledge (e.g., M&As) or by finding a niche market (e.g., risk-based pricing)	Low, but possible through local bank branch network	High	Possible through acquiring local knowledge and exploiting it through large, standardized volumes
Globalization of firms	Yes, very likely	Yes, very likely for banks, but less likely for intermediaries	Yes, most likely	Less likely, but possible
Globalization of regulation	To a limited degree	To a very limited degree	Not completely, but far-reaching	To an extremely limited degree
Globalization of markets	No	No	Yes	No

Sources: partly based on Clark and O'Connor 1997; Drahos and Braithwaite 2001.

and will surely become more regulated, but it would be hard to imagine a massive return to portfolio lending. Also, in primary mortgage markets we will not see the end of globalization. Currently we see that international market penetration is decreasing: several lenders have retreated from foreign markets, such as is the case with foreign lenders like HBOS, GMAC, and ELQ (which was owned by Lehman Brothers) who all had small shares of the Dutch mortgage market, always based on a securitization model, in several cases of subprime mortgages. At the same time, foreign investors are also buying up stocks of banks and other lenders. Next, a new merger and acquisition wave will lead to more lending activities being owned by foreign companies. In addition, we see new, *ad hoc*, national regulation, but we also see – and will see more – new, international regulation to enable improved supervision of global financial markets. In sum, we can simultaneously witness decreasing and increasing globalization of mortgage regulation, firms, and markets.

This brings us to the conclusion that, after a period of decline, we can expect a further globalization of the funding market – that is, the secondary mortgage market – but not of the other parts of the mortgage market – that is, the primary mortgage market (lending), distribution, and servicing. Indeed, the globalization of firms can take place in the absence of globalization of regulation and markets (Drahos and Braithwaite 2001). The globalization of regulation remains partial, while the globalization of firms is limited, but will reach higher levels in the near future. The introduction of the Euro had effectively created more similar markets, notably because its foreshadow as well as its implementation have resulted in lower inflation rates and lower interest rates in Southern Europe; although this convergence is not being challenged by the sovereign debt crisis in many European countries. In addition, the Basel regulations institutionalize and speed up convergence in credit risk management and solvency standards resulting in a flattening of the context of market regulation. Even though regulation is being increasingly harmonized, many differences remain and are not easily erased: cultural differences, tax differences, and juridical differences remain. Earlier proposals by the European Commission (2005) will result in more convergence if implemented, but are unable to take away all barriers. This implies a further convergence of regulation, but not the creation of one European market. Aside from the secondary mortgage market, the European financial landscape will remain one of different national mortgage *markets* that increasingly resemble each other; the creation of one mortgage *market*, however, is an illusion.

Notes

1   In 2000, two online mortgage intermediaries – Mortgage Operation from the UK and Haus & Capital from Germany – merged into Creditweb, but the

merger turned out unviable and was split into two. The German part then merged with a French company which was subsequently bought by American mortgage company GMAC RFC (Kasparova 2004: 37). Although GMAC discontinued its activities in the Netherlands, at the time of writing it was still involved in the operations of Creditweb Limited in France and Germany.

2 The aim of this worldwide standardization is to increase the liquidity of the market, so that financial actors can know the risks and certainties of particular investments, and thus the prices of financial products, *irrespective of their location* (Carruthers and Stinchcombe 1999: 354). The financial crisis may have demonstrated that many RMBS are not as transparent as they were believed to be. This may make it harder to securitize subprime, predatory and exotic loans, but I believe that, in the long run, the securitization of standardized, prime, and basic mortgage loans is here to stay.

References

Aalbers, M.B. (2007) Geographies of housing finance: The mortgage market in Milan, Italy. *Growth and Change* 38(2): 174–99.

Aalbers, M.B. (2008) The financialization of home and the mortgage market crisis. *Competition & Change* 12(2): 148–66.

Aalbers, M.B. (2009) Geographies of the financial crisis. *Area* 41(1): 34–42.

Aalbers, M.B. (2011) *Place, Exclusion, and Mortgage Markets*. Oxford: Wiley-Blackwell.

Aalbers, M.B., Engelen, E., and Glasmacher, A. (2011) 'Cognitive closure' in the Netherlands: Mortgage securitization in a hybrid European political economy. *Environment and Planning A* 43(8): 1779–95.

Aglietta, M. (1979) *A theory of capitalist regulation: The US experience*. London: New Left.

Agnew, J. (1993) Representing space: Space, scale and culture in social science. In: J. Duncan and D. Ley (eds.) *Place/Culture/Representation*, London: Routledge.

Allen, J., Barlow, J., Leal, J., Maloutas, T., and Padovani, L. (2004) *Housing and Welfare in Southern Europe*. Oxford: Blackwell.

Arbaci, S. (2002) Patterns of ethnic and socio-spatial segregation in European cities: Are welfare regimes making a difference? In: M. Fonseca *et al.* (eds.) *Immigration and Place in Mediterranean Metropolises*, Lisbon: FLAD Luso-American Foundation.

Ball, M. (2005) *RICS European Housing Review 2005*. Coventry: Royal Institute of Chartered Surveyors.

Bayoumi, T. (1997) *Financial integration and real activity*. Ann Arbor, MI: University of Michigan Press.

Braithwaite, J. and Drahos, P. (2000) *Global Business Regulation*. Cambridge: University Press.

Brenner, N. (2000) The urban question as a scale question: reflections on Henri Lefebvre, urban theory and the politics of scale. *International Journal of Urban and Regional Research* 24(2): 361–78.

Carruthers, B.G. and Stinchcombe, A.L. (1999) The social structure of liquidity: Flexibility, markets, and state. *Theory and Society* 28(3): 353–82.

Castles, F. and Ferrera, M. (1996) Home ownership and the welfare state: is southern Europe different? *South European Society and Politics* 1(2): 163–85.

Clark, G. and O'Connor, K. (1997) The informational content of financial products and the spatial structure of the global finance industry. In: K.R. Cox (ed.) *Spaces of Globalization: Reasserting the Power of the Local*, New York: Guilford Press.

CML. (2005) *Overview of Developments.* London: Council of Mortgage Lenders.

Corbridge, S., Thrift, N., and Martin, R. (eds.) (1994) *Money, Power and Space.* Cambridge: Blackwell.

Cox, K.R. (ed.) (1997) *Spaces of Globalization: Reasserting the Power of the Local.* New York: Guildford Press.

De Goede, M. (2004) Repoliticizing financial risk. *Economy and Society* 33(2): 197–217.

Dennis, M.W. and Pinkowish, T.J. (2004) *Residential Mortgage Lending. Principles and Practices.* (Fifth edition) Mason, OH: Thomson South-Western.

Dicken, P. (1998) *Global Shift: Transforming the World Economy.* (Third edition) London: Sage.

Dijkink, G. (2000) Europe 2000 and national regulation discourses. *Tijdschrift voor Economische en Sociale Geografie* 91(3): 219–26.

DNB. (2000) *Het bancaire hypotheekbedrijf onder de loep. Rapport over de ontwikkelingen op de hypotheekmarkt in de periode 1994–1999 gebaseerd op onderzoek naar de hypothecaire krediet-verlening bij Nederlandse financiële instellingen.* Amsterdam: De Nederlandse Bank.

Drahos, P. and Braithwaite, J. (2001) The globalization of regulation. *The Journal of Political Philosophy* 9(1): 103–28.

Dymski, G.A. (2002) The global bank merger wave: implications for developing countries. *The Developing Economies* 40(4): 435–66.

ECB. (2004) *European Mortgage Markets.* Frankfurt am Main: European Central Bank (ECHP). (2004) *European Community Household Panel.* Luxembourg: Eurostat.

EMF. (2001) *Key Figures.* Brussels: European Mortgage Federation.

EMF. (2003) *Hypostat 2003.* Brussels: European Mortgage Federation.

EMF. (2004) *Annual Report 2004.* Brussels: European Mortgage Federation.

EMF. (2005) *Hypostat 2004.* Brussels: European Mortgage Federation.

Engelen, E. (2003) The logic of funding European pension restructuring and the dangers of financialisation. *Environment and Planning A* 35: 1357–72.

ESF. (2006) *ESF Securitisation Data Report. Winter 2006.* London: European Securitisation Forum.

European Commission. (2005) *Green Book. Mortgage Credit in de EU.* Brussels: European Commission.

Forum Group on Mortgage Credit. (2004) *The Integration of the EU Mortgage Credit Markets.* Brussels: European Commission.

Gardener, E.P.M. and Molyneux, P. (1990) *Changes in Western European Banking.* London: Unwin Hyman.

Gotham, K.F. (2006) The secondary circuit of capital reconsidered: Globalization and the U.S. real estate sector. *American Journal of Sociology* 112(1): 231–75.

Hacker, J.S. (2006) *The Great Risk Shift: The Assault on American Jobs, Families, Health Care and Retirement – And How You Can Fight Back.* New York: Oxford University Press.

Hancher, L. and Moran, M. (1989) Introduction: Regulation and deregulation. *European Journal of Political Research* 17: 129–36.

Hirst, P. and Thompson, G. (1996) *Globalization in question.* Oxford: Polity Press.

Hollingsworth, J.R. and Boyer, R. (eds.) (1997) *Contemporary Capitalism: The Embeddedness Institutions.* Cambridge: Cambridge University Press.

Hudson, R. (2003) European integration and new forms of uneven development. But not the end of territorially distinctive capitalism in Europe. *European Urban and Regional Studies* 10(1): 49–67.

IFS. (2006) *Securitisation.* London: International Financial Services.

Kasparova, D. (2004) Mortgage pricing in the EU. Paper presented at the ENHR conference, July 2nd-6th, Cambridge, UK.

Kemeny, J. and Lowe, S. (1998) Schools of comparative housing research: From convergence to divergence. *Housing Studies* 13(2): 161–76.

Koechlin, T. (1995) The globalization of investment. *Contemporary Economic Policy* 13: 92–100.

Levine, R. (1997) Financial development and economic growth: views and agenda. *Journal of Economic Literature* 35(2): 688–726.

Leyshon, A. and Thrift, N. (1997) *Money/Space. Geographies of Monetary Transformation.* London: Routledge.

Lindblom, T. and Von Koch, C. (2002) Cross-border bank mergers and acquisitions in the EU. *The Service Industries Journal* 22(4): 41–72.

Low, S., Sebag-Montefiore, M., and Dübel, A. (2003) *Study on the Financial Integration of European Mortgage Markets.* London/Brussels: Mercer Oliver Wyman/European Mortgage Federation.

Mamadouh, V. (2001) A place called Europe. National political cultures and the making of the new territorial order known as the European Union. In: G. Dijkink and H. Knippenberg (eds.) *The Territorial Factor: Political Geography in a Globalising World,* Amsterdam: Vossiuspers.

Massey, D. (1993) Politics and space/time. In: M. Keith and S. Pile (eds.) *Place and the Politics of Identity,* London: Routledge.

Neuteboom, P. (2003) A European comparison of the costs and risks of mortgages for owner-occupation. *European Journal of Housing Policy* 3(2): 155–71.

Neuteboom, P. (2004) A comparative analysis of the net cost of a mortgage for homeowners in Europe. *Journal of Housing and the Built Environment* 19: 169–86.

O'Brien, R. (1992) *Global Financial Integration: The End of Geography.* London: Pinter.

Ohmae, K. (1990) *The Borderless World: Power and Strategy in an Interdependent Economy.* New York: Harper.

Porter, M.E. (1990) *The competitive advantage of nations.* London: Macmillan.

Sassen, S. (1998) *Globalization and its Discontents: Essays on the New Mobility of People and Money.* New York: New Press.

Sassen, S. (2001) *The Global City: New York, London, Tokyo.* (Second edition) Princeton, NJ: Princeton University Press.

Sassen, S. (2003) Globalization or denationalization? *Review of International Political Economy* 10(1): 1–22.

Scanlon, K. and Whitehead, C. (2004) *International trends in housing tenure and mortgage finance.* London: Council of Mortgage Lenders.

Scott, A. (1988) *New industrial spaces: Flexible Production organization and regional development in North American and Western Europe.* London: Pion.

Scott, A. (1998) *Regions and the world economy: The coming shape of global production, competition, and political order.* Oxford: Oxford University Press.

Stephens, M. (2003) Globalization and housing finance systems in advanced and transition countries. *Urban Studies* 40(5):-6, 1011-26.

Storper, M. (1997) *The Regional World: Territorial Development in a Global Economy.* New York: Guilford Press.

Storper, M. and Walker, R. (1989) *The Capitalist Imperative: Territory, Technology and IGdustrial growth.* Oxford: Blackwell.

Swyngedouw, E. (1997) Neither global not local: "Glocalization" and the politics of scale. In: K.R. Cox (ed.) *Spaces of Globalization: Reasserting the Power of the Local,* New York: Guilford Press.

Therborn, G. (1999) "Europe" as issues of sociology. In: T.P. Boje, B. van Steenbergen, and S. Walby (eds.) *European Societies: Fusion or Fission?,* London: Routledge.

Wachtel, H.M. (1986) *The money mandarins: the making of a supranational economic order.* New York: Pantheon.

Whitley, R. (1998) Internationalization and varieties of capitalism: the limited effects of cross-national coordination of economic activities on the nature of business systems. *Review of International Political Economy* 5(3): 445-81.

Wójcik, D. (2002) Cross-border corporate ownership and capital market integration in Europe: some evidence from portfolio and industrial holdings. *Journal of Economic Geography* 2: 455-91.

Ziltener, P. (2004) The economic effects of the European Single Market Project: projections, simulations – and the reality. *Review of International Political Economy* 11(5): 953-79.

6

The Reinvention of Banking and the Subprime Crisis

On the Origins of Subprime Loans, and How Economists Missed the Crisis

Gary A. Dymski

Introduction

The proximate cause of the subprime lending crisis was the end of the US housing bubble, which triggered an avalanche of mortgage delinquencies, especially among subprime mortgages, at the base of the financial food-chain; these eventually led to seismic financial-market eruptions at the top. This chapter develops new answers to two fundamental questions about this crisis:

- Why were subprime loans made in the first place?
- Why did economists miss it?

The two questions are interlinked: to know how economists missed it, pay attention to how they have explained it. Most explanations of the crisis have been drawn from economists' theories about why credit markets malfunction. One approach asserts that lenders and borrowers were jointly myopic about the true riskiness of housing prices and the subprime loans that fed the housing bubble; so these loans appeared rational for both borrowers and lenders when they were made. Other arguments build on the idea that subprime loans were inherently irrational because of moral hazard. One claim is that lenders made loans they shouldn't have made to people who shouldn't have been permitted to borrow. The second is that banks were forced into making highly risky mortgage loans to low-income borrowers

Subprime Cities: The Political Economy of Mortgage Markets, First Edition. Edited by Manuel B. Aalbers.
© 2012 Blackwell Publishing Ltd. Published 2012 by Blackwell Publishing Ltd.

and in unstable areas due to the pressures exerted on lenders that are subject to the Community Reinvestment Act (CRA) of 1977.

This chapter responds to these two moral hazard arguments, in two steps.[1] First, it offers an alternative micro-level explanation of why the subprime crisis emerged, rooted in the unique historical context underlying the emergence of subprime lending. We emphasize two factors that are largely overlooked in other dissections of this crisis: the strategic transformation of banking at the onset of the neoliberal era; and long-established patterns of racial exclusion in US credit markets. The collision of these two factors, during a period in which US financial markets had become a global liquidity sink, generated the spark that lit the fuse of the current economic crisis.

Second, the historical approach taken here suggests why other micro-level accounts of the subprime crisis – the moral hazard and political force approaches – are mistaken. The credit excesses of the subprime-lending era are rooted in the credit-market starvation of prior decades. Once we understand why some prospective borrowers were historically denied access to the housing credit market, we can begin to understand how risky mortgage loans began flowing to these neighborhoods and borrowers. Unfolding the underlying logic of this shift will also help us find some blind spots in credit-market microeconomics, enabling us to understand how these markets could go so wrong in ways that were invisible to the economists who study these markets.

Banking Risks and the Transformation of US Banking and Mortgage Markets

By definition, banks are financial firms that accept liquid deposits and create credit. Performing these two functions for the economy entails default risk, the possibility that borrowers may not meet their repayment obligations in a timely manner, and liquidity risk, which arises for any economic entity that finances a longer-term asset position with liabilities of shorter duration. Tensions can arise between banks' liquidity-provision and credit-creation functions, because the risks inherent in these functions are interlinked: when banks respond to improved investment and consumption prospects in upturns, banks simultaneously increase the level of systemic liquidity and default risk. Banks wishing to meet robust loan demand can do so by drawing more heavily on the interbank (Federal Funds) and other contingent borrowing markets. Loan commitments funded in this way increase systemic liquidity risk (in addition to default risk). This is barely noticed in periods of sustained growth, since deposit volumes rise and money markets are flush. However, in downturns or periods of heightened uncertainty, being liquid commands a premium: it is preferable to hold assets that are readily convertible into money, rather than non-monetary assets that may be impossible to sell except at a steep discount. Non-bank economic units will be more able to survive such periods if banks provide them with fresh infusions of credit; but to do so banks must sacrifice their own liquidity (Dymski 1988).

When banks generate default risks and liquidity risks through loan-making, and absorb those risks on their balance sheets, there are built-in brakes on tendencies toward speculative and overly risky lending. For example, banks can lend more if they are willing to borrow more funds in short-term money markets. Then in the latter stages of an expansion, banks must consider both that default risk will worsen on marginal loans, and that the liquidity risks on funds borrowed to make those loans will rise as well. This curbs bank credit expansion and slows economic growth.

This self-braking feature would be lost if banks no longer absorb default and liquidity risk when they lend. If banks could make loans without being in any way accountable for the resulting default risk, then a slowdown in credit growth linked to credit quality would have to originate with whatever entity was underwriting banks' growing default risk. Even in this case, banks might slow lending over the cycle if the cost of the funds they borrowed to support lending climbed systematically. If this liquidity risk too was eliminated (in this extreme case), banks could make as many loans as they wanted without any risk. The potential for disjuncture between the systemic and individual levels of default and liquidity-risk generation is clear.

Banking and mortgage market turbulence

Prior to the 1980s, loans made by US banks stayed on their own balance sheets, as did lending-related risks. Operating with geographic and product-line prohibitions inherited from the 1930s, banks focused primarily on local depositors and borrowers. As Figure 6.1 illustrates, savings and loan associations and mutual savings banks ("thrifts") provided half of all mortgages, funding them primarily with savings deposits.

This method of funding mortgages was always subject to substantial volatility over the business cycle, as Figure 6.2 shows. However, amidst the macroeconomic turmoil of the late 1970s, the US banking structure and mortgage system proved unsustainable. Interest rates spiked well above the rates that banks were permitted to pay, leading to disintermediation – banks' loss of depositors to innovative savings outlets, such as money-market money instruments. Their credit supply threatened, large non-financial firms expanded the scope and depth of the commercial paper market and of corporate bond markets. Disintermediation combined with an inverted yield-curve also decimated the thrift industry and the mortgage market.

This led to the passage, in 1980 and 1982, of legislation designed to modernize, respectively, commercial-banking and thrift regulation. A period of

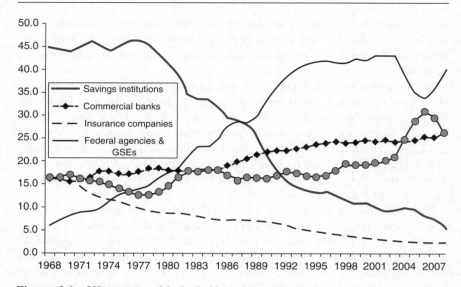

Figure 6.1   US mortgage debt by holder, 1968–2007
Source: Board of Governors of the Federal Reserve System, Release 1.54.

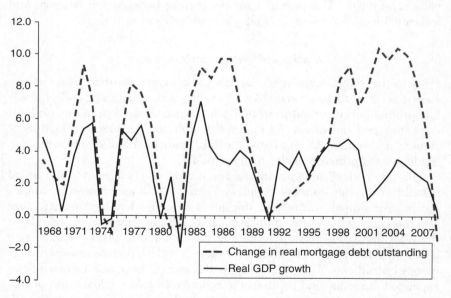

Figure 6.2   Annual percentage growth in US real GDP and outstanding mortgage debt, 1968–2007
Note: Based on GDP deflator data, drawn from the Bureau of Economic Analysis, National Income and Product Accounts for the US.

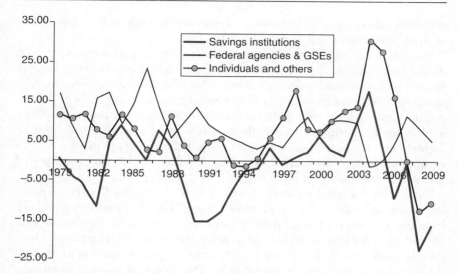

Figure 6.3 Annual percentage change in US mortgage debt outstanding for selected holders, 1979–2009
Note: Based on GDP deflator data, drawn from the Bureau of Economic Analysis, National Income and Product Accounts for the US.

competitive deregulation between the federal and state regulators of thrifts followed. As Figure 6.3 illustrates, this temporarily rescued thrifts' overall mortgage capacity: between 1983 and 1985, thrifts increased their mortgage holdings. At the same time, many thrifts took advantage of deregulation by undertaking speculative investments that often proved ill-advised. By the late 1980s, the problem of thrift illiquidity had been transformed into a crisis of thrift insolvency. A number of spectacular crashes of savings and loan institutions followed, as did 1989 legislation that permitted a federal industry bailout. The thrift industry shrank dramatically, and with it, its capacity to generate and hold mortgages (see Figures 6.1 and 6.3). The 1980s were no less troubled for commercial banks: the Latin American debt crisis, loan problems in oil-patch states, and other troubles generated widespread industry losses and a surge in bank failures.

The next several years brought mergers and institutional innovations that reshaped the competitive and institutional terrain of US banking and mortgage markets. Banks shifted their strategic focus from earnings based on interest margin to earnings based on the fees they could earn from providing services. In the 1980s, banks began to focus on creating a complete menu of financial products for upscale (asset-owning, income-secure) customers. In wholesale markets, banks began to bundle and sell off some of their credit contracts with commercial customers. Banks also accounted for a large share of mortgage originations (see Figure 6.1).

Indeed, banks' need to find new revenue sources corresponded with thrifts' reduced capacity to provide mortgage loans. Consequently, housing finance was transformed from an intermediary-based to a securities-market-based system. Lenders no longer held mortgages to maturity, along with the default and liquidity risks associated with these assets; in the new system, lenders made mortgages to sell them. Banks generated their earnings by high-volume fee-based operations. They split the mortgage process into its constituent parts – origination, servicing, holding, and so on – and priced and performed each part separately.

Establishing a mass securities-based system of housing finance required the commodification of risky mortgage assets. The first step was standard-izing the instruments being bundled and sold. In the 1980s, this was accomplished by adopting standardized criteria for mortgage eligibility. These criteria made "relationship" lending unnecessary, permitting non-local, non-thrift lenders to originate mortgage debt. The second step was generating a demand for these claims. Investors were readily found because of government and private underwriting of mortgage debt. Two federally chartered agencies, FNMA (the Federal National Mortgage Association) and FHLMC (the Federal Home Loan Mortgage Corporation), underwrote a secondary market for qualifying mortgages.[2] These agencies ensured market-wide homogeneity in terms and conditions by establishing balance-sheet and contractual thresholds that "conforming" mortgages had to meet. The resulting "plain vanilla" loans met prescribed parameters: no more than 30 percent of income spent on housing and 20 percent down on any mortgage loan. The substantial down-payments and conservative mortgage payment-to-income criteria made them extremely low-risk.[3]

This shift toward securitization radically changed the landscape of financial risks in the mortgage system. Default risk, monitored increasingly via riskiness criteria established centrally, not by individual lenders, appeared to decline. Further, financial market participants widely held the view that FNMA underwriting implied government insurance against mortgage defaults. Liquidity risk, which was shifted from mortgage originators to mortgage holders, appeared to decline as well.[4]

From the mid-1980s to the mid-1990s, most mortgages were conforming conventional loans, underwritten by these agencies. These agencies accommodated the larger flow demand for securitized mortgages by increasing their proportion of pass-through securities (securities whose owners have claims on the underlying mortgage cash-flows). Accompanying this new epoch of securitization was ambiguity about the extent and locus of risk-bearing. Banks appeared to have shed much risk; but it wasn't clear to what extent risks were lower, and to what extent shifted. In the face of these shifts, the risk "absorption" function of banks as lenders became ever more remote, even as the competition to be risk originators grew ever more intense. Facing banks on this new competitive field were the far more lightly regulated mortgage companies.

From Financial Exclusion to Predatory Lending

From the 1930s until the late 1960s, federal guidelines under the Federal Housing Administration established "redlining" – the refusal to make mortgage credit available to neighborhoods with large minority populations – as government policy. The result, given the extensive segregation in US cities, was stagnation of housing values and lower homeownership rates among minorities. This began to change in the 1960s. The 1968 Fair Housing Act and 1974 Equal Credit Opportunity Act extended the anti-discrimination principles of civil rights law to housing and credit markets, respectively.[5] The Home Mortgage Disclosure Act (HMDA) of 1975 and the Community Reinvestment Act (CRA) of 1977, in turn, permitted urban residents to monitor bank loan-making and discouraged redlining.

Community advocates used this legislative framework to advocate that banks meet credit and banking needs in minority and lower-income ("inner city") communities, as they did elsewhere in their market areas. They demanded that banks and thrifts make "mainstream" loans to qualifying households and businesses. Depository institutions objected to these demands, using an evolving set of rationales. They first argued that there was a lack of home-purchase demand in the inner city. When this was disproven, banks pointed to the excessive riskiness of lending in the inner city. So from the 1970s to the mid-1990s, community reinvestment struggles focused on whether, first, all bank customers were provided with equal access to credit, and second, banking services were uniformly available. The demand for racial equality encompassed both households who qualified for but were denied access to plain-vanilla loans, and households with fewer resources who needed access to basic financial services.

For years, basic financial services were provided to minorities and to low-income households largely by check-cashing stores, finance companies, and pawn-brokers; these were usually poorly capitalized and locally run. But with the increasing number of lower-income households and the growing market for cross-border remittances, the huge fees available from the unbanked and under-banked households in these financial-market niches attracted the attention of major financial companies and megabanks. Banks had only a miniscule market share in these markets.[6]

In the mid-1990s, banks began focusing – both directly and via subsidiaries – on the lower-income and minority customers they had previously overlooked. They designed special instruments aimed at these customer bases, including what became known as "predatory loans." This term refers to borrowing instruments characterized by excessively high rates, high fees, and high penalties for non-payment; these loans are deemed "predatory" in two cases: first, when they are higher than warranted by borrower risk; second, when the payment requirements they impose on borrowers makes default more likely than non-default. The long-term effect of reducing borrowers' wealth is more likely with the second type of predatory loan. Predatory loans grew at a frenetic pace in neighborhoods historically subject to financial exclusion, leading to high rates of personal financial distress and dispossession well *before* the 2007 mortgage-market meltdown. The two principle vehicles for predatory lending are payday loans and subprime mortgage loans.

Payday loans

Payday loans advance workers a portion of the money they will be due from their next paycheck. The customers for these loans are not the unbanked: receipt of a payday loan requires a checking account. This form of credit has spread very fast; virtually unheard of 15 years ago, one recent study estimates that as of 2005, 22,000 store locations offered payday loans, with a market volume of $40 billion and fees of $4.4 billion.[7] Four years earlier, there were 15,000 stores and $2.6 billion in fees. Most customers use payday loans 7–12 times per annum. Megabanks have provided much of the financing for these loans. The average fee for a $100 check is $18. Some 41 percent of borrowers are homeowners. Among borrowers, African Americans and military families are overrepresented, as are lower-income households: 29 percent earn less than $25,000 per year, and 52 percent earn $25,000–50,000 per year.

The payday loan industry has grown rapidly for several reasons. First, banks have steadily raised the fees they impose when a customer account lacks sufficient funds to pay all checks written against it. Second, late fees for rent, credit-card, and utility payments have risen dramatically. Some $22 billion in NSF fees and $57 billion in late fees were collected in 2003 (Bair 2005). Third, lower-income US households have much more volatile incomes than do other households, and hence are more likely than others to need credit to close income-expenditure gaps (Gosselin 2004). And since many such households lack the financial track record required to qualify for credit cards or bank loans (Information Policy Institute 2005), they turn to payday loans instead.

Subprime mortgage lending

The term "subprime mortgage" refers generally to loans made against residential real estate whose terms and conditions are harsher than the market norm. These harsher terms – higher fees and penalties, higher interest rates, shorter terms to maturity – are designed to increase the lender's expected return in compensation for the greater-than-average risk of the loan. These loans have often been described as predatory, for two reasons: first, they are sometimes supplied to households that could have qualified for mainstream mortgage loans; second, subprime mortgages often put borrowers into situations where default can be avoided only under a low-probability set of circumstances (such as continued explosive growth in housing prices). Subprime mortgages arose in the 1990s when mortgage brokers began to aggressively market second mortgages to homeowners (especially minorities) in neighborhoods that had historically been denied equal access to credit (California Reinvestment Coalition 2001). While costly, they permitted owners of modest homes to gain access to money for whatever financial contingencies they faced. This class of subprime mortgage was readily classified as predatory, as it was normally made against homeowners' equity in their homes.

Soon, loans with these characteristics were being marketed to those seeking to acquire homes – again, primarily to minority borrowers, and disproportionately for homes in high-minority and lower-income areas. Whether subprime loans for home purchase are predatory has been a source of continuing controversy: are these loans' high costs and penalties predatory, or do they represent legitimate responses to homeseekers' higher-than-normal risk?

In any event, from the beginning, subprime loans have been made disproportionately to the elderly, people of color, and people in minority neighborhoods. Many low-income and minority borrowers have obtained loans at high interest rates and with very unfavorable terms from housing-related and payday lenders (Williams 1999). For example, Canner *et al.* (1999: 709) found that in 1998, subprime and manufactured housing lenders accounted for 34 percent of all home purchase mortgage applications and 14 percent of originations. These lenders' impact on low-income and minority individuals is even more pronounced. According to Canner *et al.*, in 1998, subprime and manufactured housing lenders made a fifth of all mortgages extended to lower-income and Latino borrowers, and a third of all those made to African American borrowers. According to ACORN (2000), subprime lending grew 900 percent in inner-city areas in the period 1993–99, while other mortgage lending actually declined. A nationwide study of 2000 HMDA data by Bradford (2002) found that African Americans were, on average, more than twice as likely as Whites to receive subprime loans, and Latinos 40–220 percent more likely.[8]

Available evidence suggests that lower-income and minority borrowers have been targeted for subprime loans. Community-reinvestment advocates and consumers have continually challenged business practices that victimize borrowers. In one high-profile case, Ameriquest Mortgage Company of

Orange, California settled a consumer protection lawsuit for $325 million in January 2006. Tellingly, this was second in dollar value, in US history, only to Household Finance Corporation's $484 million settlement in 2002 (after its sale to HSBC). A *Washington Post* story summarizing the agreement indicates some of this industry's perverse practices:

> Ameriquest loan officers will be required to tell borrowers such things as what a loan's interest rate will be, how much it could rise and whether the loan includes a prepayment penalty. Loan officers who do not make that disclosure will be subject to discipline. The company would also be forbidden from giving sales agents financial incentives for pushing consumers into higher-interest loans or prepayment penalties.[9]

Why payday and subprime lending grew

The payday and subprime markets took off when lenders were able to move this paper systematically off their balance sheets. Using new technologies of securitization and risk-pooling, megabanks began converting this credit into instruments that wealth-holding institutions seeking above-market returns (and thus higher-risk assets) would readily accept. Wall Street investment banks channeled ever more funds to subprime lenders; indeed, these securitizations already averaged $80 billion annually by 1998 and 1999. Figure 6.3 illustrates the upward spike as of the late 1990s in mortgage-holding by "individuals and others," a category that consists primarily of jumbo and subprime mortgages. Further, Wall Street insurers backed the securities that subprime lenders sold off.[10]

Some bank holding companies purchased subprime lenders and finance companies. Citicorp acquired Associates First Capital Corporation, which was then under investigation by the Federal Trade Commission and the Justice Department.[11] Associates First represented a step toward Citi's goal of establishing its Citifinancial subsidiary as the nation's largest consumer finance company.[12] This consumer-lending subsidiary stabilized Citi's cash-flow during a period in which most megabanks' earnings slumped.[13] So, by the early 2000s, payday and subprime lending markets were ever more intertwined with megabank operations and securities markets.

Enabling these macro-market changes was a new consumer-banking business model for lower-income households: riskier customers were provided access to credit in exchange for either fees paid up front, or for loans made on the basis of attachable assets. Since homes are most households' primary asset, the growth of the subprime mortgage lending market is readily grasped. The logic of the payday loan industry is very similar – next month's paycheck serves as a guarantee against loss. Data for the period 1989–2004 from the Survey of Consumer Finances shows that households in the two lowest-income quintiles have had surging levels of debt, not paralleled by proportionate increases in asset levels.

In sum, by the end of the 1990s, banks – and their proxies and subsidiaries – rushed to make and securitize subprime and payday loans in inner-city areas. Both prime-heavy and subprime-heavy areas were awash with credit: the difference was that much of the debt in subprime-heavy areas was contracted at terms and conditions that threatened borrowers' future financial sustainability. Indeed, banks and markets learned to regard aggressive and even expectationally unsustainable terms and conditions on borrowers as normal business practices. And these practices soon migrated from inner-city areas to the broader markets.

From the Margins of the City to the Core of Global Finance

The initial premise of mortgage securitization was the homogenization of risks: bundling involved loans to borrowers who were expected to pay, and whose risks were readily calculable and implicitly backed by the federal government through government-sponsored enterprises. The 1990s and 2000s, however, transformed this premise. Heightened competition in financial markets, more risk-tolerance, and increases in computability permitted lenders to originate and sell off heterogeneous loans, sometimes made to borrowers whose longer-term viability was doubtful. Fees, penalties, and margins were set sufficiently high that these loans would turn a profit even if the lender–borrower relationship broke down. Figure 6.4 illustrates the emerging system for originating and distributing risk. A subprime lender makes mortgage loans, and sells them to banks that securitize them. This lender is most likely funded by money-market borrowing. Note that no bank or thrift appears: in effect, banks simply connect originators with investors. A bank can be a mortgage originator; but mortgage originators need not be banks.

Increasingly, the buyers of the loans thus originated were structured investment vehicles (SIVs).[14] Whereas plain-vanilla mortgages had formerly been bundled into securities with relatively homogeneous risks, now many different forms of collateralized debt could be combined on the asset side of SIVs. This permitted diverse forms of paper to be moved off lenders' balance sheets. The liabilities used to support SIVs also became more complex. Funds might be obtained from private equity funds, hedge funds, or money markets (especially the commercial paper market). SIVs, unlike pass-through securities, were opaque; and it was not clear whether their holders took on underlying default risk. Relative transparency associated with pass-through securities was eviscerated in most SIVs. Whether this meant that investors in SIVs were taking on the default and other risks implicit in such financial

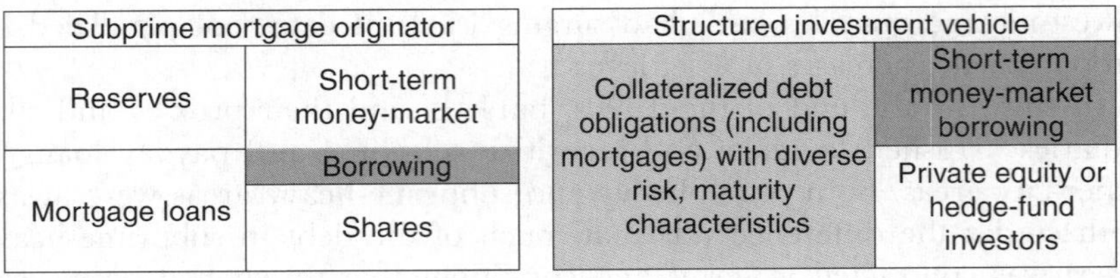

Subprime mortgage originator		Structured investment vehicle	
Reserves	Short-term money-market	Collateralized debt obligations (including mortgages) with diverse risk, maturity characteristics	Short-term money-market borrowing
Mortgage loans	Borrowing		Private equity or hedge-fund investors
	Shares		

Figure 6.4 Subprime lenders and structured investment vehicles
Note: Light grey shading indicates default risk and dark grey shading indicates liquidity risk.

instruments was unclear. Credit-risk derivatives were used in many cases to shift these risks onto third parties.[15] In any case, SIVs quickly became a $400 billion industry. As the *Wall Street Journal* put it, SIVs "boomed because they allowed banks to reap profits from investments in newfangled securities, but without setting aside capital to mitigate the risk."[16]

Once securitization markets learned to accept asset heterogeneity not backed by iron-clad underwriting, the door was open for the further evolution both of mortgages and of securities. The financial markets were no strangers to non-homogeneous risks in securitized mortgage debt. In the 1970s, REITs (real-estate investment trusts) had been marketed and sold to investors.[17] In many cities, residential real estate began climbing in value in the late 1990s, blossoming into a housing price boom in the 2000s. Those who had homes wanted bigger ones; those who did not wanted to enter the housing market. While the US has experienced other periods of sustained housing price increases, this one occurred amidst a global upsurge: many nations' housing prices rocketed upward far more than in the US. This fed the desperation to enter this market.

The fact that many potential buyers had neither the income nor the savings to support plain-vanilla mortgages created a special challenge. Encouraged by the continual upward shifts in housing prices, lenders created loans that compensated for the risks of homebuyers whose income and down-payment levels were falling increasingly short of time-honored price/income and down-payment-percentage benchmarks. Loans were made for more than 80 percent of their homes' prices; or buyers were given two loans, one for the 80 percent – making the loan potentially sellable to FNMA – and another for the remaining 20 percent of the sales price. Loans were increasingly made at below-market "teaser" rates for the first two years of a mortgage (Wray 2007: 9). When the "teaser rate" expired, any gaps over those two years would be amoritized, and the entire mortgage refinanced at a risk-adjusted market rate. The premise was that, with time, housing-price appreciation would eliminate the risks inherent in 100 percent-financed, below-market-rate home purchases.

The ever more valuable asset itself would permit the renegotiation of non-viable terms and conditions into sustainable longer-term payment streams.

Thus, subprime loans were increasingly made to homebuyers with income and down-payment resources that might have sufficed for plain-vanilla mortgages in the 1990s, but were no longer adequate in the 2000s. This was especially true in regional hot spots. But, in any case, while housing-market euphoria explains only part of the growth of the demand for subprime mortgage loans. Mortgage brokers manufactured some of it themselves. Brooks and Simon (2007), in a survey of those acquiring subprime mortgages in 2005 and 2006, found that 55 percent and 61 percent of these mortgagees, respectively, had credit scores high enough to obtain conventional loans. The fees earned by the mortgage brokers on these subprime loans were substantially higher than they would otherwise have been. In any event, brokers earned higher fees on subprime loans.

And if demand for funds was robust, funds were plentiful on the supply side of the housing finance market. Macro circumstances remained favorable: the US current account remained strongly negative, so that funds continually funneled into the US through its capital accounts. Foreign fund-holders were familiar with US mortgage-backed securities, which had been the largest global securities market for over a decade. Many European banks rushed to buy subprime paper.[18] While East Asian sovereign wealth funds did not,[19] their marginal demand for more Treasuries kept US interest rates low and, thus, indirectly sustained the subprime market.

Micro-circumstances also favored a ready supply of subprime loans. As noted, megabanks were offloading risk and shifting to fee-based income. Hyper-competition broke out among these lenders. Anderson and Bajaj (2007) describe the "once-lucrative partnership" between Wall Street and subprime lenders. These authors quote a Wall Street insider, Ronald Greenspan, as follows: "There was fierce competition for these loans … They were a major source of revenues and perceived profits for both the investors and the investment banks."

Some banks slowed their involvement as the market moved toward its mid-2005 peak; Credit Suisse, for example, reduced its underwriting in 2006 by 22 percent compared with 2004. Others plunged ahead. Morgan Stanley increased its subprime underwriting by 25 percent between 2004 and 2006, developing a special relationship with New Century Financial, a large subprime lender. According to these reporters, Morgan paid above-market so as to lock in a monthly flow of $2 billion from this firm alone. New Century, whose subprime loans' delinquency rate was twice that of Wells Fargo, filed for bankruptcy in March 2007. Anderson and Bajaj quote Jeffrey Kirch, president of a firm that buys home loans, as saying, "The easiest way to grab market share was by paying more than your competitors."

These arrangements were lucrative; total 2006 compensation for managing directors in investment banks averaged $2.5 million.

Subprime loan volumes exploded in 2004–06, even as the housing boom peaked. In the 2001–03 period mortgage originations totaled $9.04 trillion, of which 8.4 percent were subprime loans; and 55 percent of subprime originations, or $418 billion, were securitized. In the 2004–06 period total mortgage originations were the same in nominal terms, $9.02 trillion. However, 19.6 percent of all originations consisted of subprime loans, of which 78.8 percent – some $1391 billion – were securitized.[20] Figures 6.1 and 6.3 demonstrate the impact of this surge on mortgage-holding – note the huge spike in the "individuals and others" categories in both graphics. Figure 6.2, in turn, shows the spectacular surge in real mortgage volumes from 1999 to 2006: this chart demonstrates that in this period, real mortgage growth exceeded real-GDP growth by more and for longer than it had previously done.

The inherently flexible and non-transparent nature of SIVs soon opened the door for more types of credit.[21] For example, private equity funds required a huge volume of bridge loans to support their efforts to undertake leveraged buyouts of ever-larger target firms; many such loans were incorporated into SIVs. So too were other categories of firm and household loan.

How Subprime Lending Became "Rational"

We now shift from the historical basis of this crisis to two conceptual problems: first, why analysts specializing in credit and finance so completely misassessed (or simply missed) the riskiness of subprime lending; second, why explanations that trace the subprime crisis back to moral hazard forced onto lenders by political factors, such as Community Reinvestment Act requirements that lenders make loans in lower-income and minority areas of cities, are mistaken. As it happens, these two problems are interlinked.

As noted in the introduction, there are two keys to attacking these two problems. First, we must take into account the historical development of economic theories of lending to highly risky, inner-city areas – that is, to put economic theory itself into historical context. We do this by first sketching out a well-known model of the credit market. This model readily explains why lenders have redlined minority and/or high-minority neighborhoods. We can use this model to explain how previously excluded customers and areas were granted access to credit in the late 1990s. We then go further and explain how, in the early 2000s, this access to credit was granted on increasingly easy terms.

The second key to the analysis undertaken below is to distinguish between lender-based and finance-based approaches to the credit market. This contrast involves differentiating the asymmetric-information approach of Stiglitz and Weiss (1981) from the complete-information, efficient markets approach that underlies the modern theory of finance. Emphasizing this distinction will help to explain why economists missed the hyper-riskiness of subprime (and other adventurous forms of home-purchase) credit, and also why explanations that cast blame on government-sponsored enterprises such as FNMA or on the CRA are unconvincing.

Two credit-market approaches: efficient markets and asymmetric information

Economists prefer to develop explanations based on the motivations, constrained choices, and incentives of participants interacting in markets. Some begin with the premise that agents supplying and demanding goods can achieve socially optimal allocations autarchically; others postulate that government regulations and mandates may be needed to generate social optima.

Two basic approaches dominate contemporary models of credit markets: the efficient market and asymmetric-information approaches. The efficient market framework builds on the idea that buyers and sellers in credit markets (and in secondary markets for credit instruments) generally operate with common information sets. These agents cannot avoid the risks stemming from the fact that some outcomes are not known in advance. But agents' rationality leads them to construct the most reliable possible expectations about such outcomes. When some agents know less than others, the less-informed agents can use market prices as an indicator of what better informed agents know. The efficient market view of credit markets leads to the conclusion that, except in special circumstances, unconstrained market processes generate the highest feasible levels of economic welfare for society. Forced participation in markets should be avoided and free movement into and out of market transactions permitted to the fullest extent possible.

An alternative approach to credit markets assumes instead that critically important information for rational decision making is unequally distributed between potential participants. This creates a principal–agent problem, wherein one party (the principal) controls a scarce resource (in this case, access to credit); but he or she can only extract value from this resource by contracting (with borrowers) to work with this scarce resource. If principals had full information about the capability and intentions of those agents, principals could use the market to efficiently choose agents. But they don't. Principals are, by assumption, not fully informed prior to contracting about agents' capabilities, intentions, or both. Agents need the principal's resource, and thus cannot be trusted to disclose information about themselves truthfully.

In the credit market, potential borrowers may have informational advantages of two kinds over lenders: information concerning their competence, which affects their probability of success (their "type"); and their plans for using and repaying the loans they receive, which affect the likelihood of repayment (their "effort"). Because of information asymmetry (of either kind), lenders cannot rely on market forces *per se* to achieve optimal outcomes. Suppose there are more agents demanding credit than a bank is able to supply. First consider the case in which a lender faces borrowers of variable competence. If the lender raises the borrowing rate to reduce the quantity of credit demanded, the quality of the borrower pool is likely to decline, because more competent applicants are more likely to withdraw. This is the problem of adverse selection. Now consider the case in which the lender fears that borrowers may use the monies obtained for overly risky projects. Again market forces *per se* don't resolve the problem, since borrowers can do whatever they want once they get the money. This is the problem of moral hazard.

Many analysts have discussed how lenders can best respond to these problems. Here, we can focus on two responses that will limit the damage from each. Faced with adverse selection, the lender will seek out indicators (signals) of which borrowers may be better than others; faced with moral hazard, the lender will fund only a portion of credit demand, so that those funded understand that other prospective borrowers will take their places if they behave badly. Fundamental in the asymmetric-information approach is that lenders are able to set prices. That is, lenders do not confront given levels of risk, which they must price appropriately; instead, the loan rates that lenders decide on determine the riskiness of the loans they make.

Explaining redlining and subprime lending in urban areas

We mentioned above that federal mortgage policy redlined minority neighborhoods until the 1960s, by refusing to underwrite mortgages in areas with many minority residents. At this point, we need to introduce a second definition of redlining, based not on Federal Housing Administration guidelines set aside in the 1960s, but instead on lender behavior that has been disputed from the 1970s to the present. Lenders redline when they charge higher interest rates to, or reject loan applications more frequently from, residents and local businesses (or those intending to become residents and local businesses) of minority-dominated areas within cities.[22] For example, redlining would arise if White-owned businesses located in high-minority neighborhoods were charged higher interest rates on their loans than White-owned businesses in all-White neighborhoods. Similarly, when redlining occurs, Black homeowners in a low-income inner-city neighborhood are more likely to be turned down for a home-repair loan than economically identical Black homeowners in an affluent suburban neighborhood.

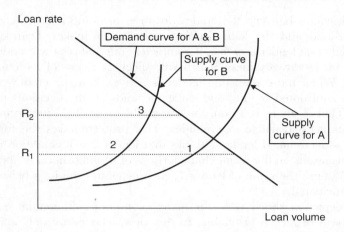

Figure 6.5   Redlining and subprime outcomes in a credit market

A 1981 article in the *American Economic Review* by Stiglitz and Weiss provided a theoretical framework for credit-market behavior under asymmetric information and explicitly addressed the phenomenon of redlining. They posited that there are two neighborhoods, with residents who differ in terms of their race and also their average riskiness as borrowers. Suppose the minority neighborhood is deemed riskier, for two reasons: first, the fundamentals (competence) of potential borrowers who live there are worse (adverse selection); second, potential borrowers there are more likely to use loans obtained for overly risky purposes (moral hazard).

If lenders offer just one borrowing rate, then redlining emerges as an optimal response to this situation. Figure 6.5 provides a graphical depiction. Suppose there are two neighborhoods, A and B; and for simplicity, residents of both A and B have identical demand curves for housing credit. The bank lender serving these neighborhoods views B as riskier, for reasons just noted. Thus, it constructs one supply curve for A and another for B. At any interest rate, it is willing to offer B residents only a fraction of the credit that A residents are offered. Suppose R_l is the lender's profit-maximizing loan rate. In this case, the lender will make loans from the origin to point 1 for A, and from the origin to point 2 for B. Neighborhood B gets less credit because it is inherently riskier (adverse selection); and there are more unserved credit customers waiting in line – and disciplining those who do get credit – in B than in A (moral hazard).

We have described Figure 6.5 as pertaining to one lender; and of course it is likely that several lenders will be active in any city and even in every neighborhood. Introducing more than one lender generates a new set of possibilities in our simple scenario. It is reasonable to suppose there are feedback effects between the creditworthiness of home loans made in any neighborhood and the loan decisions any lender makes (Dymski 1995). When only one lender is active, it completely internalizes these endogenous impacts on creditworthiness, which will affect the locus of its loan-supply curve(s). When more than one lender is active, then the creditworthiness scenario confronted by any one lender depends on the decisions made by others. That is, there is a coordination problem involved in capturing the credit market's available externalities. This problem takes the form of a prisoner's dilemma. If lender 1 thinks that lender 2 will condition its loan-market decisions on the racial characteristics of neighborhood A and B, and lender 2 thinks the same of lender 1, each generates the loan behavior the other anticipated.

This depiction shows why, for many economists, differential treatment on the basis of race is justifiable. In this view, lenders are only apparently conditioning their behavior on the contrasting racial compositions of neighborhoods A and B: instead, lenders are reacting to creditworthiness factors that are correlated with race. In this view, lenders should not bear the costs of racial differentials that work to the disadvantage of minorities; that they react to these differentials is not problematic (Dymski 2006).

We can now turn back to Figure 6.5 to show analytically how the introduction of predatory lending affects the Stiglitz and Weiss outcome. As long as lenders set one loan rate for all borrowers, they react to what they assess to be the greater riskiness of minority areas by establishing far higher denial rates in minority areas than elsewhere. Suppose, however, that the lender is willing and able to make loans at a higher rate than for its "mainstream" customers. In Figure 6.5, the lender offers loans to its higher-risk – neighborhood B – customers at rate R_2. The lender may also require higher fees; while not shown here, such fees would shift the neighborhood-B supply curve "out" (to the right), all else equal.[23] The equilibrium for subprime loans – or for other higher-rate, higher-risk loans – would be at point 3. Note that the volume of funded subprime loans (from the origin to point 3) would be more than the volume of mainstream (prime) loans formerly made in neighborhood B (origin to point 2); but the rate is, of course, substantially higher. In this very simple case, neighborhood B essentially gives up on its tenuous claim on any share of the mainstream market, in exchange for a larger volume of higher-cost loans. Since some of the loans now made in B at rate R_2 were previously made at R_1, this shift introduces predatory lending into B. Some of the loans the lender makes there are at higher rates than could be charged in equilibrium if the affected borrowers lived in another neighborhood.

Figure 6.5 represents, in effect, the 1990s phase of subprime lending. In the 2000s, as we have seen, both the secondary market for securities comprised (in whole or part) of subprime mortgages grew substantially, and so too did

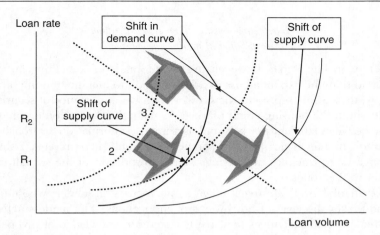

Figure 6.6 Demand and supply shifts in the mortgage market during the 2000s due to housing/securitization boom

the volume of subprime loans. As noted above, this expansion involved shifts on both the demand and the supply sides of the housing-credit market. On one hand, households (and investors) convinced that housing prices could never fall became willing to take on higher and higher loan burdens relative to their income levels; borrowers also became more dependent on high-risk mortgage loans because they *were* riskier. Figure 6.6 shows the implication: the demand for housing credit shifted decisively out to the right.

Had the credit supply curves stayed in place, mortgage rates would have risen and slowed the growth of home purchases. But the supply curves did not remain in place. Instead, the widespread use of credit-default swaps led banks to believe that their subprime loan positions were insured. Further, structured investment vehicles and lenders themselves increased their purchases of mortgage-backed securities. This enhanced demand increased banks' desire to supply this paper to the market (or to their own off-balance-sheet SIVs). That is, as Figure 6.6 shows, the two credit-supply curves also shifted out (to the right).

All these rightward shifts in Figure 6.6 increase the volume of housing credit. Whether interest rates in the mainstream or subprime segments of this market rise or fall depends on whether supply shifts outpace demand shifts. Figure 6.6 does not resolve this, nor are new market-rate equilibria drawn; instead, points 1, 2, and 3 from Figure 6.6 – the former equilibria – are preserved for reference. Note that the growth of subprime credit helped to invert the prisoners-dilemma starvation of bank lending in formerly red-lined areas. Before, banks would be reluctant to make any loans in inner-city areas; now, there was substantial fee-based income to be made there.

Interpreting housing finance securitization
as an efficient market phenomenon

The shifts in Figure 6.6, however, are symptomatic of something far more profound than the expanded use of housing credit to fuel the housing bubble. That is, these shifts represent the growing relative importance of securitized credit within the housing-credit market. As such, the distinction emphasized above between efficient markets and asymmetric-information approaches to the credit market is not just a theoretical curiosum: it represents a shift in the operating principles underlying a large proportion of the overall credit market in the 2000s.

The "bank-based" approach taken above focuses on lenders whose price-setting makes the level of borrower risk endogenous. The lenders active in loan-making had incentives to strive for accurate knowledge of prospective borrower's present and future creditworthiness; for this would permit them to make loan deals at terms reflecting borrower risk (rightly or wrongly calculated). So lenders themselves set up "mainstream" credit markets for low-risk customers, and "subprime" (and possibly predatory) markets for those unable to qualify for (or denied the chance to apply for) the mainstream market. There would be an entire cascade of such markets.

However, the shifts shown in Figure 6.6 created a brave new world of lending – the "originate and distribute" model. This model shifts the locus of control away from lenders engaged in efforts to manage risk under asymmetric information, and toward securities markets concerned with the bundling and pricing of given levels of risk. Increasingly, lenders simply executed deals to whose consequences they were relatively indifferent. And why not? The credit so created was to be insured against and held in third-party portfolios (or off-balance-sheet, at the very least).

This shift in the locus of control in credit markets, and in perceptions of market participants' roles, was appreciated amidst the heady atmosphere of the securitized-lending boom of the 2000s. Participants and analysts imagined that they were reinventing banking. Fender and Mitchell (2005a: 2) argued that structured finance overcomes "adverse selection and segmentation." Jobst (2003) asserted that collateralized loan obligations (one form of structured finance) reduce risk for investors and make investment less costly. He wrote,

> As the origination of loans and portfolio investment is unbundled, the *risk-oriented determination of credit conditions and increased efficiency in the lending process through standardized credit terms are essential components* of a new organizational model of bank lending. (Jobst 2003: 79–80)

In this new model of bank lending, one key question was unanswered: what was the *raison d'etre* for banks in this regime? Banks were no longer needed, per Diamond's (1984) model, as "delegated monitors," able to capitalize on economies of scale in acquiring information about prospective borrowers. Instead, it seemed that credit-rating agencies could evaluate risk more efficiently than banks. Banks could, thus, offload their credit-evaluation function and instead play the roles of bundler and distributor of securities. But banks *per se* were not uniquely qualified to perform these diminished roles. Instead, they had become inessential. This inessentiality reflects Fama's (1980) view that banks can have no effect on outcomes in efficient financial markets. And indeed, the key to understanding how credit securitization worked is to see that banks' core functions were now performed by agents integrated into centralized financial markets.

A more satisfactory conceptual basis for structured finance emerges in the complete-information world of efficient markets theory. Oldfield provides the clue when he writes, "Briefly, an underwriter must defeat arbitrage between pass-throughs and derivatives" (2000: 445). If information were complete, transactions costless, assets infinitely scaleable, and a complete set of contingent (derivatives) markets existed, then no structured finance could arise: any agent seeking the particular combination of risk–return characteristics available through the acquisition of a given set of securities could efficiently acquire those securities him- or herself – no intermediary (that is, no seller of a structured investment vehicle) would be needed by any wealth-owning agent. The SIV can efficiently exist only if it embodies a set of contingent and underlying claims that a wealth-owner cannot access directly. The efficiency of the SIV can thus be due either to transaction costs, the imperfect scaleability of assets, or both. In effect, in this approach, structured finance vehicles help to make markets more complete. Oldfield writes:

> A structured finance transaction transforms a pool of more or less similar loans into a set of derivative instruments collateralized by the pool. An underwriter who structures a transaction has a simple purpose: to sell the set of derivatives for more money than a direct sale of the pool or a pass-through instrument alone would fetch. The underwriter accomplishes a transaction by establishing an independent entity, usually a trust, which becomes the mechanism for structuring the derivatives. This entity represents a passive financial intermediary. (2000: 446)

Partnoy and Skeel (2007: 11) describe this as using "financial engineering" to complete markets. The term "passive" in the above passage is not anomalous. For the efficient markets hypothesis as a whole characterizes financial markets as passive carriers of the price signals and fundamental values that are continually being determined in the "real" (non-financial) side of the economy. This, after all, is the essential message of the Modigliani-Miller theorem about the irrelevance of financial structure: financial structure (say, whether debt or equity is used to finance a firm's investment) doesn't matter because financial markets will unearth firms' true value(s) and price its financial assets accordingly.[24]

In this perspective, innovations such as subprime lending and securitization promise to improve credit allocation and to expand access to capital. For example, Fender and Mitchell (2005: 2) argue that structured finance overcomes "adverse selection and segmentation" while Partnoy and Skeel (2007) discuss how "financial engineering [can be used] to complete markets." They write: "Because synthetic CDOs ... essentially create new instruments, instead of using assets already on bank balance sheets ... complete markets by providing new financial instruments at lower prices." (2007: 11–12) On the side of borrowers, more complete markets provide a wider range of contractual choice.[25] As Barth *et al.* put it:

> Those individuals choosing adjustable-rate mortgages typically receive an initial interest rate that is lower than one with a fixed-rate mortgage, but then face the prospect of higher rates if market interest rates rise. At the same time, the development and wide use of credit scores for individual borrowers and credit ratings for individual issuances of mortgage-backed securities provided more information for both lenders and borrowers to better assess and price risk. (2008: 4)

This perspective on finance in capitalist processes leads to a peculiar impasse for those who study it. On one hand, finance is only a mirror of the real. This leads to the idea of the sector's passivity. But on the other hand, the work of analysts, brokers, and traders in financial markets is to reveal the correct set of relative prices for the financial assets emitted in support of real-sector activities. An incorrect price for any one financial asset relative to other assets' prices will be eliminated vigorously by arbitrage. So the financial sector is simultaneously a ruthless cauldron of competition.

For those committed to the efficient market perspective, the tension between the passivity and hyperactivity of the financial sector leads to only one analytical conclusion: if an asset has been sold and bought on a financial market, especially a liquid market with many buyers and sellers, any analyst or economist has to assume it is efficiently priced. The fact that it exists and is vigorously traded means that it has real value. For the financial sector relentlessly polices itself, using dog-eat-dog competitive processes to guard against any deviation from rigorous market logic. Thus, the perspective that financial markets are a passive reflection of real values leads to an analytical passivity in the evaluation of those markets' performance.

Those working within the efficient market framework, including those evaluating the rise of the new securitization-based credit channel, have indicated their discomfort in being forced into this analytical posture – albeit, within the constraints imposed by their adherence to this view. Unanswered questions arise about the securitization of subprime lending, which lead in turn to implicit warnings. For example, in the Diamond model, why do banks exist if they are not delegated risk-monitors? And if credit rating agencies were introduced into the Diamond world, efficiency requires that risk assessment be subject to competition, and that risk assessors be hired by the savers, not by the lenders. As it turns out, rating agencies were seen as "particularly significant in situations where investors face relatively high costs in assessing the structure and risk profile of a given instrument – that is, in structured finance" (Committee on the Global Financial System 2005: 3). But neither condition – competition in credit assessment and payment by buyers, not sellers, of assets – was met in the real world.

Turning to Oldfield, completing financial markets through offering hitherto-unavailable risk–return combinations requires his "passive intermediary" to assemble a dizzying array of derivative and stripped assets. In Oldfield's argument, the only way that an SIV can offer unique risk–return combinations to the market is by creating opaque combinations of the risk–return characteristics of the underlying securities. Doing this in a well-informed manner that permits the bundler or lender to make normal profits, in real time, would be a herculean task. Again, real-world passive intermediaries were not up to it.

The slim analytical literature on the emerging synthetic credit instruments reflects this ambivalence: on one hand, faith that rational behavior will ultimately generate efficient market outcomes; on the other, skepticism about the plausibility of what rational agents are being asked to do. An example is a 2005 paper on risks in structured finance by Fender and Mitchell (2005a), which includes the following passages:

> This paper ... argues that certain structural features of structured finance products raise special governance issues and create important risks that are not directly related to the default risk of the assets comprising the underlying portfolios, but which may ultimately be as important to the performance of structured finance products as are the default properties of the asset pool.
>
> ... structured finance instruments also transform risk in unique ways via the tranching of claims, generating exposures to different, transaction-specific "slices" of the underlying asset pool's loss distribution. As a result of this "slicing" and the contractual structures needed to achieve it, tranche risk-return characteristics can be quite difficult to assess. (1–2)
>
> Ratings, though important, are argued to be inappropriate for gauging the risk of structured securities, despite the fact that the complexity of structured finance transactions gives investors incentives to rely more heavily on ratings than for other types of rated securities. (8)

When this paper was published in the June 2005 issue of the *BIS Quarterly Review* (Fender and Mitchell 2005b), these passages were no longer included.

Why Economists Missed the Crisis

The doubts expressed above by analysts pre-committed to the efficient markets perspective did not leak into widespread skepticism among economists about the rationality of subprime lending and the securitization of credit. Rather, the efficient markets framework dictates that steps such as these toward market-completion must necessarily lead to more socially optimal equilibria. After all, subprime mortgages expand credit-market choice and permit more efficient financial risk-sharing. This positive assessment of subprime lending is embodied in assessments by Goolsbee (2007) and Gerardi *et al.* (2007). Most economists' conceptual pre-commitments also blinded them to the possibility that the subprime market had come into being not as a rational response to well-documented risk, but instead as a vehicle for predatory loans that could be made to communities whose members were cash-short and lacked access to competitive financial markets, and thus would even pay high or exploitative prices to gain access to liquid resources.

Not surprisingly, then, when the performance of securitized credit instruments began to erode, economists steeped in the efficient market perspective sprang to their defense: for these instruments must have emerged as solutions to credit-access problems, not as vehicles for rent extraction. For example, Downs (2007) and Calomiris (2007) initially denied that the emerging subprime crisis would do much damage. But as the crisis worsened, suspicion centered on the likelihood that market forces, which would otherwise have been perfect (and gotten the prices right), must have been interfered with. The problem could not be in the strategic thrust and institutional trajectory that had created subprime loans, but in impediments that knocked this trajectory off the path of market efficiency. Wallison and Calomiris, for example, discuss the "inherent conflict between their government mission and their private ownership" (2008: 1). Calomiris was more specific in an article written a month later; claiming that the subprime crisis arose because of

> agency problems in asset management. In the current debacle, as in previous real estate-related financial shocks, government financial subsidies for bearing risk seem to have been key triggering factors, along with accommodative monetary policy. (2008: 1)

This is not to suggest that all proponents of efficient markets place responsibility on government subsidies. Nor should the reader imagine that all such proponents adhere to doctrinaire versions of efficient market theory. Instead, the deeply held assumption that efficient market processes allocate capital well leads many to ask what might have knocked markets away from what should have been an optimal course of action. Those holding this assumption are unlikely to explore the possibility that the very development of markets – and not market oversight – is a root cause of the troubles being experienced. Quigley, for example, emphasizes inadequate regulation, which provided incentives for undue risk-taking. He writes:

> One does not need to invoke the menace of unscrupulous and imprudent lenders or of equally predatory borrowers to explain the rapid collapse of the mortgage market ... There were certainly enough unscrupulous lenders and predatory borrowers in the market, but the incentives faced by decent people – mortgagors and mortgagees – made their behavior much less sensitive to the underlying risks.
>
> How, you may wonder, could contracts with such poor incentives have evolved? To some extent, that remains a mystery. But to a large extent, the system worked just fine, as long as property values were rising and interest rates falling. (2008: 2–3)

Quigley opens up two possibilities beyond Calomiris's "perverse government policies" narrative: first, unscrupulous players could exploit the unwary and naive in under-regulated markets; second, people can be systematically fooled when caught in an asset bubble. Morris (2008) and Shiller (2008), in turn, offer versions of the first and second possibilities. The first possibility leads back, of course, to a call for more effective regulation. The second either leads us to Minskyian financial instability (Minsky 1986), or to the analytical impasse implicit in the efficient market view set out above. For if one is forced to conclude that markets are efficient due to competitive pressures that lead them to incorporate all available information into pricing and trading assets – except when they are not, because they are caught in an asset bubble.[26] We do not follow this line of reasoning further here – it leads either to an internal contradiction regarding how prices are formed, or to a rejection of efficient markets theory itself.

Are FNMA or the CRA to blame?

As the subprime crisis has deepened, some micro-level explanations have been offered that do take account of some portions of the historical development of home-mortgage lending. Indeed, they focus directly on communities most profoundly affected by subprime lending. However, rather than presenting a narrative like that developed above, in which mortgage securitization emerges step by step due to the US banking sector's crisis and strategic transformation, a counter-narrative is proposed. In this narrative, an efficient market for housing finance existed; but then government initiatives intended to interject social purposes or political factors into market outcomes interfered with the market and generated the subsequent subprime crisis.

This narrative emphasizes moral hazard. The notion is that lenders willfully made excessively risky loans because their impulses toward moral hazard were encouraged not restrained. This sort of explanation featured prominently in dissections of the 1980s savings-and-loan crisis; Kareken and Wallace (1978) and Kane (2007), among others, have argued that moral hazard problems brought down the industry. Among these problems were inadequate supervision of risk-taking owners and managers, revolving-door relationships between regulators and industry, and the perverse effect of deposit insurance – specifically, it insures depositors against excessive risk-taking by the intermediaries to which they have entrusted their funds. In the current crisis, this notion that some participants were insured against a concern about excessive risk by government guarantees has been repackaged. Specifically, FNMA and FHLMC, the two government-sponsored enterprises (GSEs) that operate in the housing finance realm, have been blamed for the plethora of unviable loans made in the recent housing bubble. For example, Wallison (2008) has argued that the GSEs engaged in purchases of excessively risky subprime loans because they enjoyed the umbrella of federal protection (if only implicitly).

This is a misreading of history. As noted in the above historical narrative, these entities initially facilitated the creation of the mortgage-backed securities market by underwriting "plain-vanilla" mortgage loans. This salvaged the US system of housing finance after the thrift collapse of the 1980s. However, as our narrative has recounted, the growth of non-"plain-vanilla" loans – jumbo loans and subprime loans, in particular – was underwritten by other entities. The GSEs participated only as purchasers of these bundled loans for their own portfolios. These purchases hardly drove the market. Figure 6.1 shows that during the immediate build-up to the subprime crisis, the period 2003–06, GSEs' share of mortgage holdings fell sharply.

Another assertion some analysts have made (Wallison 2009) is that the insertion of political criteria into the bank-evaluation process forced banks into irrational loan-making. Specifically, banks had to make loans to excessively risky borrowers to meet their CRA requirements.

Lenders' hands were forced: they are victims, not perpetrators. At face value, this argument is contradictory. How is it that banks willingly helped to create and expand the subprime market – through purchases of non-bank lenders, the creation of securitization departments, and so on – as key components of their strategic realignments and yet were pushed into it?

In addition, this explanation ignores history. For one thing, most subprime loans were not made by lenders required to report under the CRA (Center for Responsible Lending 2008). For another, the CRA has imposed soft, not hard, performance requirements on covered intermediaries. Third, the CRA became law in 1977, two decades before banks apparently started making hyper-risky loans in response to CRA (in that account). The fact is that the CRA itself was passed in response to the political demand of many inner-city organizations and residents that banks be forced to cease their credit starvation of inner-city areas – especially, their refusal to make home-purchase loans. CRA advocates fought against the spread of subprime loans and viewed them as contrary to the purposes of the Act (Engel and McCoy 2002).

Theoretical pre-commitments and understandings of the subprime crisis

A pre-commitment to an efficient markets perspective makes it difficult to construct an accurate micro-level understanding of how subprime lending came into being, and why it led to crisis. This is not a matter of most economists' excessive zealotry for free markets against all evidence, but rather a case in which economists are inclined to believe that deep markets with many participants are likely to better allocate resources than other methods. The shift of housing finance – and of the struggle for fair access to credit by historically excluded communities – from a bank-centered to a market-centered perspective, thus, plays to economists' preconception that more efficiency and better outcomes must be the result. And this view gets built into their interpretations of what happened and why.

Subprime lending is seen as one component of an emerging securitized credit system that forms a continuum with an integrated set of sophisticated financial markets. Economists' narratives about what could go wrong in such a system are then informed far more by inferences from theory than from institutional developments. Racial redlining does not receive even a mention in the economics references mentioned above, nor does predatory lending. There is also no exploration of the possible analytical or policy implications of the fact that racial minorities were disproportionately excluded from mortgage lending in the "plain-vanilla" era, disproportionately targeted for subprime loans and subject to foreclosure.

Similarly, banks' solvency crisis of the early 1980s and the transformation of banking strategy in the subsequent decade are not discussed; nor is there any analytical dissection of the consequences of the wholesale securitization and recombination of a large proportion of the economy's credit contracts. Instead, in this approach, analysis of incentives, asset bubbles, and government–market interaction is sufficient to formulate hypotheses about "what went wrong."

This explains why the shift from a bank-centered to an efficient market perspective on credit markets is so fundamentally important in this history: a theoretical approach that incorporates analytical suspicion that markets may malfunction due to fraud, ignorance, or inequality is replaced by one that assumes expanding market linkages should always bring us closer to having the best outcomes in the best and most efficient of all possible worlds. The fact that neither theoretical approach was well-prepared to incorporate the implications of the profound institutional changes in the generation and distribution of mortgages from the mid-1990s to the mid-2000s only shows that economic models formulated too close to pure theoretical cases are not easily adapted to explaining institutional dynamics in the real economy.

Conclusion

We have argued here that the micro-level explanations of the subprime crisis that have dominated debate represent a very unsatisfactory and incomplete view of what happened and why. Our challenge to these explanations has unfolded in two steps. First, we have shown that the strategic transformation of banking led step-by-step to the current crisis. The behavioral shifts that banks made in the 1980s permitted them to generate substantial lending risks without absorbing them. In the 1990s, this allowed the transformation of racial exclusion in US credit markets. A scenario of loan denial was replaced by one in which minority households were awarded high-cost, high-risk loans. In the early 2000s, these predatory loan-making practices were adapted and brought into the broader housing market. This led, on one hand, to the unsustainable explosion of prices in the US housing market and, on the other, to unsustainable pressure on market liquidity. In sum, the perverse interaction between America's legacy of racial discrimination and social inequality and its hyper-competitive, world-straddling financial sector were among the triggers of the subprime crisis.

Second, we have explored what is lacking in other micro-level explanations of the subprime crisis. The root of the problem is that two competing and incompatible logics are used to explain creditor–borrower relations: a bank-centered credit-market approach; and an investor-centered financial-market approach. One approach assumes information is inherently flawed and that lenders must discipline borrowers; the other assumes information is boundlessly available and that borrowers can find lenders who will accommodate their risk characteristics. What happened is that the lending model used to describe lending to "inherently risky" urban areas shifted: the Stiglitz and Weiss model was readily adapted to explain why credit starvation in some areas was an optimal and inevitable outcome; but a financial-market-based model was used to explain how securitization could bring credit to previously redlined areas and people. So those focusing on the growth of securitized debt did not work with the problematic of lenders' control of risk: their governing approach asserted that lenders should price risk properly, not control it. Those focusing on principal–agent models of lender-rationed risk failed to consider the implications of the emergence of a class of lenders indifferent to risk.

This approach makes it readily apparent why the moral hazard and political-force approaches are misbegotten: both assume that lenders "got it wrong" and need to be disciplined. But these are ex-post explanations predicated on an ex-ante lending environment whose dismantling was a precondition for the very lending these analysts are trying to explain. Working from an alternative model of the subprime lending boom, which emphasizes the strategic transformation of banking, provides a more accurate picture of what happened. Borrowers fearful they would not otherwise qualify for credit allowing them into the housing market were glad to have the money. Lenders assumed they were inoculated against the risks these borrowers' loan and income positions posed. Financial market analysts believed that a new model of banking had emerged; one based on securitized lending flows governed by experts' assessments of risk. Since experts had evaluated these securities' risk, their opacity to everyone else was of no concern.

Clearly, this chain of events and interactions created a rationality for subprime lending that had nothing to do with the Community Reinvestment Act (CRA). The CRA had existed for nearly two decades before subprime loans were created. The notion that banks were forced into the crisis by loans made against their will is superfluous; banks made these loans willingly, due to the fortuitous intersection between the rise of a new lending model for home mortgages, the emergence of a new approach to banking strategy, and the explosion of securitization.

In sum, this chapter has tried to introduce some historical perspective into the micro-level understanding of why the subprime crisis came about. The history uncovered here has suggested patterns that warn us against the theoretical pre-conception that build in the assumption that market forces work well unless political forces or social concerns interfere. Reality tends to be far more complicated, as in the case considered here. And expositions of any history, including that of the subprime lending boom and bust, do not lend themselves to simple lessons about how best to draw the line between government and market. But if that history, however complicated, is ignored, then the historically contingent can be mistaken for the timeless.

Notes

1   This chapter does not address arguments about myopia, nor other causes of the current crisis, such as global imbalances, regulatory failures, and financial instability. Instead, see Dymski (2009, 2010).

2   A third agency, the Government National Mortgage Association (GNMA or Ginnie Mae), provided a secondary market for FHA, VA, and FmHA mortgages.

3   FNMA and FHLMC did not underwrite all mortgages in the 1980s. Several private mortgage insurers provided underwriting for "jumbo" mortgages that exceeded FNMA's maximum mortgage size.

4   Another factor keeping mortgage flows resilient was the United States' unique position within the global neoliberal regime, which could be traced to the fact that the US was both a supplier of global reserve currency and a safe haven in this period. See Dymski (2009a).

5   Racial discrimination in credit markets occurs when economically identical borrowers are treated differently by lenders on the basis of borrower race.

6   The unbanked generated $6.2 billion in fees, an average of $200 per household per year, in the early 2000s (Katkov 2002). At that time, banks had only 3 percent the remittance market (Orozco 2004).

7   The statistics on payday lending in this subsection are drawn from Bair (2005).

8   Also see United States HUD (2000), Joint HUD-Treasury Task Force (2000), Staten and Yezer (2004), and McCoy and Wyly (2004).

9   Downey (2006).

10   Henriques and Bergman (2000).

11   In another case, First Union Bancorp bought the Money Store in June 1998. First Union subsequently closed this unit in mid-2000 due to massive losses (Berman *et al.* 2006). In 2003, HSBC bought the Household Finance Company, after settling charges that it had engaged in predatory lending.

12   Oppel and McGeehan (2000). One protest by a community advocate described Associates as "a rogue company [that] may alone account for 20 percent of all abusive home loans in the nation" (Oppel, 2001).

13   Sapsford *et al.* (2001a), *Business Week* (2002).

14   The first SIVs were created for Citigroup in 1988 (Mollenkamp, Taylor, and MacDonald 2007).

15   *The Economist* (2007). The largest of these was, of course, AIG.

16   Mollenkamp, Solomon, Sidel, and Bauerlein (2007).

17   Indeed, REIT investments by the Franklin National Bank led to its 1974 failure (Sinkey 1981).

18   See, for example, Mollenkamp, Taylor and McDonald (2007).

19   "China exposure to U.S. subprime ills limited." *Reuters*, August 28, 2007. Web-accessed on December 10, 2007 at http://www.reuters.com/article/gc06/idUSPEK26110220070828

20   See Table 1 of Wray (2007: 30).

21   As Hyman Minsky put it in a 1987 memo on securitization that Randy Wray unearthed at the Levy Institute, "That which can be securitized will be securitized" (see Wray 2007: 5).

22   Redlining intersects in important and subtle ways with racial discrimination. Dymski (2006) reviews the literature in this area. Holloway and Wyly (2001) provide a vivid example (using an Atlanta case study) of how spatial and individual effects can interact in subtle ways.

23   If indeed the lender shown in Figure 6.4 shifts from offering one loan rate to all its customers to offering two different rates – one to safer, and another to riskier, customers – then it is quite likely that *R1* would also have to be redrawn (most likely, lower than in its current location).

24   The argument in this paragraph is brilliantly exposited by Justin Fox (2009).

25   Ashton (2009) also explores the notion that subprime lending represents market completion.

26   This tension was already present in Shiller's 1989 book, *Market Volatility*. There, he attempted to show that markets were more volatile than was consistent with efficient market theory. To establish this empirically within the bounds of efficient market theory requires both a theory of price and a theory of expectations formation. There aren't enough degrees of freedom to derive both from empirical data. If one focuses on expectations, as Shiller did, then one has to grant that prices are set efficiently – that is, they passively reflect the real value of the firms whose assets are being traded.

References

ACORN (Association of Community Organizations for Action Now). (2000) *Separate and Unequal: Predatory Lending in America*. Sacramento, CA: California ACORN, October 31.

Anderson, J. and Bajaj, V. (2007) Wary of risk, bankers sold shaky debt. *New York Times*, December 6, p. A1.

Ashton, P. (2009) An appetite for yield: The anatomy of the subprime mortgage crisis. *Environment & Planning A* 41(6): 1420–41.

Bair, S. (2005) *Low-Cost Payday Loans: Obstacles and Opportunities*. Amherst: Isenberg School of Management, University of Massachusetts.

Barth, J.R., Li, T., Phumiwasana, T., and Yago, G. (2008) A short history of the sub-prime mortgage market meltdown. *GH Bank Housing Journal*.

Berman, D.K., Mollenkamp, C., and Bauerlein, V. (2006) Wachovia strikes $26 billion deal for Golden West. *Wall Street Journal*, May 8, A1.

Bradford, C. (2002) *Risk or Race? Racial Disparities and the Subprime Refinance Market*. Washington, DC: Center for Community Change.

Brooks, R. and Simon, R. (2007) As housing boomed, industry pushed loans to a broader market. *Wall Street Journal*, December 3, A1.

Business Week. (2002) The besieged banker: Bill Harrison must prove J.P. Morgan Chase wasn't a star-crossed merger. April 22.

California Reinvestment Coalition. (2001) *Inequities in California's Subprime Mortgage Market*. San Francisco: California Research Coalition.

Calomiris, C.W. (2007) 'Not (yet) a "Minsky moment." American Enterprise Institute website, accessed at http://www.aei.org/docLib/20071010_Not(Yet)AMinsky Moment.pdf.

Calomiris, C.W. (2008) The subprime turmoil: What's old, what's new, and what's next. Working paper, American Enterprise Institute October 1.

Canner, G.B., Passmore, W., and Laderman, E. (1999) The role of specialized lenders in extending mortgages to lower-income and minority homebuyers. *Federal Reserve Bulletin*, November: 709–23.

Center for Responsible Lending. (2008) CRA is not to blame for the mortgage meltdown. CRL Issue Brief, Washington, DC: Center for Responsible Lending, October 3. Accessed at http://www.responsiblelending.org/mortgage-lending/policy-legislation/congress/cra-not-to-blame-for-crisis.pdf on December 28, 2009.

Committee on the Global Financial System. (2005) 'The role of ratings in structured finance: issues and implications. Bank for International Settlements, Basel, Switzerland. January: 3.

Diamond, D. (1984) Financial intermediation and delegated monitoring." *Review of Economic Studies* 51: 393–414.

Downey, K. (2006) Mortgage lender settles lawsuit: Ameriquest will pay $325 million. *Washington Post*, January 24: D01.

Downs, A. (2007) Credit crisis: the sky is not falling. Policy Brief #164, Economic Studies, The Brookings Institution, October 31.

Dymski, G.A. (1988) A Keynesian theory of bank behavior. *Journal of Post Keynesian Economics*, 10(4): 499–526.

Dymski, G.A. (1995) The theory of bank redlining and discrimination: An exploration. *Review of Black Political Economy* 23(3): 37–74.

Dymski, G.A. (2006) Discrimination in the credit and housing markets: Findings and challenges. In: *Handbook on the Economics of Discrimination*, William Rodgers (ed.) Cheltenham, UK: Edward Elgar, pp. 215–59.

Dymski, G.A. (2009) Financial risk and governance in the neoliberal era.I In: *Managing Financial Risks: From Global to Local*, Gordon L. Clark, Adam D. Dixon, and Ashby H.B. Monk (eds.) Oxford: Oxford University Press, pp. 48–68.

Dymski, G.A. (2010) From financial exploitation to global banking instability: Two overlooked roots of the subprime crisis. In: *The Great Credit Crash*, Martijn Konings (ed.) London: Verso Press, pp. 72–102.

Engel, K. and McCoy, P.A. (2002) The CRA implications of predatory lending. *Fordham Urban Law Journal*, 29(4): 1571–606.

Fama, E. (1980) Banking in the theory of finance. *Journal of Monetary Economics* 6(1): 39–57.

Fender, I. and Mitchell, J. (2005a) Risk, complexity, and the use of ratings in structured finance. Working paper, Bank for International Settlements and National Bank of Belgium, March.

Fender, I. and Mitchell, J. (2005b) Structured finance: Complexity, risk and the use of ratings. *BIS Quarterly Review* June: 67–87.

Fox, J. (2009) *The Myth of the Rational Market*. New York: HarperBusiness.

Gerardi, K., Rosen, H.S., and Willen, P. (2007) Do households benefit from financial deregulation and innovation? The case of the mortgage market. Working Paper 12967, National Bureau of Economic Research, Cambridge MA: March.

Goolsbee, A. (2007) "Irresponsible" mortgages have opened doors to many of the excluded. *New York Times*, March 29: C3.

Gosselin, P. (2004) The poor have more things today – Including wild income swings. *Los Angeles Times*, December 1.

Henriques, D.B. and Bergman, L. (2000) Profiting from fine print with Wall Street's help. *Wall Street Journal*, March 15.

Holloway, S.R. and Wyly, E.K. (2001) The color of money extended: Geographic contingency and race in Atlanta. *Journal of Housing Research* 12(1): 55–90.

Information Policy Institute. (2005) *Giving Underserved Customers Better Access to the Credit System: The Promise of Non-Traditional Data.* New York: Information Policy Institute.

Jobst, A.A. (2003) Collateralized loan obligations: A primer. Mimeo, London School of Economics.

Kane, E.J. (2007) Dangers of capital forbearance: The case of the FSLIC and "zombie" S&Ls. *Contemporary Economic Policy* 5(1): 77–83.

Kareken, J.H. and Wallace, N. (1978) Deposit insurance and bank regulation: A partial-equilibrium exposition. *Journal of Business* 51(3): 413–38.

Katkov, N. (2002) *ATMs: Self-Service for the Unbanked.* Tokyo: Celent Communications.

McCoy, P. and Wyly, E. (2004) Special Issue on Market Failures and Predatory Lending. *Housing Policy Debate* 15(3).

Minsky, H.P. (1986) *Stabilizing the Unstable Economy.* New Haven: Yale University Press.

Mollenkamp, C., Solomon, D., Sidel, R., and Bauerlein, V. (2007) How London created a snarl in global markets. *Wall Street Journal*, October 18: A1.

Mollenkamp, C., Taylor, E., and McDonald, I. (2007) How the subprime mess ensnared German bank; IKB gets a bailout. *Wall Street Journal*, August 10: A1.

Morris, C. (2008) *Trillion-Dollar Meltdown.* Jackson, TN: PublicAffairs.

Oldfield, G.S. (2000) Making markets for structured mortgage derivatives. *Journal of Financial Economics* 57(3): 445–71.

Oppel, Jr. R.A. (2001) Citigroup to pay up to $20 million in deceptive-lending case. *New York Times*, September 7.

Oppel, R. and McGeehan, P. (2000) Citigroup announces changes to guard against abusive loan practices. *New York Times*, November 8.

Orozco, M. (2004) *The Remittance Marketplace: Prices, Policy and Financial Institutions.* Washington, DC: Pew Hispanic Center.

Partnoy, F. and Skeel, Jr. D.A. (2007) The promise and perils of credit derivatives. *University of Cincinnati Law Review* 75(2): 1027.

Quigley, J.M. (2008) Compensation and incentives in the mortgage business. *Economists' Voice*, October.

Sapsford, J. Cohen, L.P., and Langley, M. (2004) High finance: J.P. Morgan Chase to buy Bank One. *Wall Street Journal*, January 15: A1.

Shiller, R.J. (1989) *Market Volatility.* Cambridge, MA: MIT Press.

Shiller, R.J. (2008) *The Subprime Solution.* Princeton: Princeton University Press.

Sinkey, Jr., Joseph F. (1981) *Problem and Failed Institutions in the Commercial Banking Industry.* Greenwich, Connecticut: JAI Press.

Staten, M.E. and Yezer, A.M. (2004) Introduction to the Special Issue. Special Issue: "Subprime Lending: Empirical Studies." *Journal of Real Estate Finance and Economics* 29(4): 359–63.

Stiglitz, J.E. and Weiss, A. (1981) Credit rationing in markets with incomplete information. *American Economic Review* 71(3): 393–410.

The Economist. (2007) At the risky end of finance. August 21: 80–2.

US Department of Housing and Urban Development. (2000) Unequal burden: Income and racial disparities in subprime lending in America. Washington, DC: Department of Housing and Urban Development, April.

Wallison, P.J. (2008) Cause and effect: Government policies and the financial crisis. *AEI Outlook Series*. Washington, DC: American Enterprise Institute, November.

Wallison, P.J. (2009) The true origins of this financial crisis. *American Spectator*, February.

Wallison, P.J. and Calomiris, C.W. (2008) The last trillion-dollar commitment: The destruction of Fannie Mae and Freddie Mac. *AEI Financial Services Outlook*. Washington, DC: American Enterprise Institute, November.

Williams, R. (1999) The effect of GSEs, CRA, and institutional characteristics on home mortgage lending to underserved markets. HUD Final Report, December.

Wray, L.R. (2007) Lessons from the subprime meltdown. Working paper no. 522, Levy Economics Institute of Bard College, December.

Part III
Cities, Race, and the Subprime Crisis

7

Redlining Revisited
Mortgage Lending Patterns in Sacramento 1930–2004

Jesus Hernandez

Introduction

For quite some time, housing activists and scholars have documented the concentration of subprime loans in US neighborhoods highly populated with non-White residents (Bradford 2002; ACORN 2005), and the targeting of non-White borrowers by subprime lenders (Immergluck and Wiles 1999; Wyly *et al.* 2006). The racial and geographic concentration of subprime loans suggests that contemporary lending patterns may be repeating the punitive mortgage redlining practices of past years that aided the decline of many inner cities throughout the US. Squires (2005) notes that the exploitative terms of subprime loans and their concentration in non-White neighborhoods may be just as harmful as the race- and place-based withdrawal of financial services previously imposed on formerly redlined neighborhoods. This "reverse redlining" referred to by Squires, and the accompanying concentration of mortgage defaults and foreclosures, suggests a long-standing relationship between geography, race, and contemporary housing and credit markets.

Subprime lending can be simply described as mortgage credit with interest rates substantially higher than those for conventional financing. Generally, subprime lenders target borrowers who have poor credit histories with mortgage products that bring an unusually high yield to lending institutions and their investors. Such excessive profit margins, realized through a pricing structure that includes periodic interest rate increases, prepayment penalties, and balloon payments, place a heavy financial burden on

Subprime Cities: The Political Economy of Mortgage Markets, First Edition. Edited by Manuel B. Aalbers.
© 2012 Blackwell Publishing Ltd. Published 2012 by Blackwell Publishing Ltd.

borrowers. Consequently, subprime borrowers are six to nine times more likely to be in foreclosure (Renuart 2004; Schloemer *et al.* 2006; Girardi *et al.* 2007). Because homeowner equity remains the largest component of wealth for non-White households in the US (Oliver and Shapiro 1995; Conley 1999), subprime lending, with its higher propensity for foreclosures, undermines and discourages the wealth-building capacity of affected homeowners and targeted communities (Farris and Richardson 2004); a process that mirrors the disinvestment practices and the loss of wealth-building opportunities from past episodes of redlining. Contemporary lending patterns in cities, therefore, continue to reflect the uneven distribution of wealth in US communities while giving local racialized geographies an intergenerational quality. Consequently, the concentration of loans with high foreclosure rates brings a social and financial vulnerability to targeted neighborhoods leaving them highly unstable in times of economic crisis.

I use the county of Sacramento, California, an area populated by 1.2 million residents at the time of the 2000 Census, as the site to examine conditions that led to increased subprime loan activity and its concentration in racialized space; geography created by the historical process of organizing space along racial categories (Iglesias 2000; Haynes 2001). Four key practices established the racial geography that now defines the Sacramento area: the explicit use of racially restrictive covenants; the informal enforcement of those covenants; central city urban renewal programs; and mortgage redlining. Preliminary observations suggest that subprime loan activity is highly concentrated in neighborhoods with high ratios of non-Whites shaped by these long-standing practices of housing segregation. Moreover, housing industry information service providers, for example RealtyTrac, report that these neighborhoods currently experience some of the highest mortgage default and foreclosure rates in the US. These observations suggest a tendency to racialize the flow of housing finance capital and that housing finance capital flows are geographically related to historically racialized housing policies. Sacramento also provides a typical example of urban processes such as segregation and sprawl that shape the social and physical landscapes of cities throughout the US. For these reasons, Sacramento provides an opportunity to understand contemporary housing credit markets as part of a larger historical process that takes form socially as well as spatially.

Finally, the "greenlining" of credit-starved neighborhoods (see Newman Chapter 8 in this volume) signals a major change in housing finance policy and demonstrates how housing credit transforms historically undercapitalized sites of racial segregation to new sites of capital accumulation. This conversion of racialized space from a place of exclusion to a place of extraction is critical to understanding the changing role of race in the post-Civil Rights economy. This study, therefore, investigates how the fusion of both explicit and supposedly race-neutral or "colorblind" housing market practices set the stage for present-day subprime mortgage activity in the city of Sacramento.

Analytical Lens

I focus on the role of capital in urban inequality, the role of the state in market (re)organization, and the role of human agency and social interaction that guide policy and decision-making to investigate the deep-rooted patterns of spatial and racial inequality in the US. The merging of these three themes provides a powerful analytical lens through which to view the nexus of race and economy as a historical process that utilizes racial segregation to advance capital accumulation.

Harvey (1985) contends that space is produced actively with the primary force behind spatial production being capital accumulation. The process of uneven urban development is the result of different levels of return on investment in specific locations. Therefore, the market in land and buildings orders urban phenomena and determines what city life can be (Logan and Molotch 1987: 17). Consequently, the logic of profit-making governs spatial development with real estate markets being one of the key ways in which cities and regions grow (Gottdiener 1994).

However, we also know that markets do not operate independently as governments promulgate and enforce formal property rights through contract law so that those exchanging in the marketplace can create binding agreements that ensure the safety of their investment in property (Carruthers and Babb 2000). Property relations, therefore, become one of the ways in which states and economy intersect. Because the state's ability to manipulate property rights is historically important in shaping market organization (Campbell and Lindberg 1990), property rights can be seen as social relations that define who has claims on profits from the exchange of property (Fligstein 1996). Hence, governments assume a varied but active role in establishing the conditions for property exchange, market activity, and market outcomes.

Housing credit extends the manner in which the state controls the exchange of property rights in the market place. Gotham (2006) informs us that real estate, a fixed immobile asset, was made the object of a standardized transparent financial instrument exchangeable through global markets and that this new financial product largely remains a product of state action. Housing credit, through the process of securitization, is a fundamental part of this conversion and reflects the state's active involvement in the creation of markets, market products, and market demand. In this manner, housing credit extends the way in which the state oversees exchanges in the market place. The subprime loan market, therefore, is an important and telling example of the federal government's expanding role in the conversion of space to sites for capital accumulation.

We know that real estate market activity is not solely a function of private enterprise because it involves direct governmental action in many ways. From regulating property rights to facilitating the movement of capital flows between regions, the state's active role suggests that the creation of spatial environments reflects decisions based on the social, political, and cultural dimensions of our society (Gottdiener and Hutchinson 2006). Although individuals participate in markets, Squires (2002) correctly notes that public policy and the private sector constrain individual choice and guide market operations. Hence, we can see that changes to the urban environment are both socially and politically generated and mediated (Smith 1988; Squires 1989).

If we can consider economic action as socially situated (Granovetter 1985; Granovetter and Swedberg 1992), then the above theoretical notions provide important clues for investigating the role of human agency in the use of racial hierarchies to valuate space and in allocating housing credit. These clues give an understanding of the relationship between the social constructions of race and economy in the US, how they inform each other, and how they interact on multiple scales, that is spatial (local, regional, national, global) and social (individual, group, institution, society). Although these scales are distinct, there are dialectical relations between them that place the social critique at the center of economic analysis (Pulido 2004). This case study, then, focuses on how social factors directly influence the price of space (Logan and Molotch 1987) while legitimizing unequal access to market opportunities (Smith 1988). Through this lens, US housing markets can be seen as social constructions that reflect and aid in the managing of social relations in the city.

I follow the lead of Gotham (2002: 3) who situates the origins and growth of racial residential segregation within "the broader processes of capitalist development, the changing dynamics of real estate activities and investment, and federal housing programs." This allows us to see how housing inequality takes form through a partnership between politicians who shape public policy and the private sector that benefits from such policy, a partnership that does not always work equally for all urban residents. This partnership between polity and business comes at a great cost to urban neighborhoods, since they rarely see the positive effects of housing policy and privatism but rather the uneven economic development so typical of cities today (Squires 1989, 1994).

In Gotham's analysis, the uneven development and residential segregation that take place concomitantly in cities can be viewed as "analogous, reciprocally related, and mutually constitutive of each other" (Gotham 2002: 3). This view insists on acknowledging the linkage between race and markets. Accordingly, my analysis of subprime lending also considers how contemporary market structures and outcomes are connected to historical

events and processes of stratification. We can, therefore, view the US housing finance market as a racialized structure that produces racial inequity
through specific practices, mechanisms, and social relations (Bonilla-Silva,
1997; Dymski, Chapter 6).

Historically, race has long been associated with property value in the US.
During the 1920s, real estate professionals tied property values to color as
a means of legitimizing racial exclusion and protecting racial boundaries.
Realtors used racial categories in property valuation and promoted differential treatment as an industry standard during an early and critical stage
of US suburban growth (Helper 1969). Working from the notions that the
racial integration of a neighborhood can lead to a very rapid decline in
property value (McMichael and Bingham 1928), and that the value of land
partially depends on the racial heritage of the people living on it (Babcock
1932; Hoyt 1933), New Deal housing finance programs institutionalized
the use of racial categories in assigning space and allocating social goods
(Freund 2006).

Although New Deal housing finance programs were important in
modernizing the mortgage industry, two federal loan requirements promoting
segregation resulted from these programs and are significant for this analysis.
During the period 1930–50, Federal Housing Administration (FHA) home
mortgage programs mandated the use of racially restrictive covenants that
prohibited non-White occupancy of homes in White neighborhoods, and
FHA-mandated mortgage redlining prohibited the use of federally insured
mortgages in racially integrated neighborhoods (Freund 2006). The FHA
issued guidelines that specifically directed banks to use racially restrictive
covenants as an indicator of the stability and security of a neighborhood
when making lending decisions (Vose 1959; Bradford 1979; Jackson 1985;
Freund 2006). Under the pretext of reducing the risk exposure to lending
institutions, the FHA systematically excluded non-Whites from obtaining
home loans and openly used racial categories to exclude minorities from
suburban areas of growth (Stuart 2003; Freund 2006). Hence, the use of
race to determine eligibility for housing credit became both an accepted and
expected business practice. The evidence suggests that race functioned as a
key determinant for assigning households into neighborhoods (Weaver 1948;
Abrams 1955; Hirsch 1983; Haynes 2001), and that this intergenerational
process of racial sorting by geography occurred persistently in urban areas
throughout the US (Jackson 1985; Massey and Denton 1993; Cutler *et al.*
1999; Gotham 2000).

The incorporation of race into urban policy triggered a series of institutional
mechanisms that separated city residents according to racial categories. The
resulting residential segregation, best described as the residual effects of how
we designed our cities, has shaped and continues to shape the quality of
life experienced by members of different racial and ethnic groups. Hence,

residential segregation is an institution that took form through discriminatory government policies and local acts of racism, reflecting the desire
for segregated housing (Kushner 1980). This trend continued well into the
1960s until the urban riots forced institutional changes to federal and state
housing policy (Sugrue 1996).

Acknowledging the historical racialization of US housing markets at an
early and critical stage in the development of US cities helps us understand
how social context informs the construction of risk as a factor in accessing housing credit (Stuart 2003). Stuart argues that race-based differential
treatment in housing was simply reduced to a matter of risk assessment and,
as a result, an acceptable business practice formalized under the pretext of
protecting investment capital from perceived risk. Risk management was
translated into a mandate for exclusion achieved through the use of boundaries to organize and guide market access. It is this socially constructed
relationship between race and risk that remains at the root of historically
disparate housing opportunities in the US. Consequently, race maintains
a powerful role in the shape and opportunities of US cities, remains an
integral factor in urban development, and must be placed at the center of
serious urban analysis (Feagin 1998).

I use this analytical lens to investigate the pre-existing conditions that
contributed to concentrating subprime loans in specific localities and within
specific populations. I examine how these conditions work over time to
contribute to the current housing crisis in the US and reproduce the
geography of racialized space. Despite decades of housing finance reform,
which have managed to improve levels of minority homeownership and
access to mortgage credit, inequalities in access to housing credit somehow
remain concentrated in those geographies characterized by past forms of
deliberate racial segregation. Therefore, this study of contemporary housing credit markets in Sacramento can provide some insight to an emerging
intergenerational quality of race-based housing inequity and its potential
impact on neighborhoods in crisis.

Method and Data

I use a case study approach to investigate the concentration of subprime
loans within areas predominantly populated by non-White residents in
Sacramento. Yin (1994) recommends the case study approach when research
questions are more explanatory and are likely to deal with operational links
needing to be traced over time. Moreover, the case study has an ability
to deal with the full variety of evidence needed to explain why certain
phenomena, in this case racialization, take place over time and within a
particular place (Creswell 1998). Two important contemporary examples

of how the case study method is used to reveal the racialization of space as an historical and contested intergenerational process can be found in Bruce Haynes' study of suburban Runyon Heights (2001) and Kevin Gotham's study of Kansas City (2002). Haynes reveals how the historical formation of a community along racial lines set the stage for racially segregated educational, social, and religious institutional life. Gotham demonstrates how the segregationist ideology of real estate elites operated to link race and culturally specific behavior to place of residence. Like these examples, the racializing of housing credit in Sacramento is a phenomenon bounded by space and time rather than just a measurement of frequency.

The case study approach in this investigation provides the opportunity to reveal power-dependent relationships between race and market processes that occur over extensive periods of time and serve to manage the flow of capital to particular localities. Moreover, the case study approach reveals the racialized ordering of the city's social relations, the communities in which they take place, and "the historical structure of domination and subordination" (Smith and Feagin 1995: 4) that is characteristic of racializing space. Thus, the case study approach helps us to properly contextualize the settings in which the subprime loan industry operates in Sacramento and provides particular advantages in investigating the convergence of local and external forces associated with credit practices and how they interact to shape social and physical landscapes.

Using multiple data sources in this case study helps to properly contextualize the settings in which the subprime loan industry operates in Sacramento. I rely on original Home Owners Loan Corporation (HOLC) Residential Security maps and appraisal data from 1938, census data from 1950 to 2000, interviews with residents, and local government records to identify historically race-based market practices. I utilize a series of oral histories captured by community activists to document racialized housing practices of real estate professionals in Sacramento from 1950 to 1980. Newspaper articles, county records and conversations with real estate agents and escrow officers were used to compile a preliminary list of census tracts with racially restrictive covenants. The number of tracts with such covenants identified by my research appears conservative. The Sacramento County Assessor estimates over 2500 subdivisions with such covenants (Magagnini 2005). Although these tracts account for a small portion of what is now a large metropolitan area, at the time restrictive covenants were imposed they represented important areas of economic and residential expansion during the post-war suburban boom and reflected the overt use of racial categories in designating neighborhood boundaries. The geography of these restrictions aids our understanding of how racial categories impacted urban planning and housing finance decisions, and influenced patterns of residential settlement over time. However, an exact accounting of the use of these covenants throughout the county requires a more comprehensive research effort. The possibility exists that any failure to identify all tracts with restrictive covenants may unintentionally skew the findings of this research.

I use the 2004 Home Mortgage Disclosure Act (HMDA) data for Sacramento County consisting of 273,286 loan applications for the calendar year. The collected information includes loan type, loan amount, property location, loan disposition, loan fees, and applicant demographic information required for federal monitoring of lending activity throughout the US. Like previous research on subprime lending, I use the Department of Housing and Urban Development's (HUD) annual list of HMDA reporting lenders that specialize in subprime loans to identify subprime lenders and their activity in Sacramento County. Although problems exist with the HUD subprime lender list that may result in understating the actual influence of the subprime market (Lax *et al.* 2004; Calem *et al.* 2004), a review of the pertinent literature indicates that the HUD subprime lender list, when used with HMDA data, still represents the most widely accepted method in terms of identifying subprime loan activity. The year 2004 marks the peak of subprime loan activity in Sacramento.[1] Moreover, subprime loans originated in this year are for the most part the vintage of toxic loans that brought about the dramatic increase in foreclosures that took place in 2007. For these reasons, I focus on 2004 HMDA data. Finally, I compare ratios of subprime activity by census tract with the geographies of restrictive covenants and redlining.

The remainder of this chapter is organized as follows. Three sections discuss critical periods of change in the housing credit industry. The period 1930–50 reveals the initial period of redlining initiated by FHA and the official use of racial categories in determining access to housing credit that established racial segregation as an accepted practice in US cities. The period 1950–80 is marked by the effects of urban renewal programs, highway construction projects, the resulting mass relocation of non-White communities, the subsequent redlining of neighborhoods integrated as a result of these projects, and the actions of local real estate professionals. The period 1980–2004 brings to the fore the emerging subprime loan market and the concentration of these loans in racialized space created by national housing policy and private actions. For each period, I describe the role of national housing policy in creating conditions necessary for the subprime mortgage market to take hold in Sacramento. These sections are followed by a cartographic summary of 2004 HMDA data and concluding remarks.

Redlining Phase I: Racializing Housing Credit (1930–50)

Racially restrictive covenants in Sacramento took root in the 1920s when local developer J.C. Carly subdivided farmland for residential development just south of the city limits. Carly, one of the founding fathers of the local real estate board, followed in step with the National Association of Real Estate Boards (NAREB), which, during this period, mandated real estate agents to honor restrictive covenants and provided local real estate boards with templates for drafting covenants that created and maintained segregated neighborhoods (Helper 1969). County Assessor records show that Carly's residential developments used racial covenants and began a trend of overt discriminatory institutional actions to establish separate residential spaces for Whites. Hence, property value in Sacramento became associated with race as early as 1920.

New Deal housing programs, initiated in the 1930s, subsequently mandated the use of racially restrictive covenants as a condition of loan approval (Jackson 1985) to avoid introducing "incompatible" racial groups into White residential enclaves (Freund 2006). Developers of new suburban tracts in elite neighborhoods used racial covenants as a means to attract buyers as developers advertised the use of "wise restrictions" along with FHA Title II financing to assure buyers of the safety of their investment (Isidro 2005). Since FHA financing aided both construction and sales of new homes, developers of new communities in Sacramento during this period eagerly complied with FHA mandates for racial restrictions on residency by excluding non-Whites from housing tracts in elite neighborhoods and areas adjacent to the northern part of the city undergoing rapid growth. The use of FHA loan programs during this period institutionalized the practice of racial segregation in new suburban housing tracts throughout the city and county.[2]

By 1950, the distinct dual geographies of the city were clearly evident (see Figure 7.1). Racial restrictions on Sacramento residential real estate controlled the location of ethnic groups according to a perceived risk on property values. Segregation, therefore, became a method of risk containment sanctioned by federal housing credit policy as necessary to maintain the value of White residential space. Consequently, a racial divide grew that would eventually concentrate non-Whites in older, "non-restricted" residential tracts.

During this same period, federal housing policy also restricted the flow of housing capital into racially integrated neighborhoods (Jackson 1985). In Sacramento, the HOLC residential security map of 1938 identified the Sacramento neighborhood known as the "West End," the northwest area of downtown Sacramento between the State Capitol building on 10th Street to the east and the Sacramento River to the west, as the location that presented the primary risk to lenders (see Figure 7.1). The redlining of the West End severely altered the property owners' ability to finance repairs and maintain their property.[3] Moreover, with redlining preventing buyers from obtaining conventional or government-sponsored financing, West End property owners were unable to participate in normal real estate market practices.[4]

As suburban growth took hold and the city became more decentralized, the inability of West End property owners to participate in traditional

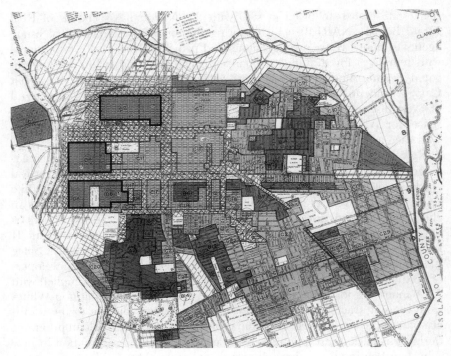

Figure 7.1 1938 Sacramento residential security map
Source: Federal Home Loan Bank Board, National Archives: Record Group 195; map courtesy of
T-Races [Testbed for the Redlining Archives of California's Exclusionary Spaces]).
Note: Redlined areas of the West End are identified by the highlighted borders.

market exchanges contributed to the drastic decline in the value of redlined
real estate. From 1938, the beginning of West End redlining by the FHA, to
1949, property in Sacramento experienced a 46 percent increase in value. But
during this same period, redlined property decreased in value by 30 percent
(Sacramento City Planning 1950). Clearly, the city's racialized geography
took shape around the ability to participate in housing markets. While the
FHA actively protected the property rights of the new homogeneous White
suburban communities, it prohibited non-Whites access to wealth accumulation opportunities gained only through housing credit and homeownership.

City redevelopment planning documents indicate West End property
owners resorted to converting homes into multiple units and obtaining
more rents to compensate for lost value. This transformed a neighborhood
designed for single-family occupancy to one of conversions for multiple-
family tenant use and accelerated the deterioration of the area's residential
quality. As a result, the greatest concentration of non-Whites in the city was

in the West End. Some city blocks in the West End were reported as having 90–99 percent of dwelling units occupied by non-Whites in 1940, a fact that planning documents attributed in part to the housing restrictions imposed by racial restrictive covenants. These strategically enforced racial restrictions on residency led absentee landlords to capitalize on market constraints by renting converted units to non-Whites unable to leave the neighborhood (Sacramento City Planning 1950).

Adding to the racial concentration in the West End was the signing of Executive Order 8802 by President Roosevelt in 1942 that allowed Blacks to work in military installations and initiated a flow of Black labor to Sacramento that increased with each episode of military involvement. Another factor was the importing of Mexican labor via the Labor Importation Program of 1942, better known as the Bracero Act, to compensate for labor shortages caused in part by Japanese internment during the Second World War. Originally intended for agricultural support, Braceros found themselves in a number of varied industries as agriculture capitalized on improvements in transportation technology. When farmers began to transport products throughout the nation, Mexican labor soon migrated to the city to meet the demands of local food processing canneries, making up almost 50 percent of all employment in Sacramento canneries during the 1940s. An expanding railway system placed additional demands on Mexican labor and Sacramento's Southern Pacific rail yards located on the northern border of the city contributed to the large Mexican presence in the West End (Avella 2003).

Census data provide further evidence of how racial covenants and redlining helped shape city neighborhoods. By 1950, almost 70 percent of the city's minority population was located in the West End with 87 percent of the city's Mexican residents, 75 percent of the city's Asian population, and 60 percent of the city's Black community residing there. The enforcement of restrictive covenants in the city for the most part contained non-White residents within the boundaries of the West End while steadily reducing property values. As improvements to transportation technology and suburban growth set in motion the movement of business and employment to the city's outer rings, this state-sponsored decline now set the stage for the devastating urban renewal phase of city building and the forced exodus of entire non-White communities from the West End.

Redlining Phase II: Redevelopment and Relocation (1950–80)

Since 1939, city leaders have openly struggled with how to address the social problems related to the declining West End.[5] City government soon found its cure to the West End slum problem when the California State

Legislature passed the Community Redevelopment Act. The Act allowed local governments to clear "blighted" land and transfer it to private interests for development via eminent domain. Shortly thereafter, Congress passed the Federal Housing Act of 1949, which focused on eliminating substandard living conditions through the clearance of slum areas and provided federal subsidies for cities attempting to remedy serious housing shortages. The Act was originally centered on improving the housing stock in "blighted" communities, but amendments to it in 1954 changed the approach to urban renewal, weakening the requirement for predominantly residential construction in redevelopment sites (Gelfand 1975). Despite strong objections from residents, Sacramento city planners seized the opportunity to alter proposed housing plans that initially accommodated low-income minority residents and turned to private commercial development as the mechanism to generate tax dollars and encourage the return of business to the West End.[6]

Figure 7.2 shows how urban renewal sites, identified by the black boundary in the urban redevelopment survey map for Sacramento in 1949, were located in precisely the same areas previously redlined by the FHA in their 1938 residential security map. The switch in urban renewal plans from affordable housing to commercial development required the eviction of thousands of West End residents occupying redlined space.

Public highway construction also began during the 1950s and reconfigured Sacramento's physical and social geography, becoming the perfect complement to redevelopment. Federal transportation funds provided up to 90 percent of the construction costs for expressways that connected the racially homogeneous suburban tracts in the northeast, east, and southwest parts of the county to the redevelopment projects that brought employment and commercial centers to the West End.[7] But the placement of these roads also created a physical barrier between neighborhoods with restrictive covenants and areas soon to be racially integrated by forced West End migration. These massive transportation thoroughfares, along with urban renewal plans, would accelerate changes to the city's racial landscape and ultimately the way Sacramentans would organize their lives and communities.

Other national events also altered the racial mix of Sacramento's population and intensified the already urgent housing need of non-Whites. The military build-up in response to the Korean and Vietnam Wars brought a new civilian and military workforce of approximately 25,000 to Sacramento's three military installations. Black employees constituted 10 percent of this new workforce (Mueller 1966). Bracero labor continued to flow into the city beyond the official end of the program in 1964. Together, these politically produced market pressures threatened the homogeneous quality of traditionally restricted neighborhoods throughout the Sacramento area. The demand on housing now included approximately 2500 Black households from military installations and another 3000 Blacks residing in the redevelopment

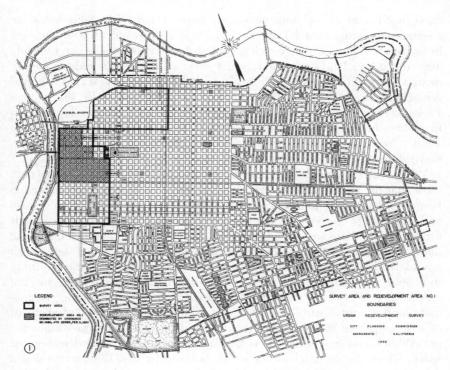

Figure 7.2 1949 redevelopment survey area map of Sacramento
Source: Sacramento City Planning, 1950.
Note: Highlighted borders identify West End areas impacted by urban renewal programs and are
strikingly similar to areas redlined by FHA in the above Residential Security Map.

survey area and in the path of the W/X freeway interchange. Another 4900
non-Whites (predominantly Asian) and 3500 Mexican residents, classified as
White Spanish surname in the 1950 US Census, also resided in the redevelopment survey area. The combination of military involvement, migrant
labor, and government-sponsored construction projects that pushed non-
Whites out of the West End brought an immediate need to house thousands
of non-White residents exiled from the newly created redevelopment survey
area – a need that proved difficult to meet in a city actively engaged in, and
shaped by, segregationist housing policies.

By the late 1950s through the mid-1960s, residents in the path of West End
renewal and freeway construction projects reported the push by landlords
and the city to relocate. When these projects pushed non-Whites out of
the West End, realtors, property managers, and private property owners
directed the flow of non-White residents who quickly filled available housing

units in older neighborhoods previously unprotected by racially restrictive covenants. Census data for the period 1950–70 provide us with the best indication of how quickly redevelopment and racial restrictions can radically alter the urban landscape. As the first stage of downtown redevelopment neared completion, the percentage of non-Whites in the West End dropped remarkably from 42.6 percent in 1950 to 5.4 percent in 1970. But in Oak Park, for example, a neighborhood without restrictive covenants located less than three miles southeast of the West End, the exact opposite occurred. In 1950, 6.5 percent of the neighborhood's residents were non-White. By 1970, non-Whites made up close to 48 percent of Oak Park's residents.

While Oak Park experienced drastic changes to its population, census data show that the adjacent racially restricted neighborhoods remain consistently homogeneous to this date. The potential spill-over from West End migration and incoming non-White military personnel to White neighborhoods threatened the homogeneity of restricted suburban space and prompted the informal actions of realtors and homeowners to protect established racial boundaries.[8] And the expansion of statewide administrative agencies during the 1960s, now centralized in newly constructed state office buildings in the redeveloped West End, triggered a sudden increase in non-White employment opportunities with the state of California. The strict enforcement of new employee discrimination laws provided access to employment for non-Whites who now sought new housing opportunities beyond segregated space. Thus, the demand for suburban housing by non-Whites revealed a resistance on the part of local developers, real estate professionals, and property owners to open traditionally White housing tracts to non-White buyers.

The period 1960–70 shows housing market principals engaged in organized housing segregation. Racial steering and the refusal to sell or rent to non-Whites by real estate professionals and property owners, a direct response to increased non-White housing demands, effectively halted integration of White neighborhoods. Using surveys, housing audits and oral histories, local housing activists such as the Sacramento Community for Fair Housing documented discriminatory actions of realtors who routinely discouraged and denied purchase offers from non-Whites attempting to move into new suburban tracts in Land Park and in northeast Sacramento, such as Arden and Carmichael (Duff 1963). These efforts helped activists shift protest strategies from the streets to the legal arena. Also, over 90 percent of the rental market in the area remained closed to non-Whites (Mueller 1966). Non-White military personnel were forced to live in predominantly low-income, non-White communities following multiple refusals from property managers restricting access to housing in White neighborhoods (Mueller and Crown 1965). Finally, realtors and property managers openly organized the overturn of fair housing laws that prohibited racial discrimination in property sales and rentals.[9] These unconcealed, organized, and deliberate acts of protecting racial boundaries helped maintain the segregated geographies created by restrictive covenants despite the groundbreaking federal and state fair housing laws of the 1960s.

Meanwhile, fears of high risks for lenders, based on the area's rapidly changing demographics, led to a systematic disinvestment by financial institutions from older inner-city communities, now integrated as a result of West End migration, and helped initiate their eventual decline. With access to mortgage capital still contingent upon borrower racial characteristics and neighborhood racial composition, the rapid ethnic shift in Sacramento's population brought a new wave of mortgage redlining. Interview data show that redlining occurred in neighborhoods that absorbed urban renewal emigrants and coincided with the escalation of redevelopment activities in Sacramento. One informant, a resident of Oak Park since the 1930s, confirms the practice of redlining in the neighborhood while discussing the city's housing problems of the 1950s:

> But what they, you know back then when I was a young man, they had something called the red liners. See, yeah, see and blacks couldn't buy out in this area. So what they did, a black would get a white person to get the home for them, and then they would move in, then they would somehow take the title later.

Confirming the rise of redlining in Sacramento, property owners looking to sell homes to non-Whites navigated around the lack of available financing in redlined areas by using installment contracts that gave physical possession to buyers but kept legal ownership in the name of the seller. One former West End resident describes her relocation to Oak Park in 1957.

> We were lucky to find our house. We rented a small house in back of our landlord's house on 3rd Avenue. When she evicted a renter from the house she owned next door, we asked her if we could buy it. She called her attorney who wrote up some kind of contract and we made payments right to her. I don't remember seeing any paperwork until we paid the house off. Then she sent us the papers that said we owned the house. ... We bought our second house on 11th Avenue the same way.

Through the 1970s, redlining was an accepted practice in Sacramento and created a vacuum of disinvestment in neighborhoods experiencing rapid integration. During the summer of 1969, racial tensions between White and Black residents, fueled in part by housing discrimination, led to civil unrest and riots in the Oak Park community mirroring similar episodes of violence in cities across the US. Based on the success of national grassroots campaigns in the 1970s by coalitions such as the Association for Community Reforms Now (ACORN), the National Association for the Advancement of

Colored People (NAACP), the National Urban League, and the National Training and Information Center, local groups such as the Sacramento Urban League, and regional advocacy by the NAACP and the Western Center on Law and Poverty pushed for formal administrative action on the area's housing problem. These coordinated multi-scaled advocacy efforts led to a series of local and statewide public hearings to address the lack of housing credit and the continued neglect of predominantly non-White neighborhoods by savings and loan corporations throughout the city and the state (California State Legislature 1976).

Hearing testimony revealed how lenders associated the growing numbers and concentrations of non-Whites in certain communities with increased financial risk to mortgage funders. The hearings led to investigations by the Department of Savings and Loan (DSL) that subsequently identified "mortgage deficient areas" in Sacramento and in other major California cities (State of California 1977). Mortgage deficient areas were defined as census tracts with a loan volume per capita less than 25 percent of the county average. The DSL findings for Sacramento documented how redlining in 1975 remained concentrated in the northern and southern parts of the county undergoing racial integration as indicated by census data, areas that over time became economically and socially unstable from financial disinvestment. In Sacramento, redlining meant the steady flow of capital to historically restricted neighborhoods while closing off capital investment to neighborhoods without racially restrictive covenants.

During this period long-standing segregationist housing policies, coupled with the actions of real estate professionals, worked to safeguard and maintain Sacramento's existing racial boundaries while creating new racial boundaries for housing credit. Thus, the racially oriented organization of the city's social, political, and economic actions resulted in resettlements that reinforced racial segregation and relations of powerlessness that immobilized certain groups and constrained their free market participation (Iglesias 2000).

Redlining Phase III: Deregulation and the Subprime Mortgage Market (1980–2004)

By 1980, federal legislation had aggressively extended access to lending products for residents of areas once redlined by banks. The Home Mortgage Disclosure Act of 1975 (HMDA) and the Community Reinvestment Act of 1977 (CRA) provided for the monitoring of lending activity by neighborhood and the threat of sanctions for lenders failing to underwrite loans in previously under-served areas. But during this time, federal policymakers, responding to the push by institutional lenders and banks for federal deregulation of lending activity, unknowingly laid the foundation for the subprime market crisis we see today under the guise of opening credit opportunities to financially starved redlined neighborhoods. As we shall see, lending deregulation provided the market conditions necessary for a disproportionate concentration of alternative credit products in predominantly non-White neighborhoods while institutionalizing the subprime mortgage industry. Thus, a series of what appeared to be abstract administrative financial regulations actually had very localized implications.

Gotham, in Chapter 1, outlines a series of legislative acts beginning in 1980 that essentially deregulated the mortgage industry. Rule-makers eliminated all usury controls on first lien mortgage rates, permitting lenders to charge higher interest rates to borrowers with presumed higher credit risks. These new rules also encouraged the development and use of credit scoring in the mortgage arena to better gauge risk and enabled lenders to establish price differentials (interest rates) for higher-risk borrowers (Gramlich 2004, 2007). Rather than just rejecting high-risk applicants with poor credit as in the prime mortgage market, lenders could now select loan terms that reflected their exposure to risk by adjusting interest rates and loan fees, and imposing balloon payments. The new regulations also permitted the use of variable interest rates and balloon payments while specifically overriding local government restrictions on alternative lending products. Thus, two important characteristics of subprime mortgage credit, high interest rates and adjustable interest rates, directly resulted from federal responses to the housing finance industry's push to create new opportunities for profit. McCoy and Renuart (2008) argue that by liberalizing the permissible features of loan products and facilitating risk-based pricing, federal legislation provided the legal consent necessary for the rapid growth of the subprime market in the coming years.

As part of this regulatory redesign of the financial industry, federal rule-making also promoted the issuance of Mortgage Backed Securities (MBS), which featured varying maturities issued according to different risk characteristics, and significantly increased the demand for subprime mortgage products (see Chapter 1 by Gotham and Chapter 9 by Wyly *et al.*). Investors now had the option of selecting the level of credit risk and the accompanying rate of return. Federal support of MBS expansion successfully attracted a new pool of secondary market investors to purchase subprime MBS. The legislation also removed long-standing regulations that purposely separated commercial banking activities from insurance companies and non-banking investment finance on Wall Street and gave banks of all sizes the ability to engage in a much wider range of financial activities without regulatory restraint. Commercial banks could now offer financial services similar to investment bankers, merge with investment banks, and compete with their relatively unregulated Wall Street competitors (Wray 2007). The easing of these restrictions subsequently triggered a wave of mergers and provided unparalleled opportunities for marketing subprime mortgage products.

The 1980s signaled the formalizing of the subprime market and a dramatic shift in the mortgage industry away from the traditional fixed rate loan to nontraditional loans such as adjustable rate mortgages (ARMs) (Gruenberg 2007). Federal responses to the housing finance industry's push to create new opportunities for profit produced policies that removed mortgage interest rate limits, facilitated the use of adjustable interest rates and enhanced opportunities for recycling mortgage funds via securitization. The state, therefore, assumed an active and important role in establishing the necessary market conditions for rapid subprime growth. The combination of ARMs, relaxed underwriting guidelines, and steady pools of lending capital made available through securitization, intensified both investor activity in the MBS market and consumer use of subprime products.[10]

Subprime loan originations rose 25 percent per year during the period 1994–2003, nearly a tenfold increase in just nine years (Gramlich 2004). In 2001, subprime mortgages accounted for 5 percent of total mortgage originations, but by 2006 accounted for over 20 percent (Gruenberg 2007). In 2003, the Federal Reserve Board (FED), monitoring the steady rise in subprime lending activity, became aware of deteriorating credit standards used by lenders in approving loan applications. The FED then collected data that clearly indicated lenders had eased lending standards by 2004 (Dodd 2007). Congressional Hearing testimony further revealed that despite these early warning signs of subprime market problems, the FED in February 2004 actually promoted the use of ARMs and encouraged lenders to develop and market alternative ARM products while the FED was preparing to raise short-term interest rates. Shortly thereafter, the FED raised interest rates 17 times, taking the FED funds rate from 1 percent to 5.25 percent, overlooking the fact that the steady increase would soon trigger a massive reset of ARM interest rates in 2006 and 2007.

Fueling the demand for subprime mortgages were low start rates and loose credit guidelines making them more attractive to both investors and borrowers than traditional fixed rate mortgages. In June 2005, former FED chair Alan Greenspan warned that 25 percent of loans originated were "interest only" (Dodd 2007). By 2006, the lax underwriting guidelines used for subprime mortgages became alarmingly clear as over 40 percent of loan approvals did not consider the applicant's income (Western Asset 2007). In 2005 and 2006, annual subprime loan volume ballooned to well over $600 billion (Schloemer *et al.* 2006). Thus, federal regulators actually set the stage for the intense subprime activity that occurred during the period 2003–06.

But this rapid growth also came with problems. Community activists discovered that a large portion of subprime loan activity throughout the US was concentrated among black and Latino borrowers (Bradford 2002; ACORN 2005), and in the neighborhoods in which they live (Wyly *et al.* 2006). National organizations such as ACORN, the National Fair

Housing Alliance, the Center for Responsible Lending, and the National Community Reinvestment Coalition pressured federal regulators while aiding local affiliates in organizing public awareness efforts. This combination of local and national level advocacy resulted in federal acknowledgement of subprime loan concentration as early as 2000 (US Department of Housing and Urban Development 2000). In 2006, the FED, relying on HMDA data from 2005, revealed that 55 percent of Blacks and 46 percent of Latinos received subprime loans with interest rates exceeding the Treasury rate by three percentage points (Avery *et al.* 2006). Despite this information and intensive advocacy efforts that conveyed the disproportionate activity of subprime lending in minority neighborhoods, federal regulators refused to take the necessary steps to head off the looming foreclosure crisis.

In Sacramento, the first signs of subprime loan concentration appeared in 2000 when ACORN organized "sit-in" protests by borrowers in local branches of the Household Finance Corporation, one of the largest subprime originators in the area (Casa 2000). Advocacy efforts also focused on local and state regulators. In 2001, the California Reinvestment Coalition (CRC) identified Sacramento as one of the major cities in California experiencing racial and spatial subprime loan concentration. Meanwhile, ACORN worked with city council members to draft a resolution that would prohibit the city from doing business with any financial organization that had ties to those engaged in predatory lending (Jones 2001). The persistent efforts of housing activists revealed how the demographic targeting of non-White neighborhoods by subprime lenders and the exploitative terms of their credit resulted in dangerous subprime loan concentrations in Sacramento neighborhoods well before the housing crisis of 2007 occurred (CRC 2001; ACORN 2005).

The area's real estate boom beginning in 2000 also aided the racial concentration of subprime loans. The influx of investors and new residents from the San Francisco Bay area and other California areas seeking affordable housing created a rush on Sacramento property. Recent estimates suggest that San Francisco Bay area buyers purchased up to 40 percent of new homes in the Elk Grove and Natomas communities (Sadovi 2005). Sacramento soon became one of the least affordable US real estate markets (Woolsey 2007). House prices quickly inflated throughout the entire region, even in areas concentrated with non-White residents, making home buying more difficult for all.

Consistently low FHA maximum loan limits failed to keep pace with the area's escalating home prices and accelerated the demand for subprime loans. Moreover, FHA mortgages usually consisted of fixed rate loans with high credit requirements thus making "teaser rate" adjustable loans and the low- or no-income requirements of many subprime loan products significantly easier to qualify for than FHA loans.[11] For many, subprime financing became the only way to participate in the housing market. However, as we shall see, in Sacramento, subprime loan activity remained concentrated in areas previously redlined and shaped by state-sponsored segregation.

Spatial Comparisons

In the US, we know that the use of subprime loans is higher for Black and Latino borrowers than for Whites, and also for Black and Latino neighborhoods than for White ones (Wyly *et al.* 2006, Chapter 9 in this volume). As expected, 2004 HMDA data show similar patterns of subprime activity in Sacramento. But not well-known is how the seemingly placeless economic and regulatory functions associated with contemporary housing credit markets remain linked to spaces shaped by historically racialized housing policy. To demonstrate the relationship between long-standing spatial patterns of racial segregation and contemporary housing policy, I map out the geographic history of racialized space and housing policy. Figure 7.3 summarizes the geography of racialized space in Sacramento by overlaying DSL findings on census tracts redlined by lenders during the 1970s with census tracts that used racially restrictive covenants, providing an image of how housing policy shaped the Sacramento social and physical landscape. Historical patterns of redlining appear in the northern and southern parts of the city while areas with restrictive covenants show a west to east geography.

Figure 7.4 shows the percentage of loan denials by census tract. Wyly *et al.* (2006) found that loan applicants who are denied are five times as likely to approach a subprime lender. Therefore, denials could conceivably provide some evidence of increased subprime activity as well as of neighborhoods excluded from the prime mortgage market. Figure 7.4 also shows that the geography of loan denials in Sacramento bears a strikingly similar pattern to the geography of redlined areas and racially restrictive covenants identified in Figure 7.3. Redlined neighborhoods located to the north and south of the central business district contain the highest proportion of loan denials. Also, high concentrations of loan denials appear near former military installations where concentrations of non-Whites formed during the period 1950–70. Conversely, census tracts with racially restricted covenants and those areas previously protected by private actions in the northeast area of the county incurred significantly lower rates of loan denials.

Finally, Figure 7.5 shows the percentage of subprime loan activity by census tract and clearly indicates that neighborhoods with a history of restricted access to lending products, or redlined areas, received a disproportionate share of subprime loans. A critical point here is that newer development (between 1960 and 1980) located in areas without racially restrictive covenants also shows high concentrations of subprime activity in addition to high loan denial rates. These integrated housing tracts experienced significant

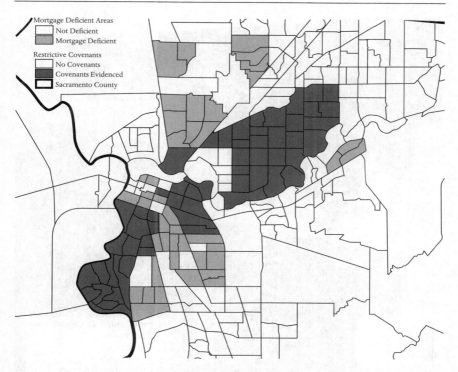

Figure 7.3 Preliminary map of areas with racially restrictive covenants and mortgage deficient areas in Sacramento County
Source: For covenants: author's review of public records. For mortgage deficient areas: State of California (1977) Department of Savings and Loan fair lending report No. 1, Vol. II. State of California Library, Sacramento.

economic decline during the redlining of the 1970s and remain unstable to this date. South Sacramento, an area highly populated with low-income and non-White residents, serves as a prime example of this decline.

But suburban tracts with restrictive covenants built during the same period and areas adjacent to the northeast previously protected by the actions of realtors show a much lower rate of subprime usage and loan denials. Similarly, we can see that subprime loan distribution in these tracts approximates the geography shaped by housing policies captured in Figure 7.3. The data show that census tracts with racially restrictive covenants today experience a lower rate of subprime activity than non-protected communities (tracts without racially restrictive covenants). Hence, this spatial comparison provides some evidence that access to mortgage financing remains consistently positive for neighborhoods over time once restraints on residency are in

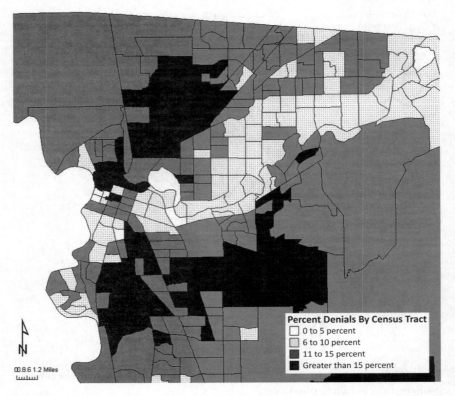

Figure 7.4 Percentage of prime loan denials by census tract for Sacramento County in 2004
Source: FFIEC HMDA raw data, 2004.

place. Moreover, census data confirm that neighborhoods with access to suitable housing credit have remained economically stable and for the most part racially homogeneous since 1950. Conversely, the higher rate of subprime financing in tracts without restrictive covenants means those property owners incur higher risks, pay a higher price to finance the purchase of their home, and have more difficulty accessing their equity when seeking financial and social mobility.

We have yet to see the full effects of high-cost subprime lending in Sacramento. The expansion of subprime mortgage products occurred at a time when interest rates were at their lowest while housing prices were at record highs. A good portion of these recently obtained ARMs have reached their first adjustment date. As these ARMs adjusted upward and area housing prices declined 44 percent from 2005 values, homeowners

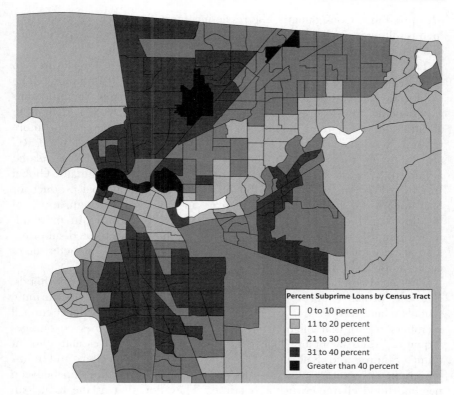

Figure 7.5 Percentage of subprime loans by census tract for Sacramento County in 2004
Source: FFIEC HMDA raw data, 2004.

faced higher loan-to-value ratios and encountered difficulty in refinancing their mortgages especially when applying for a fixed rate loan.[12]

The sudden loss in equity from declining values coupled with higher mortgage payments means we now see higher rates of payment delinquencies, mortgage defaults, lender repossessions, properties listed as "short sales," and foreclosures in areas with concentrations of subprime loan activity.[13] In fact, South Sacramento neighborhoods have experienced some of the highest fore-closure rates in the US (Christie 2007). As property values decline in these neighborhoods, homebuyers looking to establish a sense of community and earn equity are less inclined to purchase in unstable locations. Neighborhood renters, the most likely to buy in distressed areas, are unable to afford the purchase of foreclosed property without the use of subprime loans or down payment assistance programs, two resources now with limited access due to the declining investor market for subprime MBSs and recent changes to FHA loan programs. Consequently, the resale inventory for foreclosed property is high resulting in declining values, opportunities for investors and speculators, and leaves neighborhoods vulnerable to even further decline.

The economic and social costs of subprime related foreclosures to homeowners, neighborhoods, and the city are indeed substantial. The California Reinvestment Coalition (CRC) (2008) estimates Sacramentans experiencing foreclosure in 2007 collectively lost nearly $54 million in addition to losing their homes. Census tracts with 45 percent or more minority residents accounted for almost 40 percent of this loss.[14] The CRC also estimates a loss of $40 million to the city in 2007 foreclosure related administrative costs such as decreased property tax revenues. Finally, Global Insight (2007) estimates a $1.73 billion loss in gross municipal product for Sacramento due to the dramatic increase in foreclosures. Again, much of this loss can be attributed to the high rate of foreclosures in predominately minority neighborhoods. So, we can see how concentrated subprime loan activity mirrors the destructive disinvestment practices characteristic of earlier episodes of redlining in the city.

The social costs of foreclosure also weigh heavy on these neighborhoods. Reduced property tax revenues means less funding for low-performing schools where foreclosures are concentrated. Support staff for local council members report that blight from boarded and vacant homes encourages "squatters" and facilitates illicit drug sales, which in turn escalate violent crime. Squires and Kubrin (2006) note that homeownership and housing credit opportunity play an important role in the relationship between neighborhood characteristics and crime.. They find that as the total loan amount in a neighborhood increases, crime rates tend to decrease. Simply stated, crime rates are lower in neighborhoods where homeownership is high. Consequently, the residential instability that subprime lending and foreclosures bring to a neighborhood also means a heavy social cost.

Conclusion

Subprime lending, a seemingly placeless and colorblind market phenomenon, plays an important but potentially divisive role in reorganizing space initially shaped by race-based housing policies. We can now see that the combination of historical and contemporary housing policies created a set of structural conditions in neighborhoods that made them vulnerable to capital extraction and the resulting economic catastrophes brought on by the meltdown of the globally leveraged deregulated subprime loan industry in 2007. As the patterns of foreclosures in Sacramento begin to mirror subprime activity, these vulnerabilities clearly produce racially disparate social and economic outcomes for residents of cities experiencing stress and change.

This analysis of subprime loan activity demonstrates how socially and politically produced market interventions shape the life chances of residents and their communities, granting advantage and privilege to dominant groups while promoting inequitable market outcomes for others. The evidence shows that race and geography influenced capital flows in a way that cannot be explained by traditional neo-classical market forces. The relationship between capital flows and geography in Sacramento leads to three hypotheses on how space was allocated in the city: (1) the use of racial categories in market interventions created structural conditions that dictated a specific course for market operations, laying the foundation for markets to operate as a form of exclusion as well as a form of extraction; (2) housing markets are embedded in adverse social relationships – therefore, economic activity today is somewhat shaped by social influences rather than simply the result of consumer market adaptation; and (3) although restrictive covenants, redevelopment, redlining, and subprime lending appear to be distinct and separate processes, local geography links them as one intergenerational practice that racializes market outcomes. Hence, race plays an historical as well as a contemporary role in the way housing markets shape cities. We can see, as Smith (1988) reminds us, that economic forces work through historically, geographically, and racially specific social and political processes. Markets, contends Smith, do not operate in isolation from government policy. Although theoretical "supply and demand" markets are colorblind, real markets remain race-minded.

The fact that contemporary lending patterns in Sacramento are tied to past housing practices that shaped the social geography of the city shows how subprime lending continues historical practices of exclusion. We need to pay more attention to how past practices and public policies shape and influence markets. This will help us understand how markets operate as extensions of social and political processes and identify the embeddedness of social relations in allocating public resources. Social and economic inequities must not be seen as solely the result of free market practices and individual deficiencies. As we continue to rely on market practices to solve problems of urban planning and fix racialized inner-city space, we must recognize how urban policy implemented through market structures can perpetuate inequality in the US. The way we regulate and control access to housing credit sets the conditions for who wins or loses in our cities.

Acknowledgments

The author thanks Manuel Aalbers, Bruce Haynes, Fred Block, Elvin Wyly, and two anonymous reviewers for helpful comments on previous drafts of this chapter. The author also thanks Richard Marciano and the Testbed for

Redlining Archives of California's Exclusionary Spaces (T-Races) project for access to maps and records of the Federal Home Loan Bank Board, National Archives: Record Group 195. The author claims responsibility for all errors and opinions contained in this chapter.

Notes

1   HMDA raw data for 2003–6 shows that the peak year for subprime activity in Sacramento was 2004. Also, HMDA data may not include a number of subprime loans originated during this period as not all subprime lenders are subject to reporting. Thus we may not be able to realize the true size of the subprime market in Sacramento. Using the list of subprime lenders from HUD to identify subprime lenders, we see that just over 31 percent of loans in the 2004 HMDA data were classified as subprime. Although analysts now look at high cost or rate spread loans as the basis for identifying subprime lending, this method fails to identify the bulk of subprime loans. For example, in Sacramento, the 2004 HMDA data only show that 6 percent of loans are high cost and thus fails to provide any useful measurement of the magnitude of subprime lending in the area. The danger in using high cost loans as a proxy for identifying subprime loans is that it conflates high cost with subprime lending, which significantly undercounts the number of such loans. A subprime loan is characterized more by its unsustainable repayment terms rather than its cost. By charging higher overall interest rates, building in rapid interest rate reset periods and penalties for early loan payoff, a lender can earn substantial revenues from loan investors in the form of rebates and avoid "high cost" reporting requirements. Thus, lenders do not need to originate high cost loans subject to federal reporting in order to earn high fees. It is not high fees that trigger foreclosures but adjustable payments and other harsh credit terms characteristic of subprime lending.

2   During the late 1930s, the bulk of mortgage activity in Sacramento consisted of new construction loans. Banks, through the use of federal Title II loans, supplanted individuals as the principal mortgage lenders in the area and dominated mortgage origination activity. In 1938, almost 80 percent of mortgages for the top five banks and trust companies in Sacramento were Title II loans. See Summary, HOLC Survey of Sacramento, California by the Division of Research and Statistics Field Report dated December 2, 1938 (source: Testbed for Redlining Archives of California's Exclusionary Spaces (T-Races)).

3   HOLC appraisal worksheets for 1937 identified areas of the city where mortgage credit was difficult to obtain, thus indicating that some informal redlining by lenders occurred in Sacramento prior to the creation of the Residential Security Maps (source: T-Races). The formalizing of race-based underwriting guidelines by the FHA provided real estate professionals with organized race-based policies that intensified redlining practices during this period when the primary source of mortgage credit in the city shifted from individuals to federally regulated banks via the use of Title II loans.

4   Sacramento Urban Redevelopment: Existing Conditions in Blighted Areas. Sacramento City Planning Commission. October 1950.

5 Ibid.
6 Local residents actively resisted West End redevelopment and organized a public awareness media campaign that resulted in voters defeating Proposition 'B', a bond proposal to finance the first stage of West End redevelopment (see series of paid political advertisements in The Sacramento Union, October 21–31, 1954). Despite the defeat of Proposition 'B' by voters on November 2, 1954, city council members subsequently approved the sale of tax allocation bonds to proceed with redevelopment plans (see Land purchase in blight area is set to begin, The Sacramento Bee, August 8, 1956).
7 See the National Interstate and Defense Highway Act of 1956.
8 See, for example, Ming v. Horgan *et al.* (Calif. Super. Ct., Sacramento Co., #97130.) where the court clearly recognized and spelled out the various methods of consistent discrimination used by area subdividers, owners, builders and real estate agents in the absolute prohibition of Negroes from buying new housing in the area. The court ruled that, as recipients of federal governmental assistance through FHA and VA financing, defendants were required not to flout the federal policy of equal rights established in Brown v. Board of Education.
9 The California Real Estate Association and the California Apartment Owners Association formed the Committee for Home Protection to sponsor "Proposition 14" in 1964, a statewide referendum to overturn the fair housing laws contained in the Rumford Act of 1963. The Sacramento Apartment House and Property Owners Association, along with the Sacramento Real Estate Board actively supported the committee's efforts (Cain 1964; Mueller1966; see also Sacramento Association of Realtors Archives – minutes from various executive staff meeting in 1963 through 1966). Sixty-two percent of Sacramentans voted in favor of Proposition 14 (source: Supplement to Statement of Vote, State of California General Election November 3, 1964). The US Supreme Court later overturned this Proposition (see Reitman v. Mulkey, 387 US 369, 87 S.Ct. 1627, 18 L.Ed.2d 830 (1967).
10 See Chapter 9 by Wyly *et al.* for a more detailed discussion on risk-based pricing and Chapter 1 by Gotham for a more detailed discussion on securitization.
11 The author's review of HMDA raw data for Sacramento County shows that FHA loans accounted for only 1.13 percent of total loan activity for 2004 and only 1.58 percent of loan activity during the period 2003–6.
12 Source: California Association of Realtors 2009 Market Forecast. October 15, 2008.
13 Using raw foreclosure data from DataQuick, the author calculates that 68 percent of foreclosures in Sacramento between January 1997 and June 2008 occurred within the period January 2006–December 2008.
14 Author's calculation using CRC methodology, 2006 Federal Financial Institutions Examination Council Census Estimates and DataQuick raw foreclosure data for 2007.

References

Abrams, C. (1955) *Forbidden Neighbors: A Study of Prejudice in Housing.* Harper and Brothers: New York.

ACORN (Association of Community Organizations for Reform Now). (2005) Separate and unequal: predatory lending in America. ACORN Fair Housing. [WWW document]. URL http://www.acorn.org/fileadmin/Community_Reinvestment/ Reports/ S_and_E_2004/separate_and_unequal_2004.pdf (accessed May 10, 2009).

Avella, S. (2003) *Sacramento, Indomitable City.* Arcadia Publishing: San Francisco.

Avery, R., Brevoort, K., and Canner, G. (2006) Higher-priced home lending and the 2005 HMDA data. *Federal Reserve Bulletin*, 92: a123–a126.

Babcock, F. (1932) *The Valuation of Real Estate.* McGraw-Hill: New York.

Bonilla-Silva, E. (1997) Rethinking racism: toward a structural interpretation. *American Sociological Review* 2: 465–80.

Bradford, C. (1979) Financing home ownership: the federal role in neighborhood decline. *Urban Affairs Quarterly*, 14(3): 313–35.

Bradford, C. (2002) Risk or race? Racial disparities and the subprime refinance market. Neighborhood Revitalization Project, Center for Community Change [WWW document]. URL http://www.knowledgeplex.org/showdoc.html?id=1032 (last accessed May 10, 2009).

Cain, L. (1964) Absolute discretion? The California controversy over fair housing laws. Research Bulletin No. 7, April. Sacramento: Sacramento Committee for Fair Housing.

Calem, P., Hershaff, J., and Wachter, S. (2004) Neighborhood patterns of subprime lending: evidence from disparate cities. *Housing Policy Debate* 15(3): 603–22.

California State Legislature. (1976) Summary of interim hearings: redlining in California. Senate Local Government Committee. October 1976. State of California Library, Sacramento.

Campbell, J. and Lindberg, L. (1990) Property rights and the organization of economic activity by the state. *American Sociological Review* 55(5): 634–57.

Carruthers, B. and Babb, S. (2000) *Economy/Society: Markets, Meanings, and Social Structure.* Pine Forge Press: Thousand Oaks.

Casa, K. (2000) Preying on predators: nonprofits fight back against predatory lending practices. *Sacramento News and Review.* 23 August. [WWW document]. URL http://www.newsreview.com/sacramento/content?oid=3363 (accessed May 10, 2009).

CRC (California Reinvestment Coalition). (2001) Stolen wealth: inequities in California's subprime market [WWW document]. URL http://calreinvest.org/system/assets/16.pdf (accessed May 10, 2009).

CRC (California Reinvestment Coalition). (2008) Foreclosure trends in Sacramento and recommended policy options. [WWW document]. URL http://www.sacbee.com/static/weblogs/real_estate/archives/28778290425200808332418l.PDF (last accessed May 10, 2009).

Christie, L. (2007) Foreclosures drift to Sun Belt from Rust Belt. CNNMoney.com. 13 August. [WWW document]. URL http://money.cnn.com/2007/06/18/real_estate/foreclosures_hardest_hit_zips/ index.htm (accessed May 10, 2009).

Conley, D. (1999) *Being Black, Living in the Red: Race, Wealth, and Social Policy in America.* Berkeley: University of California Press.

Creswell, J. (1998) *Qualitative Inquiry and Research Design: Choosing Among the Five Traditions.* Thousand Oaks: Sage Publications.

Cutler, D., Glaeser, E., and Vigdor, J. (1999) The rise and decline of the American ghetto. *Journal of Political Economy*, 107(3): 455–506.

Dodd, C. (2007) Opening statements: hearing on mortgage market turmoil. US Senate Committee on Banking, Housing and Urban Affairs. 22 March. [WWW document]. URL http://banking.senate.gov/public/index.cfm?FuseAction =Hearings. Hearing&Hearing_ID=4ccca4e6-b9dc- 40b1-bab5–137b3a77364d (accessed May 10, 2009).

Duff, E. (1963) Federal employee sues for blocked home. Sacramento Committee for Fair Housing, Sacramento. May.

Farris, J. and Richardson, C. (2004) The geography of subprime mortgage prepayment penalty patterns. *Housing Policy Debate* 15(3): 687–714.

Feagin, J. (1998) *The New Urban Paradigm: Critical Perspectives on the City*. Boulder, CO: Rowman and Littlefield.

Fligstein, N. (1996) Markets as politics: a political-cultural approach to market institutions. *American Sociological Review* 61(4): 656–74.

Freund, D. (2006) Marketing the free market: state intervention and the politics of prosperity in metropolitan America. In: K. Kruse and T. Sugrue (eds.) *The New Suburban History*. Chicago: University of Chicago Press.

Gelfand, M. (1975) *A Nation of Cities: The Federal Government and Urban America, 1933–1965*. New York: Oxford University Press.

Girardi, K., Shapiro, A., and Willen, P. (2007) Subprime outcomes: risky mortgages, homeownership experiences, and foreclosures. Working Paper 07–15, Federal Reserve Bank of Boston. [WWW document]. URL http://www.bos.frb.org /economic/wp/wp2007/wp0715.pdf (accessed May 10, 2009).

Global Insight. (2007) The mortgage crisis: economic and fiscal implications. November 2007. [WWW document]. URL http://www.globalinsight.com/ Highlight/ HighlightDetail11078.htm (accessed December 20, 2008).

Gotham, K. (2000) Racialization and the state: the Housing Act of 1934 and the creation of the Federal Housing Administration. *Sociological Perspectives* 43(2): 291–317.

Gotham, K. (2002) *Race, Real Estate and Uneven Development: The Kansas City Experience 1900–2000*. Lawrence: University Press of Kansas.

Gotham, K. (2006) The secondary circuit of capital reconsidered: globalization and the US real estate sector. *American Journal of Sociology* 112(1): 231–75.

Gottdiener, M. (1994) *The Social Production of Space*. Austin: University of Texas Press.

Gottdiener, M. and Hutchinson, R. (2006) *The New Urban Sociology*. Boulder: Westview Press.

Gramlich, E. (2004) Remarks at the financial services roundtable annual housing policy meeting. Chicago, Illinois. 21 May. [WWW document]. URL http://www. kc.frb.org/PUBLICAT/ECONREV/PDF/4q07Gramlich.pdf (accessed May 12, 2009).

Gramlich, E. (2007) *Subprime Mortgages: America's Latest Boom and Bust*. Washington, DC: The Urban Institute Press.

Granovetter, M. (1985) Economic action and social structure: the problem of embeddedness. *American Journal of Sociology* 91: 481–510.

Granovetter, M. and Swedberg, R. (eds.) (1992) *The sociology of economic life*. Oxford: Westview Press.

Gruenberg, M. (2007) Vice Chairman, Federal Deposit Insurance Corporation. Remarks to the American Banker's Association Stonier Graduate School, University of Pennsylvannia. 11 June. [WWW document]. http://news/news/speeches/ archives/2007/chairman/spjun1107.html (accessed May 12, 2009).

Harvey, D. (1985) *The Urbanization of Capital: Studies in the History and Theory of Capitalist Urbanization*. Baltimore: Johns Hopkins University Press.

Haynes, B. (2001) *Red Lines, Black Spaces*. New Haven: Yale University Press.

Helper, R. (1969) *Racial Policies and Practices of Real Estate Brokers*. Minneapolis: University of Minnesota Press.

Hirsch, A. (1983) *Making the Second Ghetto: Race and Housing in Chicago 1940–1960*. Chicago: University of Chicago Press.

Hoyt, H. (1933) *One Hundred Years of Real Estate in Chicago*. Chicago: University of Chicago Press.

Iglesias, E. (2000) Global markets, racial spaces and the role of critical race theory in the struggle for community control of investments: an institutional class analysis. *Villanova Law Review* 45: 1037–73.

Immergluck, D. and Wiles, M. (1999) *Two Steps Back: The Dual Mortgage Market, Predatory Lending, and the Undoing of Community Development*. Chicago: Woodstock Institute.

Isidro, J. (2005) *Images of America: Sacramento's Land Park*. San Francisco: Arcadia.

Jackson, K. (1985) *Crabgrass frontier: the suburbanization of the United States*. New York: Oxford University Press.

Jones, S. (2001) Circling the sharks: legal opinions differ on whether Sacramento can ban predatory lending practices. *Sacramento News and Review* 16 August. [WWW document]. URL http://www.newsreview.com/sacramento/content?oid=8117 (accessed May 10, 2009).

Kushner, J. (1980) *Apartheid in America: An Historical and Legal Analysis of Contemporary Racial Segregation in the United States*. Arlington: Carrollton Press.

Lax, H., Manti, M., Raca, P., and Zorn, P. (2004) Subprime lending: an investigation of economic efficiency. *Housing Policy Debate* 5(3): 533–71.

Logan, J. and Molotch, H. (1987) *Urban fortunes: the political economy of place*. Berkeley: University of California Press.

Magagnini, S. (2005) Racist housing clauses stricken. *The Sacramento Bee*. 13 January. [WWW document]. URL http://www.sacbee.com/content.homes/re_news v-print/story/13553680p-14394400c.html (accessed April 2, 2007).

Massey, D. and Denton, N. (1993) *American Apartheid: Segregation and the Making of the Underclass*. Cambridge: Harvard University Press.

McCoy, P. and Renuart, E. (2008) The legal infrastructure of subprime and non-traditional home mortgages. In: N. Restinas and E. Belsky (eds.) *Borrowing to Live: Consumer and Mortgage Credit Revisited*. Washington, DC: The Brookings Institution.

McMichael, S. and Bingham, R. (1928) *City Growth Essentials*. Cleveland: The Stanley McMichael Publishing Organization.

Mueller, P. (1966) Effects of housing discrimination on residential segregation patterns in Sacramento 1960–1966. The Sacramento Community Integration Project, Sacramento.

Mueller, P. and Crown, M. (1965) McClellan Air Force Base area rental survey. Research Bulletin No. 9, Sacramento Committee for Fair Housing, Sacramento.

Oliver, M. and Shapiro, T. (1995) *Black wealth/white wealth*. Routledge, New York.

Pulido, L. (2004) Environmental racism and urban development. In: J. Wolch, M. Pastor Jr., and P. Dreier (eds.) *Up Against the Sprawl: Public Policy and the Making of Southern California*. Minneapolis: University of Minnesota Press.

Renuart, E. (2004) An overview of the predatory mortgage lending process. *Housing Policy Debate* 15(3): 467–502.

Sacramento City Planning. (1950) Sacramento urban redevelopment: existing conditions in blighted areas. October 1950. City of Sacramento, Sacramento.

Sadovi, M. (2005) Home buyers see value in Sacramento. Real Estate Journal.com. 20 July. [WWW document]. URL http://www.realestatejournal.com/columnists /livingthere/20050720-blueprint.html (accessed May 12, 2009).

Schloemer, E., Li, W., Ernst, K., and Keest, K. (2006) Losing ground: foreclosures in the subprime market and their cost to homeowners. Center for Responsible Lending. December 2006. [WWW document]. URL ftp://www. responsiblelending.org/ mortgage-lending/research-analysis/foreclosure-paper-report-2–17.pdf (accessed May 12, 2009).

Smith, M.P. (1988) *City, State and Market: The Political Economy of Urban Society*. Oxford: Basil Blackwell.

Smith, M.P. and Feagin, J. (eds.) (1995) *The Bubbling Cauldron: Race, Ethnicity and the Urban Crisis*. Minneapolis: University of Minnesota Press.

Squires, G. (ed.) (1989) *Unequal Partnerships: The Political Economy of Urban Redevelopment in Postwar America*. New Brunswick: Rutgers University Press.

Squires, G. (1994) Capital and Communities in Black and White: The Intersections of Race, Class and Uneven Development. Albany: SUNY Press.

Squires, G. (ed.) (2002) *Urban Sprawl: Causes, Consequences, and Policy Responses*. Washington, DC: Urban Institute Press.

Squires, G. (2005) Predatory lending: redlining in reverse. *Shelterforce Online* Issue 139. [WWW document]. URL http://www.nhi.org/online/issues/139/redlining. html (accessed May 10, 2009).

Squires, G. and Kubrin, C. (2006) *Privileged Places: Race, Residence and the Structure of Opportunity*. Boulder: Lynne Rienner.

State of California. (1977) Department of Savings and Loan fair lending report No. 1, Vol. II. State of California Library, Sacramento.

Stuart, G. (2003) *Discriminating Risk: The US Mortgage Lending Industry in the Twentieth Century*. Ithaca, NY: Cornell University Press.

Sugrue, T. (1996) *The Origins of the Urban Crisis: Race and Inequality in Post War Detroit*. Princeton: Princeton University Press.

US Department of Housing and Urban Development. (2000) Unequal burden: income and racial disparities in subprime lending in America. [WWW document]. URL http://www.hud.gov/library/bookshelf18/pressrel/subprime.html (accessed December 12, 2005).

Vose, C. (1959) *Caucasians Only: The Supreme Court, the NAACP, and the Restrictive Covenant Cases*. Berkeley: University of California Press.

Weaver, R. (1948) *The Negro ghetto*. New York: Harcourt, Brace and Company.

Western Asset Management. (2007) Subprime mortgages. Commentary/Insights 22 March [WWW document]. URL http:// www.westernasset.com/us/en/ commentary/subprime_mortgages_200703.cfm (accessed May 10, 2009).

Woolsey, M. (2007) Least affordable US real estate markets. Housing Trends, Forbes. com. 23 July. [WWW document]. URL http://www.forbes.com/2007/07/20/unaffordable-housing-property-forbeslife-cx_mw_0723realestate.html (accessed May 10, 2009).

Wray, L.R. (2007) Lessons from the subprime meltdown. Working Paper No. 522. The Levy Economics Institute of Bard College.

Wyly, E., Atia, M., Foxcroft, H., Hammel, D., and Phillips-Watts, K. (2006) American home: predatory mortgage capital and neighborhood spaces of race and class exploitation in the United States. *Geografiska Annaler B* 88(1): 105–32.

Yin, R. (1994) *Case Study Research: Design and Methods*. Thousand Oaks: Sage Publications.

8

The New Economy and the City
Foreclosures in Essex County New Jersey

Kathe Newman

Seventeen ZIP Codes in Newark, NJ., pulled in about $1.5 billion. In all of those ZIP Codes, subprime mortgages comprised more than half of all home loans made. (Whitehouse 2007)

The American Dream

Homeownership has been lauded in the US as a tool to build wealth, revive failing neighborhoods and cities, reduce poverty, and engage the civically disengaged. When the US homeownership rate reached 69 percent in 2006, many celebrated as vast scores of Americans, including many people of color, achieved the much-celebrated American Dream – acquiring a home. But not everyone was celebrating. After decades of work to reverse redlining and disinvestment, some community organizations found themselves in the unusual position of questioning whether the influx of capital their neighborhoods experienced since the mid-1990s was beneficial or harmful. While some celebrated, others began to question whether their neighborhoods had increased access to capital or capital had increased its access to them. The dispute concerned whether access to capital produced a net benefit for homeowners and communities or whether it facilitated capital accumulation with little public benefit. Housing, of course, in addition to being "home" is also a major component of the US and other countries' economies.

Subprime Cities: The Political Economy of Mortgage Markets, First Edition. Edited by Manuel B. Aalbers.
© 2012 Blackwell Publishing Ltd. Published 2012 by Blackwell Publishing Ltd.

Since the early 1990s, community concerns about access to capital have focused on the quality of lending within the subprime market. Subprime loans have higher fees and interest rates to offset the risk of lending to risky borrowers. The subprime market expanded from its emergence in the early 1990s in two waves, one during the 1990s and another between 2002 and 2007. The second wave introduced new loan products (prime and subprime) and institutional relationships and lending processes. Regulatory changes, technological advances, credit scoring, and credit enhancements enabled lenders to more finely assess risk and quickly process loans. The secondary market facilitated access to capital for financial institutions to originate those loans (Immergluck 2009; Apgar, Bendimerad, and Essene 2007).

In the early 1990s, subprime lending appeared to have the potential to transform disinvested communities, and the borrowers in them. But even in the mid-1990s, long before the recent financial crisis, there were questions about whether abuses within the subprime market were withdrawing capital from neighborhoods and consumers instead of helping them. Until the economic crisis of 2007, the problems within the subprime market were often attributed to the actions of a small group of lenders rather than a reflection of industry-wide practices. As liquidity dried up, foreclosures skyrocketed, and the US plunged into a recession, it became clear that this interpretation failed to capture the complexity of the contemporary financial system and its relationship to home mortgages.

If the subprime crisis is conceptualized as the action of a minor group of predatory lenders or of inexperienced and overly exuberant borrowers, the problem is individualized, segmented, and inherently local. If instead it is conceptualized as embedded in the financialization of the economy, the problem looks quite different. In Harvey's (1982; 1989) initial conception of capital flows and the relationship to the built environment, he argued that investment in the built environment was the result of a surplus in the primary circuit of production. To avert crisis, capital switched from the primary circuit of production to the secondary circuit of the built environment. Since Harvey's initial work, others have sought to tease out how capital switching works and how switching is related to the production and reproduction of the city. For some, capital doesn't switch so much as it expands in both circuits simultaneously (Beauregard 1994). Others argue that it switches opportunities or sectors rather than circuits (Charney 2001). However it works, it is clear that the expanded role of finance in the broader economy has transformed capital flows and their relationship to place (Harvey 1982, 1989; Beauregard 1994; Charney 2001).

As finance has taken an increasing share of the deindustrialized economy, financial institutions and processes have started to resemble Fordist production processes of the industrial era. Mortgages could be thought of as the equivalent of the post-industrial widget, an important raw ingredient for financial expansion. Homes, the place necessary for the origination of the mortgage, become intricately tied into the web of global capital flows. Mortgage brokers and lenders link global (and local) capital to urban places by providing the connection – the node – to facilitate capital accumulation, completing the flow from the ethereal world of securities and investment in the secondary circuit of capital to the real-world place of extraction in communities. Financialization, increases in homeownership, and housing price increases, until the bubble burst, were celebrated as economic growth at multiple scales. Cities announced that they were back and states and the national government took pains to avoid limiting growth in this sector (Gotham 2006; Harvey 1989).

To better understand the connections between the financialization of the economy and urban change, I examine foreclosures in one city. I explore the role of the financial sector in the expansion of the post-industrial economy and place the emergence of subprime lending within that context. I am interested in the role of the state in the development of these processes and institutional structures and in their relationship to place. I review the emerging literature on the role of the state in the expansion of the post-industrial economy with particular emphasis on changes in the prime and subprime mortgage markets. While I am interested in understanding capital flows and the rules and structures that enable capital mobility, I am also interested in what happens as that capital touches ground and transforms urban communities. To illustrate the relationship between financialization and place, I look at mortgage foreclosure filings in Essex County, New Jersey. Until recently, foreclosures had been explained as the result of job loss during economic downturns, housing price decline, or personal events such as divorce and illness. More recently foreclosures have been explained as the result of poor quality lending and over exuberant borrowing. The unraveling of the financial crisis of 2007 suggests that many lenders were engaging in risky lending practices during the mid 2000s. Some of that lending took place in communities that had been the sites of prior disinvestment and predatory lending. The events magnify the effects of these long-term practices on disadvantaged communities and populations.

To illustrate these trends, I turn to a case study of foreclosures in Essex County. I use data on foreclosure filings from 2004 to capture foreclosure processes at the start of the major expansion of the subprime market.[1] I complement this data with Sheriff sales, the point at which a property in foreclosure is sold at auction, during the period 1991–2002 to explore the historical concentrations of foreclosures in these communities. Focus groups with neighborhood residents in one Newark neighborhood provide a glimpse of how capital reaches community residents as home mortgages. I conclude by considering the relationship between foreclosures, financialization, and economic growth.

Mortgages, the New Economy, and the City

Harvey (1982, 1989) linked the development of the built environment to the production of surplus capital in the primary circuit of production. Capital switching from the primary to the secondary circuit ensured continued opportunities for accumulation. Since his initial work, other researchers have sought to understand how capital flows between the circuits and to tease out the relationship of capital to the built environment. Exploring capital switching in the New York City economic boom of the 1980s, Beauregard (1994) found that instead of switching, capital expanded in production and the built environment simultaneously. More recently Charney (2001) argued that capital switched sectors rather than circuits. Harvey and those who followed were seeking to understand the structure of the post-industrial economy and its relationship to place during a period of transformation when the shape of the post-industrial economy was just coming into view. Even at these early stages, the structure of financial arrangements was beginning to play an increasingly central role in facilitating capital's movement globally from one sector or circuit to another, and into investment in the built environment. Harvey (1989) suggested an increasingly integral relationship between the production of the new economy and the production of place:

> The effect, however, was to tie the production of urban infrastructures more tightly into the overall logic of capital flow, primarily through movements in the demand and supply of money capital as reflected in the interest rate. The "urban construction cycle" therefore became much more emphatic, as did the rhythmic movement of uneven urban development in geographic space. (Harvey 1989: 36)

This increased centrality of credit, finance, and banking has been loosely termed "financialization" (*Growth and Change* 2007; Krippner 2005; French and Leyshon 2004; Martin and Turner 2000). While the term is used to describe different aspects of finance and the economy, here we are particularly interested in the role that Krippner (2005), building on earlier work by Arrighi, explores, namely a shift from commodity production to finance production. Banks and other financial institutions create financial products such as mortgages, derivatives, securities, credit default swaps, and a broad array of other things. Harvey (1999, 1989) anticipated that the state would play an increasingly important role as fictitious commodities, especially land and money, play larger roles in the economy but he saw finance as distinct from production.

> Financial markets separate out from commodity and labor markets and acquire a certain autonomy vis-à-vis production. Urban centers can then become centers of coordination, decision-making, and control, usually within a hierarchically organized geographical structure. (Harvey 1989: 22)

Harvey's ideas about production, finance and credit, and the built environment present a jumping off point for considering these relationships.

Reflecting the growing importance of finance in the national economy, the US federal government (largely viewed as pursuing deregulation policies and a reduction in social policymaking since the Reagan revolution of the 1980s) was intimately involved in creating policies to increase demand for mortgage products and constructing an institutional framework that enabled financial institutions and actors, to flourish.[2] In much the same way that Keynesianism guided state policy to address the underconsumption problems of the 1930s, in the post-Keynesian neoliberal age, the state has played an aggressive role in ensuring the expansion of the new economy by increasing demand for mortgage products, facilitating investment by de-linking property investment from place, creating and supporting the expansion of the secondary mortgage market, and changing tax laws to use housing to further commodity consumption (Apgar, Bendimerad, and Essene 2007; Gotham 2006; Howell 2006; Chomsisengphet and Pennington-Cross 2006; NHS 2004).

The federal role in supporting demand dates back to efforts to transform housing policies in the 1970s and to revive urban markets by attracting private capital. Nixon's moratorium on public housing construction was complemented by a shift to housing vouchers, support for federally assisted private multi-family housing, and later an aggressive push to increase homeownership. A central urban program since the 1990s, HOPE VI has facilitated public housing demolition and the resurgence of private markets, re-linking capital to communities (Crump 2002; Wyly and Hammel 1999). Similar policy efforts were at work in the UK. Beaverstock *et al.* (1992) see a relationship between policies that "enthusiastically promote home ownership" and the desire to increase the production and expanded use of credit, or in other words, to help produce growth by expanding the new economy.

The expansion of mortgage production and homeownership was dependent on resolving two issues - fixity and liquidity (Gotham 2006). Fixity poses two interrelated problems. First, the market value of a property is dependent in part on its location. Second, the investment in real estate at a fixed location requires some in-depth knowledge of the property and the place in which it is situated. A series of policy changes initiated in the 1980s helped to de-link property from place by increasing the ease with which investors – even those located on the other side of the globe – could transcend the fixity of property investment (Gotham 2006; French and Leyshon 2004).

Once property was de-linked from place, liquidity was necessary to turn properties into commodities (Gotham 2006). Until the 1980s, most mortgages in the US were originated by depository institutions, whose capacity to make loans was limited by their dependence on deposits and by the need to ensure timely repayment on the mortgages they originated (Stiglitz and Weiss 1981). The emergence and rapid growth of the US-backed government sponsored enterprises (GSEs) changed the calculus for mortgage lending by creating a secondary mortgage market. The ability to package and sell loans to outside buyers meant that originators could increase loan origination volume (dependent on purchases in the secondary market), lower the cost of lending, and loosen underwriting standards. The government's backing of the secondary market provided the support necessary to attract secondary market investors (Immergluck 2009; Follain and Zorn 1990; Lea 1990).

Since the 1980s, banks, financial investment firms, and government have enhanced the expansion of the secondary market by increasing liquidity through sophisticated investment tools that, until recently, were thought to all but eliminate investment risk. Collatoralized Mortgage Obligations (CMOs) "tranched" or divided mortgage income into categories of risk allowing investors to invest based on their desired risk and investment return (Immergluck 2009; Wyly *et al.* 2006; Kendall and Fishman 2000). Changes to federal legislation in the 1980s, such as the 1984 Secondary Mortgage Market Enhancement Act (SMMEA), expanded Wall Street's ability to use these new flexible multi-class securities. And the 1989 Financial Institutions Reform, Recovery, and Enforcement Act further encouraged secondary market expansion by mandating higher capital requirements for thrifts, pushing them to sell loans they originated into the secondary market (Immergluck 2009; Gotham 2006; NHS 2004; Follain and Zorn 1990). Securitizing, tranching, credit enhancement, and loan terms such as prepayment penalties helped to de-link investment from place and, thus, further commodify real estate (Immergluck 2009; Gotham 2006; Beauregard 1994). As these processes expanded, investment in housing was further woven into the US economy. The Tax Reform Act of 1986 changed the rules on tax deductions creating an incentive for homeowners to tap into home equity to fund college educations, purchase new cars, and finance home renovation, further installing housing and finance as a critical segment in the broader economy (Immergluck 2009; Apgar, Bendimerad, and Essene 2007; NHS 2004; Howell 2006; Chomsisengphet and Pennington-Cross 2006).

Subprime Lending

These regulatory and legislative transformations created an infrastructure for lending that made it possible for lenders to increase home mortgage lending and, therefore, to increase opportunities for many borrowers who had been previously shut out of home lending networks. The expansion of the subprime market is usually explained as the result of increased liquidity and of complicated risk management strategies produced through the secondary market and a suite of technological innovations that include automated underwriting and credit scoring, which enable lenders to quickly and more finely estimate risk. Such developments, not incidentally, also fueled the growth of the prime mortgage market and, many argue, reduced the cost of lending (Crews Cutts and Van Order 2004). Subprime lending can be viewed as an evolutionary innovation that increased the avenues for capital accumulation in the land and housing markets. The later introduction of exotic or nontraditional mortgages and expanded use of ARMs (in the prime or subprime markets) can be thought of in much the same way (Beaverstock *et al.* 1992). Mortgages are products and in order for the financial industry to expand it needed to originate more loans. Given finite demand for loans, the only way to increase production is to find new markets, which could mean providing loans to borrowers with different risk profiles.

Securitization played an important role in facilitating this; reducing the regulatory impact of the Community Reinvestment Act (CRA) since it gave an advantage to non-bank lending institutions by creating an alternative source of capital divorced from place (Follain and Zorn 1990). Just as the federal government was gearing up for one of the most significant reductions in federal social welfare, heralding a New Federalism that increasingly devolved responsibility to local government, the federal government was restricting state controls over lending. The 1980 federal Depository Institutions Deregulation and Monetary Control Act (DIDMCA) allowed lenders to exceed state interest rate caps, allowing high cost sub-prime lending. Two years later, congress passed the Alternative Mortgage Transaction Parity Act (AMTPA) allowing negative amortization, adjustable interest rates, and balloon payments (Immergluck 2009; Chomsisengphet and Pennington-Cross 2006; Mansfield 2000).

The growth of subprime lending shifted concerns about access to capital to concerns about access to quality capital. Some concern stems from the racial disparities in subprime lending, which suggest that the mortgage market is racially segmented with Whites more likely to receive prime low cost loans and people of color, including people of color with good credit, likely to receive higher cost subprime loans (Apgar, Bendimerad, and Essene 2007; Wyly *et al.* 2006; Howell 2006; Chomsisengphet and Pennington-Cross 2006; US Departments of Treasury and HUD 2000). Moreover, subprime lenders have little incentive to turn away overqualified borrowers and Fannie Mae estimates that half of subprime borrowers qualify for prime credit, which means that borrowers are unnecessarily paying high fees and interest rates and damaging their credit (Stein and Libby 2001; TRF 2005; Squires and O'Connor 2001; Carr and Schuetz 2001).

Since the financial implosion of 2007, some have blamed overly exuberant borrowers for the collapse. But Engel and McCoy argue that residents of inner city communities have become "disconnected from the credit market and hence are vulnerable to predatory lending hard sell tactics." They add that lenders can use "information asymmetries" to exploit such market disconnection (Engel and McCoy 2002). Throughout the lending process, lenders and mortgage brokers have more information than borrowers. Borrowers often lack a complete understanding of the borrowing process and their legal rights and rarely obtain their own legal representation (Engel and McCoy 2002; TRF 2005). In surveys and interviews with borrowers, the Community Reinvestment Committee (CRC) (Stein and Libby 2001) and The Reinvestment Fund (TRF) (2005) found that many predatory lending victims do not understand the lending process, do not shop for their loan, use subprime credit even when they qualify for prime credit, do not understand the terms of their loans, and do not read documents at closing. In the CRC study, 36 percent of respondents did not read their loan documents. The rationales for not reading are telling: "61.9% reported that the documents were too lengthy; 38.1% felt pressured; 23.8% reported that the documents were too complex; and 19% reported that they trusted their loan representative" (Stein and Libby 2001 27). The information asymmetries especially within the subprime market are so great that even the savviest consumers have little chance of identifying the best priced loan.

There is mounting evidence that subprime lenders, often the mortgage brokers, use sophisticated marketing techniques to reach people with little lending experience, education, mobility, or access to alternatives (Quercia, Stegmen, and Davis 2004; Carr and Kolluri 2001). In its survey of borrowers, CRC found that 80 percent of African American borrowers with incomes above $45,000, who thought they had good credit, did not approach a bank before approaching a subprime lender for a loan (Stein and Libby 2001). Internet technology and mortgage brokers enable subprime lenders to reduce costs by eliminating branch offices. Lenders reach consumers through direct marketing, mortgage brokers, as well as home improvement contractors. As subprime lending boomed, the number of mortgage brokerage firms also increased, growing from 7000 in 1987 to 44,000 in 2002. Brokers originated 45 percent of subprime loans in 2002 (Harnick 2008).

Broker-originated lending is considerably different from direct institution lending and broker-originated loans are more likely to have poor terms. "Borrowers with broker-originated loans were more likely to pay points (25 versus 15 percent) and more likely to have a loan with a prepayment penalty (26 versus 12 percent)" (Harnick 2008). Despite the potential for abuse, brokers and home improvement contractors are not closely regulated (Gale 2001). Once identified as within a subprime market, residents received mailings and phone calls. For those who are most in need, with little time or lack of ability to shop, these offers can be appealing. In one study, 38 percent of respondents reported that the idea to take out a loan for home purchase or consumption came from marketing, and the proportions reached 40 percent for African American respondents and 44 percent for Latino respondents (Stein and Libby 2001).

We might expect that subprime credit is closely regulated because of the risks to borrowers, lenders, and financial markets; instead, from the brokers on the ground to the investors in the secondary market, it is not. Most prime lenders are regulated by one of the four federal regulatory agencies and are subject to periodic reviews and CRA requirements (Immergluck 2009; Immergluck and Smith 2005). But subprime capital flows through different conduits and a different regulatory structure (Apgar, Bendimerad, and Essene 2007; MacDonald 1996). Less than 2 percent of subprime loans are sold to GSEs, producing what Apgar, Bendimerad, and Essene (2007) refer to as "channel specialization." Channel specialization has distinct racial implications with White borrowers accessing credit that is more closely regulated.

> [S]ome 44.2 percent of all blacks (versus 30.1 percent of whites) obtain a loan from less heavily regulated independent mortgage companies. (Apgar, Bendimerad, and Essene 2007: iv)

Even though some states have passed legislation to limit lending practices associated with predatory lending, such as repeated refinancing without benefit to the consumer and balloon loans, states face significant capital regulating limitations (Quercia, Stegman, and Davis 2004). Federal preemption, capital's flexibility, and assignee liability, along with media campaigns and pressure from lenders, rating agencies, and investment groups that threaten to withdraw from lending activities, limit state regulatory ability and effectiveness. States that seek to regulate predatory lending face aggressive campaigns by lenders and lending institutions (Newman and Wyly 2004). And regulatory safeguards have not kept pace with the financialization of the economy.

In summary, the state has facilitated financialization and its link to the urban built environment. US housing policy, macroeconomic policy (artificially low interests rates), and legislative changes, which spurred the expansion of the secondary market and encouraged borrowers to use their homes as banks, all helped drive demand for mortgage production. But the expansion of the subprime market occurred in a space relatively free from regulation, and its spatial concentration in certain places meant that risk was also concentrated in certain places nationally and within metropolitan areas.

Measuring Foreclosure

Subprime lending held the promise of erasing urban disinvestment by increasing access to capital for borrowers and communities that lacked it in the past. The mounting scale of housing foreclosures, however, signaled the failure of that promise. The expansion of subprime lending also brought fears of high cost risky lending and foreclosures that could harm borrowers and communities. Since subprime lending emerged in the 1990s, researchers and advocacy groups have sought to measure the incidence of foreclosure, understand the extent to which it happens in the subprime market, and explore what it means in urban communities.

Studying foreclosure is complicated by a few intersecting problems. First, foreclosure is a process rather than a single event that introduces measurement and data collection problems. Foreclosures can be measured at the foreclosure filing stage, when mortgage owners announce their intent to foreclose, or at any point along the process such as when properties are sold at auction. Measuring the process at the foreclosure filing stage may overestimate the problem as some borrowers may resolve the delinquency, refinance, or negotiate a short sale. Measuring foreclosure at the auction stage misses borrowers who sell properties early, a problem in both hot and declining markets where buyers sell to avoid the costs of foreclosure and to preserve their credit. Second, measuring the extent to which foreclosure is a problem is complicated by the challenges involved in calculating a foreclosure rate that meaningfully captures the foreclosure problem and is comparable across places. The numerator could be foreclosure filings or auctions and the denominator could be the total number of housing units, occupied housing units, number of loans originated, or mortgageable properties (Immergluck 2009). These different possible measures mean that, few foreclosure rates are comparable. A 5 percent foreclosure rate might be extraordinarily high in one context and negligible in the next, depending on how foreclosures were measured. Third and not inconsequentially, foreclosure data in most places are not digitally available from public sources and purchasing the data privately is costly. This introduces data quality problems, and some data contained within the foreclosure documents is not included in these for-purchase datasets. The Home Mortgage Disclosure Act (HMDA) provides for an annual national dataset on mortgage applications and originations, but no comparable dataset exists for foreclosures. Fourth, the role of subprime lenders in foreclosure is a primary concern but gathering data that identify the originating lender and/or provide sufficient information about loan terms to characterize loans as subprime is often difficult, if not impossible. Instead, proxies are often used such as identifying subprime loans based on the characteristics of the lender rather than the loan.

The National Training and Information Center (NTIC) (1999), a historic participant in the US community reinvestment movement, conducted one of the earliest foreclosure studies in Chicago and a three county surrounding area based on mortgage foreclosure filings for foreclosures that went to auction between 1993 and 1998. Foreclosures doubled during the study period, subprime lenders accounted for 36 percent of foreclosures in 1998, and many loans foreclosed in less than four years. Subsequent studies replicated this initial study and produced similar findings including short times to foreclosure, increasing foreclosure rates over time, and active subprime participation. Gruenstein and Herbert (2000) studied foreclosures in Atlanta between June 1996 and December 1999 and found a decrease in total fore- closures, a 232 percent increase in subprime foreclosures, and that subprime loans foreclosed in half the time (two years) of non subprime foreclosures. Foreclosures in Cuyahoga County, Ohio increased from 2582 in 1995 to more than 12,000 in 2005 (Dimora, Hagan, and Jones 2005). Foreclosure starts in Chicago and a five county area skyrocketed from 7433 in 1995 to 25,145 in 2002 (Immergluck and Smith 2005). Many were in neighbor- hoods with high minority populations and extensive subprime penetration. Newman and Wyly (2004) also identified a connection between foreclosures and subprime lending that was not explained by borrower characteristics.

The Reinvestment Fund (TRF) has conducted some of the most comprehensive and far reaching foreclosure studies in Philadelphia, Pennsylvania, Delaware, and New Jersey. TRF matches foreclosure starts and auctions with loan level data, including originating lender and loan histories for individual properties. Their understanding of local markets and lenders allowed them to more accurately identify subprime lenders, including those not included in HUD's subprime list, presenting a more complete picture of subprime involvement in local foreclosures. When com- bined with interviews with borrowers, industry representatives, and other actors involved in mortgage lending, TRF's studies present a comprehensive account of mortgage foreclosure. In a study of foreclosure starts between 2000 and 2003 for the Pennsylvania Department of Banking, they found that subprime lenders originated 60–75 percent of foreclosure starts. Because many of these loans were concentrated in moderate income communities, many of which had sizable minority populations, even if there is nothing predatory about the loans, the fact that so many go to foreclosure and the concentration of subprime lending means that foreclosure too is spatially concentrated, a point that TRF has made to great effect (TRF 2005).

As researchers struggled to gather data and craft methodologies that would explore whether there was a relationship between subprime lending and foreclosures, the link was visibly made in 2007 when the number of foreclosures surged and an international fiscal crisis followed. Before the economic downturn of late 2007, researchers and policymakers anticipated that foreclosure rates on subprime loans originated between 1998 and 2006 would reach 18–20 percent (JEC 2007; Schloemer *et al.* 2006).

The incidence and characteristics of foreclosure can be illustrated through a case study of Essex County, New Jersey. These loans were originated before the problems in the subprime market grew worse and when underwriting practices were more cautious.

Foreclosures in Essex County

Essex County is situated a mere 20-minute train ride west of New York City in Northern New Jersey. It is home to Newark, the state's largest city and some of the state's wealthiest suburban communities lie on its western edge. In between is a ring of once-thriving inner suburban communities that have suffered severe disinvestment for more than two decades. The county and most of its constituent communities, including Newark, experienced a rapid upswing in real estate prices from the end of the 1990s. Community organizations that previously were able to access land for free from the city found themselves in competition with for-profit private developers as early as the late 1990s. Essex County was selected for a case study to expand on prior work and to build capacity to analyze these processes over time (Community Development Studio 2006; Newman and Wyly 2004; Community Finance Research Initiative 2001; Zimmerman, Wyly, Botein 2002).

The data for this study are 2004 foreclosure filings contained in public court records at the Administrative Office of the Courts Foreclosure Division in Trenton, NJ.[3] Removing non-bank filings, tax foreclosures, commercial foreclosures, and multi-family buildings produced a dataset of 2191 bank foreclosures.[4] The database was enhanced by identifying originators as subprime using the list prepared by the US Department of Housing and Urban Development (HUD) (Scheessele 2005 FFIEC annual). The HUD list identifies lenders as subprime if more than half of their loans are subprime in any given year. This procedure is limited because subprime is defined by the characteristics of the lender rather than the loan. Also, some small lenders are not required to file HMDA data and in some cases, it is impossible to identify the originating lender in the court records. To find the percentage of subprime loans in the 2004 foreclosure dataset, HMDA identification codes were identified for 77 percent of the loans originated between 1992 and 2004.[5] The data were cleaned and geo-coded producing 2083 records that matched 80–100 percent and 51 that matched at less than 80 percent.[6]

Two additional data sources provide context to understand the foreclosures in Essex County. First, we mapped Sheriff sales from 1991 to 2002, which suggest the concentration and spatial distribution of foreclosures during the period of subprime expansion (Community Development Studio 2006). In partnership with the New Jersey Institute for Social Justice, I also conducted four focus groups in 2003 with 23 homeowners in the Vailsburg section of Newark to help understand the process through which borrowers got loans, the role of home improvement contractors, mortgage brokers, and other local actors, and borrower experience with home loans and lending processes in their community. Vailsburg lies on Newark's western edge between the inner-ring suburbs of Irvington and East Orange, both of which have suffered disinvestment.

Geography of foreclosure

Mapping the spatial concentration of foreclosures offers only a piece of the picture. Calculating foreclosure rates using loan originations as the denominator provides a numerical indication of areas with severe foreclosure concentrations. The foreclosure rate, calculated as the number of loans originated between 2000 and 2003 in foreclosure in 2004 divided by total mortgage originations, looks similar to the analysis using owner occupied housing as the denominator and provides an intuitive way of understanding the impact (see Figure 8.1) (FFIEC, annual).[7] Seven of the 213 Census tracts in Essex County had 10 percent or more of the loans originated between 2000 and 2003 enter foreclosure in 2004 (three tracts in Newark, three tracts in Irvington, and one tract in East Orange).[8] The foreclosure rate exceeded 5 percent in 54 Census tracts. In some neighborhoods and regions, the foreclosure rate was much higher. The Upper Clinton Hill neighborhood in Newark's South Ward and the north section of Irvington saw 7 percent of the loans originated between 2000 and 2003 enter foreclosure in 2004.

The geography of the 2004 foreclosure filings matches spatial patterns identified in earlier work (Newman and Wyly 2004). Foreclosure filings in Essex County are concentrated in predominantly African American and Latino neighborhoods in Newark and in the adjacent inner ring cities/suburbs of Irvington, East Orange, and Orange. They are sparsely distributed in the County's wealthy western suburbs. Within the city of Newark, foreclosures are absent from areas that were targets of mid-century urban renewal projects that involved major land clearance for the construction of public and federally assisted housing. Maps and planning documents from Urban Renewal and Model Cities programs of the 1960s and 1970s show these neighborhoods as places that did not experience the extent of disinvestment and arson that plagued other parts of Newark during that period. They were not torn up by highway construction, nor were they the sites of massive scale high-rise public housing construction. They are low-rise residential neighborhoods, many of which have been the target of focused community development efforts, receiving governmental, private foundation, and bank resources. Foreclosures are also notably absent in the predominantly White communities and in the Ironbound, a predominantly immigrant Portuguese and Brazilian community on Newark's south east corner.

The foreclosure filings mapped here suggest that a foreclosure problem was underway before 2005. Sheriff sales data for 1991–2002 suggest a concentration that looks strikingly like that exhibited by the 2004 foreclosures filings. Of the 8763 Sheriff sales in Essex County during the decade, most, 3255, were concentrated in Newark and the surrounding inner-ring cities of Irvington with 1573 and East Orange with 1268.

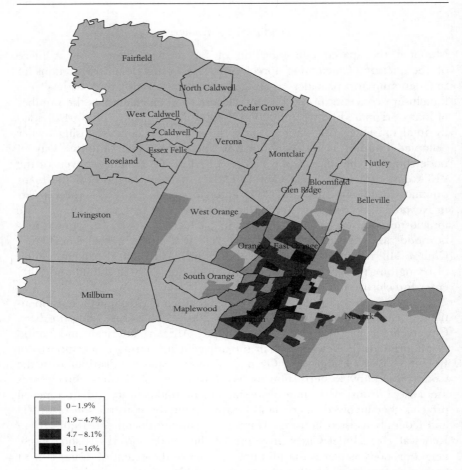

Figure 8.1 Percentage of loans originated 2000–03 in foreclosure in 2004, Essex County, New Jersey
Source: Based on author's calculations of mortgage foreclosure filings, 2004, Trenton; FFIEC, 1993–2004 created by Kathe Newman based on public FFIEC for HMDA data.

The foreclosure filings include information that sheds some light on the processes, institutions, and actors at work. The top ten originators of loans with foreclosure filings in 2004 account for one-quarter of foreclosure filings. Half of these are subprime lenders: and half of originated loans that fore-closed did so within two years of origination. The average interest rate for loans originated in 2003 that went into foreclosure in 2004 is only slightly above the average prime rate. If interest rate reflects the risk of lending, then these loans to not-so-risky borrowers went into foreclosure very quickly.

Another group of lenders originated loans with much higher average interest rates that exceed 11 percent. These loans took longer to foreclose and women appear to have accounted for 44 percent to 63 percent of the borrowers.

While interest rates taken alone do not indicate a definitive loan cost, they do provide a picture of the lending that produced the foreclosures. A handful of foreclosures have astronomically high interest rates that look like high credit card rates rather than home mortgage rates. These include a 23.89 percent interest rate on a $21,680 20-year loan originated in 2002 in Bloomfield and a 21.9 percent interest rate on a 30-year $30,000 loan in Newark. The interest rates on nearly a fifth of the foreclosure starts were 10 percent or more.[9] To compare the foreclosure filing interest rate with the prime rate at the time of origination, I calculated an average interest rate for the foreclosure filings each year for 30-year loans and compared it with the average annual interest rate on prime 30-year loans (Freddie Mac 2007).[10] The two interest rate curves look similar until 1995 when they diverge and the foreclosure filings interest rate exceeds the prime rate. Between 2000 and 2004, the foreclosure filings interest rate is 1.41–1.7 points above the prime rate. The average interest rate on subprime loans is higher than the average foreclosure filing interest rate but it does not fully make up the difference suggesting that at least some of the other loans are subprime.

The length of time between loan origination and foreclosure provides yet another piece of the puzzle regarding loan quality and/or borrower stability. The 2004 Essex County foreclosure filings went into foreclosure on average in 3.9 years; subprime loans entered foreclosure in an average 2.6 years. Sixty-three percent of all 2004 foreclosure filings were originated between 2001 and 2004 and a quarter originated in 2003. Eighteen percent started the foreclosure process less than a year after origination.

To understand the role of non-bank lenders in Essex County, using HMDA, I identified financial institutions and their regulators. Lenders sometimes change regulators so for each foreclosure filing, the originating lender was matched to the corresponding HMDA record for each year between 1993 and 2004. This provided the name of the regulating institution at the time of origination. For loans originated in 2003, lenders not regulated by one of the four federal regulatory agencies accounted for at least 60 percent of the foreclosure filings in Essex County. Between 1993 and 2004, 45 percent of the foreclosure filings were originated by lenders that were not regulated by the four federal agencies; 15 percent were regulated by the Office of the Comptroller of the Currency, 7 percent by the Federal Reserve System, 4 percent by the Federal Deposit Insurance Company, 7 percent by the Office of Thrift Supervision, and 21 percent were unidentifiable. The data appear to suggest that nonbank lenders played a significant role in originating loans that went into foreclosure and may indicate an increased role for these lenders in 2003 compared to 2000.

The concentration of foreclosures in particular communities, relatively short times to foreclosure, high interest rates, and a possibly increasing role for nonbank lenders that are not regulated by one of the four federal regulatory agencies provides some insight into the processes at work but offers little to explain processes within neighborhoods on the ground. Foreclosures are usually explained by life events and recently they have been described as loans people took out because they were not careful. But how did these borrowers get the loans and why? To better understand the processes that produced the foreclosure filings and the context within a neighborhood, we turn now to the Newark neighborhood of Vailsburg.

The View from Vailsburg

Vailsburg is a moderate-income predominantly African American neighborhood on the west side of Newark between the city of East Orange to its north and the city of Irvington to its south. Vailsburg began to shift from White to Black in the 1970s. New residents were middle class but lacked access to mortgage loans because of redlining. Focus groups with Vailsburg homeowners presented a different picture of access to capital after 2000. Residents describe a neighborhood bombarded by capital's intermediaries – home improvement contractors, lenders, and mortgage brokers – who sought to increase their business through mailings, phone calls, and in-house visits. One resident explained: "I get a lot of mail, two or three letters, pieces a day, approved refinancing, sometimes five or six." Another lamented: "My shredder is full of junk mail. I get stacks of information about home improvement loans ..." Residents pointed out that the advertisements often sell products unaffordable to the borrower. One resident explained: "My husband is retired but they are always offering him loans for $50,000 or $88,000. He can hardly pay the mortgage."

Even though the advertisements are a nuisance, some residents bought the services offered because they found it difficult to identify alternatives. But those services often came at a high cost. Many of the interviewees noted that contractors often ask about financing before they look at the job that needs to be done and they offer to link homeowners up to financing if they don't already have it. One homeowner explained his experience of getting quotes for his roof:

> I wanted to put a new roof on my house. The guy went directly to my house. He didn't look at the roof and he started talking about financing to me directly. He didn't look at the roof! He walked directly from the car to the house and [said] you want to talk to me about how much it would cost to put a roof on?

Residents indicated that they were encouraged to take out loans that exceeded their immediate needs. Home improvement contractors suggested that residents could take out home improvement loans that exceeded their home improvement needs and they could use the extra money to pay for vacations, cars, education, or simply the bills. One resident explained: "Home improvement contractors send you a letter and it says the balance of your home is 'X' and we can give you 'X' amount of dollars to do home repair or more if you want to buy a new car ..."

A frequently heard criticism suggests that borrowers would not fall into these lending traps if they were more financially literate and/or had adequate disclosure of loan terms. But Engel and McCoy (2002) have dispelled this notion by pointing out the extreme information asymmetries between borrowers and lenders. The Vailsburg residents were savvy and experienced. Nearly all were banked, more than half knew what a credit score was, and two monitored their credit scores. But having access to a savings account and knowing a credit score are not much protection considering the complexity of the mortgage process. Few, in Vailsburg or anywhere else, fully understand points, interest rates, loan durations, fees, adjustable rates, or exotic mortgages.

Residents identified closings as a particularly confusing and stressful time. The volume of legal papers and the complexity of the disclosure rules are overwhelming. More importantly, some homeowners, who discovered problems at closing or at some earlier point during the lending process, found that they had little choice but to proceed. In some cases, residents had to close to purchase new homes. In other cases, homeowners had invested time and money; each fee that residents pay puts them further into the process and the further in, the more compromised they feel. Walking away from a lender midway has practical implications – lost time from work, the time to find new lenders, lost fees, and possibly the loss of their home. The only resident who seemed entirely confident that he had been treated fairly at his mortgage closing used an attorney.

Residents of Vailsburg felt that their neighborhood was a target for unscrupulous actors. One resident explained:

> Minority neighborhoods are more susceptible to being victimized. We're seen as being less knowledgeable about obtaining contractors for repairs. We're charged a higher rate and higher fee and usually the quality of the work is substandard. And the financing is suspect ... they will query you about how you can repay the loan, personal savings, have a line of credit or they are willing to establish a line of credit with a lending institution.

Homeowners in Vailsburg, like homeowners in other neighborhoods that have lack of access to financial institutions, are vulnerable to high cost and abusive lending. The residents were clear that they are subjected to aggressive home loan and home improvement marketing and lack accessible alternatives. Vailsburg residents offer some insight into how loans reach community residents. They offer a portrait of a neighborhood that is subject to aggressive home mortgage marketing and residents who lack alternatives.

The case study of Essex County illustrates some of the processes through which capital is extracted from communities. Previously harmed by disinvestment related to redlining, the urban areas of Essex County are now being devastated as borrowers are unable to hold onto their homes. The pattern of foreclosures shows concentrations in majority Black and Latino neighborhoods with larger homes and equity to strip. Homeownership in these communities was not an avenue to wealth, neighborhood stability, or urban revitalization. Instead, for many, it was a path to urban decline and further disinvestment.

Conclusion

Mortgage foreclosures can be understood as the plight of individual borrowers who are in financial difficulties well over their heads; as the product of a handful of unscrupulous lenders seeking to make a profit; or even as the result of disintermediation in which each lending function is performed by a specialist with brokers originating loans for which they bear little subsequent responsibility. Or we can expand the scale of explanation and view the foreclosure crisis as related to broader efforts to expand economic growth with little regulation. Subprime lending transformed access to capital. And, mortgage lending and "home" became even more intricately woven into the economy. In the new economy, mortgage loans are the modern day widget and financial institutions needed to produce more widgets to fuel expansion. The state helped to fuel financial expansion through a series of regulatory and tax decisions over a period of decades with the hope that economic growth would provide great public benefits. But the effect on disadvantaged populations and urban places has been devastating and the structure became unstable enough to threaten the global economy.

Homeownership has been heralded as the "American Dream," a tool to build intergenerational wealth, revitalize disinvested cities, and stabilize neighborhoods. In recent years, an increasing number of borrowers, communities, and local governments have woken up to find that the dream was instead a nightmare. Vacant boarded buildings line urban neighborhoods, borrowers and renters seek alternative housing and communities desperately seek strategies and funding to rescue people, homes, communities, and investments. Home mortgage lending can provide benefits for many but some regulation is necessary to ensure that the lending produces public benefits that outweigh the costs.

Acknowledgments

Many thanks to Gretchen Minneman and the Spring 2006 Rutgers University Community Development Studio for gathering mortgage foreclosure filings. A very special thanks to the staff at the foreclosure division of the New Jersey Administrative Office of the Courts, to Ken Zimmerman and Ellen Brown at the New Jersey Institute for Social Justice and to Michael Farley, Doris Lewis, Moises Serrano, members of UVSO's predatory lending advisory panel and to the many homeowners who graciously spent their evenings with us. Manuel Aalbers, Robert Lake, Elvin K. Wyly, Norman Glickman, Phil Ashton, Dan Hammel, Tom Slater, and IJURR reviewers provided helpful comments on the chapter and thoughts along the way. All errors or misinterpretations are the responsibility of the author.

Notes

1   I chose 2004 because that was the New Jersey Courts had a full year of data for 2004 when I began this project towards the end of 2005.
2   The UK adopted similar policies (Martin and Turner, 2000).
3   Foreclosure data in New Jersey are available from state court files, county *lis pendens* filings, or from private firms that specialize in foreclosure data collection.
4   The initial list totaled 3008 MFF: 22 (1 percent) private sales, 54 (2 percent) home equity lines of credit, 75 (3 percent) non residential, 666 (22 percent) tax foreclosures reducing our list to 2191 (73 percent) bank foreclosures. In retrospect, removing the tax sales may result in underestimating the problem. Some borrowers may not realize that their taxes are not in escrow and while they manage to pay the lender, they may not pay their taxes and lose the home to tax foreclosure.
5   The unidentified lenders include lenders that do not file HMDA reports and unclear lender names based on the way the name was recorded in the foreclosure documents.
6   Addresses were checked using Google Maps to correct misspelling, zip code changes, and other errors. Missing addresses were identified using block and lot numbers through the New Jersey Association of County Tax Boards online parcel identification system (http://njactb.org/).
7   Both efforts underestimate the extent of the foreclosure problem because they only capture loans that foreclosed in 2004 missing those that foreclosed before and after and it also misses the cumulative effect of foreclosures over time. Foreclosure rate calculated as the number of foreclosure starts by owner occupied housing units, produces a 5 percent foreclosure rate in Irvington and East Orange, 3.7 percent in Newark, 3.5 percent in Orange, and 1.3 percent in Belleville and South Orange, similar to what was produced using loan originations.

8   This does not mean that only 10 percent of loans originated during that period went into foreclosures; it means that 10 percent or so foreclosed in 2004 so it likely underestimates the total foreclosure rate of loans originated during that period.

9   Loan position was not identifiable from the foreclosure filings.

10 Many of the loans with excessively high interest rates were for terms shorter than 30 years.

References

Apgar, W., Bendimerad, A., and Essene, R. (2007) *Mortgage market channels and fair lending: An analysis of HMDA data*. Joint Center for Housing Studies. Boston: Harvard University. http://www.jchs.harvard.edu/publications/finance/mm07-2_mortgage_market_channels.pdf. Accessed July 30, 2007.

Beauregard, R. (1994) Capital switching and the built environment: United States, 1970–89. *Environment and Planning A* 26: 715–32.

Beaverstock, J., Leyshon, A., Rutherford, T., Thrift, N., and Williams, P. (1992) Moving houses: The geographical reorganization of the estate agency industry in England and Wales in the 1980s. *Transactions of the Institute of British Geographers* 17(2): 166–82.

Carr, J. and Kolluri, L. (2001) Predatory lending: an overview. Washington, DC: Fannie Mae Foundation.

Carr, J. and Schuetz, J. (2001) Financial services in distressed communities: framing the issue, finding solutions. Washington, DC: Fannie Mae Foundation. http://www.fanniemaefoundation.org/programs/financial.PDF

Charney, I. (2001) Three dimensions of capital switching within the real estate sector: A Canadian case study. *International Journal of Urban and Regional Research* 25(4): 740–58.

Chomsisengphet, S. and Pennington-Cross, A. (2006) The evolution of the subprime mortgage market. *Federal Reserve Bank of St. Louis Review* 88(1): 31–56.

Community Development Studio, Rutgers University. (2006) *Mortgage market transformation and foreclosure*. Report to the New Jersey Institute for Social Justice. New Brunswick. http://www.policy.rutgers.edu/academics/studios/index.html

Community Finance Research Initiative. (2001) *A report on predatory lending in the greater Newark, New Jersey area*. Submitted to The New Jersey Institute for Social Justice. New Brunswick, New Jersey.

Crews Cutts, A. and Van Order, R. (2004) On the economics of subprime lending. Freddie Mac Working Paper #04–01 January. http://www.freddiemac.com/news/pdf/subprime_012704.pdf Accessed July 30, 2007.

Crump, J. (2002) Deconcentration by demolition: public housing, poverty, and urban policy. *Environment and Planning D: Society and Space* 10: 581–96.

Dimora, J., Hagan, T., and Lawson Jones, P. (2005) Commissioners' report and recommendations on foreclosures. Cuyahoga County of Ohio. http://development.cuyahogacounty.us/PDF/foreclosure_rpt.pdf Accessed December 28, 2006.

Engel, K. and McCoy, P. (2002) A tale of three markets: the law and economics of predatory lending. *Texas Law Review* 80(6): 1255–381.

Federal Financial Institutions Examination Council (FFIEC). (Annual) *Home Mortgage Disclosure Act, raw loan application register data, CD ROM.* Washington, DC: Federal Reserve Board.

Follain, J. and Zorn, P. (1990) The unbundling of residential mortgage finance. *Journal of Housing Research* 1(1): 63–89.

Freddie Mac. (2007) Weekly primary mortgage market survey. 30-year fixed-rate historic tables. http://www.freddiemac.com/dlink/html/PMMS/display/PMMSOutputYr.jsp?year=2007 Accessed August, 2007.

French, S. and Leyshon, A. (2004) The new financial system? Towards a conceptualization of financial reintermediation. *Review of International Political Economy* 11(2): 263–88.

Gale, D. (2001) Subprime and predatory mortgage refinancing: information technology, credit scoring, and vulnerable borrowers. Paper presented at the American Real Estate and Economics Association Midyear Meeting. Washington, DC May 31.

Gotham, K. (2006) The secondary circuit of capital reconsidered: globalization and the U.S. real estate sector. *American Journal of Sociology* 112(1): 231–75.

Growth and Change. (2007) special issue on European Financial Geographies 38(2).

Gruenstein, D. and Herbert, C. (2000) Analyzing trends in subprime originations and foreclosures: a case study of the Atlanta metro area. Prepared for The Neighborhood Reinvestment Corporation. Abt Associates, Inc. https://www.abtassociates.com/reports/20006470781991.pdf Accessed July 30, 2007.

Harnick, E. (2008) http://www.responsiblelending.org/mortgage-lending/policy-legislation/congress/ellen-harnick-testimony-veterans-affairs-feb-08.pdf

Harvey, D. (1989, 1985). *The Urban Experience.* Baltimore: The Johns Hopkins University Press.

Harvey, D. (1999, 1982) *Limits to Capital.* NY: Verso.

Howell, B. (2006) Exploiting race and space: concentrated subprime lending as housing discrimination. *California Law Review* 94: 101–47.

Immergluck, D. (2009) *Foreclosed: High-Risk Lending, Deregulation, and the Undermining of America's Mortgage Market* Ithaca, NY: Cornell University Press.

Immergluck, D. and Smith, G. (2005) Measuring the effect of subprime lending on neighborhood foreclosures: evidence from Chicago. *Urban Affairs Review* 40(3): 362–89.

Immergluck, D. and Smith, G. (2006) The external costs of foreclosure: the impact of single-family mortgage foreclosures on property values. *Housing Policy Debate* 17(1): 57–79.

Joint Center for Housing Studies. (2006a) *State of the nation's housing 2006.* Graduate School of Design, Kennedy School of Government, Harvard University, Boston. http://www.jchs.harvard.edu/publications/markets/son2006/index.htm Accessed on July 30, 2007.

Joint Center for Housing Studies. (2006b) *Fact Sheet. state of the nation's housing.* Graduate School of Design, Kennedy School of Government, Harvard University, Boston. http://www.jchs.harvard.edu/media/son2006_fact_sheet.pdf Accessed on July 20, 2007.

Joint Economic Committee (JEC). (2007) *The Subprime lending crisis: The economic impact on wealth, property values and tax revenues, and how we got here.* Report and

Recommendations by the Majority Staff of the Joint Economic Committee of the United States Senate. October. http://www.jec.senate.gov/Documents/Reports/ 10.25.07OctoberSubprimeReport.pdf Accessed on January 26, 2008.

Kendall, L. and Fishman, M. (ed.) (2000) *A Primer on Securitization*. Cambridge: MIT Press.

Krippner, G. (2005) The financialization of the American economy. *Socio-Economic Review* 3: 173–208.

Lea, M. (1990) Sources of funds for mortgage finance. *Journal of Housing Research* 1(1): 139–62.

MacDonald, H. (1996) The rise of mortgage-backed securities: struggles to reshape access to credit in the USA. *Environment and Planning A* 28(7): 1179–198.

Mansfield, C.L. (2000) The road to subprime "HEL" was paved with good congressional intentions: usury deregulation and the subprime home equity market. *S.C.L Rev* 51: 476, 476–587.

Martin, R. and Turner, D. (2000) Demutualization and the remapping of financial landscapes. *Transactions of the Institute of British Geographers* 25(2): 221–41.

National Housing Services of Chicago (NHS). (2004) Preserving homeownership: community-development implications of the new mortgage market. Chicago: NHS. http://www.nw.org/network/pubs/studies/documents/ preservingHomeownershipRpt2004_000.pdf Accessed on July 30, 2007.

National Training and Information Center (NTIC). (1999) *Preying on neighborhoods: subprime mortgage lending and Chicagoland foreclosures*. September 21. Chicago: IL. http://www.ntic-us.org/preying/preying.pdf. Last accessed June 22, 2007.

Newman, K. and Wyly, E. (2004) Geographies of mortgage market segmentation in Essex County, New Jersey. *Housing Studies* 19(1): 53–83.

Quercia, R.G., Stegman, M., and Davis, W.R. (2004) Assessing the impact of North Carolina's anti-predatory lending law. *Housing Policy Debate* 15(3): 573–602.

Scheessele, R. (2005) HUD subprime and manufactured home lender list. Annually updated dataset available at http://www.huduser.org/datasets/manu.html. US Department of Housing and Urban Development, Washington, DC.

Schloemer, E., Li, W., Ernst, K., and Keest, K. (2006) Losing ground: foreclosures in the subprime market and their cost to homeowners. Center for Responsible Lending. December. http://www.responsiblelending.org/pdfs/FC-paper-12–19-new-cover-1.pdf

Squires, G. and O'Connor, S. (2001) *Color of Money*. Albany: State University of New York Press.

Stein, K. and Libby, M. (2001) *Stolen Wealth: Inequities in California's Subprime Mortgage Market*. California: California Reinvestment Committee.

Stiglitz, J.E. and Weiss, A. (1981) Credit rationing in markets with imperfect information. *The American Economic Review* 71(3): 393–410.

The Reinvestment Fund (TRF). (2005) *Mortgage foreclosure filings in Pennsylvania*. TRF. A Study for the Pennsylvania Department of Banking, Philadelphia. www.trfund.com/policy/pa_foreclosures.htm

US Departments of Treasury and Housing and Urban Development. (2000) *Curbing Predatory Home Mortgage Lending*. (HUD-Treasury Report) http://www.huduser.org/ publications/pdf/treasury

Whitehouse, M. (2007) Day of reckoning. "Subprime" aftermath: losing the family home. *Wall Street Journal.* May 30.

Wyly, E., Atia, M., Foxcroft, H., Hammel, D., and Phillips-Watts, K. (2006) American home: predatory mortgage capital and neighbourhood spaces of race and class exploitation in the United States. *Geografiska Annaler* 88(B): 105–32.

Zimmerman, K., Wyly, E., and Botein, H. (2002) *Predatory lending in New Jersey: the rising threat to low-income homeowners.* Newark: New Jersey Institute for Social Justice. http://www.njisj.org/reports/predatory_lending.html.

9

Race, Class, and Rent in America's Subprime Cities

Elvin Wyly, Markus Moos, and Daniel J. Hammel

Introduction

Beginning in early 2007, the collapse of an obscure corner of the US housing market began to cascade through the entire American economy, eventually spreading worldwide and triggering the first truly global recession since the Great Depression of the 1930s. Credit and lending practices that had been justified on the basis of free-market doctrines of individual opportunity, consumer sovereignty, and competitive innovation had driven a wave of accelerated increases in present-day consumption purchased through vastly increased long-term debt commitments. While the boom flourished, mainstream and conservative analysts praised the rationality of consumers using low borrowing costs to leverage buoyant house prices and stock market portfolios. When the boom collapsed, conservatives moved quickly to frame the crisis as a failure of personal responsibility among "risky" borrowers – especially racial and ethnic minorities who were supposedly the beneficiaries of ill-conceived government policies – thereby obscuring the systemic nature of a generational transformation in the financial services sector (Malkin 2008; Will 2008; Thomas *et al.* 2008). In the last 15 years, an industry that historically maximized profits by class, racial, and ethnic exclusion and state-subsidized, long-term arbitrage had evolved into something very different: a deregulated entrepreneurial environment in which brokers, lenders, and investment banks pushed high-cost, exploitative credit into minority and working-class communities, earning up-front profits while competing to

Subprime Cities: The Political Economy of Mortgage Markets, First Edition. Edited by Manuel B. Aalbers.
© 2012 Blackwell Publishing Ltd. Published 2012 by Blackwell Publishing Ltd.

off-load the long-term risks to other institutions, investors, governments, and vulnerable borrowers themselves.

In this chapter, we analyze the urban geography of this transformation. We begin with an empirical narrative of events during the crisis that exposed the contradictions of an entrenched theoretical and policy infrastructure favoring the agents and institutions of mortgage capital. We then review the economic doctrines – credit rationing and risk-based pricing – that underwrote the subprime boom, before offering a theoretical-political challenge. Racial-ethnic inequalities in high-risk lending should be understood not as market-equilibrium responses to consumer demand and borrower credit characteristics, but as contemporary reincarnations of a previous generation of urban exploitation – class-monopoly rent (Harvey 1974). Subprime lending exploits the legal and regulatory loopholes created and justified by risk-based pricing in order to provide profitable opportunities to extract class-monopoly rent. These opportunities, however, are fundamentally geographical: class-monopoly rents are based on the strategic exploitation of a scale mismatch between the social and cultural use values of place-based homeownership, and the mobile circuits of exchange value speculative investment and regulatory arbitrage. To measure these geographical dynamics, we develop a simple protocol for measuring and mapping the racial and class dimensions of class-monopoly rent. This protocol is used to map the geography of the subprime boom at its peak (2004–06) across several hundred metropolitan areas in the US. Several complementary approaches are used to test whether variations in market penetration simply mirror borrower qualifications (as predicted by risk-based pricing) or reflect systemic, fundamental inequalities of contemporary class-monopoly rent.

Rethinking "How the World Works"

In early 2007, the collapse of a once-obscure segment of the US mortgage market began to cascade through the financial system, triggering multiple waves of crisis that eventually shook the pillars of the entire global financial infrastructure. The first clear signs of the present crisis, appropriately enough, were announced by a large transnational bank that had always distinguished itself by understanding the geography of global–local relations: HSBC, "the world's local bank," issued an unprecedented earnings warning in late February, along with reassurances that the problem was confined to a batch of faster-than-expected defaults on the 2006 vintage of high-cost "subprime" loans made by its US-based subsidiary, Household International. In response to HSBC's announcement, "stock markets around the world plummeted … in a wave of selling" (Norris and Peters 2007), offering a preview of the global devastation to come. By the late summer of 2008, the world economy was in freefall towards the first truly global recession since the Great Depression of the 1930s – offering a belated reminder that the post-Cold War "end of history" had not resolved the internal contradictions of finance capital. Indeed, the intensifying disasters brought a resurgent interest in the lessons of political economy from surprising quarters. The most conservative daily newspaper in America published the *Wall Street Journal Guide to the End of Wall Street as We Know It* (Kansas 2009). Francis Fukuyama himself coauthored a comprehensive attack on the free-market dogmas of economics itself, under the title, "What were they thinking?" In stark contrast to the "historically unprecedented rates of growth" achieved by China's pragmatic approach to finance policy, Fukuyama pointed to the continuation of America's stagnant and crisis-ridden path thanks to a stubborn commitment to the efficient-markets hypothesis and theoretically derived virtues of financial-sector liberalization:

> Americans ... have proven to be remarkably rigid in their economic thinking and – there is no other word for it – ideological. ... Unjustified and empirically unsupported economic ideas sowed the groundwork that has prompted the worst economic crisis in 75 years. Any academic discipline that developed and communicated ideas of such devastating effects has some soul-searching to do. (Fukuyama and Colby 2009: 23, 25)

Alan Greenspan (2008), long revered as the brilliant objectivist architect of deregulated growth and the maestro of impenetrable macroeconomic discourse, was finally forced to explain things in clear terms:

> those of us who have looked to the self-interest of lending institutions to protect shareholders' equity (myself included) are in a state of shocked disbelief. Such counterparty surveillance is a central pillar of our financial markets' state of balance ... So the problem here is something which looked to be a very solid edifice, and indeed, a critical pillar to market competition and free markets, did indeed break down. And I think that, as I said, did shock me. I still do not understand fully why it happened and, obviously, to the extent that I figure out where it happened and why, I will change my views. I found a flaw in the model that I perceived is the critical functioning structure that defines how the world works, so to speak.

As the crisis worsened in the summer and fall of 2008, a rare, clear image of America's political economy could be glimpsed through a parallax view of epistemology and power. Each week brought new revelations, new collapses that exposed the crumbling foundations of economic theory and institutional practice; yet each week also brought state interventions designed to shock and awe, to showcase the unquestioned power of the sovereign. Free markets suddenly questioned the metaphysical reality of the "value" of a vast array of assets and instruments that had been cemented into the foundation of the transnational financial system. With house prices collapsing, investors could find no basis in reality to set trading values for mortgage-backed securities (MBSs), collateralized debt obligations (CDOs), or credit default swaps (CDSs). Investors quickly lost confidence in the value of any institution with any perceived exposure to these financial instruments. Confronted with the terrifying abyss of unreality – an edifice of trillions of dollars of leveraged market capitalization in suspended animation – state actors responded with a hyper-real force of power and performativity. On Friday, July 11, 2008, market rumors erased nearly half the value of the government sponsored enterprises (GSEs) Fannie Mae and Freddie Mac, which together owned or insured some $5.3 trillion in residential mortgages. Literally overnight, the US Treasury reversed a generation of bipartisan policy commitments, and moved to inject billions to prevent a cascade that would have hit innumerable institutions around the world. Treasury Secretary Henry M. Paulson, Jr. used a provocative metaphor to convince angry senators why unlimited authority was required:

> If you've got a squirt gun in your pocket, you may have to take it out. If you've got a bazooka, and people know you have it, then you may not have to take it out. By making it unspecified, it will greatly expand the likelihood it will not have to be used. (quoted in Labaton and Herszenhorn 2008: A1)

Paulson got his bazooka with unlimited ammunition, but it soon became clear that bigger artillery would be required. The government seized Fannie and Freddie on September 7, and announced the first of many unprecedented plans designed to shore up the prices of MBS that had been judged worthless and unreal by the open market. Markets virtually disappeared for credit transactions or financial institutions with any suspected MBS exposure. Investors understood that MBS bids could no longer be premised on recent asset prices, but would have to be based on precisely those textbook finance valuation concepts that had been rendered epistemically untenable and unknowable. An estimate of the discounted net present value of a stream of future payments from millions of borrowers – many of them pushed into complex loans with deceptive, hidden terms – arrayed in risk tranches that had been rendered meaningless by the failure of securities with triple-A ratings. In the last weeks of 2006 alone, the three dominant ratings agencies had downgraded more than 1300 CDOs, "many of them straight from AAA to junk" (McDonald and Robinson 2009: 200). The entire analytical infrastructure of Wall Street was crumbling, as the "seemingly safely framed and profitable 'credit risk' " overflowed "into 'market risk' in which asset prices fell in unexpected ways, and 'counterparty risk' where fear of potential exposure to others' losses quite literally brought credit markets to a standstill" (Robertson and Jones 2009: 859). Conditions worsened within a week, when Treasury and the US Federal Reserve claimed there was no legal authority permitting a government guarantee on Lehman Brothers' toxic MBS assets in order to find a buyer for the troubled firm. Lehman filed for bankruptcy on September 15, sending shock waves through global financial markets. The next day, Paulson and Fed Chair Ben Bernanke reversed course with an infusion of $85 billion into the American International Group. Paulson and Bernanke reluctantly agreed that they needed Congressional authorization for the increasingly aggressive interventions, culminating in several weeks of market anxiety and political theater before the passage of a $700 billion Troubled Asset Relief Program (TARP).

TARP quickly evolved "into a program of unprecedented scope, scale, and complexity" (SIGTARP 2009: 3). Even its dozen separate programs constituted only a small fraction of the remarkable, raw demonstration of state power: the Fed repeatedly cited the "unusual and exigent circumstances" provisions of Depression-era amendments to the Federal Reserve Act to justify opening the discount window to more and more kinds of institutions. As the market freefall steadily exposed the bottomless unreality of model-based asset prices, it became imperative to expand the scope and scale of the response in order to demonstrate sovereign power. Almost 50 programs or initiatives were created by US federal agencies, providing direct infusions as well as guarantees and other "potential support" totaling more than $23 trillion (SIGTARP 2009: 137). From March 2008 to May 2009, the Fed made nearly $9 trillion in short-term loans to 18 large financial institutions under a single program, one of the highlights of more than 21,000 transactions. Citigroup, Merrill Lynch, and Morgan Stanley each returned to the well more than 100 times (Chan and McGinty 2010).

The extraordinary measures that became standard procedures in the last year of the Bush Administration set the template for many of the early efforts of the Obama Administration. Obama's first months required balancing a precarious progressive coalition amidst the immediate policy demands of a wide range of geopolitical, economic, and institutional threats around the world. Obama moved quickly to reassure Wall Street with an economic team dominated by veterans of earlier eras of deregulation. As a painful recession deepened and the housing market was hit by a "perfect storm" of foreclosures (Newman 2008), three interrelated features of the crisis began to clarify what was new, and what was not, in this most recent financial panic.

First, race was central to the material and discursive constitution of subprime and its collapse – and yet the subject of race was quickly whitewashed as the crisis exposed the systemic failures of the financial system. To make the loans that could be packaged into MBSs to feed the "appetite for yield" of global investors between 2001 and 2007, lenders and brokers used many of the high-pressure sales tactics and underwriting approaches first devised in the Federal Housing Administration (FHA) scandals that devastated Black neighborhoods in the late 1960s and early 1970s (Boyer 1973). These deceptive practices were further perfected in the subprime refinance and home improvement abuses of the 1990s (Immergluck 2009; Squires 2003; Williams *et al.* 2005). When the cascade of failures hit the riskiest front-line originators in 2007 and 2008, conservatives moved quickly to construct "subprime" as the housing equivalent of affirmative action. The crisis was suddenly portrayed as the collateral damage of interference with race-neutral free markets, in the form of fair housing laws, the Community Reinvestment Act (CRA), and policy support for an expansion of minority homeownership (Malkin 2008; Sowell 2007; Will 2008). Peter Wallison, the American Enterprise Institute's senior analyst in financial policy studies, explicitly blamed "the U.S. government's efforts to increase home owner-ship, especially among minority, low-income, and other underserved groups, through hidden financial subsidies rather than through direct government expenditures." (Wallison 2009: 365). Wallison was subsequently appointed as one of the Republican members of the Financial Crisis Inquiry Commission, and coauthored a pre-emptive dissent highlighting how government policy contributed to declining lending standards:

> Through the GSEs, FHA loans, VA loans, the Federal Home Loan Banks, and the Community Reinvestment Act, among other programs, the government subsidized and, in some cases, mandated the extension of credit to high-risk borrowers, propagating risks for financial firms, the mortgage market, taxpayers, and ultimately the financial system. (Thomas *et al.* 2010: 3)

At a speech delivered to the right-wing think tank of the 1980s junk-bond king Michael Milken, the chief executive of the nation's largest subprime lender famously blamed the crisis on "special pressure from minority advocates to help people buy homes," which forced lenders to "lower their mortgage standards." (Angelo Mozilo, quoted in Morgenson and Fabrikant 2007).

Second, the crisis exposed the new interdependency between two separate facets of subprime finance. As a regime of racial or ethnic exploitation, various forms of subprime lending have a long history (Boyer 1973; Engel and McCoy 2002; HUD-Treasury Joint Task Force 2000; Immergluck 2004; Sorkin 2002; Squires 2003, 2004; Williams *et al.* 2005). Yet the boom after 2001 was unique in the way that the old racialized inequalities first intensi-fied and then went mainstream in a form of hyper-competition that reflected and reinforced the dramatic escalation of house prices. Innovation diffusion reversed the hierarchy to go upscale, and to go White. High-risk advances in underwriting, loan terms, and consumer deception that had been pioneered in the racialized, low-income subprime refinance market in the 1990s were increasingly used, especially after 2003, in the "Alt-A" market. "Subprime" innovations paved the way for "exotic" instruments to help middle-income buyers, including many non-Hispanic Whites, stretch to qualify for the escalating home prices of California, Florida, and other expensive growth centers (Immergluck 2008, 2009). Gotham, in Chapter 1, and Sassen, in Chapter 3, analyze how this shift reflected the use of credit innovation and securitization technologies to lengthen the distance between a financial instrument and its underlying asset; such innovations served as major (if ultimately failed) crisis-management strategies to deal with the contradictions of capital accumulation in housing. In this chapter, we seek to measure and map the local, urban, and regional expression of these circuit-crisis dynamics.

A third feature of the crisis offered stern lessons on the importance of power and ideology. Both the Bush and Obama economic teams were forced into virtually unlimited commitments and assurances to stabilize the institutions that had created vast transnational networks of leveraged risk. By contrast, efforts to provide even small amounts of direct assistance to the millions of people facing foreclosure and eviction – many as a direct result of predatory subprime abuses – have been met with fierce resistance. The opposition has several sources. The biased electoral geography of the US Senate exacerbates an "institutional strangulation" (Carpenter 2010) funded by lobbyists advancing the class interests of finance capital (Harvey 2005). Influential economic theory underpins a stubborn preference for self-correcting markets over clear regulatory prohibitions (Peterson 2005, 2007). More than half a century of implicit and explicit preference in public policy and American culture have encouraged homeownership (Krueckeberg 1999), maintaining a deep suspicion of any regulatory intervention that might limit access to the "American Dream." Taken together, all of these factors mean that the "subprime cities" analyzed in this volume provide textbook case studies of urban legal geographies: "living in cities is one way of realizing the raw force of law," and indeed "law is sought as a mediator and a weapon" quite frequently in this crisis (Clark 2001: x). Caught between the legal quagmire of fragmented mortgage ownership among securitized loan pools and the unpopularity of direct financial assistance to borrowers, the Obama Administration offered financial incentives for lenders and loan servicers to voluntarily modify the terms of troubled loans. Through various programs a total of 467,000 permanent loan modifications have been completed so far, out of a total of 5.5 million homes that have received foreclosure notices since January 2009 (SIGTARP 2010: 6). Yet a proposal that would require not a penny of public expenditure – revising the personal bankruptcy code to permit judges to modify the terms of first-lien mortgages – has been repeatedly killed in the Senate. For banks and institutional investors holding securities backed by distressed mortgages, the threat was only partly about profits – which remain uncertain given the elevated default risk of un-modified, usurious loans. The true threat is the precedent of altering the terms of class power in the market for mortgage finance:

The proposal would have shifted negotiating power to the millions of troubled homeowners who could use the threat of bankruptcy to wrest lower payments from lenders. The banks claimed that would force them to raise rates. (Labaton 2009: A1)

It came as no surprise that financial sector lobbyists would offer this logic, and it is to be expected that conservative Senators and political operatives would press the argument at every opportunity. What defied expectations, however, was the refusal of centrist Democrats and a Democratic executive to challenge the raw assertion of class power so soon after what Greenspan himself had confessed was a "once in a lifetime" shock in which "the whole intellectual edifice" of self-correction markets as a risk-management paradigm had "collapsed" (quoted in Andrews 2008). Even the *possibility* of helping individual borrowers became a powerful catalyst for right-wing American populism: less than two years after CNBC correspondent Rick Santelli yelled from the trading floor of the Chicago Mercantile Exchange, "do we really want to subsidize the loser's mortgage?" and called for a "Tea Party" response, 41 percent of voters in the 2010 midterm election expressed support for the movement (Pew Research Center 2010; 86 percent of this support came from self-identified Republicans). To understand the speed of the realignment back to the old, discredited ideological equilibrium – government is the problem, free markets are the solution – we need to analyze the economic doctrines sustaining the popular faith that deregulated credit markets will open doors to the American Dream of homeownership. Two theoretical frameworks serve this purpose: credit rationing and risk-based pricing. We now turn to the history of these theories, before offering a theoretical and empirical challenge.

Credit Rationing, Risk, and Race

Credit is fascinating for economists (and especially neoclassical economists), because it is vulnerable to a dilemma first identified by Adam Smith. If the interest rate is set too high, "the greater part of the money to be lent, would be lent to prodigals and profectors" (*Wealth of Nations* 1776, cited in Stiglitz and Weiss 1992: 694). Two centuries on, "The fundamental problem facing capital markets can be put starkly: there is an infinite supply of charlatans in the market" (Greenwald and Stiglitz 1991: 8). Charlatans disrupt the entire system, because credit is not like other commodities. Money circulates not for current goods and services, but in exchange for contingent promises about the future that take the form of "I will pay a certain amount, provided that I can; and if I can't, other consequences follow" (Greenwald and Stiglitz 1991: 5). The economics of such contingent promises rely on borrowers' individual assessments of the need for credit and the severity of consequences for default – and on lenders' ability to discern the true intentions of borrowers who make promises. Markets fail under conditions of asymmetric information, when lenders have insufficient and/or unreliable information on borrowers' willingness and commitment to honor their obligations. In this situation, a perverse problem of adverse selection sets in when lenders raise the cost of credit to cover the expected losses on borrowers who appear to be more risky. The higher price will deter the prudent borrowers who will work hard to honor the debt, but it will not discourage the charlatans who have no intention of repaying. Instead of reducing loss risks, raising prices worsens the average risk profile of the lender's portfolio – undermining profits and exacerbating the risk of systemic disequilibrium and insolvency. When lenders do not have the information required to distinguish good customers from bad, in other words, the paramount instrument of neoclassical economic theory (the price mechanism) fails to achieve its axiomatic role. Lenders respond to this dilemma by rationing credit on the basis of supply rather than price, setting qualification standards unreasonably high, rejecting many qualified borrowers, and resorting to idiosyncratic or irrational criteria in attempts to avoid the charlatans. The result is a systemic credit shortage for many qualified borrowers (Stiglitz and Weiss 1981).

Credit rationing is the dominant neoclassical explanation for the racial redlining and discrimination that plagued American cities for generations (Berkovec *et al.* 1994; Stiglitz and Weiss 1981; Vandell 1984). For conservatives, credit rationing has irresistible ontological appeal: racial inequality is not the result of bigoted lenders or misguided industry practices, but simply reflects a market imperfection. The policy solution is obvious: get more and better information on consumers to eliminate information asymmetries. As lenders are able to acquire more relevant and reliable information to help distinguish borrowers with good and bad intentions, they will once again be able to use the price mechanism to allocate credit more efficiently to more people. This expanded screening capacity arrived in the 1990s, with a revolution in consumer credit reporting and surveillance systems, credit scoring algorithms, automated underwriting software, and finely tuned delinquency and default models (Miller 2003; Saunders and Allen 2002; White 2002). With the growth of an increasingly sophisticated subprime sector in the 1990s, lenders, brokers, lobbyists, and conservative industry advocates began to herald a new era of "risk-based pricing" – an efficient, innovative, and benevolent market in which lenders are able to accurately measure borrower risk and provide expanded credit access for "weaker" borrowers and racial or ethnic minorities. Meanwhile, de-regulated competition will ensure that the higher prices charged to serve high-risk customers are just sufficient to provide a normal rate of risk-adjusted profit (Litan 2001; Chinloy and Macdonald 2005; cf. Ashton 2009). Expanded access to credit, at a higher but justified price, provides new opportunities to marginal borrowers who would otherwise be excluded under credit rationing. But, if risk-based pricing emerged logically from the axioms of neoclassical thought, in other ways the theoretical justifications were devised *post hoc* to defend a rapidly growing industry that had become the center of controversy: "It was at that point that a group of industry advocates and economists began to articulate an interpretation of the mortgage market that is increasingly referred to as the market completion model" (Ashton 2009: 2).

There is now a compelling body of evidence that contradicts the rosy predictions of risk-based pricing and the market completion model (for reviews, see Ashton 2009; Engel and McCoy 2002, 2007; Immergluck 2009; White 2004). The information asymmetries at the heart of credit rationing theory are often reversed when lenders and brokers hide important information about complex loan instruments in order to deceive borrowers. Credit risk premiums – portrayed in theory as legitimate compensation for elevated long-term borrower risks – are, in practice, pursued by many industry actors as up-front revenue streams. Borrower credit risks (delinquency, default) are overshadowed in declining interest rate environments by prepayment risks – which are largely driven by the aggressive efforts of competing lenders seeking up-front fees from refinancing. Adverse selection and information asymmetries between borrowers and lenders are dwarfed by the asymmetries among brokers and lenders, lenders and Wall Street investment houses, and investment banks and thousands of individual and institutional investors.

Unfortunately, all of these flaws in the market completion model are routinely dismissed, in favor of a self-referential doctrine that privileges the virtues of unregulated market innovation, unfettered consumer choice, and – perhaps most important of all – the American Dream of home-ownership. Nearly every regulatory proposal – even modest attempts to limit the freedom of lenders and brokers to engage in the most deceptive and abusive tactics – is immediately attacked as a betrayal of innovation, choice, and American opportunity. "Innovative loan options" are serving people and places that would otherwise be excluded from credit, as the President of the National Association of Mortgage Brokers declared in testimony at a Senate hearing on the eve of the current crisis. Senators were urged to resist the temptation to regulate any lending terms or practices. Lawmakers should "not risk 'turning back the clock' to a pre-Fair Housing Act era where certain population segments were unfairly denied access to loan financing options" (Dinham 2007: 10). Any restrictions on the freedom of brokers and lenders to devise any kind of "innovative loan option" would threaten consumer sovereignty: "Only the consumer can determine the 'best' combination of factors that fit their needs," and regulation will "upset the balance created by the market that provides homeownership opportunities to so many Americans" (Dinham 2007: 9).

This logic is widespread, compelling, and deeply entrenched in American politics and popular culture. It seems only logical, reasonable, and fair that lenders and brokers should be encouraged to serve people in need, and to be allowed to charge higher rates to compensate for the increased risk. Even in the wake of the subprime catastrophe, legislators routinely warn against "throwing the baby out with the bathwater," by imposing restrictions that might choke off a recovery in the subprime sector that will once again provide expanded access to low-income and minority consumers struggling to achieve the American Dream of homeownership.

Unfortunately, the material meaning of homeownership has changed dramatically in recent years – particularly for the poor and working classes, and for racially marginalized consumers. Millions of debt-strapped "owners" have only the most precarious, tenuous rights to "have" or "possess" implied by the etymology of the Old English *āgnian* and *agen*. Many owners are in fact renters, with capital as the landlord.

Renting Capital

If risk-based pricing and credit rationing boast a genealogy to the great Adam Smith himself, so does the theory of class-monopoly rent:

> The rent of land, considered as a price paid for the use of the land, is naturally a monopoly price. It is not at all proportioned to what the landlord may have laid out upon the improvement of the land, or to what he can afford to take; but to what the farmer can afford to give. (*Wealth of Nations* 1776, cited in Evans 1991: 2)

For unimproved land, the cost of "production" for the landowner is zero, and yet still the owner receives a price for its use. The class of landowners, by definition, enjoys a monopoly that commands rent. This insight was "a feature of classical economics" (Evans 1991: 4) in the eras of Ricardo, Smith, Mill, and Marx. But it "virtually disappears from the literature" (p. 3) in the twentieth century, and "class" was virtually erased from the literature on rent until Harvey's (1974: 240) reminder of the inescapably social relations of tenure:

> Tenants are not easily convinced that the rent collector merely represents a scarce factor of production. The social consequences of rent are important and cannot be ignored simply because rent appears so innocently in the neoclassical doctrine of social harmony through competition.

Through the 1960s, considerable attention focused on the adaptation of agricultural land-rent theory – especially differential land rent – to understand the spatial structure of cities. For Harvey, however, urban industrialization blurred the landlord and capitalist distinction of classical political economy, and gave rise to class-monopoly rent: the price that owners can demand for an essential resource, on the basis of their collective power of ownership. Each element of class-monopoly rent is crucial. *Class* matters because in all capitalist societies, the rights and privileges of ownership are central to power relations, political conflict, and social inequality – all of which are concentrated and intensified by urbanization. *Monopoly* matters not primarily because as Marx suggests the supply of land is limited, nor because landowners can become price makers, but rather because of the inherent monopoly associated with the legal status of ownership. Owners enjoy a collective power in the marketplace by virtue of the fact that they are not renters. Owners' rights are codified in law and backed up by state protection, and, if necessary, armed police force: owners' protection is by no means absolute or unconditional, but it is much more than the security given to renters. Finally, *rent* is the simple yet crucial economic measure enabling owners' claims on the use of any capitalizable asset with a rate of return subject to the "outcome of a conflict with a class of consumers of that resource" (Harvey 1974: 239).

These conflicts are mediated by various financial institutions providing credit for those who can only become owners through mortgage debt: "All of these institutions … operate together to relate national policies to local and individual decisions and, in the process create localized structures within which class-monopoly rents can be realized" (Harvey 1974: 245). For empirical illustration, Harvey mapped the anatomy of class-monopoly rent in neighborhood submarkets of Baltimore, Maryland. Although part of his analysis dealt with conflicts between speculator-developers and suburban middle- and upper-income homebuyers, the most shocking exploitation was apparent in the urban core, where urban and regional context inscribed localized variations on the deeply entrenched and fundamental American dilemma of White racism against African Americans. In one inner-city submarket, home and land sales were "dominated by cash and private loan transactions with scarcely a vestige of institutional or government involvement in the used housing market" (Harvey 1974: 245). The most severe class-monopoly rent inequalities in this submarket follow the landlord–tenant binary, as mediated by American urban racism. "Professional landlords are anxious to disinvest" from real estate so they can earn higher returns in the financial markets,

> but they still manage to get a rate of return around 13 percent. … The tenants are low-income and for the most part black. They are poorly organized, exercise little political control and are effectively trapped in this sub-market. Class-monopoly rents are here realized by professional landlords who calculate their rate of return to match the opportunity cost of capital. (Harvey 1974: 245)

In a separate submarket of West Baltimore, by contrast, lower-middle class Blacks had sufficient incomes to consider homeownership. Yet they faced discrimination from mainstream financial institutions, and could only access ownership through the land-installment contract: a usurious and precarious path to homeownership. Only if this course was successfully navigated for several years could a "buyer" reduce the principal enough to obtain conventional financing and achieve "true" ownership. These types of schemes were common in US cities through the 1960s, and allowed speculators to charge steep premiums to African Americans excluded from mainstream credit flows. Most of these "owners" were really the tenants of capital.

Class-monopoly rent and the subprime mortgage market

The fundamental essence of the subprime lending boom involves the use of highly mortgaged "homeownership" to connect national and transnational capital markets to the lucrative profit margins of local class-monopoly rents. Two long-term shifts established and strengthened these connections. First, a durable bipartisan Washington consensus on the virtues of homeownership has steadily undermined rental housing markets, especially for low-cost units. Second, deregulated financial innovation and creative debt management became key instruments of privatized public policy. Especially in housing, spending, and redistribution, policies were downplayed in favor of a new emphasis on tax credits and other incentives to encourage market-based solutions. This shift was bipartisan, too: Reagan championed regressive tax cuts, while Clinton permitted unprecedented banking-sector consolidation while using a combination of deregulatory carrots and fair-lending enforcement sticks to encourage private market solutions to problems (like redlining, urban disinvestment, discrimination) that had insufficient public support for direct government intervention (Listokin *et al.* 2000). The financial services industry had already begun searching for new market opportunities as growth rates moderated among its traditional demand base, and Wall Street was creating an ever-broader array of new kinds of credit default swaps and asset-backed securities markets for every conceivable debt instrument (Fabozzi 2001). After the landmark deficit-taming budget deals of the first year of the Clinton Administration in 1993 reduced long-term interest rates amidst a climate of expanded free trade and transnational investment, the mortgage industry began to accelerate its reorientation away from a business model premised on long-term repayments to a pass-through model earning up-front fees on mortgages quickly sold in the secondary market. Through most of the 1990s, the Federal Housing Administration (FHA) and the GSEs Fannie Mae and Freddie Mac led the effort to encourage traditional but flexible lending to underserved markets – a record that conservatives are now working to distort with claims that the worldwide financial crisis resulted from misguided government efforts to encourage easy credit for minorities. In fact, the subprime boom was in direct competition with publicly subsidized affordable lending, and most subprime lenders preferred to avoid the rules and regulations of FHA insurance and the loan-screening policies of the GSEs in favor of un-regulated private securitization through Wall Street investment banks. Thanks to a series of laws made in the 1980s that had exempted certain types of lenders and certain kinds of loans from state usury limits (Engel and McCoy 2007), and after the Bush Administration began to fight state-level efforts to crack down on predatory practices, more and more institutions and investors began to pursue the higher up-front fees of subprime lending.

The combined effects of state and federal regulatory structures and competition in the lending industry encouraged what Dymski diagnoses in Chapter 6 as the strategic transformation of banking at the dawn of contemporary neoliberalism. The details of institutional structure were crucial to this transformation. In the early 1990s, many large lenders facing increased fair-lending oversight were reluctant to make fundamental changes to their outreach, underwriting, and product development practices – but they were willing to create specialized affordable lending divisions to make loans to underserved markets. As a wave of consolidation spread through the financial services sector, banks became more eager for quick regulatory approvals of applications for mergers and acquisitions – and, thus, tried to pre-empt challenges filed under the provisions of the Community Reinvestment Act (CRA). Many large banks began to regard affordable lending divisions – even when subsidized with below-market interest rate loans and other costly concessions – as regulatory investments that paid rich dividends in good public relations. By the late 1990s, however, more and more traditional banks were facing competitive threats from thinly capitalized, non-bank mortgage companies that were exempt from most state interest rate caps and had direct sources of capital from Wall Street investment banks (Ashton 2009; Immergluck 2009). A growing number of large banks bought up existing subprime firms and organized them as national subsidiaries exempt from state regulation; other banks created their own subsidiaries to cash in on the boom. In Chapter 8, Newman astutely analyzes the effects of this transformation: communities that had struggled for years to gain access to (traditional, safe, sustainable) mortgage credit were soon devastated by high-risk, predatory capital aggressively seeking access to communities where a history of financial exclusion had made it easy to deceive consumers into expensive debt obligations. The old problems of *limited access to mainstream* capital evolved into new problems of *vulnerability to predatory* capital. Steadily rising home values allowed predators to refinance borrowers who fell behind, earning more fees and hiding abusive practices behind artificially low default rates. Together, these changes propelled an unprecedented wave of capital investment targeted mostly, but not exclusively, at low-income people and places, racially and ethnically marginalized borrowers and communities, and other "new markets."

Of course these markets were new only for mainstream financial institutions, and for Wall Street investment conduits. "Underserved" markets have long been familiar to slum landlords, abusive storefront lenders, payday lenders, pawn shops, and foreclosure specialists. Subsidiary structure and securitization, however, allowed large national banks and Wall Street investment houses to tap into the extractive profits of "new markets" while avoiding state usury law and the reputational risks of deceptive, abusive business practices. Citigroup, HSBC, and many other global banking brands bought up notorious subprime firms and moved aggressively into high-cost lending. Industry competition combined with federal preemption of state law led to the selective replacement and de-localization of many of the individual actors described by Harvey. Yesterday's local landlords and speculators financed by local or regional banks have been replaced by today's network of local brokers, working independently or for various kinds of non-bank mortgage companies or bank subsidiaries. Nearly all of them sell loans to obtain fresh capital flows from private investors and SPVs working with national lenders and Wall Street investment banks.

Since the 1970s, the individual actors have changed but the material relations of exploitation are the same. Today, fewer inner-city African American renters are forced to pay class-monopoly rent to slum landlords, and fewer aspiring Black homeowners are forced to accept the terms of speculators peddling land installment contracts. Yet many more African Americans (as well as Latinas and Latinos, and others) are pushed into high-cost subprime mortgage credit – even when they are qualified for better-priced prime credit, and often (in the case of home improvement and refinance loans) when they are not even seeking credit in the first place (Lax *et al.* 2004; Peterson 2005; Renuart 2004; Squires 2004; Stein 2001). Anyone trapped in the web of high-cost subprime credit is forced to pay a wide range of interest-rate premiums and complex fees and charges, many of them carefully disguised (Engel and McCoy 2002; White 2004). These excessive payments are sustained by information asymmetries (the econometric term for deception) and by savvy exploitation of many consumers' belief that they are unable to qualify for mainstream credit. The excessive payment stream is allocated, by negotiation as well as competition, amongst brokers, lenders, appraisers, home-improvement contractors, investment banks, and investors seeking maximum risk-adjusted yields in MBS shares.

It is entirely possible for abusive, racially discriminatory subprime lending to flourish even when all of the individual actors involved have honorable intentions of providing fair treatment to the customers they deal with directly. A subsidiary develops an innovative, flexible mortgage available to all, but markets its products heavily through racialized minority advertising channels and broker networks; a broker working in a low-income, inner-city neighborhood treats all borrowers the same regardless of race or ethnicity, but happens to specialized only in high-cost subprime adjustable-rate mortgages with stiff pre-payment penalties; a Wall Street investment banker can truthfully claim to have no knowledge of the racial identities of individuals struggling with monthly payments collateralizing subprime MBS shares. Even when individuals have honorable intentions, however, the transformation of the collateralized house into a traded financial instrument that stretches the distance between the underlying asset and global financial markets (see Sassen Chapter 3 in this volume) also breaks the ethical and economic interdependencies between savers, lenders, and borrowers. The new actors involved in what Sassen diagnoses as the global circulation of mortgages – local brokers and lenders, transnational banks, investment houses and hedge funds, and worldwide MBS investors – have for the most part replaced the slum landlords and land-installment speculators of a previous age. But just as in Harvey's account of Baltimore, "owners" have only the weakest rights of possession and security. Millions of home "owners" drawn into the subprime system are, in material and housing-class terms, barely distinguishable from renters. In the subprime market, homeowners are simply paying rent to the new landlord, subprime mortgage capital. In these circumstances, the cultural symbolism of homeownership mutates into a deceptive illusion (Krueckeberg 1999).

The question of scale

The relations of class-monopoly rent appear most clearly in localized submarkets, but also shape inequalities across entire national and transnational urban systems. Three issues of scale are significant. First, the balance between competition and cooperation was reconfigured, but remained otherwise durable through a turbulent period of economic and regulatory change. In Harvey's Baltimore of the 1970s, rents were appropriated by a loosely organized network of landlords who were willing to cooperate just enough to ensure that their individual competitive maneuvers did not undermine the collective, shared rewards available to them as a dominant local landlord class. Clearly, the dramatic de-localization and transnationalization of housing finance over the past generation has rendered local collusion impossible and irrelevant. But national deregulation accomplished very similar results. Amidst the dominance of the standard, fixed-rate 30-year mortgage through the 1980s, lender competition was a zero-sum game war for market share, fought through offers of improved customer service, reductions of service charges, and the cultivation of advertising images of bankers' local corporate citizenship. With the proliferation of ever more complex mortgage instruments between the early 1990s and the market peak in 2006, however, lenders and brokers were able to compete on new terms without undermining their aggregate profits: the entire market expanded first through competitive deception of borrowers in the home equity credit, renovation, and refinance markets, and then in the purchase market as home values escalated with the flood of Wall Street securitization funds after 2001. In this new environment, competition did not undermine collective class interests among subprime lenders – so long as the entire industry remained united in its opposition to threats that would reduce the freedom to use any kind of financial instrument, no matter how risky or abusive, in the competitive pursuit of profitable market niches.

Second, the local limits to exploitation were destroyed by the expanding scale of mortgage markets. Harvey analyzed informal mechanisms that prevented landlords in Baltimore from extracting usurious rents beyond what the captive low-income tenants could bear. Such mechanisms ensured the sustained reproduction of local circuits of accumulation and exploitation; but these limits became irrelevant as class-monopoly rent was extracted through national and transnational networks far removed from the day-to-day experiences of individual borrowers and neighborhoods. Leveraged lending was freed from the immediate material constraints of borrowers struggling to make monthly payments.

Third, the growth of private securitization expanded the potential for traditional kinds of transaction profits – and created a wide variety of new kinds of fees and commissions – for industry actors working at a variety of spatial scales. Lucrative new revenue streams – ranging from local brokers' yield-spread premiums to the securities underwriting fees of Wall Street investment banks and the ratings charges of bond-rating firms – built a vast, lucrative, and spatially dispersed infrastructure of "predatory structured finance" (Peterson 2007). This dispersed web of profits was ultimately built atop the millions of quotidian interpersonal actions of front-line brokers and loan officers, who negotiated between the vast array of choices of mortgage instruments and the individual needs of consumers trying to gain access to the material and cultural benefits of homeownership in their particular, distinctive, and inherently local housing market.

Once consummated within the particularity of a local borrower's decision and trust of a broker or loan officer, however, the mortgage acquires the legal force of state powers over foreclosure, eviction, and bankruptcy, and becomes an attractive commodity for trading and investment at all geographical scales. With subprime securitization, "The lender," Harvey emphasizes, "holds a piece of paper, the value of which is backed by an unsold commodity. This piece of paper may be characterized as *fictitious value*. ... If this credit money is loaned out as capital, then it becomes *fictitious capital*" (Harvey 1981: 369). Whether it is fictitious when understood in terms of theories of late-industrial capitalism, or quite real when seen from the vantage point of theories of postindustrialism, there can be no doubt that capital backed by subprime home loans began to trade at an accelerated velocity through the new instruments of structured finance. The front-end, origination side of the subprime market, which peaked at about $625 billion annually, provided healthy up-front fees for neighborhood brokers, appraisers, and contractors, as well as local, regional, and national banks and mortgage companies. However, once the loans were securitized, insured, and traded, they generated new kinds of revenues and the possibility of capital gains for all of the individuals and institutions with specialized expertise and access to key nodes of the transnational city-systems of financial services. In the subprime boom after 2000, a single Wall Street law firm, McKee Nelson, earned fees by helping investment banks prepare regulatory filings for more than three thousand mortgage securities deals worth some $2.7 trillion (Browning 2008). When Greenspan went on the lecture circuit to promote his autobiography in 2007 and confronted harsh questions about his role in the housing bubble, he tried to reassure investors who were fearful about subprime write-offs then projected at a worst-case scenario of $400 billion: thanks to the "extraordinary" growth of globalization, Greenspan (2007) noted, "arbitrageable long-term assets are worth close to a hundred trillion dollars" worldwide. Arbitrageable long-term assets are not worth much, however, when speculative investment capital no longer floods into the housing finance system, and when mortgage securities must be valued in terms of the only value that counts: the discounted net present value of the debt payments of millions of borrowers, many of whom find themselves in a labor market that provides inflation-adjusted earnings that fall short of the wages prevailing when Harvey first came to Baltimore. The labor theory of value, easily forgotten and sidelined during the investor euphoria of securitization and the "global savings glut" of investments flooding into US capital markets, reasserted itself with a vengeance in the crisis. Even now, as analysts and policymakers struggle to ascertain the "true value" of subprime mortgage-backed securities, the wild uncertainty of the varied estimates reflects the fact that we still do not know the true magnitude of exploitation and accumulation that was built upon the needs and circumstances of borrowers struggling to achieve gains in the housing market that have been denied to so many wage workers over the past generation.

It is now universally recognized that the risk management systems of structured finance failed spectacularly. Nevertheless, the trillions of dollars of investor losses in the 2007–09 crisis have not weakened the structured inequalities of class-monopoly rent. Federal policy interventions to help homeowners facing foreclosure have been severely limited: the federal response in the final year of the Bush Administration consisted almost exclusively of voluntary programs to encourage servicers to consider mild forms of forbearance. When the Obama Administration refused to commit political capital to persuade the Senate to consider a watered-down provision allowing bankruptcy judges to modify first-lien mortgages, the stakes had nothing to do with public expenditure: the true threat involved the precedent that would have placed limits on the rights of one class of investors and debt-holders to demand full repayment from a subordinated class of consumers struggling to make payments on unsustainable, usurious, and often inherently exploitative debt. By contrast, payments, subsidies, and guarantees to the institutions and large investors of finance capital are designed to be nearly unlimited – sufficient to restore investor confidence. A previous generation's discourse of class conflict and class struggle was replaced with a new, carefully disguised class vocabulary. We can't afford to spend money to subsidize irresponsible borrowers, and we can't risk the moral hazard that would prevent them from learning from their mistakes. But we can't afford not to invest to stabilize the troubled assets held by institutions deemed too big to fail. This is triple-A rated class war.

Metropolitan Market Penetration and Racial–Geographic Segmentation

Our perspective on class-monopoly rent is not new. The argument was sketched clearly by Harvey in 1974, and refined in the subsequent decade (Harvey 1978, 1981, 1985). Our theory is implicit in, and complementary to, other lines of inquiry in a rich literature, including historiographies of the Community Reinvestment Movement (Squires 1992, 2003, 2004), legal-economic diagnoses of segmented subprime credit markets and global finance (Engel and McCoy 2002, 2007), long-term measures of the transformation from the old inequalities of exclusion to the new inequalities of stratified inclusion (Ashton 2008; Hernandez Chapter 7 in this volume; Immergluck 2008; Williams *et al.* 2005), and especially Peterson's (2007) notion of "predatory structured finance" and Gotham's (2006) analysis of securitization as the secondary circuit of capital. Our purpose is to add an explicit, consistent, and multivariate urban and regional dimension to this literature. If we were to map Harvey's (1974) relations of class-monopoly rent as it circulates through Berry's (1964) cities as systems within systems of cities, what would we see in this cartography of capital?

Our analysis rests upon two claims, which we evaluate during the peak of the subprime boom from 2004 to 2006. First, we examine *metropolitan market penetration* by beginning with the risk-based pricing notion that subprime credit will be most common in places marginalized by urban and regional inequalities of deindustrialization and uneven development. Even after accounting for these factors, however, we hypothesize that the geography of race and ethnicity still matter. In the distorted world of subprime marketing, targeting racially and ethnically marginalized communities is an efficient, economically rational way to find consumers who feel excluded from mainstream credit markets, and who are likely to be more vulnerable to deception and abuse. Second, we hypothesize that the *racial-geographic segmentation* of class-monopoly rent can best be understood by analyzing mortgage-industry subsidiary structure and secondary-market circuits – rather than the presumed credit blemishes of individual borrowers at the heart of risk-based pricing.

Data

Many different kinds of data sources provide complementary yet partial views of specific facets of the subprime market (Immergluck 2008; see also Newman Chapter 8 in this volume). Since we wish to measure the market consistently across nearly all cities and suburbs throughout the nation, the only comprehensive source comes from the annual application-level records reported by lending institutions that comply with the Home Mortgage Disclosure Act (HMDA) (FFIEC, annual). HMDA provides, *inter alia*, the requested loan amount, purpose, and income of each consumer applying for a mortgage loan from a covered lender, along with the location of the collateral property, the outcome of the application, and (for loans approved and originated) information on whether the loan was sold in the same calendar year to a secondary-market investor.

HMDA has many well-documented limitations, but (1) unlike specialized industry datasets, it provides unparalleled coverage of most of the market, (2) unlike specialized housing surveys or internal lender files, it is a full enumeration rather than a sample, and (3) it is the only comprehensive source of information on applicants' racial and ethnic identities for specific types of loans in particular places. Additionally, some of the limitations of HMDA ensure that it will understate the true extent of exploitation and bias.[1] Beginning in 2004, expanded disclosure rules required lenders to identify originations classified as high-cost, or "rate-spread" loans[2] – where the annual percentage rate cost of borrowing, including up-front points and fees, is more than three percentage points higher than the reported yield for US Treasury securities of comparable maturity for first mortgages, and five percentage points higher for subordinate liens (see FDIC 2005).

Consider a simple illustration of the interpretive dilemma between risk-based pricing and class-monopoly rent, as seen through the geography of HMDA data. Figure 9.1 presents a simple summary of rate-spread loan shares and conventional application denial rates across all of the nation's metropolitan areas. The common-sense understanding of risk-based pricing seems inescapable: subprime credit achieves the greatest market penetration where it is needed the most. This is in cities where higher shares of applicants are turned away from conventional credit.

Metropolitan denial rates alone account for more than one-third of the variance in subprime market share, from the worst-case scenarios of Detroit and Texas border cities (where rate-spread loans account for more than two out of five loans) to the best-case outcomes in small college towns like Boulder, Colorado, Madison, Wisconsin, and Iowa City, Iowa – where only one out of seven loans is subprime. But if we account for denial rates and other factors associated with the logic of risk-based pricing, is there any evidence of the kinds of racial–geographic disparities predicted by class-monopoly rent?

To address this question, we narrowed the full database used for Figure 9.1 to make it possible to match lending information to other metropolitan characteristics. We also applied several quality-control screens for individual application records in order to ensure precise measures that build in a conservative bias against any finding of race–class–geographical exploitation and discrimination.[3] The final database provides information on 16.1 million applicants in 2004, and 17.4 million in 2006 (Table 9.1). Between 2004 and 2006, denial rates edged up slightly, a reminder that relaxed underwriting did not quite allow credit for "anyone this side of life support" (Stiglitz 2007), as almost a quarter of requests in 2006 were rejected.

Yet among those who did get loans, the share exceeding the rate-spread (high cost) trigger shot up from 16.6 percent in 2004 to 29.7 percent in 2006. Lenders retained only a third of the loans they made, and sold the other two-thirds. A growing share of secondary-market sales is bypassing the GSEs in favor of a wide variety of private investor conduits. The dataset also confirms the deeply racialized character of the subprime boom (Table 9.2). Non-Hispanic Whites comprise an absolute majority of subprime borrowers, and the share of Whites with high-cost loans jumped from 13 percent to 22 percent. But market penetration was far higher for Blacks and Latinos. The ratio of Black-to-White subprime share fell slightly, from 2.86 to 2.44, but the secular expansion of subprime share meant that, by 2006, an outright majority of all African American borrowers were pushed into high-cost loans. For Hispanics, the disparities with Whites jumped from 1.95 to 2.07.

Results

Metropolitan market segmentation

Our first hypothesis is that subprime credit proliferates in economically marginalized areas, but that risk factors cannot fully explain the sharp patterns of racial and ethnic inequality documented by so many researchers and

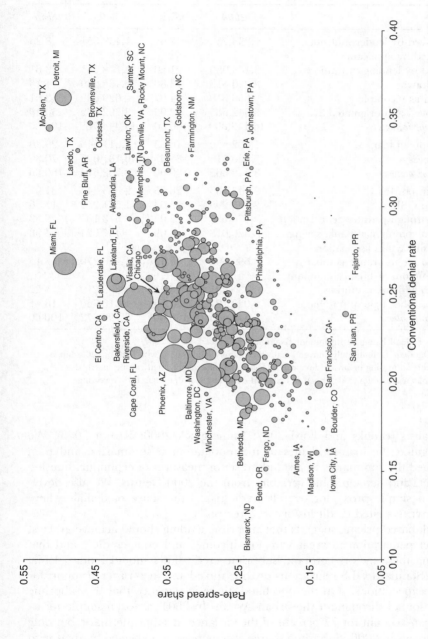

Figure 9.1 Denial rate for conventional mortgage applications, vs. rate-spread share of conventional loan originations, by metropolitan area, 2006

Source: FFIEC 2007.

Note: Circle sizes are proportional to the number of rate-spread originations (e.g., 618 in Iowa City, 72,022 in Miami, 124,215 in Riverside, CA).

Table 9.1   Action taken on loan applications, 2004–06

	2004	Share	2006	Share
Approved by lender, but not accepted by applicant	1,233,253	7.64	1,438,651	8.25
Denied by lending institution	3,469,950	21.50	4,118,251	23.61
Withdrawn	2,240,413	13.88	2,465,289	14.13
Closed as incomplete	656,618	4.07	629,899	3.61
Approved and originated	8,542,665	52.92	8,792,672	50.40
Total applications	16,142,899	100.00	17,444,762	100.00
Rate-spread loans	1,422,550	16.65	2,611,646	29.70
All others	7,120,115	83.35	6,181,026	70.30
Total originations	8,542,665	100.00	8,792,672	100.00
Held in portfolio	2,447,105	28.65	2,805,347	31.91
Sold to GSE	2,138,295	25.03	1,561,259	17.76
Sold through private securitization	176,637	2.07	578,185	6.58
Sold to commercial bank, savings bank, or savings association	520,018	6.09	437,624	4.98
Sold to life insurance company, credit union, or finance company	699,604	8.19	1,156,270	13.15
Sold to affiliate institution	531,885	6.23	635,219	7.22
Sold to other type of purchaser	2,029,121	23.75	1,618,768	18.41
Total originations	8,542,665	100.00	8,792,672	100.00

Source: Federal Financial Institutions Examination Council, 2005, 2007.
Note: Database includes only conventional, single-family applications with first- or subordinate liens, with no missing or invalid financial or locational information, that can be matched to metropolitan area data as described in text, and excluding loans purchased by reporting institutions.

journalists (Brooks and Ford 2007; Immergluck 2008; Rivera 2008). We aggregated the loan-level files to metropolitan-area summaries, and then matched the summaries to a standard set of measures of economic, housing market, and demographic variables from the 2000 Census. We also developed a simple proxy for overall credit risk – the share of denials where underwriters cited credit history as a reason.[4]

Risk-based pricing suggests that subprime lending should achieve greatest market penetration in areas with low incomes and poor credit – and that holding these factors constant, subprime credit flows should reduce denial rates. Standard OLS regressions provide mixed and inconsistent support for these expectations.[5] On the one hand, there is evidence that the subprime flood spread throughout the urban system. In 2004, a dozen simple measures can account for 77 percent of the variance in subprime share, but only 65 percent in 2006. Subprime shares also increase as expected in areas with

Table 9.2 Race/ethnicity and subprime lending, 2004–06

	2004			2006		
	Rate-spread	*All others*	*Rate-spread share*	*Rate-spread*	*All others*	*Rate-spread share*
Non-Hispanic White	673,925	4,582,813	12.8	1,145,948	4,051,650	22.0
Non-Hispanic Black	217,811	375,624	36.7	435,478	375,915	53.7
Hispanic[1]	233,438	700,283	25.0	553,839	660,871	45.6
Demographic information incomplete[2]	293,987	1,182,673	19.9	422,832	803,428	34.5
Native American	7,694	24,852	23.6	9,474	19,630	32.6
Asian, Hawaiian Native, Pacific Islander	37,603	383,259	8.9	92,718	327,771	22.1

Source: FFIEC 2005, 2007.
Notes: [1]Includes some applicants who provided no information on race.
[2]Includes some applicants who provided information on ethnicity and race, but no information on gender.

higher denial rates, lower per capita incomes, and greater market shares of applicants rejected for bad credit.

Even after accounting for these factors, racial segmentation remains crucial – and its impact worsened at the height of the boom. In 2004, a one standard-deviation increase in the metropolitan share of non-Hispanic Blacks increases subprime market penetration by 0.32 standard deviations; this elasticity of racial inequality increased to 0.36 two years later. Subprime penetration showed no significant bias towards cities with large Latino populations in 2004 (after accounting for income and other controls in the models), but yields a 0.34 standardized beta in 2006. For many years, subprime credit was most pervasive in African American communities (HUD-Treasury Joint Task Force 2000; Squires 2003), whereas predators found it more difficult to penetrate Hispanic communities and other minority ethnic niches. This seems to have changed rapidly as brokers and lenders responded to Wall Street pressures to find more "underserved" markets.

Table 9.3   Model fit diagnostics for credit history instrument

Probability Range	Number of Applications	Average model-predicted probability of bad-credit rejection	Actual proportion rejected for bad credit
0.1–4.9%	54,974	0.027	0.026
5.0–9.9	29,679	0.070	0.071
10.0–14.9	11,113	0.122	0.122
15.0–19.9	5,487	0.172	0.183
20.0–24.9	3,055	0.223	0.220
25.0–29.9	1,655	0.273	0.262
30.0–34.9	1,025	0.323	0.322
35.0–39.9	642	0.373	0.388
40.0–44.9	479	0.423	0.441
45.0–49.9	345	0.475	0.464
50.0–54.9	235	0.522	0.519
55.0–59.9	162	0.574	0.549
60.0–64.9	138	0.625	0.696
65.0–69.9	100	0.670	0.640
70.0–74.9	102	0.725	0.657
75.0–79.9	57	0.779	0.754
80.0–84.9	31	0.822	0.774
85.0–89.9	6	0.867	0.833
90.0–94.9	–		
95.0–99.9	–		

Source: FFIEC 2005, 2007.
Note: Model estimated on a randomly selected sample (109,285) of all applications.

Racial–geographic segmentation

Aggregate measures of market segmentation are helpful in mapping the broad contours of credit inequalities, but precise measurements require the analysis of outcomes for individual borrowers. To evaluate our second hypothesis – that lending industry dynamics and class monopoly rent account for racially unequal credit better than risk-based pricing – we analyze the 8.54 million loans in the dataset that were approved and originated in 2004, and the 8.79 million for 2006. We use logistic regression, the standard workhorse of the banking and lending literatures, augmented with an instrumental variable technique that provides an estimate of the credit risk for each individual applicant (see Abariotes *et al.* 1993; Holloway 1998).

This instrument is derived from the stated judgments of underwriters and lenders on their reasons for refusing to make loans to certain applicants, and it thus provides conservative insurance against any results that would unfairly place blame on the lending industry. Our instrumental variable model, estimated on a random sample of all applications, is quite "good" at predicting the characteristics of those viewed as unacceptable by underwriters (Table 9.3). We use the parameters from this bad-credit model to calculate a risk proxy for each of the applicants who eventually did receive loans. We then estimate several models to measure the factors that distinguish those who wound up with high-cost, rate-spread loans.

We estimated four models each for 2004 and 2006, beginning with (1) basic applicant financial measures, loan purpose, and demographic characteristics, then adding measures of (2) lending industry structure, (3) estimated credit risk, and (4) metropolitan housing market context (see Table 9.4). Five results stand out. First, measures of fit declined slightly across all model specifications, attesting to the generalized spread of subprime credit throughout the market. Second, the effects of core underwriting measures weakened. Odds ratios for income and income-to-loan ratios moved closer to unity, as various forms of high-cost loans became more common among middle-income borrowers struggling to cope with the high costs of many markets. The odds ratio for owner-occupancy fell, as subprime credit became more closely linked to investment and speculative purposes; but the effect (from 0.89 to 0.69; see Model 1) is not nearly as large as implied by press coverage of legions of speculative flippers using "exotic" loan instruments.

Third, racial disparities worsened. For Blacks and Latinos, the results are striking across all specifications. Subprime disparities increased from 3.5 to 3.8 for African Americans, and from 2.0 to 2.9 for Hispanic borrowers.[6] Accounting for differences in lender type (Model 2) and estimated credit risk (Model 3) certainly reduces these inequalities. However, even after giving every benefit of the doubt to lenders with an instrumental variable that itself captures disparate-impact racial discrimination, African Americans are 1.6 times more likely than non-Hispanic Whites to have subprime credit in 2004, and 2.3 times more likely in 2006. For Latinos, the corresponding increase is from 1.1 to 1.9. This result aligns with the aggregate, metropolitan-level analysis, and confirms that the subprime boom consolidated African American segmentation even as the industry made new inroads into Latino communities. At the same time, the central plank to justify risk-based pricing slid away; in 2004, increasing the credit risk measure by one standard deviation increased the likelihood that a borrower received a subprime loan by a factor of 1.43; only two years later, this ratio slipped to 1.24.

The fourth finding confirms the crucial role of institutional processes and capital circuits in connecting individual borrowers to transnational investment networks. Subprime lending has traditionally been most common among small, thinly capitalized independent mortgage companies, which disclose their activity to the US Department of Housing and Urban Development (HUD), but escape the closer supervision of the four main

Table 9.4 Subprime segmentation models

	Odds ratios from logit models							
	Model 1		Model 2		Model 3		Model 4	
	2004	2006	2004	2006	2004	2006	2004	2006
Income (log)	0.592	0.789	0.540	0.702	0.666	0.794	0.737	0.846
Income-to-loan ratio (log)	1.400	1.107	1.738	1.320	1.524	1.263	1.329	1.157
Owner-occupied	0.886	0.693	0.954	0.673	0.855	0.648	0.827	0.640
Subordinate lien	1.755	1.427	0.849	0.865	0.910	0.853	1.220	0.995*
Pre-approval requested	0.660	0.336	0.516	0.301	0.702	0.362	0.691	0.359
Home improvement	0.603	0.486	0.648	0.679	0.294	0.541	0.322	0.560
Refinance	1.111	1.011	1.128	0.999*	0.898	0.898	0.932	0.911
Incomplete demographic information	1.579	1.728	1.197	1.466	1.075	1.235	1.108	1.259
Female primary applicant	1.244	1.203	1.160	1.152	1.150	1.079	1.174	1.094
Hispanic or Latino	2.037	2.863	1.662	2.400	1.138	1.951	1.239	1.972
Native American	1.975	1.690	1.747	1.709	1.026*	1.002*	1.091	1.031*
Asian	0.843	1.076	0.868	1.068	0.756	0.878	0.849	0.937
Black or African American	3.480	3.783	2.645	3.267	1.659	2.326	1.638	2.360
OCC-regulated bank			0.269	0.351	0.208	0.331	0.207	0.333
OTS-regulated thrift			0.219	0.912	0.199	0.845	0.208	0.853
FDIC-regulated bank			0.407	0.466	0.323	0.445	0.332	0.452
HUD-supervised mortgage company			2.258	1.377	1.921	1.329	1.973	1.350
Sold to GSE			0.046	0.154	0.043	0.151	0.043	0.151
Sold to private investor			0.779	3.282	0.731	3.199	0.745	3.233
Sold to bank			0.871	1.352	0.789	1.339	0.806	1.344
Sold to life insurance co., credit union, mtg. bank, or finance co.			0.575	1.803	0.559	1.796	0.565	1.790
Sold to affiliate institution			0.796	1.201	0.771	1.189	0.762	1.191
Sold to other type of purchaser			0.931	2.056	0.908	2.042	0.923	2.061

	(1)	(2)	(3)	(4)	(5)	(6)	(7)	(8)
Credit history instrument					1.433	1.239	1.420	1.235
Conventional denial rate							1.048	1.110
Share of applications requesting FHA insurance							0.980	0.972
Non-Hispanic Black population							1.053	0.962
Hispanic population							0.981	0.959
Per capita income							0.908	0.905
Ratio of non-Hispanic White to Black per capita income							1.057	1.068
Ratio of non-Hispanic White to Hispanic per capita income							0.951	0.965
Share of owner-occupied housing built before 1950							0.982	0.983
Share of owner-occupied housing built 1995–2000							0.970	0.949
Median gross rent as share of household income							0.924	0.960
Median owner-occupied value as share of household income							0.927	0.943
Share of owner-occupied housing units with no mortgage							1.036	0.976
Share of mortgaged units with a second mortgage							0.954	0.991
Nagelkerke max R-squared	0.131	0.116	0.333	0.303	0.338	0.305	0.346	0.310
Percent concordant	71.0	67.7	83.4	79.1	83.8	79.2	84.1	79.5

Observations for 2004 models: 8,542,665

Observations for 2006 models: 8,792,672

Source: FFIEC 2005, 2007.

Notes: *Not significant at $P < 0.01$; all other coefficients significant at $P < 0.001$. For continuous variables (income, income-to-loan ratio, credit instrument, and metropolitan variables), odds ratios report the change in odds with a one standard deviation increase in the respective predictor.

banking regulators. Yet, as the federal banking regulators "shrugged" when confronted with proliferating abuses (Andrews 2007), many traditional banks began to pursue the profits of the subprime boom by purchasing or establishing their own subprime subdivisions. The odds ratio comparing independent mortgage companies to large national banks regulated by the Federal Reserve (the reference category) fell from 1.92 in 2004 to 1.32 two years later (Model 3). Traditional, locally oriented savings and loan institutions reporting to the Office of Thrift Supervision (OTS) became almost indistinguishable from the national, Federal Reserve-regulated banks. Moreover, as banking structures evolved to create new channels for subprime credit on the front end, the back end was also shifting, as lenders accelerated their sales to the secondary market.

For quite a few years, the majority of home loans have been securitized. Until recently, however, most lenders held many of the non-conforming, non-traditional, or high-risk loans in their own portfolio for a year or more. This practice, known as "seasoning," was particularly important in the 1990s as secondary-market investors reacted cautiously to front-line lenders who were relaxing underwriting criteria in order to reach new markets (Listokin *et al.* 2000). Our analysis reveals that this practice changed dramatically between 2004 and 2006. In 2004, subprime loans posted low odds ratios for all types of secondary purchasers. Compared to prime loans (which are commonly sold quickly to the GSEs), subprime loans were, overall, more likely to be held in portfolio long enough to stretch past the same-year sale reporting requirements of HMDA.

As investors flooded the MBS market and investment banks became more aggressive, front-line lenders responded with more risky loans passed on to the secondary market more quickly. In 2006, a loan approved and sold to a private investor was 3.2 times more likely to be subprime compared to an otherwise identical loan that was held in portfolio past the end of the year. A loan sold to an "other type of purchaser" – usually an SPV that packages the loans before passing on to a trust or SIV – was more than twice as likely to be subprime. In light of what is now known about the deteriorating quality of loans made in the latter months of 2006, it is clear that the securitization system had fused a toxic brew from the most volatile compounds of economic chemistry (adverse selection, principal-agents dilemmas, information asymmetries) to create perverse incentives encouraging loans destined to end in foreclosure (Dymski 2007; Immergluck 2008).

The fifth finding suggests no clear role for urban and regional context. Adding a vector of theoretically relevant metropolitan measures adds almost nothing to model fit, and yields standardized odds ratios that all fall in a narrow range between 0.94 and 1.11 (Model 4). The largest effects are for metropolitan denial rates and White–Black income inequality (both positive) but the effects are modest for all metropolitan indicators. After accounting for secondary investment networks, banking industry structure, and applicant characteristics, it seems that class-monopoly rent displays no contextual bias towards particular kinds of places. This finding appears to undermine one of our important hypotheses.

Acknowledging geographical contingency

Adding "metropolitan indicators" to a model is only one way to capture the distinctions of place. Another approach is to recognize that the processes summarized in a particular model may vary across different settings. There are several intricate ways to analyze this variation (expansion techniques, multilevel models) but here we consider the simplest approach: estimating Model 3 (Table 9.4) separately for all metropolitan areas. This boosts model fit considerably for most places, and yields varied coefficient estimates for relations of particular concern. We focus here on the geographical contingency of racial subprime segmentation for African Americans (Figure 9.2) and Latinas or Latinos (Figure 9.3), and the nexus of subprime segmentation, applicant income, and secondary-market sales networks (Figure 9.4).

These graphs offer vivid portraits of the contextual landscape of capital flows. Subprime credit is deeply racialized across most, but not all, housing markets. Most metropolitan areas appear in the top portion of the graphs in Figures 9.2 and 9.3. For African Americans, many of the larger cities post coefficients between 0.75 and 1.00 – all else constant, Blacks are between 2.1 and 2.7 times more likely than otherwise identical non-Hispanic Whites to wind up with subprime credit. For Hispanics, most of the odds ratios range from 1.65 to 2.7. Likewise, the general pattern of class segmentation and secondary-market sales conduits is clear. Most metropolitan areas in Figure 9.4 appear in the upper-left quadrant. All else constant, in most places subprime loans are targeted towards lower-income borrowers, and are more likely than prime loans to be sold immediately to SPVs and other purchasers. These general patterns conform well to the hypothesis that class-monopoly rents are extracted from across the urban system – but in uneven ways that inscribe distinctive local credit environments.

Nevertheless, urban and regional contingencies matter. Quite a few metropolitan areas cluster along one of the axes, indicating no statistically significant segmentation for race or ethnicity (Figures 9.2 and 9.3) or class/secondary circuits (Figure 9.4). In several metropolitan areas, the prevailing patterns are reversed. Subprime segmentation is significantly less likely for African Americans in places like Flint, Michigan, Rochester, New York, and Pensacola, Florida; for Latinas and Latinos, these effects appear in Pueblo, Colorado, and the locally transnationalized, multi-generational Texas border cities of El Paso and Laredo.

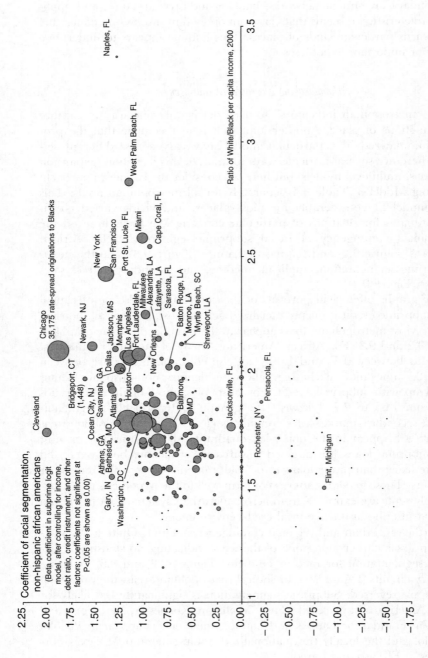

Figure 9.2 Metropolitan coefficients of racial segmentation, non-Hispanic African American borrowers, 2006
Sources: FFIEC 2007, US Census 2000 (per capita income data).
Note: Circle sizes are proportional to the number of rate-spread originations to non-Hispanic Blacks.

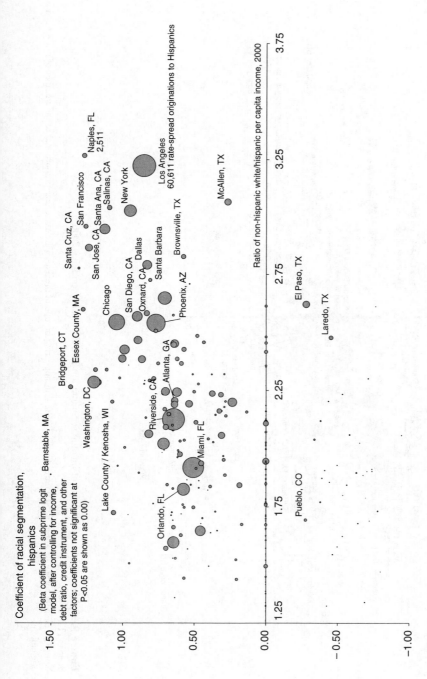

Figure 9.3 Metropolitan coefficients of racial segmentation, Latino/Latina borrowers, 2006

Sources: FFIEC 2007, US Census 2000 (per capita income data).

Note: Circle sizes are proportional to the number of rate-spread originations to Hispanics.

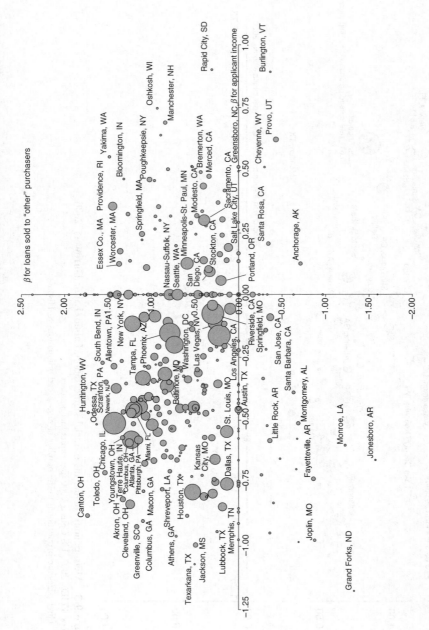

Figure 9.4 Metropolitan coefficients of income segmentation and SPV sales conduits, 2006
Source: FFIEC 2007.
Note: Coefficients not significant at P<0.05 are shown as 0.00, thus appearing on one of the axes. Circle sizes are proportional to the number of rate-spread originations.

There are even more exceptional cases for income and loan-sales networks: in four dozen metropolitan areas, subprime credit is *ceteris paribus* more likely for higher-income applicants. The effects are not substantively large,[7] but they provide a direct counterpart to the general trend. Given the controls included in the models, these effects cannot be attributed to compositional factors: a greater incidence of subprime credit for higher-income borrowers in certain places does not mean that these places have more investor-buyers, borrowers with higher debt ratios, or that there is a different mixture of buyers and owners seeking to refinance. Even after accounting for these factors, part of the subprime boom appears to have involved higher-income applicants responding to the imperatives of extremely tight housing markets in a number of large cities – such as the Twin Cities, San Diego, Salt Lake City, Portland, and Sacramento. But even stronger effects appear in smaller regional trade centers, and in exurban towns transformed by dramatic increases in long-distance commuter suburbs. Some of these places – San Diego, Minneapolis-St. Paul, Portland – are highlighted in Immergluck's (2008) analysis of the expansion of ARMs and zero-downpayment loans in the cumulative-causation cycle of "exotic" mortgages in the home purchase market. Rising prices in overheated markets induce lenders and buyers to use more flexible instruments, which in turn enable sellers to demand still higher prices. Yet many other cities on our graph do not correspond so neatly to Immergluck's (2008) analysis. Compared with the durable historical geographies of race and ethnicity, the class focus of subprime capital exhibits considerable metropolitan contingency.

As with so many other dimensions of housing, subprime mortgage capital reflects and reproduces the complex local environments of demographic continuity and change. This environment also interacts with the partially autonomous legal realm of state attempts to regulate the worst of the lending abuses over the past decade. We can gain a glimpse of one highly simplified representation of the results of these processes if we map all metropolitan counties where severe racial and ethnic inequalities go hand in hand with strong connections to Wall Street securitization networks; we can then add a map of the innovative and valuable index of state predatory lending protections measured by Bostic *et al.* (2007).[8]

There is no perfect, simple correlation here (Figure 9.5). There is no easy correspondence between weak state laws and racialized circuits fed by Wall Street securitization. Even if a suggestive visual match were to appear, the correlation would be an illusory relationship concealing the profound contingency reproduced by the history of American banking and federalism. Even the most restrictive state laws are rendered meaningless for certain parts of the market. While the primary division between state and local institutions versus national commercial banks was formalized shortly after the Civil War, the contemporary legal landscape also reflects a deregulatory

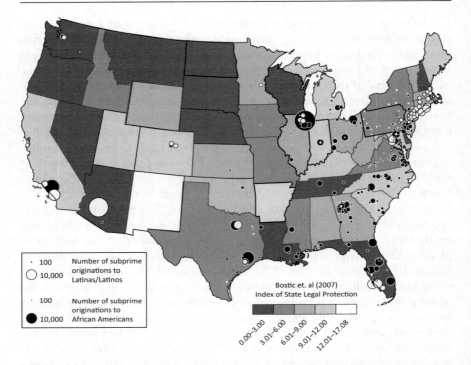

Figure 9.5 Racialized circuits of capital and extent of state legal protections from predatory lending, 2006

Sources: FFIEC 2007, Bostic *et al.* 2007.

Note: The circles represent counties that meet two conditions: (1) African American and Hispanic borrowers are at least 2.5 times more likely than non-Hispanic Whites to wind up with subprime loans, after controlling for income, estimated debt burden, and loan type; and (2) loans sold to SPVs are at least 2.5 times more likely than portfolio loans to be subprime. States outlined in bold represent net Senate-seat gains by Republican candidates in the November 2010 midterm elections.

legal cartography drawn since the early 1980s. The Depository Institutions Deregulation and Monetary Control Act of 1980 exempted *certain types of lenders* from state usury limits on first-lien mortgages, while the Alternative Mortgage Transactions Parity Act of 1982 pre-empted state restrictions on *certain types of loans* (regardless of who made them). Federal regulatory decisions in the Clinton and Bush years further liberated large national lenders and independent mortgage companies. A 2007 Supreme Court decision (*Watters v. Wachovia*) held that mortgage-company subsidiaries of national banks were not subject to even the minimal level of state oversight – the requirement to register to obtain a license to do business in a state. Legal, regulatory, and competitive struggles have stretched, torn, and folded the seemingly straightforward map of the US into a discontinuous, multi-scalar field of power relations. The map changes, of course, every time state legislatures and governors take action on banking, lending, or consumer protection law – or when they capitulate in the face of ratings-agency threats to shut down all credit if predatory credit is restricted in any way. Parts of the map also change, of course, with every election (note the six states where Republicans gained Senate seats in the 2010 midterm elections). In Pennsylvania, Arlen Specter's seat was won by a former derivatives trader, Pat Toomey, who repackaged his Wall Street experience into an angry, winning message that "Congress bailed out the Wall Street companies, then homeowners who borrowed too much, and then the auto industry" (Toomey 2010).

The state legal environment portrayed in Figure 9.5, therefore, cannot be taken as a simple, causally predictive explanation. But it is indispensable for a thick description of the state of play in the politics of capital. Federalism is marked by a complex mosaic of different settings reproduced by industry innovation, regulatory response, and activist mobilization. On the one hand, most of the high plains and the mountainous West have few state restrictions; but the racial and ethnic inequalities in these regions tend to be somewhat more localized, without strong connections to Wall Street investment circuits. State legislatures have been more responsive in California, Michigan, Indiana, Maryland, New Jersey, and the Carolinas, in part because responses were so desperately needed. Even so, federal preemptions ensure that the deeply unequal subprime flows in these states remain a battleground over the rights of consumers facing off against servicers, lenders, and other investors working to extract subprime class-monopoly rents. The legal climate matters: states can be located in regulatory space with the multivariate technique of multidimensional scaling, and the resulting state-by-state contrasts entered as an additional explanatory variable in the segmentation models (Table 9.5). While the effects of state regulation are far from smooth and linear, they are nevertheless significant and meaningful: all else constant, moving "away" from the most aggressive anti-predatory legal regime achieved in New Mexico elevates the odds of subprime segmentation by a factor between 1.1 and 1.7.

For African Americans, the dominant centers of this complex, multi-scaled geography of capital and law etch out a familiar urban system (Figure 9.5): Chicago, Los Angeles, Atlanta, and Houston appear, serving as reminders of the network of cities where Myrdal's (1944) *American Dilemma* of abundant economic opportunity paired with retrograde racial oppression was becoming so vivid and undeniable. But we also see the scores of small cities across the broad regional, post-bellum legacies from Virginia to Louisiana through rural Georgia, where W.E.B. du Bois (2003[1903]: 92) diagnosed a neo-slavery sharecropping landscape where "the merchants are in debt

Table 9.5　Segmentation and state regulatory space, 2004–06

Deciles for distance in state regulatory space	Odds ratios for subprime segmentation	
	2004	2006
1	1.076	1.196
2	1.325	1.543
3	1.111	1.329
4	0.962*	1.104
5	1.205	1.202
6	1.194	1.692
7	0.897	1.064
8	1.285	1.379
9	1.191	1.359
10	1.094	1.326

Source: FFIEC 2005, 2007.
Notes: Reference category (distance = 0) is New Mexico, with the best anti-predatory regulatory regime in 2004. Segmentation models include controls for all variables shown in Table 9.4, Model 4. *Coefficient not significant at $P < 0.001$.

to the wholesalers, the planters are in debt to the merchants, the tenants owe the planters, and laborers bow and bend beneath the burden of it all." Significant Black–White inequalities also appear throughout the corridor of postindustrialization from Baltimore to Philadelphia, Camden, Trenton, Newark, and the mosaic of working-class counties across the broader New York region. For Latinas and Latinos, capital flows highlight a pattern that is somewhat different at the peak of the hierarchy – Phoenix, Southern California, Dallas, Southwest Florida – while overlapping and reinforcing the Black–White inequalities of the Boston–Washington corridor.

This northeastern corridor is the vast territory described as the "main street of the nation" in Gottman's (1961) landmark study of *Megalopolis*, a place and time emblematic of dramatic postwar growth, rapid suburbanization, increasing city–suburban interdependence, and rapid technological innovation during the early years of postindustrial tertiary growth – in an era when such development did not yet imply the slow, painful death of the Fordist industrial city. Today, the optimistic, modernist facets of Gottman's analysis have been replaced by more turbulent, deregulated regimes of unequal growth and decline. Today's Megalopolis often still appears distinctive on national maps, but, if the pattern closely resembles Gottman's mid-century cartography, the processes creating it could not be more different. Our analysis reveals persistent and severe racial inequalities of capital and securitization that shape Black–White and Latino–White inequalities in homeownership throughout Megalopolis.

Today's geographies of subprime lending reflect not only the historic imprint of regional racial geographies, but also the historical legacies of American urbanization itself. In recent years, the iconography of the mid-twentieth century American Dream of (White, middle-class) homeownership was repackaged and aggressively marketed to African Americans, Latinos, and others long excluded from its opportunities. Yet that mythical, mid-twentieth century model was built in part on a series of Fordist-era bargains of regulation, wage-productivity increases, mass public subsidy, and stabilized, managed economic growth. This material base was actively destroyed in the 1980s. Without this foundation, the new image of expanded access to homeownership turned out to be a mirage. The inequalities of places shaped by the financial speculations of this new mirage – declining industrial cities of the Midwest rustbelt, the enduring mosaic of urban and suburban counties across Megalopolis, the ever-exploding subdivisions of California's Inland Empire, the piedmont South, and Florida – demonstrate that the urban imprint of the contemporary American Dream is a risky, borrowed one, paid for with the high costs of unequal exploitation enabled and encouraged by a doctrine of market freedom and market justice.

Conclusions

As America's subprime lending boom reached its crescendo, the share of African Americans pushed into high-cost loans shot up from 37 percent to 54 percent, and the share for Latinas and Latinos jumped from 25 to 46 percent. Even after accounting for a wide range of demand-side factors, African Americans and Latinas and Latinos approved for credit were still twice as likely as otherwise identical non-Hispanic Whites to wind up with high-cost loans in 2006. Inequalities are even more severe for African Americans in cities like Cleveland, Chicago, Newark, and New York; for Latinos, in smaller cities in Massachusetts, Bridgeport, Connecticut, Washington, DC, Chicago, and the San Francisco Bay Area. Securitization reinforced these effects, and overshadowed demand-side factors associated with the needs of borrowers. The evidence demonstrates the bankruptcy of the dominant risk-based pricing framework, and of attempts to blame the crisis on irresponsible consumers. The racial inequalities and urban expressions of the subprime boom were inscribed through the mutual interplay between regional histories of race and uneven urban development across the American urban system and the competitive moves of brokers, lenders, and Wall Street investment houses working to maximize short-term profits in an anti-regulation climate that favors the class interests of financial capital over the needs of consumers. Although our findings are tempered by significant data limitations, our results complement and amplify the historical analysis, in Hernandez' Chapter 7, of the "seemingly place-less and colorblind" wave of subprime capital that reorganized the spaces of vulnerability created in previous generations of racialized exclusion. Our measures of the rapid changes in securitization networks at the height of the boom also complement Gotham's Chapter 1, with its important Lefebvrian analysis of the role of securitization innovations in accelerating the fluidity and velocity of leveraged market transactions – annihilating space by time in a dangerous shift to unsustainable, short-term relations of extraction and exploitation (see also Burton 2008; Langley 2007).

For more than a generation, risk-based pricing and similar orthodox neoclassical theoretical frameworks have sustained an unquestioned policy doctrine of market sovereignty. This framework has been used to blame consumers for the consequences of an abusive industry, to justify a deregulatory stance that encourages usury as a form of innovation, and to sustain the mirage of the "American Dream" of homeownership backed by high-risk, predatory credit. While certain elements of economic theory can be refined and adapted to explain the perverse behavioral incentives of the credit boom (Greenwald and Stiglitz 1991; Engel and McCoy 2007), emancipatory social science demands a more critical and ambitious analysis of the gaps and contradictions within the process of reproduction of dominant ideologies of capital, power, and law (Wright 2010). These contradictions have been exposed repeatedly in vivid detail since this crisis emerged in early 2007 – and they highlight the paradox of de-materialized unreality backed up by the very real force of law and threats of violence (usually presented when the local sheriff's deputy arrives to enforce an eviction order). On the one hand, the wholesale destruction of fictitious capital opens a space for the exploration of alternatives: Dymski notes in his chapter that in economic theory, finance "is only a mirror of the real," and yet it is simultaneously "a ruthless cauldron of competition" to find arbitrage opportunities. The scale of wealth destruction presents an opening to challenge the entrenched presumption in favor of financial innovation. National home prices in the United States collapsed 32 percent from April 2006 to the trough of March 2009, while the Dow Jones Industrial Average plummeted 54 percent from October 2007 to March 2009 (Thomas *et al.* 2010: 8). The crisis destroyed trillions in presumed wealth, in no small part because of the new linkages connecting the localized use values of house and home with the fictitious capital machines of speculative capitalist innovations like credit default swaps; "Innovation has now cost us $7 trillion," as one analyst put it, referring to the liquidation of household wealth in the US alone; "That's a pretty high price to pay for innovation" (quoted in Morgenson 2010). Critical perspectives on class-monopoly rent and financial exploitation (Harvey 1974; Krueckeberg 1999;

Peterson 2005, 2007; Squires 2003; Ashton 2008, 2009) help to challenge the deceptive illusion of homeownership when delivered via usurious, deceptive finance. Class-monopoly rent places the focus squarely where it belongs – on the people and communities working to protect the non-commodified social use values of shelter, neighborhood, and community from those with the class power to benefit from exploitation.

At the same time, the ongoing crisis is repeatedly showcasing the power of a deeply structured political economy to reconstruct certain kinds of material realities – even in a world of widespread poststructuralist suspicion of the idea of objective, metaphysical reality itself. While the crisis vaporized trillions in stock and housing markets in 2008 and 2009, unprecedented state power stabilized most of the legal, political, and economic infrastructure that sustains the daily realities of accumulation and financial exploitation. By the end of 2010, US Treasury Secretary Timothy Geithner was able to note rebounding asset values that would permit the $700 billion TARP initiative to earn such good returns on its "investments" that the total cost would amount to less than 1 percent of US GDP. Perhaps the trillions of lost wealth in 2008–09 was never quite real in the first place; with sufficient state power, however, fictitious capital becomes real, and performative – while always ensuring that it is addressed by the proper name. The wide array of initiatives launched for the benefit of *foie gras* financial institutions are clearly defined as *investments* that "will likely, in the aggregate, ultimately yield a positive return for taxpayers." (Geithner 2010: 5). And so "The *cost* of TARP is likely to be no greater than the amount *spent* on the program's housing initiatives." (Geithner 2010: 5, emphasis added). Those housing initiatives, of course, are limited, temporary, and heavily biased towards the provision of further incentives for banks and mortgage servicers. Still, even these most limited of efforts to help consumers fit easily into the angry narrative of a Tea Party rebellion, which appeals to homeowners who are absolutely convinced that every bit of equity accumulated in their home is theirs alone, are the product of individual work and entrepreneurial skill. It is no surprise that these owners were ready to respond when Santelli asked, "do we really want to subsidize the loser's mortgage?"Critical perspectives on class-monopoly rent offer a powerful, strategic corrective. The exchange value rewards of debt-backed homeownership are a direct function of the terms of credit, while the use value advantages are paid for through the corresponding reduction of rights available to renters in most jurisdictions (Krueckeberg 1999). Recently, it has been made clear how little the distinction between owning and renting matters when it comes time to seize assets in an age of automated, predatory capitalism. Companies servicing some $6.4 trillion in residential mortgages have been caught evading legally required steps in foreclosure proceedings, backdating paperwork and falsifying statements on the facts of mortgage obligations. In a wide range of cases, where homeowners have fought foreclosure, depositions have revealed servicer employees engaging in "robo-signing" – signing hundreds of documents per day, violating the explicit legal mandate to have personal knowledge of the facts of the case and to attest on the facts justifying a company's legal authority to foreclose. (The recent revelations were foreshadowed early on in the crisis, when a federal judge in Ohio refused to allow Deutsche Bank to foreclose without proving it had the right to do so; see Bokyo 2007). In order to perform the transformation of housing into an electronic instrument that Sassen describes in Chapter 3, the industry had to develop an electronic transfer mechanism to reconcile the contradictions of today's transnational investment circuits and yesterday's place-based property law: "the financial industry developed an electronic transfer process that bypasses county property offices. This electronic process has, however, faced legal challenges that could, in an extreme scenario, call into question the validity of 33 million mortgage loans" (Congressional Oversight Panel 2010: 5).

Validity – *validus*: the Latin word for "strong" – is precisely what is at issue here, in a struggle of class power. The search for gaps and contradictions in the reproduction of capitalist inequality seems radical; and perhaps even a bit utopian (Wright 2010). Yet the opening in which to discuss alternatives is real and viable when we realize how frequently these contradictions are being exposed by the growing conflicts *amongst capitalists themselves*, with serious battles among different factions of industrial and financial capital and various alliances of state-backed capitalists in Europe, Russia, China, and elsewhere. In the shadow of these conflicts, class-monopoly rent provides coherent theoretical guidelines for progressive organizing through a politics of scale that must remain alert and flexible to an evolving legal and regulatory landscape. The Dodd–Frank financial reform legislation, signed in July 2010, has the potential to reduce the worst abuses and offers a partial reversal of a longstanding federal deregulatory agenda that undermined consumer protection efforts at the state and local levels. Yet major compromises were required to secure passage, and resurgent conservative power is now being directed to stalling reform through legal challenges, lobbying in the rulemaking process, and attempts to cut off funding for the consumer protection agency mandated by the legislation. Mobilization must, therefore, be divided between Washington and the evolving mosaic of state and local government. Regionally contingent relations of race, class, and rent will be central to the efforts of community organizations fighting the dispossessions of foreclosures, as Newman demonstrates in Chapter 8. Chapter 5 by Aalbers and Chapter 4 by Wainwright show how the details of national and multilateral political economy can shape the landscape of possible alternatives in conflicts over reforms of bank supervision, accounting regulations, and disclosure regimes.

As the financial crisis of speculative accumulation was mortgaged into a transnational sovereign debt crisis, it was clear that the crisis would not be resolved anytime soon. Yet the politics and struggles of America's housing markets will continue to be an important venue, where the contradictions of predatory capitalism are sometimes undeniable even to the most conservative of voters. In this crucible, we may find surprising opportunities for progressive alternatives amidst intensifying transnational tensions. A quarter of a century ago the US was "draining a large share of the world's savings – about $100 billion per year – to underwrite ... unstable and unproductive adventures" (Adams 1986: 236). The contradictions have only grown worse in the years since, intensified by what Schwartz analyzes in Chapter 2 as "nested political concerns" from the geopolitical to the local levels that helped to create serious problems of excessive leverage and maturity mismatch. We may not know exactly where the limits to capital are, but the speculative promises of a self-styled postindustrial capitalism cannot be infinite. Harvey's (1974, 1981, 1985) crisis predictions, once ahead of their time as theoretical analysis, seemed almost to have been plagiarized on a daily basis by central bankers and bond analysts quoted in the frantic news stories of 2008 and 2009. And so too, perhaps Adams' (1986: 234) glimpse of a post-materialist reconsideration of the meaning of housing may now resonate with a broader alliance of individuals and families deceived by the financial cult of the American Dream of debt-financed homeownership.

> In the twilight of materialism, the meaning of housing will be simplified and clarified, with a renewed emphasis on shelter and neighborhood. The false hope that everyone can get rich from real estate investment will be laid to rest for another fifty years, or perhaps for all time.

Notes

1   Lenders below specified size and lending activity thresholds are not required to report HMDA records. Some operators craft their business to escape disclosure requirements, while other fly-by-night shops simply refuse to comply. Between 2004 and 2006, the Federal Reserve cited almost 300 banks for violations of HMDA (Braunstein 2007). Discriminatory and/or fraudulent practices are likely to be much more prevalent among institutions that refuse to disclose their activities.
2   Rate-spread loans are proxies for subprime loans. The analysis does not estimate the actual class-monopoly rent extracted, but demonstrates that subprime mortgage markets can be explained through the relations of class-monopoly rent since borrower differentials (the premise of risk-based pricing explanations) do not fully explain the observable patterns.

3 Metropolitan areas in Puerto Rico, where the industry operates in a distinctive
   legal regime, were excluded from the final database. We also excluded all files
   with missing or invalid information on income or location, applications for government-insured loans, records for multifamily properties or with no formal
   mortgage lien, and records with either validity or quality edit failures. We also
   excluded applications in many of the new micropolitan areas defined by the
   Census Bureau in 2004 – since it is not possible to match these records to the
   detailed socioeconomic and housing characteristics reported in the 2000 Census.
   Finally, we sought to distinguish the subprime crisis from other disasters: Tables
   9.1, 9.2, 9.3, and 9.4 exclude applications on properties located in New Orleans
   and Houma, Louisiana, and Gulfport-Biloxi, Mississippi.
4 HMDA does not provide credit history information for all applicants, but certain
   types of lenders are required to cite up to three reasons when they decide to
   reject an application. "Credit history" is one of nine options lenders can choose
   from.
5 To conserve space, full results are not presented here. All multicollinearity tolerance statistics are well below problematic thresholds.
6 We use these categories with an understanding of the complexities of the social
   construction of race and ethnicity. In the case of HMDA data, loan applicants
   are asked to self-identify race or ethnicity by choosing from a list of categories.
   They may decline to do so.
7 For metropolitan areas near Minneapolis-St. Paul on the graph, increasing applicant income from about $100,000 to $350,000 increases the odds of subprime
   selection by a ratio of about 1.07.
8 This analysis is based on a different database from those described above. Controls
   in the logistic regression models are included for applicant income, estimated debt
   burden, and loan purpose, but the credit history instrument is omitted.

References

Abariotes, A., Ahuja, S., Feldman, H., Johnson, C., Subaiya, L., Tiller, N., Urban, J.,
   and Myers, Jr., S.L. (1993) Disparities in mortgage lending in the upper Midwest.
   Paper presented at the Fannie Mae University Colloquium on Race, Poverty, and
   Housing Policy. Minneapolis, MN, December 3.
Ambrose, B.W. and Pennington-Cross, A. (2000) Local economic risk factors and
   the primary and secondary mortgage markets. *Regional Science and Urban Economics*
   30: 683–701.
Anderson, J. and Timmons, H. (2007) Why a U.S. subprime mortgage crisis is felt
   around the world. *New York Times* 31 August: B1.
Andrews, E. (2008) Greenspan concedes error on regulation. *New York Times* 23
   October: B1.
Andrews, E. (2007) Fed and regulators shrugged as the subprime crisis spread. *New
   York Times* 18 December; A1.
Ashton, P. (2008) Advantage or disadvantage? The changing institutional landscape
   of underserved mortgage markets. *Urban Affairs Review* 43(3): 352–402.

Ashton, P. (2009) An appetite for yield: The anatomy of the subprime mortgage crisis. *Environment and Planning A* 41(6): 1420–41.

Berkovec, J.A., Canner, G.B., Gabriel, S.A., and Hanman, T.H. (1994) Race, redlining, and mortgage loan performance. *Journal of Real Estate Finance and Economics* 9(3); 263–94.

Berry, B.J.L. (1964) Cities as systems within systems of cities. *Papers of the Regional Science Association* 13: 147–63.

Bostic, R.W., Engel, K.C., McCoy, P.A., and Pennington-Cross, A. (2007) State and local anti-predatory lending laws: The effect of legal enforcement mechanisms. Working Paper, 7 August. Available at Social Science Research Network.

Boyko, C.A. (2007). *Opinion and Order, In Re Foreclosure Cases, 1:07CV2282 et al.* October 31. Cleveland: U.S. District Court, Northern District of Ohio, Eastern Division.

Braunstein, S.F. (2007) *Statement of Sandra F. Braunstein, Federal Reserve Division of Consumer Affairs.* Congressional Testimony, 25 July. Washington, DC: States News Service/Federal Reserve Board.

Brooks, R. and Ford, C.M. (2007) The United States of subprime: Data show bad loans permeate the nation. *Wall Street Journal,* 11 October: A1.

Browning, L. (2008) Small law firm at center of loan universe. *New York Times,* 1 February; C6.

Burton, D. (2008) *Credit and Consumer Society.* New York: Routledge.

Carpenter, D. (2010) Institutional strangulation: Bureaucratic politics and financial reform in the Obama Administration. *Perspectives on Politics* 8(3): 825–46.

Chan, S. and McGinty, J.C. (2010) Fed documents breadth of emergency measures. *New York Times,* December 1.

Chinloy, P. and Macdonald, N. (2005) Subprime lenders and mortgage market completion. *Journal of Real Estate Finance and Economics* 30: 153–65.

Chomsisengphet, S., and Pennington-Cross, A. (2006) The evolution of the subprime mortgage market." *Federal Reserve Bank of St. Louis Review* 88: 31–56.

Clark, G.L. (2001) Preface. In: N. Blomley, D. Delaney, and R.T. Ford, (eds.) *The Legal Geographies Reader.* Malden, MA: Blackwell, pp. x–xii.

Congressional Oversight Panel (2010) *November Oversight Report: Examining the Consequences of Mortgage Irregularities for Financial Stability and Foreclosure Mitigation.* November 16. Washington, DC: Congressional Oversight Panel for the Troubled Asset Relief Program.

Dinham, H. (2007) *Prepared Testimony of Harry Dinham on 'Preserving the American Dream: Predatory Lending Practices and Home Foreclosures.* Washington, DC: Committee on Banking, Housing, and Urban Affairs, US Senate. 7 February.

Du Bois, W.E.B. (2003[1903]) *The Souls of Black Folk.* New York: Barnes and Nobles Classics.

Dymski, G.A. (2007) *From Financial Exploitation to Global Banking Instability: Two Overlooked Roots of the Subprime Crisis.* Sacramento, CA: University of California Center Sacramento, 11 December.

Engel, K.C. and McCoy, P.A. (2002) A tale of three markets: The law and economics of predatory lending. *Texas Law Review* 80(6): 1255–381.

Engel, K.C. and McCoy, P.A. (2007) Turning a blind eye: Wall Street finance of predatory lending. *Fordham Law Review* 75(4): 2039–103.

Evans, A.W. (1991) On monopoly rent. *Land Economics* 67(1); 1–14.

Fabozzi, F. (ed.) (2001) *Handbook of Mortgage-Backed Securities*. (Fifth Edition) New York: McGraw-Hill.

Federal Deposit Insurance Corporation (2005) *Frequently Asked Questions about the New HMDA Data*. Washington, DC: FDIC.

Federal Financial Institutions Examination Council (Annual) *HMDA Raw Data Loan Application Register Data on CD-ROM*. Washington, DC: Board of Governors of the Federal Reserve.

Federal Reserve Board (2007) *Proposed Rule, Revisions to Regulation Z*. Draft Federal Register Notice and Request for Comment. December 18. Washington, DC: Board of Governors of the Federal Reserve.

Fisher, R. (2008) Dallas Fed's Fisher: Rate cuts won't cure STD (Securitization Transmitted Disease). *Wall Street Journal*, http://blogs.wsj.com/economics, September 26, accessed September 28.

Fukuyama, F., and Colby, S. (2009) What were they thinking? The role of economists in the financial debacle. *The American Interest* September/October: 18–25.

Geithner, T.F. (2010) *Written Testimony*. December 16. Washington, DC: Congressional Oversight Panel for the Troubled Asset Relief Program.

Gotham, K.F. (2006) The secondary circuit of capital reconsidered: Globalization and the U.S. real estate sector. *American Journal of Sociology* 112(1): 231–75.

Gottman, J. (1961) *Megalopolis*. New York: Twentieth Century Fund.

Greenspan, A. (2007) U.S. moving closer to recession. Appearance on *ABC News This Week* 16 December.

Greenspan, A. (2008) *Testimony of Dr. Alan Greenspan, before the Committee on Government Oversight and Reform*. October 23. Washington, DC: US House of Representatives.

Greenwald, B., and Stiglitz, J.E. (1991) Information, finance, and markets: The architecture of allocative mechanisms. Working Paper 3652. Cambridge, MA: National Bureau of Economic Research.

Harvey, D. (1974) Class-monopoly rent, finance capital and the urban revolution. *Regional Studies* 8: 239–55.

Harvey, D. (1981) *The Limits to Capital*. Chicago: University of Chicago Press.

Harvey, D. (1985) *The Urbanization of Capital*. Baltimore: Sir Johns Hopkins Press.

Harvey, D. (2005) *A Brief History of Neoliberalism*. New York: Oxford University Press.

HUD-Treasury Joint Task Force (2000) *Final Report of the Joint Task Force on Predatory Lending*. Washington, DC: US Department of Housing and Urban Development.

Hulse, C. (2008) Conservatives viewed bailout plan as last straw. *New York Times* September 26; A1.

Immergluck, D. (2004) *Credit to the Community*. Armonk, NY: M.E. Sharpe.

Immergluck, D. (2008) From the subprime to the exotic: Excessive mortgage market risk and foreclosures. *Journal of the American Planning Association* 74(1): 1–18.

Immergluck, D. (2009) *Foreclosed: High-Risk Lending, Deregulation, and the Undermining of America's Mortgage Market*. Ithaca, NY: Cornell University Press.

Kansas, D. (2009) *The Wall Street Journal Guide to the End of Wall Street as We Know It*. New York: Collins Business.

Krueckeberg, D. (1999) The grapes of rent: A history of renting in a country of owners. *Housing Policy Debate* 10(1): 9–30.

Labaton, S. (2009) Ailing, banks still field strong lobby at Capitol. *New York Times* 4 June: A1.

Labaton, S. and Herszhenhorn, D.M. (2008) Opposition from both parties over bailout plan. *New York Times* July 16: A1, A22.

Langley, P. (2007) *The Everyday Life of Global Finance: Saving and Borrowing in Anglo-America.* New York: Oxford University Press.

Lax, H., Manti, M., Raca, P., and Zorn, P. (2004) Subprime lending: An investigation of economic efficiency. *Housing Policy Debate* 15(3): 533–71.

Listokin, D., Wyly, E., Keating, L., Rengert, K., and Listokin, B. (2000) *Making New Mortgage Markets.* Washington, DC: Fannie Mae Foundation.

Litan, R.E. (2001) *A Prudent Approach to Preventing 'Predatory' Lending.* Washington, DC: Brookings.

Malkin, M. (2008) The subprime whiners: Ignoring reality. *New York Post* February 2.

McCoy, P.A. and Wyly, E. (2004) Guest Editors' introduction: Market failures and predatory lending. *Housing Policy Debate* 15(3): 453–66.

McDonald, L.G., and Robinson, P. (2009) *A Colossal Failure of Common Sense.* New York: Crown Business.

McKinnon, J.D., Mecker, L., and Cooper, C. (2008) An inside view of a stormy White House summit. *Wall Street Journal*, September 27.

Miller, M.J. (ed.) (2003) *Credit Reporting Systems and the International Economy.* Cambridge, MA: MIT Press.

Morgenson, G. (2010) It's time for swaps to lose their swagger. *New York Times* February 28.

Morgenson, G. and Fabrikant, G. (2007) Countrywide's chief salesman and defender. *New York Times* November 11; C1.

Myrdal, G. (1944). *An American Dilemma: the Negro Problem and American Democracy.* New York: Harper and Row.

Newman, K. (2009) The perfect storm: Contextualizing the foreclosure crisis. *Urban Geography* 29(8): 750–4.

Norris, F. (2007) A worrisome new wrinkle in bailouts. *New York Times* 14 December: C1, C13.

Norris, F., and Peters, J.W. (2007) Wall Street tumble adds to worries about economies. *New York Times* February 28: A1.

Pérez-Peña, R. (2008). Amid market turmoil, some journalists try to tone down emotion. *New York Times* September 22: C8.

Peterson, C. (2005) Federalism and predatory lending: Unmasking the deregulatory agenda. *Temple Law Review* 78(1): 1–98.

Peterson, C. (2007) *Predatory Structured Finance.* Gainesville: Levin College of Law, University of Florida.

Pew Research Center (2010) A clear rejection of the status quo, no consensus about future policies. November 3. Washington: Pew Research Center.

Renuart, E. (2004) An overview of the predatory lending process. *Housing Policy Debate* 15(3): 467–502.

Rivera, A., Cotto-Escalera, B., Desai, A., Huezo, J., and Muhammad, D. (2008) *Foreclosed: State of the Dream 2008.* Boston: United for a Fair Economy.

Roberts, J. and Jones, M. (2009) Accounting for self-interest in the credit crisis. *Accounting, Organizations, and Society* 34: 856–67.

Saunders, A. and Allen, L. (2002) *Credit Risk Measurement: New Approaches to Value at Risk and Other Paradigms*. Hoboken, NJ: John Wiley & Sons.

SIGTARP (2010) *Quarterly Report to Congress, October 26, 2010*. Washington, DC: Office of the Special Investigator General for the Troubled Asset Relief Program.

Sorkin, A.R. (2002) HSBC to buy U.S. lender for $14.2 billion. *New York Times* November 15: C1, C10.

Sowell, T. (2007) Political 'solutions.' *Real Clear Politics* October 30.

Squires, G.D. (ed.) (1992) *From Redlining to Reinvestment*. Philadelphia: Temple University Press.

Squires, G.D. (ed.) (2003) *Organizing Access to Capital*. Philadelphia: Temple University Press.

Squires, G.D. (ed.) (2004) *Why the Poor Pay More: How to Stop Predatory Lending*. Westport, CT: Praeger.

Stein, E. (2001) *Quantifying the Economic Cost of Predatory Lending*. Durham, NC: Center for Responsible Lending.

Stiglitz, J.E. and Weiss, A. (1981) Credit rationing in markets with imperfect information. *American Economic Review* 71(3): 393–410.

Stiglitz, J.E. and Weiss, A. (1992) Asymmetric information in credit markets and its implications for macro-economics. *Oxford Economic Papers* 44; 694–724.

Tam, J. (2007) Rare HSBC warning spawns fear. *The Standard/Financial Times* London, February 26.

Thomas, B., Hennessey, K., Holtz-Eakin, D., and Wallison, P.J. (2010) *Financial Crisis Primer*. Washington, DC: Republican Commissioners on the Financial Crisis Inquiry Commission.

Thomas, L. (2008) Buddy, can you spare a billion? *New York Times* 16 January.

Toomey, P. (2010) Toomey for U.S. Senate. http://toomeyforsenate.com, last accessed December 16.

Vandell, K.D. (1984) Imperfect information, uncertainty, and credit rationing: Comment and extension. *Quarterly Journal of Economics* 99(4): 841–63.

Walkom, T. (2007) GM layoffs show Canada not immune to turmoil in world financial markets. *The Toronto Star*, 31 August.

Wall Street Journal (2008) Treasury's financial bailout proposal to Congress. Real Time Economics blog, at http://blogs.wsj.com/economics, September 20, accessed September 20.

Wallison, P.J. (2009) Cause and effect: Government policies and the financial crisis. *Critical Review* 21(2–3): 365–76.

Wessel, D. (2008) In turmoil, capitalism in U.S. sets new course. *Wall Street Journal* September 20.

White, A.M. (2004) Risk-based mortgage pricing: Present and future research. *Housing Policy Debate* 15(3): 503–31.

White, L.J. (2002) The credit reporting industry: An industrial organization analysis. In: R.M. Levitch, C. Majnoni, and C. Reinhart (eds.) *Ratings, Ratings Agencies and the Global Financial System*. Boston: Kluwer.

Will, G.F. (2008) Alice in housing land. *Washington Post* May 15: A15.

Williams, R., Nesiba, R., and McConnel, E.D. (2005) The changing face of inequality in home mortgage lending. *Social Problems* 52(2): 181–208.

Wright, E.O. (2010) *Envisioning Real Utopias*. London: Verso.

Wyly, E.K., Atia, M., Foxcroft, H., Hammel, D.J., and Phillips-Watts, K. (2006) American home: Predatory mortgage capital and neighborhood spaces ofrace and class exploitation in the United States. *Geografiska Annaler* 88B(1): 105–32.

Zuckoff, M. (1992) Shawmut is said to settle over loan scams. *Boston Globe*, February 22, Metro/Regional Section, p. 1.

Part IV
Conclusion

10

Subprime Crisis and Urban Problematic

Gary A. Dymski

Introduction

A crucial question that must be answered in explaining the sequence of events that ended in global financial crisis is this: Why did the mortgage market generate the subprime crisis? The chapters in this book explain the mortgage market crisis as resulting from a rupture between the frenetically growing financial obligations linked to housing and the thick set of urban, spatially differentiated social relations in which this housing was embedded. Racial inequality figures centrally on both sides of this rupture – it affected both housing finance and evolving urban social relations. The subprime crisis is seen as a multi-dimensional phenomenon that arises in the context of what might be termed the urban problematic – that is, the historically evolving, racialized dynamics of social inequality and accumulation, which unfold in urban space. The authors show how this crisis represents, in many places, one stage in an urban evolutionary process that is creating subprime cities – subareas within many metropoles that are scarred by racial discrimination, disinvestment, high rates of joblessness, poor public services, and (most recently) foreclosed or abandoned housing. Mortgage markets, whose broader opening should have symbolized the possibility of full economic citizenship for some formerly excluded households, instead became the latest venue for such households' exploitation.

This shared perspective on the causes of the subprime crisis stands in stark contrast to the answers to this question that have emerged elsewhere. One focal point for blame is Wall Street. The Financial Crisis Investigation Commission (FCIC), for example, singles out the large financial institutions that generated, underwrote, and profited from the explosive growth of subprime mortgage paper, as well as the derivatives

Subprime Cities: The Political Economy of Mortgage Markets, First Edition. Edited by Manuel B. Aalbers.
© 2012 Blackwell Publishing Ltd. Published 2012 by Blackwell Publishing Ltd.

based on this paper. Financiers' and brokers' greed and even criminal fraud (Black 2010), as well as inadequate oversight, is an increasing focus of investigation by state attorney generals and the Securities and Exchange Commission.

Economists, in turn, have tended to depict the core problem as failed economic mechanisms. Their accounts do not take the urban problematic as their analytical frame; instead, they view the process of subprime lending, securitization, underwriting, as a sequence of market transactions occurring in the dimensionless terrain of financial markets. Breakdowns in market mechanisms then can be traced to design problems involving improper reward–punishment criteria in one or more parts of this sequence. This explains why major treatments of this crisis, such as Robert Shiller's *The Subprime Solution* (2008), make no mention of racial discrimination or predatory lending.

This concluding chapter first briefly sets out the preceding chapters' explanations of how the US and UK subprime crisis developed, and then summarizes economists' views. We next consider why there is such a profound explanatory gap between these answers to the same question – and, in turn, why economists' views have been more generally embraced than have views espousing the urban problematic. This last has something to do with the idea that globalization generally, and financial globalization in particular, appears to smooth over the rifts and differences between different national and regional spaces. Consider the interpretive choices available: one requires diving into the particularities of how financial institutions have affected patterns of racial/ethnic inequality, segregated urban space, and uneven urban development and investment; the other seeks to fine-tune market mechanisms that spread capital efficiently across space. The former requires assembling and interpreting rich, complex data that vary across space and reach back into time; the latter relies, more simply, on globe-spanning firms' efficient use of whatever information they deem necessary.

This will lead us into reflecting on how financial globalization is understood from the urban-problematic perspective unfolded in this volume. And this in turn will bring us back to the question of what to do about economics. The answer proposed here is this: scholars and analysts working in the critical social-science traditions that open space for the urban problematic are more likely to find *simpatico* approaches to the economy among heterodox political economists than among economists pre-committed to the notion that properly structured markets will tend to equilibrate at socially optimal levels. To close this gap, two traditions that have inexplicably lost contact must find one another again. This last chapter concludes by reflecting on why the gap between heterodox political economy and critical urban theory has arisen, and how to mend it.

Why the US Mortgage Market Generated the Subprime Crisis: A View from the Chapters

The chapters of this book present a relatively harmonious answer to the question of why the US mortgage market generated the subprime crisis. Specifically, the mortgage markets are depicted herein as a crucial link between spatially differentiated, socially unequal urban spaces, on one hand, and globally connected financial markets, on the other. Thus, the subprime crisis resulted from the collision between US mortgage markets as they have been – social institutions that reflected and deepened social exclusion and racial inequality – and US mortgage markets as global finance needed them to be – a terrain of integrated, homogenized, low-risk assets ripe for bundling and distribution into global wealth portfolios. The housing-price bubble put ever more pressure on this nexus between fixity and liquidity, until the liquid markets that supported this leveraged architecture froze, and the entire edifice came tumbling down.

These chapters' drill-down into the US and European mortgage markets showing how spatial and social inequality were central to the creation of the subprime crisis. Briefly put, the logic is as follows. While racial inequality and segregation originally excluded whole areas and subpopulations from access to credit, innovations in loan markets made an entire set of exploitative loans into a hot growth market. Once these loans went bad, the investment vehicles they underlay became non-performing, leading the money markets that supported these vehicles to shut down. This forced the banks that had bundled and sold this paper to take it back on their balance sheets, forcing massive capital losses (some still undeclared). This in turn led banks to cease lending, which dried up consumer credit and spiked consumer confidence, shaking the entirety of the housing and banking markets in numerous countries to their core. The collapse of the housing market and the contraction of bank credit led to a macroeconomic slump, which quickly spread worldwide.

This logic is embodied in many of the preceding chapters. In effect, the current crisis justifies the analyses of analysts and social scientists who have insisted that racial inequality matters. That the crisis arose from the embedded logic – the "normal" functioning – of the mortgage and banking markets would seem to have profound implications for understanding and designing policy "fixes" for these markets. Explanations of these markets' dynamics should pay explicit attention to the dynamics of racial and ethnic inequality over space and across time. Policy proposals must, in turn, pay attention to the racial and ethnic patterns of inequality. In the case of the US, this immediately creates challenges, given the shift of public discourse toward "race-free" criteria in allocating public resources.

The chapters herein embody a social science approach to conceptualizing social problems that can be characterized as the urban problematic. This approach involves a distinctive substantive focal point within the broader terrain of the field of urban studies: that is, a concern with understanding the origins and implications of social inequality in urban space.[1] It also embodies a methodological point of departure: a recognition that urban inequality unfolds in the context of thick, intertwined sets of social relations that no one conceptual entry point can cut through. Any progress made is necessarily partial and temporally bounded. Claims about generality have to be regarded with caution; and no one method of social science inquiry can be privileged as reliably superior to all others in generating insights. Given the challenging context within which knowledge is built, it is as important to connect insights derived from any one method and data set with insights from other studies and approaches, as it is to generate results in the first instance. Work on issues within the urban problematic is necessarily co-respective, time-place bounded, and partial. The notion of an urban problematic can be used to describe an entire lineage of academic inquiry, which runs from Bradford and Rubinowitz (1975) to Squires (1992) to Immergluck (2004), to cite three examples. This lineage encompasses this volume as well. Here, racial and ethnic differences in access to housing and credit markets are the particular facet of urban inequality that is highlighted.

The authors gathered together here pay special attention to how processes of redlining, racial and ethnic discrimination, and racial and ethnic segregation are interrelated. If they stopped at the level of urban populations and banks within the national context, these chapters would constitute a set of updates on the race/space/lending dynamic described in earlier work on the urban problematic (including the work cited immediately above): the central question would be whether being assigned a subprime loan in the mid-2000s is, in effect, equivalent to a loan denial in 1975. But these studies all share another characteristic: they link the race/space/lending dynamic to the growth and spread of subprime lending, to processes of financial globalization, on one hand, and to evolving governmental initiatives and policies regarding race and housing in US cities, on the other.

In solidly connecting subprime lending and crisis with racial inequality, these chapters deviate sharply from economists' accounts of the origins of this crisis. And while many authors have acknowledged the significance of past government policies of racial exclusion in shaping bank redlining and loan denial in contemporary mortgage markets, Chapter 7 by Hernandez sets a new standard in linking the history of federal discrimination in mortgage policy with urban land use decisions, and in turn with racial bias in both conventional and subprime mortgage markets.[2] Several chapters break new ground by elaborating on the links between processes of financial globalization and the subprime-lending explosion.

Economic Approaches to the Subprime Crisis

To throw the particularity of this volume into sharp relief, it will be useful to summarize the views of economists about the origins of the subprime crisis. For, whereas those working within the urban problematic start with the notion that crises of social and economic reproduction involving racial inequality are conjunctural and historically specific, many economists explain crises via a small set of fundamental principles about abstract market relationships. This is certainly the case for those using a neoclassical economics approach.

The "neoclassical" approach refers to what Schumpeter (1954) identified as an analytical pre-commitment to viewing the economy as reflecting the constrained choices and incentives of individuals and firms as they engage in market exchanges. Government regulations then affect market outcomes by influencing the incentives and potential returns available to the entrepreneurs that shape markets' evolution.

In this perspective, subprime lending and securitization are viewed as innovations that can improve credit allocation and expand access to capital. For example, Fender and Mitchell (2005: 2) argue that structured finance overcomes "adverse selection and segmentation." while Partnoy and Skeel (2007) discuss how "financial engineering [can be used] to complete markets." They write:

> Because synthetic CDOs ... essentially create new instruments, instead of using assets already on bank balance sheets ... complete markets by providing new financial instruments at lower prices. (2007: 11–12)

On the side of borrowers, more complete markets provide a wider range of contractual choice.[3] As Barth *et al.* put it:

> Those individuals choosing adjustable-rate mortgages typically receive an initial interest rate that is lower than one with a fixed-rate mortgage, but then face the prospect of higher rates if market interest rates rise. At the same time, the development and wide use of credit scores for individual borrowers and credit ratings for individual issuances of mortgage-backed securities provided more information for both lenders and borrowers to better assess and price risk. (2009: 4)

In the neoclassical framework, these developments will clearly lead to more socially optimal equilibria: subprime and Alt-A mortgages expand credit-market choice and permit more efficient financial risk sharing. Consequently, neoclassical economists – such as Downs (2007) and Calomiris (2007) initially denied that the emerging subprime crisis would do much damage.

As the crisis worsened, they conceded that market forces had been under-mined. Wallison and Calomiris (2008), for example, discuss the "inherent conflict between their government mission and their private ownership" (1). Calomiris was more specific in an article written a month later; the sub-prime crisis arose because of

> agency problems in asset management. In the current debacle, as in previous real estate-related financial shocks, government financial subsidies for bearing risk seem to have been key triggering factors, along with accommodative monetary policy. (2008: 1)

This is not to suggest that all proponents of a neoclassical view place responsibility on government subsidies. Others have emphasized inadequate regulation, which provided incentives for undue risk taking. Quigley, for example, writes:

> One does not need to invoke the menace of unscrupulous and imprudent lenders or of equally predatory borrowers to explain the rapid collapse of the mortgage market ... There were certainly enough unscrupulous lenders and predatory borrowers in the market, but the incentives faced by decent people – mortgagors and mortgagees – made their behavior much less sensitive to the underlying risks. How, you may wonder, could contracts with such poor incentives have evolved? To some extent, that remains a mystery. But to a large extent, the system worked just fine, as long as property values were rising and interest rates falling. (2008: 2–3)

Quigley opens up two possibilities here beyond the "perverse government policies" narrative that Calomiris pursues: first, unscrupulous players could exploit the unwary and naive in underregulated markets; second, people can be systematically fooled when caught in an asset bubble. These two possibilities have been explored by Morris (2008) and Shiller (2008), respectively.

The key point for our discussion is that racial discrimination and redlining do not appear in these economists' narratives, nor does predatory lending, and no spatial dimension is introduced: these terms do not receive even a mention in any of the texts referred to above. Analysis of incentives, asset bub-bles, and government–market interaction is sufficient to formulate hypotheses about "what went wrong." It is not necessary to take on the embedded logic of racial inequality and discrimination to "fix" the housing finance market.

So neoclassical economics and global structural imbalances approaches don't "need" racial/social inequality and spatial separation to generate the conditions for systemic malfunction. They are centered on aspects of social interaction in which race and space are not essential. Given the depth of the dysfunctionality demonstrated in the contemporary crisis of finance, a fix that brings financial system stability while reducing fraud and consumer abuse would be welcomed; and an analysis that stops far short of an exploration of historical legacies of racial exclusion will suffice to provide the requisite support. *Vis-à-vis* race, simple consumer protection measures built into revitalized financial oversight would, if effectively policed, disproportionately benefit minorities. This is without forcing legislators or academic experts to take on a serious analysis of how racial and ethnic dynamics have played over uneven urban spaces.

One factor that makes this disjuncture all the greater is that the urban problematic is embodied in situations that differ from place to place and over time. It is conjunctural: so ideas about what shape it and give it social meaning will vary depending on how spatial and social inequality have mattered in historic time. This quality of variability – which is of course one of the defining features of the subprime crisis – means that capturing the essential features of the urban problematic in any time and place requires the expenditure of some resources. This discourages many at the outset. But for researchers seeking to understand the shifting points of intersection between globalization, race, and space, the urban problematic is a logical point of analytical departure. As Sassen put it:

> The city and the metropolitan region emerge as one of the key sites where these macro social trends instantiate and hence can be constituted as objects of study. Among these trends are globalization and the rise of the new information technologies, the intensifying of transnational and trans-local dynamics, ... [and] the strengthening presence and voice of specific types of socio-cultural diversity. (2005: 353–54)

Globalization and New Rifts in Social Science Inquiry

This problem of whether social analysis should seek out "intensifying ... transnational and trans-local dynamics" or instead try to uncover universal organizing principles is, of course, irresolvable at the level of principle. A serious social inquiry must take on both ends of this polarity. But how one looks, and what one finds, depends on whether one is seeking thick or thin explanations; and this in turn depends in part on one's degree of confidence in the theoretical framework that guides one's inquiry.

This polarity has been widened by processes of globalization, foremost among which has been the surge of financial globalization that began in the late 1970s. This epoch eventually led, of course, to the globalization of securities markets, the digital assignment of creditworthiness scores (Sinclair 2008), the creation of vast markets for subdividing and selling risk, and eventually the subprime – and now global – financial crisis.

Shifts of similar magnitude, leading to many types of dislocation, have occurred in many social and economic spheres in this same time period (Dicken 2007). The all-embracing pace of globalization, which seems to deny the very relevance of localized space in appropriating experience, has posed a challenge to analytical work rooted in the assumption that space and place matter. Previously, social and spatial investigations could implicitly introduce their audiences to new localized contexts, the author giving the reader a window into how people in those local contexts organized their affairs and understood things. To investigate was to unfold new vistas, to find revealed the variety and strangeness and uniqueness of the world.

But globalization changed the fundamental premises of investigation. Human societies were being stripped of their "'otherness,'" their unique, isolated reference points – and instead being relentlessly homogenized. Investigations of the local would now find the local in the process of being appropriated into the global whole.[4] This is not to say that the global has swallowed the local; but at the very least, the local and global are now mutually constitutive. Many contemporary investigations by social scientists seek to decode evidence in local instantiations of the emerging logics of global structures; examples are the literatures on global cities (Sassen 1991) and on networks (Castells 1996).

This sense of an accelerating collision between local and external forces stimulated renewed interest in what different disciplinary perspectives could teach one another, and in the problem of agency itself. As Marcus notes for the case of social and cultural anthropology, "the center of the discipline [was left] intellectually weak relative to the vitality of its diverse interdisciplinary and even nonacademic engagements" (2008: 1). The decentering process described by Marcus was experienced in many social science disciplines.[5] This, of course, led to a re-centering. Everyone had to look again: idiosyncratic, non-homogenized behavior might represent the continuity of persistent traditions; or it might represent stubborn resistance to the onslaught of globalization. There was always the possibility that high-speed communications and money movements were eating away the foundations of nationally or regionally distinct patterns. With quickened global rhythms, one could know more, more quickly; but one became ever more uncertain about the ontological status of that knowledge. Cultural studies and postmodernist approaches emerged as possible alternative ways of knowing, or not-knowing.

This brings us to our central argument in this section: as the neoliberal era deepened, social scientists generally wrestled with post-modernism and cultural relativism, and with the decentering of received wisdoms – but neoclassical economics did not. Its proponents were well positioned to take advantage of the growing importance of the global *vis-à-vis* the local, for epistemological reasons. Neoclassical economics works from ideal, abstract forms to instantiations of those forms in real world contexts. To be validated in economic theory, any lived experience must be understandable as an instance of a general case with discoverable formal properties.

Neoclassical economists generally believe that eradication of the specifically local creates a wider domain of action for a more general – and thus more optimal – dynamic. The elimination of national financial policies and aid policies – that is, of distortions in capital markets – should lead to the welfare-optimizing flow of capital from rich to poor countries (Lucas 1990). Further, freer global trade means fewer restrictions on the movement of goods from their markets of production to markets where they are most sought-after; thus, globalization of production and opening of markets to foreign tradables should maximize global welfare (Bhagwati 2004). The same conclusion follows for financial markets – the fewer restrictions on the formation and movement of assets, the more optimal an equilibrium can be achieved. Global homogenization, from this point of view, means the attainment of higher welfare levels.

An obvious virtue of this approach from the viewpoint of neoclassically oriented policy economists is that "one size fits all" policy prescriptions are readily generated – countries and regions should make whatever policy steps are necessary to open the way to global flows of capital and goods. There is no need to analyze the logic of local socio-economic dynamics, or to problematize the urban problematic in any given locale. Localized inequalities in resource flows and opportunity that are not due to borrower or entrepreneurial merit should disappear once portals to global markets are fully open. The idiosyncratic local structure need not be an object of research, except insofar as analysis might examine gaps between restrictive local policies and desired globally open policies.

Clearly, many of the economic policies implemented by President Reagan and Prime Minister Thatcher and their successors – monetarism, deregulation, free-trade agreements, and so on – reflect this "one size fits all" policy approach. Of course, many dissident economists have resisted this rush to theoretical judgment: institutionalists, Keynesians, neo-Marxians, feminist economists, and others. But the crucial point is that the new phase of globalization liberated neoclassical economists to make bold and definitive statements about how markets would react to deregulation, to freer trade and financial flows, and so on – all this at a time when other social science disciplines were feeling hemmed in, and far less confident about the utility of their methodologies and the validity of their conclusions.

In sum, globalization has made the social and economic relations highlighted in the "urban problematic" approach even denser and thicker than before: efforts to define "excluded" populations must be refined, and more interrelated trajectories among different sub-populations have be traced out and understood. The world of racialized inequality is not as simple as it was before. But at the same time, the heightened ability of globally mobile actors to move across borders makes explanations that focus on the universal and ignore the local more attractive. And what social science has been more insistent on universal, context-free explanations than economics? Ironically, the idea that globalization puts the same sorts of pressures on economic actors everywhere gave renewed resonance to economists' penchant for institutions-don't-matter theorizing and policy advice. The attractiveness of this latter approach for financial-market participants and government regulators is obvious: simple truths are so much more readily digested than dense contextual analyses. The fact that some economists' (and finance theorists') blind embrace of idealized universal markets helped drive the global financial system off a cliff was recognized too late.

The Urban Problematic in the Neoliberal Transition

In contrast to its epochal implications for core social science disciplines such as anthropology and economics, the unleashing of global, post-regulationist forces did not put the urban problematic at an analytical crossroads. One reason is that the urban problematic necessarily has a multi-disciplinary character. Another is that analysts anticipate that interconnections between race and space and inequality will vary over time and place; there is no idealized case that defines how the relations among these variables "should" be. The urban problematic is a way of seeing things, not a paradigm or a discipline. One asks how spatial division, racial division, and wealth differences matter in urban space. Observations and generalizations are then made based on what has been found at a particular time and place.

The notion that "global" (non-local) and local forces are mutually conditioning, then, is inherent in all work on the urban problematic. This said, the chapters collected here, all of which use the urban problematic, wrestle with two questions about local and global dynamics: how much continuity is there in local dynamics as the global age begins? And do global dynamics eventually dominate local forces?

There is no simple answer; the global is always present in the local, and vice versa. But these authors' struggle with the questions highlights different elements of the global–local interlock. Hernandez (Chapter 7) insists that the local dynamic dominates, and there is virtually complete continuity from past to present as the global age begins. Newman (Chapter 8) argues by contrast that the global has eradicated the local, via a huge rift that destroyed all apparent continuity. Wyly *et al.* (Chapter 9) also develop their ideas on the premise that a "global" metric of exploitation is at work, one that exploits local conditions. Gotham (Chapter 1) too shows how a willing federal government created a "global" market; Sassen (Chapter 3) describes how this market was generalized. Wainwright (Chapter 4) and Aalbers (Chapter 5), however, then tell a very different story about the UK and continental Europe: in their rendering, these spaces remained distinct and "local" despite the onslaught of global forces.

These differences in the privileging of the local or global are due in part to these chapters' different starting points: Hernandez, Wainwright, and Aalbers root their analyses in the period before the neoliberal age; the other chapters focus in on the neoliberal era *per se*. In effect, pre-neoliberal and neoliberal understandings of globalization co-exist uneasily in the space of urban theory, and of these chapters. This uneasiness is reflected as well in these authors' reliance on Harvey. His pre-1990 work is cited by every author in the symposium. But can these different works use Harvey's framework consistently?

Both a strength and a limitation of Harvey's framework (as exposited in Harvey 1981, 1985) is that it rigorously applies Marx's ideas to the urban context. This provides a useful lens for understanding the contradictory, crisis-prone trajectory of accumulation with spatially fixed capital. On the other hand, Harvey has a particular vision of capital accumulation, which was built up prior to the "financialization" period that has attracted so much recent interest: that is, he views residential capital as a circuit secondary to a primary commodity-production circuit. Generally, Harvey's work on the city embodies a relatively orthodox, top-down conception of urban accumulation. Finance, for example, is discussed in terms of the roles it must perform to assure maximum overall capital accumulation in the city. In effect, Harvey's writing assumes that the accumulation imperative drives the urban agenda, and that finance is the servant of urban accumulation.

This view has been challenged in the financialization framework. For one thing, the latter framework does not privilege commodity production as a site for surplus extraction in the overall architecture of capital accumulation. For another, the financialization framework does not assume that finance subordinates itself to production, nor that it assures maximum accumulation in the city. Indeed, Harvey himself (1990) suggested, in his first book of the neoliberal era, that financial globalization makes public control of financial markets impossible, since instantaneous information transmittal compresses space by eliminating time. This conclusion is subject to challenge (Dymski and Veitch 1996); but the main point here is that Harvey's own work does not provide a unitary construct, as his own ideas have been deeply affected by the emergence of the neoliberal era. And the subprime crisis itself has emerged in the neoliberal era.

Gotham (2006) recognizes the tension between these older and newer views of global accumulation processes, but does not attempt to resolve them. He uses Lefebvre's work primarily to contrast spatial fixity and fluidity; specifically, he shows how the key to fully incorporating the potential of residential capital into the broader accumulation process is transforming an illiquid, spatially fixed asset (a home) into a liquid, aspatial asset. This shift in form involves a series of guarantees and supports for the markets involved.

This movement from nationally centered dynamics to continual global flux has shaken not just Harvey's framework, but many other reference points in urban theory as well. Molotch's (1976) notion of an urban growth machine was a powerful organizing concept for investigating urban political economy. In this heuristic, urban growth was seen as coordinated by a coalition of interests, with local political leadership guaranteeing the conditions of existence for local circuits of capital. But just eight years later, Molotch and Logan already wrote of "tensions [in the growth machine] generated by the growing international concentration of capital" (1984: 483).

The inductive approach of the growth machine concept is partly to blame here: this heuristic embraces a bottom-up methodology to study and understand global-level phenomena.[6] And in any event, global decisions – decisions made elsewhere – increasingly cross-cut and even undermine the coherence of local strategies of accumulation and political control. Some locales make sense only *vis-à-vis* the global. Urban expansion in many places (Las Vegas, the San Joaquin Valley, the Coachella Valley, and so on) now involves vast landscapes of growth, quite often encompassing multiple cities that compete to host big box retail stores that can provide them with sales tax revenue. The acres and acres of houses built in this zero-sum expansion game are then marketed as commodities stripped of any but global designations ("properties in the sun in California").

The Chicago–LA "dispute" on urban structure is also a product of this global decentering. Previously, the local urban center was the focal point around which urban resources would be deployed; it was hierarchical, concentric, and functionally separated. In the neoliberal world, unicentric development has been displaced by an LA-like spread of urban activity across space, with local activities integrated more tightly into the logic of global exchange than of local community coherence (Scott and Soja 1996).

Bringing the Urban Problematic and Heterodox Political Economy Together

This brings us back to one of our central points of reflection: how to encourage deeper and more rewarding dialogues regarding the urban problematic between non-economists and economists – that is, between social sciences other than economics, and economics? A previous section explained the relative indifference of many economists towards the urban problematic: the methodology of neoclassical economics biases its proponents toward simplified explanations drawn from first principles; but the urban problematic requires a tolerance for complexity and for multiple points of view. So, most economists working within neoclassical methodology conclude that cross-disciplinary conversations are outside the scope of serious inquiry.

Turning to the other side of the chasm, for some work on the urban problematic, the absence of economics is not important. And for many other questions, non-economist authors build analyses that include political-economy insights. The chapters in this book are an example. They are replete with political economic analysis: that is, they systematically show how economic outcomes are shaded by government regulations and by political decisions; they show the dense interpenetration of the spheres of civitas, market, and money.

Market and polity interaction is hardly the exclusive domain of those working on the urban problematic. The term "political economy" has been appropriated from different entry points by many subfields in social science. Among those is neoclassical economics itself, for which "political economy" involves the analysis of economic outcomes when market forces are affected by governmental decisions (such as the rate of money-supply growth or the scope of regulation).[7] Once economists working from this perspective take up a problem, they reduce it to a question of how equilibrium is altered by the introduction of factors extraneous to pure market dynamics. Confronting the urban problematic, these "extraneous" factors would be such things as social heterogeneity distributed over space, racial differentials in wealth and income, and so on. The point is not to explore the unfolding of inherently thick, interpenetrating social logics, but instead to isolate the impact of non-economic factors on "economic" dynamics.

This seems harmless on its face; but the economic dynamics in question are those of equilibrium analysis, wherein decentralized decision-making by self-interested agents can achieve socially optimal outcomes. And *this* is a denial of the very premise of the urban problematic.[8] To maintain the integrity of the urban problematic as such, then, its protagonists have three options: to wall themselves off from interaction with economists; to pluck ideas opportunistically from the realm of economic theory, appropriating those tools for their own uses; or to find economists who are not pre-committed to reductionist methodologies and to the centrality of pure market forces in social analysis.

There are economists who are not so pre-committed, and who work with pluralist and holistic methodologies. Many have despaired of theory and prioritized empirical and policy work. These are, in the main, economists who are working at a critical distance from the neoclassical framework, and who are suspicious of appeals to authority on the order of "what economics has to say about topic X." Many, though by no means all, of these are economists who work with heterodox frameworks – post-Keynesianism, institutionalism, Marxian economics, feminist economics, and radical political economy, among others.

Aalbers, in his introductory chapter, is sensitive to the potential alliance between heterodox economics and critical social science. But this alliance has been far from fully achieved in these pages. For example, none of the chapters herein on mortgage finance connect with the core concepts of contemporary heterodox political economy.

Where did this rift arise, and what to do about it? We must go back in time to answer these questions. Heterodox economics emerged in the US, the UK, and elsewhere, in the late 1960s in the context of the rise of Euro-communism, of the new social movements, and of resistance to the US war in Vietnam. New readings of Marx's texts by this New Left generation gave rise to new Marxian and Marx-inspired theories: to name just a few, Sraffian economics, conflict theory, underdevelopment theory, overdetermination, rational-choice Marxism, and so on.

The worsening condition of Western macroeconomies soon led to decisive shifts in the terrain of "orthodox" (neoliberal) macroeconomics. By the end of the 1970s, Keynesian economists were forced either to give lip service to a newly dominant, equilibrium-based (non-Keynesian) macroeconomic orthodoxy, or to lose their status within the mainstream. Keynesian holdouts were shunted into the heterodox camp – even in the former Keynesian citadel of Cambridge University. American institutionalist economists met the same fate. These developments, along with the rise of economists interested in exploring gender and race, created a rich tableau within heterodox economics. So by the early 1980s, heterodox political economy – while marginalized within the broader economics profession – had undergone a profound transformation. It became a set of overlapping communities of discourse united by their opposition to (and exclusion from) mainstream economics (Cohen 2007; Hayes 2007).

This history could not be more different from that of the entry of Marx's ideas into contemporary urban theory. David Harvey's interpretation and spatialization of Marxian political economy had an overwhelming impact on urban theory as a whole – not just on a marginalized segment of urban theorists. Harvey's rich and contextualized reading of Marx framework provided a sufficient framework for many critical theorists, as it achieved the status of a quasi-orthodoxy in geography. As such, it became a point of critical departure for eventual feminist and post-modern critics of his approach; and indeed, Harvey's own dialogues with his critics and his own earlier ideas have lent continued vibrancy to his voice in recent years.

There was no Harvey-equivalent in economics. In that field, heterodox theorists – whether they drew on Marx, Keynes, Schumpeter, or von Mises – never penetrated into the core of the discipline. Even when insights developed by heterodox economists gained currency, they were normally expressed in the game-theoretic terminology favored by orthodox thinkers – usually in articles making no reference to heterodox work.

This asymmetry itself has constituted a huge barrier to dialogue between two loosely constituted sets of theorists – heterodox economists and critical social scientists – that have much to teach one another. For example, geographers and urban theorists view Harvey's work as an orthodoxy itself, from which some escape is necessary. Consequently, some of the most interesting work by geographers and urbanists has been fueled by the tension between postmodern and other impulses and the neo-Marxian framework that underlies such protean constructs as the Molotch and Logan vision of the city as a growth machine.

On the side of heterodox political economy, a different dynamic has occurred. Many scholars writing on the urban problematic have been trained as heterodox political economists. Until the mid-1980s, the *Review of Radical Political Economics* (*RRPE*) regularly published articles and even sponsored a special issue on urban development; see Edel *et al.* (1978). But the *RRPE* has published virtually no recent work on urban political economy *per se*; neither has the *Cambridge Journal of Economics*.

Heterodox political economists have focused in recent years on development and inequality, but generally in the context of national or racial and ethnic-minority development. When heterodox economics journals have explored core theoretical frameworks, they have privileged aspatial models that abstract from urban processes. Heterodox theorists tend to debate issues at the level of macroeconomic structural constraints; more localized spatial scales – including the urban – are usually treated as second order. Theoretical models typically build on ideas derived from Keynes, Marx, Veblen, Minsky, and other protean figures; these models are also often developed with explicit attention to flaws or blind spots in orthodox (efficient market) approaches to the same types of problem. This continual interrogation of the conceptual roots of heterodox thinking and of the adequacy of the orthodox framework is a defining feature of work in one or more of the heterodox lineages.

The results of these two cross-cutting trends are sometimes subtle and sometimes great disjunctures between the communities of heterodox political economy and of critical urban social science. So when heterodox political economists write about poverty and development, their attention normally centers on how to extend ideas linked to heterodox sources of inspiration, or how to respond to orthodox claims and findings; they are unlikely to "drill down" analytically into how (in this case) poverty and development emerge from richly detailed social or spatial processes in cities. And while many critical social scientists, both in geography and sociology (as well as other fields and subfields) work on poverty and development, they are far less concerned with "drilling down" to whether the core social dynamics they are identifying are consistent with core concepts in Keynesian, Marxian, or other protean approaches. They may use "neoliberal economic dynamics" as a reference point; but this is likely to be done in a broad-brush manner, without the nuanced attention to which assumptions of orthodox economic theory have what implications in any arguments they are developing.

This disjuncture is readily illustrated for the chapters gathered here. Several authors make use of Harvey's class-monopoly rent framework. This poses no problems; but this approach is not unique to Harvey. Itoh and Lapavitsas (1999) and especially Lapavitsas (2008) have highlighted precisely this sort of exploitation, and attributed it to class-based power differences that can operate at macro or micro scales. Bowles and Gintis' "contested exchange" framework (1993) explains this sort of exploitation as being due not to class power but to asymmetries in contracting parties' exit options (using terminology introduced by Hirschman (1970)). The contrasting views of Itoh and Lapavitsas, on one hand, and Bowles and Gintis, on the other, are animated to a large extent by their different understandings and appropriations of Marxian theory. I am not campaigning against Harvey's conceptual approach, but instead drawing attention to extensive work by contemporary heterodox economists, which is not on these authors' radar screens. This rift between heterodox political economy and contemporary urban theorists matters because the former have developed ideas about micro and macro (generally aspatial) dynamics in contemporary capitalism; so connections are not made about the broader political economy context of issues that arise in the urban problematic.

This disjuncture occurs differently in Chapter 9, as Wyly *et al.* work effectively with economists' ideas. These authors mention the familiar insight of Stiglitz and Weiss (1981) that lenders confronted with asymmetric information about borrowers try to differentiate safer from riskier borrowers; so, these authors note, better information will ameliorate some risk-related problems in subprime lending. This is true as far as it goes. But this chapter's appropriation of these ideas would be enriched if it were informed by the heterodox critique of the asymmetric-information lending model, which is asocial and equilibrium-based.[9] Other chapters in this volume refer to Shiller's 2005 volume *Irrational Exuberance* and to concepts such as efficient markets and asymmetric information. While these references are almost uniformly critical, the chapters in which they appear contain almost no references to heterodox economists' parallel work on the subprime crisis.

The work of such contemporary heterodox-economics interpreters of Keynes as Wray, Kregel, and Davidson – all of whom have written extensively on the subprime crisis – makes no appearance. Nor is there any explicit reference to Keynes or Keynesian uncertainty. Most surprisingly from a heterodox-economics perspective, there is no mention of Minsky's financial instability hypothesis (Minsky 1986) – this being the principal heterodox framework for understanding financial crises. Wyly and his coauthors do make solid critiques of the notion that risk-based pricing could be done efficiently and create a flat subprime earth.

Does this lacuna matter? For some purposes, certainly not. But as Minsky himself used to say prior to his death in 1996, "you have to fight a theory with a theory." The theory he had in mind, of course, was that of capitalist market dynamics. Economists are as aware as any other investigators that no single factor governs that dynamic; but because they are, at the same time they are more aware than non-economists of the many nuanced ways in which the privileging of some factors over others in an explanation of those dynamics can change an entire trajectory of thinking about what is wrong and what should be done about it. There is no doubt that bringing some Minskyian ideas into focus would shore up any critique of the overconfident efficient-markets thinking that underlay the subprime disaster – including the critique(s) developed here.

But it is unfair to leave the finger of blame for this disjuncture pointed only in one direction. As noted, most published academic research by heterodox economists in recent years has overlooked the urban problematic. And heterodox economics journals have published at best a trickle of articles having anything to do with the urban problematic.

The Widgets of the Post-Industrial World?

In any event, many potential "gains from trade" can be had by increasing the connections between heterodox political economy and spatial theory. We now turn to a concrete example: Newman's description of subprime loans as the "widgets of the post-industrial order." This characterization, while provocative, raises questions about the status of subprime loans in the accumulation process. Her linking of the term "widget" with subprime loans is first of all a provocation; it implies that subprime loans are so widespread that they have become an everyday feature of contemporary capitalism. Everybody makes money from them; everybody knows somebody who has one; and so on.

The term "widget" is also a provocation. Microeconomists are so confident of the power of their purely theoretical insights that they sometimes demonstrate their ideas for a purely fictional good. This is the "widget." A widget describes a generalized commodity – an "every commodity" – that is either sold to final consumers or used as an intermediate good in production. Mentioning "widgets" reminds readers of just how decontextualized and historically disembedded economics has become. But the analogy between widget ("every commodity") and subprime loan breaks down. That is because for every widget there is, so to speak, a widget factory. But this is not the case for subprime loans. There is a housing production process, and there are factories that produce the material elements that are assembled in the construction of a house. Subprime loans are assembled on the basis of the contracts that are drawn up after or as a house is sold.

The cash-flow of the mortgage holder is insufficient to buy this combination of widgets (together with the value of the land they sit on), even for plain-vanilla mortgages. So, while capitalist accumulation previously involved the production of widgets by means of widgets, to paraphrase Sraffa (1960), we do not now have the production of subprime loans by means of subprime loans. We have first of all an expansion of shelter consumption, on a precarious basis relative to worker income levels; for shelter purchased on the housing market requires sustained income flows over time. Accomplishing this consumption requires the creation of Newman's post-industrial widgets: mortgages, which she characterizes as "the raw products necessary for the production of securities, derivatives, and the related products of a financialized economy" (Newman 2009: 315).

But there is no direct connection between one round of production (of subprime loans) and the next; the subprime loans in different rounds are connected through the housing market. As Sassen predicts – and Aalbers hints – housing itself should actually be proposed as "widget of the post-industrial world." But the subprime crisis shows us how wrong the production of housing by means of housing can go. That chain can proceed only if workers – who buy the houses so produced – draw down an ever larger share of national income. This bolsters capitalists' profits in the housing (and financial) sector, but at the expense of profits elsewhere. Eventually the links between profit growth in the housing sector and workers' real wages will be snapped.

Conclusion

This chapter has offered a terse synopsis of some of this volume's central themes and made two other points. First, it is important that critical social scientists – those involved in understanding the urban problematic – make deep contact with heterodox economists. Second, the trajectories of both globalization and the subprime crisis highlight the importance of refocusing social scientists' attention (economists included) on the urban problematic. As Sassen recently put it:

> Today ... the city is once again emerging as a strategic site for understanding some of the major new trends reconfiguring the social order, and hence potentially for producing critical knowledge not just about cities but about the larger social condition. (2005: 352)

Many of the debates and disagreements we have been describing are purely academic. But the reader should be under no illusion about what is at stake. Protagonists such as Shiller (2008) believe that, in the end, the financial markets broke down and generated a housing crisis because they lacked enough futures/derivative/insurance markets. If those existed, risk-based pricing could have been accurately done, and crisis averted. Rallying on the other side will be policy-makers and academics, and others who are skeptical that any set of futures and contingent markets can ever foresee all that they must to avoid another disaster. It is too early to know which side is right – but it is not too early to acknowledge that the subprime crisis will ultimately constitute an historical dividing line for the urban problematic, for heterodox economists, and for the future of social science. This is crucial. For if the subprime crisis is understood as being only about incentive and oversight problems, and not about racial exploitation and spatial separation, then solutions imagined even under progressive political leadership will not address the root causes this book's chapters so deftly expose.

Acknowledgments

Comments by Silvana De Paula, Kevin Fox Gotham, and the editor significantly improved this chapter. Remaining errors are the author's own.

Notes

1 Bowen *et al.* (2010) have recently defined urban studies *per se* as a "field of inquiry steered by complex, ever-changing, and often-large-scale realities and real-world problems of evolving human settlements" (page 199).
2 Outstanding examples are Dreier (1991), Squires (1992), and Stuart (2003).
3 Ashton (2009) also explores the notion that subprime lending represents market completion.
4 This shift in perspective was perhaps most acutely felt in anthropology, since ethnography had been predicated on the notion that the investigator was unfolding the "authentic" (local) cultural essence of a society and thus revealing something about "man." In the 1980s, however, critical ethnographic investigations challenged this very premise. See Clifford and Marcus (1986).
5 See, for example, May and Perry (2005).
6 The author is indebted to Gotham for this point.
7 See, for example, Drazen (2001) and Persson (2002).
8 The city itself has provided a rich field for the application of mainstream economics methods; see, for example, Fujita *et al.* (2001) and Arnott and McMillen (2007).
9 See, for example, Crotty (1996).

References

Arnott, R. and McMillen, D.P. (2007) *A Companion to urban economics*. New York: Wiley-Blackwell.

Ashton, P. (2009) An appetite for yield: The anatomy of the subprime mortgage crisis. *Environment & Planning A* 41(6): 1420–41.

Barth, J.R., Li, T., Phumiwasana, T., and Yago, G. (2008) A short history of the sub-prime mortgage market meltdown. *GH Bank Housing Journal*. Los Angeles: Milken Institute.

Bhagwati, J. (2004) *In defense of globalization*. Oxford: Oxford University Press.

Black, W.K. (2010) Neo-classical economic theories, methodology and praxis optimize criminogenic environments and produce recurrent, intensifying crises. *Social Science Research Network*: http://papers.ssrn.com/sol3/papers.cfm?abstract_id=1607124.

Bowen, W.M., Dunn, R.A., and Kasdan, D.O. (2010) What is "urban studies"? Context, internal structure, and content. *Journal of Urban Affairs* 32(2): 199–227.

Bowles, S. and Gintis, H. (1993) The revenge of homo economicus, contested exchange and the revival of political economy. *Journal of Economic Perspectives* 7(1): 83–114.

Bradford, C.P. and Rubinowitz, L.S. (1975) The urban-suburban investment-disinvestment process, consequences for older neighborhoods. *Annals of the American Academy of Political and Social Sciences* 422: 77–86.

Calomiris, C.W. (2007) Not (yet) a "Minsky moment." American Enterprise Institute website, accessed at http://www.aei.org/docLib/20071010_Not(Yet)AMinskyMoment.pdf on December 11, 2007.

Calomiris, C.W. (2008) The subprime turmoil, what's old, what's new, and what's next. Washington, DC: American Enterprise Institute, October 1.

Castells, M. (1979) *The Urban Question: A Marxist Approach*. Cambridge: MIT Press.

Castells, M. (1996) *The rise of the network society, the information age, economy, society and culture vol. I*. Oxford: Blackwell.

Clifford, J. and Marcus, G.E. (eds.) (1986) *Writing Culture, the Poetics and Politics of Ethnography*. Berkeley: University of California Press.

Cohen, P. (2007) In economics departments, a growing will to debate fundamental assumptions. *New York Times*, July 11.

Crotty, J. (1996) Is New Keynesian investment theory really "Keynesian?" Reflections on Fazzari and Variato. *Journal of Post Keynesian Economics* 18(3).

Dicken, P. (2007) *Global Shift, Mapping the changing contours of the world economy*. Fifth edition. New York: Guilford Press.

Downs, A. (2007) Credit crisis, the sky is not falling. Policy Brief #164, Economic Studies, The Brookings Institution, October 31.

Drazen, A. (2001) *Political economy in macroeconomics*. Princeton: Princeton University Press.

Dreier, P. (1991) Redlining cities: How banks color community development. *Challenge*, November/December.

Dymski, G.A. and Veitch, J.M. (1996) Financial transformation and the metropolis, booms, busts, and banking in Los Angeles. *Environment and Planning A*. 28(7): 1233–60.

Edel, C.K., Edel, M., Fox, K., Markusen, A., Meyer, P., and Vail, D. (1978) Uneven regional development, an introduction to this issue. *Review of Radical Political Economics* 10(3): 1–12.

Fender, I. and Mitchell, J. (2005) Structured finance, complexity, risk and the use of ratings. *BIS Quarterly Review*, June, 67–87.

Fujita, M., Krugman, P., and Venables, A. (2001) *The spatial economy, cities, regions, and international trade*. Cambridge: MIT Press.

Gotham, K.F. (2006) The secondary circuit of capital reconsidered, globalization and the U.S. real estate sector. *American Journal of Sociology* 112(1): 231–75.

Harvey, D. (1981) *The Limits to Capital*. Chicago: University of Chicago Press.

Harvey, D. (1985) *The Urbanization of Capital*. Baltimore: Sir Johns Hopkins Press.

Harvey, D. (1990) *The condition of postmodernity*. London, Blackwell.

Hayes, C. (2007) Hip heterodoxy. *The Nation*, May 24.

Hirschman, A.O. (1970) *Exit, voice, and loyalty*. Cambridge: Harvard University Press.

Immergluck, D. (2004) *Credit to the community. Community reinvestment and fair lending policy in the United States*. Armonk, NY: M.E. Sharpe.

Itoh, M. and Lapavitsas, C. (1999) *Political economy of money and finance*. Basingstoke: Macmillan.

Lapavitsas, C. (2008) Financialised capitalism, direct exploitation and periodic bubbles. Mimeo, Department of Economics, School of Oriental and African Studies, University of London, May.

Lucas, Jr., R.E. (1990) Why doesn't capital flow from rich to poor countries? *The American Economic Review* 80(2), Papers and Proceedings, May: 92–6.

Marcus, G. (2008) The end(s) of ethnography, social/cultural anthropology's signature form of producing, *Cultural Anthropology* 23(1): 1–14.

May, T. and Perry, B. (2005) Continuities and change in urban sociology. *Sociology* 39(2): 343–70.

Minsky, H.P. (1986) *Stabilizing the Unstable Economy*. New Haven: Yale University Press.

Molotch, H. (1976) The city as a growth machine, toward a political economy of place. *American Journal of Sociology* 82(2): 309–32.

Molotch, H. and Logan, J. (1984) Tensions in the growth machine, overcoming resistance to value-free development. *Social Problems* 31(5): 483–99.

Morris, C.R. (2008) *The trillion dollar meltdown, easy money, high rollers, and the great credit crash*. New York: Public Affairs.

Newman, K. (2009) Post-industrial widgets: Capital flows and the production of the urban. *International Journal of Urban and Regional Research* 33(2): 314–31. Partnoy, F. and Skeel, Jr., D.A. (2007) The promise and perils of credit derivatives. *University of Cincinnati Law Review* 76.

Persson, T. (2002) *Political Economics, Explaining Economic Policy*. Cambridge: MIT Press.

Quigley, J.M. (2008) Compensation and incentives in the mortgage business. *Economists' Voice*, October.

Sassen, S. (1991) *The Global City, New York, London, Tokyo*. Princeton: Princeton University Press.

Sassen, S. (2005). Cities as strategic sites. *Sociology* 39(2): 352–7.

Schumpeter, J.A. (1954) *History of economic analysis*. Cambridge: Harvard University Press.

Scott, A.J. and Soja, E.W. (1996) *The City, Los Angeles and Urban Theory at the End of the Twentieth Century*. Berkeley: University of California Press.

Shiller, R.J. (2005) *Irrational Exuberance*. Princeton: Princeton University Press.

Shiller, R.J. (2008) *The Subprime Solution, How Today's Global Financial Crisis Happened, and What to Do About it*. Princeton: Princeton University Press.

Sinclair, T.J. (2008) *The New Masters of capital, American Bond Rating Agencies and the Politics Of Creditworthiness*. Ithaca, NY: Cornell University Press.

Squires, G.D. (ed.) (1992) *From Redlining to Reinvestment, Community Response to Urban Disinvestment*. Philadelphia: Temple University.

Sraffa, P. (1960) *The Production of Commodities by Means of Commodities*. Cambridge: Cambridge University Press.

Stiglitz, J.E. and Weiss, A. (1981) Credit rationing in markets with imperfect information. *American Economic Review* 71(3): 393–410.

Stuart, G. (2003). *Discriminating Risk*. Ithaca, NY: Cornell University Press.

Wallison, P.J. and Calomiris, C.W. (2008) The last trillion-dollar commitment, the destruction of Fannie Mae and Freddie Mac. *Financial Services Outlook*, Washington, DC, American Enterprise Institute for Public Policy Research, September.

Glossary

ABS	Asset-backed security. An investment product where the bond repayments are based on the securitized revenue streams of loans, or leases. These loans or leases are often secured on assets such as automobiles, SME loans, credit cards, aircraft, and infrastructure.
Agency debt or agency RMBS	Debt or RMBS issued by the GSEs, Fannie Mae, Freddie Mac, or Ginnie Mae. Agency debt consists of direct borrowing by the GSEs. Agency RMBS are passed through securities sold by the GSEs in which they act as guarantors for the debt and servicer for the underlying mortgage loans.
Alt-A loan	Type of mortgage loan between prime and subprime in which the borrower has a good credit rating but will have housing related debt payments above the 28 percent of gross income level Fannie Mae requires for prime loans.
ARM	Adjustable-rate mortgage (also known as adjustable rate loan, variable rate mortgage, variable rate loan). A loan in which the interest rate is periodically adjusted, moving higher or lower in the same ratio as a preselected index, such as Treasury bill rates. The purpose of the interest rate adjustment is primarily to bring the interest rate on the mortgage in line with market rates. ARMs generally have initial below market interest rates in return for the borrower sharing the risk that interest rates may rise during the life of the loan. At first, this makes the ARM financially easier for a borrower than a fixed-rate mortgage for the same loan amount. But increases to the preselected index lead to higher monthly payments in the future that can lead to mortgage default and foreclosure.

Subprime Cities: The Political Economy of Mortgage Markets, First Edition. Edited by Manuel B. Aalbers.
© 2012 Blackwell Publishing Ltd. Published 2012 by Blackwell Publishing Ltd.

CDO	Collateralized debt obligation. An investment product where the bond repayments of other RMBS and ABS bonds are securitized again, to produce a new range of notes.
CDS	A Credit Default Swap is a contract between two financial entities. The first entity buys protection from the second to cover losses on a financial product, often corporate, or securitized bonds. Although this principle appears similar to insurance, CDSs are not covered by insurance regulation.
Conforming loan	In the US, a conforming loan is a mortgage loan that conforms to mortgage underwriting guidelines of Fannie Mae or Freddie Mac. These guidelines pertain to maximum loan limits, lending standards, property type, credit scores, and income verification documentation. Mortgages meeting these criteria are securitized on Wall Street as mortgage-backed bonds.
Credit scoring	Statistically based management tools for forecasting the outcome of extending credit to individuals. Credit scores are based on such common variables as occupation, length of employment, marital status, bank account, gender, and geographical address, which are analyzed by computer systems and statistical methods in order to predict credit performance.
Derivative	A derivative is a contract between two entities, and its price is based on the underlying value of another asset, or its perceived value. They often include swaps (see CDS), options, and futures and can be used to hedge against risk, or to provide leverage (see also CDO).
Disparate impact	An unnecessary discriminatory effect of a practice or standard that is neutral and non-discriminatory in its intention but, nonetheless, disproportionately affects individuals belonging to a particular group based on their age, ethnicity, race, or sex.
Disparate treatment	Intentional denial of opportunity to individuals belonging to a particular group based on their age, ethnicity, race, or sex that is available to other employees or applicants.
Equity withdrawal	Mortgage Equity Withdrawal: borrowing against the difference between the market value of one's house and the existing mortgage debt on that house for the purpose of consumption or reduction of higher interest rate credit card debt.

Fannie Mae   Nickname of the Federal National Mortgage Associate (FNMA) founded in 1938 to buy and sell mortgages as an expedient to stimulate capital investment in the residential construction industry that had collapsed because of the Great Depression. A related purpose of Fannie Mae was to stimulate cash flow to enable mortgage banks, savings and loan associations, and commercial banks to make new loans. In 1949, Fannie Mae expanded its activities to include buying and selling mortgages guaranteed by the Veterans Administration (VA). The Housing Act of 1968 removed Fannie Mae from the federal budget and privatized the agency as a shareholder-owned company (see GSE). In 1981, Fannie Mae issued its first mortgage-backed security (see RMBS). The economic downturn caused by the subprime crisis motivated the federal government to put Fannie Mae under conservatorship on September 7, 2008.

Flipping   Making a series of loans on the same property, in quick succession, in order to generate repeated rounds of fees, penalties, and other transaction costs for lenders, brokers, property appraisers, realtors, attorneys, or other industry actors. Flipping is driven not by consumers' credit needs, but by industry actors' needs for up-front revenues generated on each new loan.

Freddie Mac   The Federal Home Loan Mortgage Corporation (FHLMC), known as Freddie Mac, is a government sponsored enterprise (GSE) of the US federal government. The US Congress created the FHLMC in 1970 to attract investors to finance housing through an expanded secondary mortgage market. Freddie Mac buys mortgages on the secondary market, pools them, and sells them as a mortgage-backed security (see RMBS) to investors to increase the money available for new home purchases. In response to the savings and loan crisis, the Financial Institutions Reform, Recovery, and Enforcement Act of 1989 (FIRREA) revised the regulation of Freddie Mac and made HUD the supervisory agency of the GSE. The economic downturn caused by the subprime crisis motivated the federal government to put Freddie Mac under conservatorship on September 7, 2008.

Ginnie Mae   The Government National Mortgage Association (GNMA), known as Ginnie Mae, is a government-owned corporation that guarantees bonds backed by home mortgages that other government agencies, mainly the Federal Housing Administration and the Veterans Administration, have guaranteed. Congress created Ginnie Mae in 1968 within the Department of Housing and Urban Development (HUD). Unlike Fannie Mae and Freddie Mac, Ginnie Mae is not a publicly traded company and its insured bonds have the explicit backing of the federal government.

Greenlining
The business practice of investing energy, products, and services in low-income, minority, and disabled communities. As investments in the inner city become financially attractive, the marketing emphasis on minority, elderly, and poor communities to increase profits leads to a process by which lenders strip capital from neighborhoods and consumers.

GSE
Government-Sponsored Enterprises are privately owned corporate entities created by US federal charters and statues. GSEs make loans or loan guarantees for limited purposes such as to provide credit for specific borrowers or one economic sector. They may also raise funds by borrowing (without the backing of the federal government) or to guarantee the debt of others in unlimited amounts. As quasi-governmental organizations, GSEs do not exercise powers that are reserved to the government as sovereign (such as the power to tax or to regulate interstate commerce) and they do not have the power to commit the Government financially. The major housing GSEs – the Federal National Mortgage Association (Fannie Mae), the Federal Home Loan Mortgage Corporation (Freddie Mac), and the Federal Agricultural Mortgage Corporation (Farmer Mac) – are investor owned; the others – the Federal Home Loan Bank System and the Farm Credit System – are owned cooperatively by their borrowers.

Home loan
Loan secured by a home.

Interest rate cap
An absolute legal limit on the annual interest rate cost of credit. In response to farm foreclosures in the late nineteenth century and during the Great Depression of the 1930s, most US states imposed interest-rate caps, or "usury" laws, limiting the annual cost of various kinds of credit. Beginning in the 1970s, many of these caps were either repealed, or (more commonly) sidestepped by changes in how various kinds of lending institutions were subject to state or federal supervision (see preemption).

LIBOR
The London Interbank Offered Rate is the interest rate at which banks borrow unsecured funds from each other on the London wholesale market. The rates are set daily and are calculated from the trimmed arithmetic mean of rates charged by a group of contributor banks trading

	in the market. The rates offered for different currencies vary from lending overnight up to one year.
Mortgage deficient area	A term used to describe the unusually low amount of mortgage activity in a census tract. In 1976, the State of California Department of Savings and Loan considered census tracts as mortgage deficient if loan volume per capita was less than 25 percent of the county average.
Mortgage insurance	Mortgage Insurance, also known as mortgage guaranty, is insurance that compensates lenders or investors for losses due to the default of a mortgage loan. Mortgage insurance can be either public or private depending upon the insurer. In the US, the Federal Housing Administration (FHA) and the Veterans Administration (VA) offer public mortgage insurance. Lenders normally finance and pay the mortgage insurance premium to these government agencies on the borrower's behalf. Private Mortgage Insurance (PMI) is insurance that protects lending institutions against nonpayment should a borrower default on the mortgage loan. Lenders often require PMI due to the higher level of default risk that is associated with low down payment loans (e.g., less than 20 percent of the purchase price of the home). Those borrowers who put a down payment of 20 percent or more on a home typically are not required to pay primary mortgage insurance. Once the equity in a home falls below the 80 percent loan-to-value-ratio required by a lender, homeowners can eliminate private mortgage insurance.
Negative equity	A situation that occurs when the amount of the outstanding loan is larger than the market value for which the loan is provided, in this case a house.
OCC	Office of the Comptroller of the Currency: US agency responsible for regulating nationally chartered banks.
Originator	A lender that produces mortgage assets, often with the intention of selling them in a secondary market.
OTS	Office of Thrift Supervision: US agency responsible for regulating savings and loan banks (i.e., *sparkassen* or building societies).
Predatory lending	A sub-set of subprime lending. A form of price discrimination by unsuitable loans designed to exploit vulnerable and unsophisticated borrowers.

Preemption	The assertion of national, federal supremacy over state laws and/or regulations. In many aspects of the political economy of the US, "states' rights" is code for economic and cultural conservatism; these politics were reversed during the boom in subprime lending, when Washington, DC was dominated by advocates of deregulation. The explosive growth of abusive, high-cost lending had led to disastrous consequences in many cities across the US. With no meaningful response from the federal government, a growing number of state legislatures passed various kinds of anti-predatory lending laws. Federal agencies responded aggressively, preempting state laws (especially for nationally chartered financial institutions) in the name of an integrated national market. Several of the state-federal conflicts went all the way to the US Supreme Court, which generally upheld federal preemption authority.
Primary mortgage market	The market where borrowers and mortgage originators come together to negotiate terms and complete mortgage transaction. Mortgage brokers, mortgage bankers, credit unions, banks, and savings and loan institutions make up of the primary mortgage market.
Private-label securitization	Mortgage securitizations that involve issuances of mortgage-backed securities by entities other than Fannie Mae and Freddie Mac. The mortgages that make up these securities do not have the backing of the federal government and as a result carry a significantly greater risk. Jumbo loans, low- and no-document loans, Alt-A loans, and mortgages with low teaser rates represent types of non-conforming loans that do not conform to the criteria set by the GSEs.
Rate-spread loan	Loans with an annualized percentage rate in borrowing costs that exceed a specified benchmark by a certain "spread" or "trigger." The most widely used public database about mortgages in the US, the Home Mortgage Disclosure Act (HMDA) data, was revised in 2002 to include information on the cost of credit. The banking industry fought efforts to add new information, and as a compromise the Federal Reserve only required lenders to disclose the cost of credit for the highest-cost loans – mortgages with a spread of more than three percentage points over the yield on US Treasury Securities of comparable yield for first-lien

mortgages, and five points for subordinate liens. (First-lien lenders are first in line for repayment in the event of bankruptcy.) For loans made after October 1, 2009, these triggers were reduced to 1.5 percent and 3 percent, respectively, and the benchmark was re-defined to compare loan costs to the average prime mortgage offer rate.

Redlining — Lender behavior that denies or limits credit to specific neighborhoods, or when the loans a lender will make in those areas are significantly more expensive because of higher interest rates or large fees. The justification given for redlining is that certain areas have a higher rate of mortgage default, thus lenders refuse to lend to anyone in those areas. The designating of redlined neighborhoods has been normally associated with minority neighborhoods. Moreover, redlining unfairly restricts people's access to loans without looking at their individual creditworthiness. Together, these practices have led to legal challenges of redlining as a discriminatory practice. The term has evolved to refer to any practice that restricts services for a specific group of people.

Risk-based pricing — A theory – and a political interpretation – of how deregulation allows financial institutions to measure the risks of various kinds of consumers, and to vary the price of credit accordingly. Advances in consumer credit reporting and modeling systems seemed to have succeeded in allowing lenders to serve riskier borrowers who would otherwise have been excluded; de-regulated innovation thus seemed superior to clumsy government regulations (see interest rate caps). Risk-based pricing dominated policy discussions from the 1990s up to the financial crisis, when its flaws became clear: (1) securitization had distorted and underestimated default risks, (2) the risks that borrowers would fail to repay was only one of many different kinds of risks magnified by securitization, and (3) rising home prices had artificially suppressed foreclosure rates, hiding the growing phenomenon of defaulted borrowers forced to sell their homes without going through formal foreclosure proceedings.

RMBS — Residential mortgage-backed security. An investment product where the bond repayments are derived from securitized residential mortgages.

Savings and Loans Institution (thrift)

A financial institution that specializes in accepting savings deposits and making mortgage and other loans. From the 1930s through the 1980, savings and loan institutions (S&L's) were the main originator and manager of mortgages in the US. Using the model of the 30-year fixed-rate mortgage, S&L's regulated and controlled all phases of the mortgage process: risk assessment, origination, servicing, and investment. As a result, thrifts had strong incentive to avoid high-risk lending and maintain strong quality control over the mortgages they held in portfolio. This localized system of mortgage financing restricted cross-border flows of mortgage capital and limited the loan volume and investment potential of mortgages.

Secondary mortgage market

The market where investment banks, financial institutions, and the two major government sponsored enterprises (GSEs)—the Federal Home Loan Mortgage Corporation (FHLMC, nicknamed Freddie Mac) and the Federal National Mortgage Association (FNMA, or Fannie Mae) — repackage mortgages as securities to sell to institutional investors in national and global capital markets. While the secondary mortgage market originated during the 1930s, it was not until the 1980s that Congress passed several statutes to encourage the securitization of relatively illiquid assets, such as mortgages, and attract new sources of investment to finance real estate. Unlike the primary mortgage market where the source of profit is the payment of the mortgage to the bank that originated the home loan, the source of profit in the secondary mortgage for securitized mortgages is the sale of mortgage pools that contain hundreds or thousands of individual mortgages. The goal of the secondary mortgage market is to increase the exchangeability and liquidity of mortgages through the rationalization and standardization of mortgage features and characteristics.

Securitization

The process of transforming localized, non-standard, and opaque assets like mortgages into transparent and liquid securities that people can easily exchange on global markets. Securitization is designed to reduce the uncertainty of buying and selling atypical assets (leases, homes, loans, etc.) by transforming them into marketing investments that have common features and characteristics. Securitization has been used as a tool to obtain funding for lenders by liquefying assets and to reduce regulatory capital holdings. As a mechanism for easing the spreading and trading of risk, securitization seeks to homogenize diverse commodities and weaken the institutional buffers between local, national, and global markets. Securitization may also be used to transform mortgage default risk into a range of low risk notes (that were comparable with the risk rating of sovereign debt) whilst creating a smaller range of high risk debt.

SIV A Structured Investment Vehicle is a financial entity that purchases RMBS, ABS, and corporate bonds, and securitizes them into different classes of notes. SIVs borrow heavily from interbank money markets in order to buy greater volumes of bonds, to drive greater returns for SIV investors.

SPV A Special Purpose Vehicle is a company that fulfills a particular and narrowly defined task. An SPV does not have employees or offices and is normally used in securitization to legally separate the ownership of mortgage assets from the originator. This enables the assets to be securitized and for the investors to be able to claim all the revenue derived from the mortgages, even if the lender goes into liquidation. The legal separation also enables banks to avoid the retaining regulatory capital to cover mortgages losses, as the bank no-longer owns the mortgages. Separate SPVs are also used to issue the bonds to investors.

Subprime loan High-cost loan meant for borrowers with credit imperfections or higher default risk, but also sold to borrowers with a good credit history.

Index

Page references to figures are given in *italics*; those for tables are given in **bold**.
References relating to notes have the letter 'n' following the page number.

Subprime Cities: The Political Economy of Mortgage Markets, First Edition. Edited by Manuel B. Aalbers.
© 2012 Blackwell Publishing Ltd. Published 2012 by Blackwell Publishing Ltd.